Optical Storage Technology 1992

Optical Storage Technology 1992
A STATE OF THE ART REVIEW

William Saffady

Meckler
Westport • London

ISSN 1047-3505
ISBN 0-88736-759-3

Copyright © 1992 Meckler Publishing. All rights reserved. No part of this publication may be reproduced in any form by any means without prior permission from the publisher, except by a reviewer who may quote brief passages in review.

Portions of this publication originally appeared in **Micrographics and Optical Storage Equipment Review** 16 (1991), copyright © 1991 and **Library Computer Systems and Equipment Review** 13, no. 2 (1991), copyright © 1991 by Meckler Publishing.

Meckler Publishing, the publishing division of Meckler Corporation,
    11 Ferry Lane West, Westport, CT 06880.
Meckler Ltd., 247-249 Vauxhall Bridge Road, London SW1V 1HQ, U.K.

Printed and bound in the United States of America.

Contents

Introduction vii

Part One: Read/Write Optical Disks 3
    Write-Once Technology 4
    Rewritable Technology 9
    WORM Drives and Media 17
    Autochangers 36
    Data Storage Applications 42
    Document Imaging Applications 54
    Video and Audio Recording 70

Part Two: CD-ROM and Related Media 73
    CD-ROM Technology 73
    CD-ROM Drives 80
    Applications 89
    Standards and Software 104
    User Experiences 109
    Multimedia Technologies 111

Part Three: Optical Cards and Optical Tape 123
    Optical Cards 123
    Optical Card Applications 125
    Optical Tape 127

Bibliography 129

Index 207

Introduction

This book is the seventh in a series of annual state-of-the-art surveys of optical storage technology, concepts, research, product developments, and applications. It updates a discussion begun in *Optical Disks 1985: a State of the Art Review* (Meckler, 1985) and continued in that publication's five successors: *Optical Disks for Data and Document Storage* (Meckler, 1986); *Optical Storage Technology 1987: a State of the Art Review* (Meckler, 1987); *Optical Storage Technology 1988: a State of the Art Review* (Meckler, 1988); *Optical Storage Technology 1989: a State of the Art Review* (Meckler, 1989); and *Optical Storage Technology 1990-91: a State of the Art Review* (Meckler, 1990). Like its predecessors, this report is intended for information specialists, data processing administrators, computer systems analysts, records managers, office systems analysts, librarians, archivists, and others responsible for evaluating, planning, procuring, implementing, and/or operating optical information systems for data and document storage.

Seven years after the introduction of commercially available products, optical storage remains a subject of considerable interest to information management professionals. Addressing potential customers' demands for useful information about optical storage concepts, technology, and products, tutorial articles and other surveys have become commonplace in professional journals and trade publications, as well as in popular business and science-oriented magazines. Although they are no longer considered novel, optical storage products continue to attract large, enthusiastic crowds at professional conferences and trade meetings; continuing education short courses, seminars, and similar educational programs dealing with optical storage technology and applications are typically well attended.

In late 1984, when the first title in this series of state-of-the-art surveys was prepared, the field of optical storage was dominated by experimental systems, barely working prototypes, and premature product announcements. The few operational systems available at that time were customized, often with considerable engineering effort, for specific installations. By early 1986, when the second report in the series was published, a number of interesting products were commercially available, although optical storage remained an emerging technology with undisputed potential but an uncertain future. Product announcements and availability increased significantly in 1986. By early 1987, when the third report in this series appeared, the characteristics, advantages, and limitations of optical storage technology had been more clearly articulated by research and development activities. Since that time, some impressive new optical storage products—including rewritable and multifunctional drives, networked CD-ROM systems, a variety of jukebox retrieval units, and high-capacity optical tape recorders—have been introduced. Older products have been refined and expanded, and the number of installations—while still small relative to such well established information management technologies as magnetic storage and micrographics—has increased.

The broad scope and varied characteristics of optical storage technology have confused information management professionals since the early 1980s. This report is divided into three parts which reflect the major categories of optical storage products employed in data and document management:

— Part One covers read/write optical disks. Such media, which are purchased blank, permit the direct recording of information by end users. A small but interesting group of read/write optical disk products employs videodisc technology and can record analog signals generated by cameras, videotape recorders, or other video sources. For purposes of this discussion, however, read/write optical disk systems which employ digital recording are more significant. When configured with appropriate computer hardware and supporting software, such disks offer a high-capacity supplement, complement, or alternative to magnetic media for the storage of character-coded text and quantitative data. As an alternative to micrographics technology, read/write optical disks can store digitized document images. Regardless of the type of information they contain, read/write optical disks can be divided into two groups: write-once and rewritable. Write-once optical disks—often termed WORM disks—support direct recording of user information but do not permit the erasure and reuse of previously recorded disk segments; rewritable optical disks, in contrast, are erasable.

— Part Two of this report deals with Compact Disc-Read Only Memory (CD-ROM), the most important type of read-only optical storage product for data-oriented applications. As a group, read-only optical discs are produced by mastering processes and contain prerecorded information. Following common practice in published literature and vendor documentation, this report will employ the spelling "disc" when discussing read-only optical storage products; the spelling "disk" will be utilized for read/write optical media.

Derived from technologies originally developed for consumer applications, read-only optical discs can be divided into two major groups: compact discs and videodiscs. CD-ROM, as noted above, is the compact disc format for computer-processable data. Other formats include Compact Disc-Digital Audio (CD-DA), Compact Disc-Video (CD-V), and Compact Disc-Interactive (CD-I). While they fall outside of the scope of this report, such formats will be described briefly at appropriate points in the text. Videodiscs support both analog- and digitally-coded information—the former being employed for visual materials and the latter for computer-processable data. This report includes a brief examination of videodisc technology in the context of a discussion of multimedia applications of optical storage products. Digital Video Interactive (DVI) technology is discussed in the same context.

— While platter-shaped media are currently the focal point of information management interest in optical storage technology, the optical storage product group also includes cards and tape. Part Three of this report surveys optical card and optical tape technology, summarizing the current state of the art, product characteristics, potential advantages, and intended applications.

For readers interested in more detailed treatments of specific facets of optical storage technology, important books, articles, technical reports, conference papers, and other publications are cited at relevant points in the text, and a lengthy bibliography appears at the end of the report. Citations to recently published literature are emphasized, but references to significant older works—cited in this report's six predecessors—are also included.

While every attempt has been made to identify relevant optical disk research activities, products, and services, it is impossible to comprehensively and definitively survey any developing technology. Recognizing that no published discussion of this topic can be completely up to date, this report emphasizes the categorization of available optical storage products and an understanding of their characteristics, advantages, limitations, and current relationship to the current state-of-the-art and likely future trends. While continuing product developments will affect specific details presented in the individual sections, the report's overall conceptual presentation should retain its utility, and readers should be able to relate new optical storage products to those discussed here.

Optical Storage Technology 1992

Part One:
Read/Write Optical Disks

Optical disks are typically divided into two broad groups: read-only and read/write. Read-only optical disks, of which CD-ROM is the best known example in information management applications, are purchased with prerecorded contents. Such disks are created by a mastering process, the individual copies being stamped or molded out of plastic. The copies, which are distributed to end-users, have no recordable properties and are read by devices, such as CD-ROM drives, which have no recording capabilities. Read/write optical disks, in contrast, are purchased blank, although they are often pregrooved and may contain some prerecorded control signals. Such disks feature specially formulated coatings that support the direct recording of machine-readable information.

As computer storage media, read/write optical disks can accept data generated by keyboards, document scanners, scientific instrumentation, or other input peripherals. They can also record information transferred from magnetic disks, magnetic tapes, or other optical media. While the most widely publicized products record digitally coded information, one group of read/write optical disk systems—sometimes described as video disc recorders—accepts analog television signals generated by video cameras or transferred from prerecorded video tapes, read-only video discs, or other video sources. Examples of such products will be described later in this report.

Whether digital or analog coding is involved, read/write optical disk systems include recording/playback equipment—so-called optical disk drives—and recording media—the optical disks themselves. With the exception of those products intended for video recording, read/write optical disk drives are computer peripheral devices; read/write optical disks are platter-shaped media with optically alterable surfaces. As described later in this report, read/write optical disks are removable media. Like 3.5-inch floppy disks, they are typically encapsulated in plastic cartridges which protect their recording surfaces and facilitate mounting, dismounting, and other media handling. The optical disks utilized by certain video disc recorders are an exception; lacking protective encapsulation, they must be handled carefully to avoid damaging their exposed recording surfaces.

While the characteristics and capabilities of specific products differ in ways to be discussed in detail below, read/write optical disks and the drives that utilize them are commonly divided into write-once and rewritable varieties. Write-once optical disks are often described as WORM disks. The acronym variously stands for Write Once Read Many (times) or Write Once Read Mostly. Such disks are not erasable. The write-once designation is potentially misleading, however; WORM disks can be used for repeated recording as long space remains available, but once information is recorded in a given sector of a write-once optical disk that area cannot be reused. If previously recorded information is accidently or intentionally overwritten, it is obliterated rather than replaced. Unlike magnetic disks, with which they compete in certain information storage applications, write-once optical disks can become irrevocably full. With rewritable optical disks, in contrast, the contents of previously recorded media segments can be erased and/or overwritten with new information. Like their magnetic counterparts, rewritable optical disks are reusable media.

The following discussion outlines the most important characteristics of write-once and rewritable recording technologies. It emphasizes factors which influence the design of operational products and their suitability for information management applications. The discussion of recording technologies is followed by descriptions of typical products. As delineated above, read/write optical disk is a generic designation for a product group that includes write-once and rewritable varieties. In some publications, particularly microcomputer magazines, the terms "read/write" and "rewritable" are treated synonymously, leaving write-once optical disks as a separate product group. Such usage is imprecise and confusing. This report will treat write-once and rewritable optical disks as varieties of read/write optical disks.

WRITE-ONCE TECHNOLOGY

While some industry analysts and computer users continue to view optical storage as a new technology, it has a relatively long history when compared to such commonly encountered information processing products as personal computers, desktop laser printers, local area network interface cards, handheld document scanners, and fax boards. Laboratory experiments with write-once optical recording materials date from the 1970s. Write-once optical disk drives and media were introduced in the early 1980s, and they have been readily available to computer users since the middle of that decade. The general characteristics of write-once optical recording technology—though not as widely analyzed as principles of magnetic recording—have been described in numerous monographs, journal articles, technical reports, and conference papers, most of which were published in the 1980s. Cohen (1979), Bell (1980, 1983), Herzog (1980), Kenville (1981), Hecht (1982), Goldstein (1982, 1984), and Rothchild (1983, 1984) were among the earliest surveys of write-once recording and its potential applications. Much of their content remains interesting and relevant to readers today. Write-once optical storage is likewise described, in varying levels of technical detail, by Bracker (1987), Croucher and Hopper (1987), DeHaan (1987), Emmelius et al (1989), Harvey (1990), Harvey and Reinhardt (1990), Hecht (1987a), Lee (1989), Mendez (1988), Tanaka (1986), Tanaka et al (1987), Thomas (1987, 1988), and Zech (1988).

While media characteristics and equipment capabilities have been refined and expanded in ways described later in this report, write-once recording technologies have changed little since the late 1980s. At the time this report was prepared, five different technologies—ablative recording of tellurium thin films, dye-based recording, dual alloy recording, phase-change recording, and thermal bubble recording—were being used in write-once optical disk systems offered by various vendors. All five technologies utilize lasers to record information by irreversibly altering the reflectivity characteristics of a thermally sensitive material coated on a platter-shaped aluminum, glass, or plastic substrate. The last of these includes polycarbonate (PC) and polymethyl methacrylate (PMMA). Characteristics of optical disk substrates are discussed by Hennig (1985), Inui et al (1987), Kaempf (1987), Kaempf et al (1987), Leuschke (1989), Smith (1981), and Sudou et al (1988), among various others. Media manufacturing processes are described by Put (1990).

In write-once optical disk systems intended for computer installations, the laser-induced alterations conform to predetermined patterns of one and zero bits associated with digitally coded information. While obviously different in execution, this approach is conceptually similar to magnetic disk and tape recording in which digitally coded bits are represented by aligning magnetic particles in specified directions. With all optical storage technologies, special coding schemes are used to compensate for media defects and reduce the likelihood of unrecoverable recording errors. Such error management techniques are discussed by Brown and Earman (1988), Glover (1989), Han Vinck (1988), Howe and Meichle (1987), Livingston (1988), Saito and Takeda (1988), Takeda and Saito (1988), Turner (1988), and Van Uijen (1987). To retrieve previously recorded information, a write-once optical disk drive contains lasers and pickup mechanisms which detect the alterations and interpret the bit patterns they represent.

While they share certain conceptual similarities, the five write-once optical storage technologies differ in their specific recording processes, media attributes, and performance characteristics. A substantial number of journal articles, conference papers, technical monographs, and related publications trace the progress of particular write-once technologies and their associated equipment and media from laboratory prototypes to commercial availability. The following discussion surveys the most important characteristics of each write-once optical recording technology, citing published research reports where pertinent.

Tellurium Thin Films. In the most extensively researched, widely implemented, and frequently cited approach to write-once optical recording, a highly focused laser beam irradiates a disk that is coated with a thin film of tellurium. The tellurium is usually covered with a protective layer and alloyed with other materials, such as selenium or lead, to enhance stability. The laser's energy is converted to heat which creates microscopic holes or pits in the thermally sensitive thin film. The pit formation process is termed ablation, and this type of write-once technology is often described as ablative recording. Suh (1985) reviews its most important characteristics.

While ablation is widely identified with tellurium-based optical media, ablative techniques—as discussed below—are also employed by optical disk systems that utilize dye-based media. It should further be noted that tellurium-based optical disks are utilized in phase-change recording, which does not utilize ablative techniques. As discussed later in this report, tellurium-based phase-change optical recording is compatible with both write-once and rewritable implementations. In contrast, ablative recording of tellurium thin films is irreversible.

Tellurium thin films and ablative recording techniques are employed in write-once optical disk systems manufactured by Fujitsu, Hitachi, Laser Magnetic Storage International, Literal Corporation, Mitsubishi, Toshiba, and other companies. In most implementations, the microscopic pits represent the one bits in digitally-coded information; to represent the zero bits, spaces are left in areas where pits might otherwise have been formed. The pits and spaces are recorded serially in tracks that radiate outward from the center of an optical disk. The recorded data is read by a laser and an optical pickup mechanism that detects differences in the reflectivity characteristics of pits and spaces. To avoid accidental obliteration of information, the recording and playback lasers typically operate at different wavelengths.

The subject of more than a decade of laboratory research, tellurium thin films offer good thermal sensitivity for low-power recording, high signal-to-noise ratios, limited thermal conductivity to prevent undesirable increases in pit sizes, good resolution for high density recording, and good media stability. These characteristics are outlined in a sizable published literature, much of it reflecting Japanese and European research and development activities. Examples include Abe et al (1987), Beauvais et al (1990), Chung et al (1989), Coufal and Lee (1987), DiGiulio et al (1988), Ikemoto et al (1990), Jacobs (1985), Kivits and Bont (1981), Ohta et al (1982), and Takenaga et al (1982). Developed by Philips in the late 1970s, the much publicized "air sandwich" design features a tellurium alloy deposited on the inner surfaces of two disk-shaped substrates which are separated by a thin cushion of air that lowers the reflectivity of pitted areas. Employed by several media manufacturers, it is described by Blom (1982), Eventoff (1983), Hoekstra (1983), Lou (1977), McFarlane et al (1978), Rooijmans and Verhoeven (1983), Vries and Jacobs (1984), and Yonezawa (1979).

Other disk structures and tellurium alloys are discussed by Altman et al (1986), Gittleman and Arie (1984), Gittleman et al (1986), Goto et al (1984), Hanus and Laude (1990), Kanazawa et al (1984), Kenville (1982), Reno and Tarzaiski (1979), Schiavone et al (1984), Shiuh et al (1988), and Yamazaki and Yagi (1987). As discussed in a later section of this report, manufacturers of ablative-oriented optical disk systems have steadily refined their products to improve recording density and media capacity. Saito et al (1987) and Arai and Maeda (1990) discuss capacity improvements associated with pit-edge recording techniques and other technological refinements.

The stability of optical disks is of obvious interest and concern to computer specialists, records managers, archivists, librarians, and others responsible for the implementation and operation of data and document storage systems which utilize such media. Write-once optical disks are often described in advertisements and manufacturers' product literature as archival media. The description is typically employed in the data processing sense, in which "to archive" means to transfer inactive information from a relatively expensive online storage device—typically, a fixed magnetic disk drive—to a presumably less expensive medium for offline storage. As described later in this report, optical disks are often utilized for such purposes. The term "archival," however, implies permanence, an archival storage medium being one that will retain its original information-bearing characteristics indefinitely. By that definition, available optical storage media have no known archival properties. Over time, optical disks undergo significant chemical and physical changes that will eventually render them unsuitable for accurate recording of new information and retrieval of previously recorded information. Such changes may be induced by environmental effects, by defects associated with media manufacturing, or by media damage resulting from improper handling.

Various research reports acknowledge the impact of oxidation, corrosion, and other aging mechanisms on the tellurium thin films employed in ablative write-once recording. Examples include Blom and Lou (1984), Carcia et al (1988), Evans (1988), Gotoh et al (1989), Lee and Geiss (1983), Lee and Weider (1983), Lou (1980), Milch and Tasaico (1980), Retzler et al (1988, 1989), and Shrawagi et al (1984). While the use of oxidation-resistant alloys and barrier coatings can retard media degradation of tellurium-based media, they do not eliminate it entirely; as noted above, significant time-dependent changes will eventually render a given WORM disk unusable for its intended purpose.

Discussions of this subject typically distinguish two facets of media stability: (1) shelf stability, sometimes termed shelf life, indicates the period of time during which a given optical disk remains useful for data or document recording; (2) storage stability, sometimes termed playback stability, indicates the period of time during which previously recorded information can be reliably retrieved. In both cases, lifetime estimates are established by accelerated aging tests which subject specific optical recording media to extremely harsh environmental conditions for relatively brief periods of time. The resulting media damage is observed, and calculations are performed to determine the period of time required for comparable damage to occur under less extreme conditions. Based on such tests, manufacturers of tellurium-based write-once optical disks typically claim a useful shelf life of five years from the date of media manufacturing for recording new information on previously unused areas of a disk. After five years, a given disk may still be recordable, but manufacturers warn that users cannot have confidence that an acceptably low recording error rate will be sustained. Tellurium-based media manufacturers variously claim a useful storage life of ten to forty years for reliable retrieval of previously recorded information. Ten-year stability claims were typical of first generation products; most vendors contend that their newest tellurium-based write-once optical disks will remain stable for thirty to forty years.

Dye-Based Optical Recording. Dye-based optical recording materials—also described as dye-polymer, dye-in-polymer (DIP), and organic dye binder media—feature a transparent polymer layer which contains an infrared absorbing dye. This recording layer is coated on a plastic or glass substrate. In some cases, a reflective metal layer is deposited between the substrate and the recording material. Information is recorded by a laser which operates at the dye's absorption wavelength. The laser's energy is converted to heat, forming pits or bumps with detectable reflectivity characteristics. As with the tellurium thin films described above, the pits or bumps typically represent the one bits in digitally coded data, while the spaces represent the zero bits. Alternatively, a laser may induce the diffusion of a dye into an absorption layer, producing detectable differences in the reflectivity of diffused and pure dye areas. Dye-based recording is utilized in write-once optical disk drives manufactured by Eastman Kodak, Pioneer, and Ricoh. Ricoh's dye-based WORM products are sold in the United States by Maxtor. While dye-based materials for rewritable optical recording have been demonstrated as laboratory prototypes, only write-once products were commercially available at the time this report was prepared.

The various approaches to dye-based optical recording are described in numerous journal articles and conference papers. Examples include Brazas (1988), Burgess et al (1987), Chung (1987), Couture and Lessard (1988), Fleming (1989), Goldberg et al (1989), Graham (1987), Gravesteijn and Van der Veen (1984), Gupta (1984), Howe and Wrobel (1981), Itoh et al (1983), Jipson and Jones (1981), Kay et al (1984), Kim et al (1987),

Kobayashi et al (1990, 1991), Kowel et al (1987), Kuder (1988), Kuder and Nikles (1985), Kurtz (1987), Law and Johnson (1983), Maeda et al (1990), Maher (1987), Matsui et al (1988), Matsuzawa et al (1990), Miceli et al (1987), Miyazaki et al (1987), Molaire (1988), Nikles et al (1989, 1990), Oba et al (1985, 1986), Ogoshi et al (1985), Pearson (1986), Shepherd (1988), Shimidzu and Ohno (1989), Takagi et al (1987), Tao and Chen (1990, 1990a), Wissbrun (1987), Wrobel (1989), and Yoshino et al (1990). Proponents of dye-based optical materials claim higher read/write speeds, lower threshold energy requirements for pit formation, greater stability, and lower production costs when compared to optical recording systems that employ tellurium thin films. Manufacturers of dye-based optical disks typically claim a shelf stability of five years and a playback stability of fifteen years. As discussed below, a rewritable implementation of dye-based optical recording technology has attracted considerable research interest, but it is not utilized in commercially available products.

Dual Alloy Media. In 1986, the Sony Corporation commercialized a write-once optical disk system based on dual alloy recording technology. The technology is described by Nakane et al (1985, 1986). Dual alloy media—sometimes described as bimetallic alloy media—consists of two metal alloys coated as thin films on a platter-shaped polycarbonate substrate. One of the alloys is composed of tellurium and bismuth, the other of selenium and antimony. The recording material is layered, the tellurium-bismuth alloy being surrounded by two selenium-antimony layers. All layers are covered by a protective seal; the media are consequently described as "direct seal" disks. To record the one bits in digitally coded information, a laser fuses the three alloy layers, creating a four-element alloy with reflectivity characteristics that are distinguishable from those of the unfused alloys. Unfused areas of a disk represent the zero bits in digitally coded information.

At the time this report was prepared, dual alloy recording was employed exclusively in write-once optical drives and media manufactured by Sony. At five years, the shelf life of unrecorded dual alloy disks is comparable to that of other write-once media. As a potential advantage in applications which require long-term retention of computer-processible information, Sony claims a playback life of 100 years for information recorded on its dual alloy disks, which it advertises as "Century Media." As with other optical storage media, such claims are based on accelerated aging tests.

Skeptical observers, however, have questioned the significance of long lifetime estimates for computer-processible media which depend on specific hardware devices for playback of recorded information. They note that, while Sony's dual alloy media may remain stable for one hundred years, the optical disk drives which read such media are typically engineered for a maximum useful life of ten years. Similar reservations apply to other optical storage media and the devices which read them. When successor products are introduced, manufacturers of computer storage devices typically provide some backward compatibility which enables their new products to read media recorded by older models, but there is no guarantee that such compatibility will be continued indefinitely. On the contrary, the history of data processing suggests that equipment vendors will abandon support for older storage media and recording formats after relatively brief periods of time. Media such as seven-track magnetic tapes and hard-sectored eight-inch diskettes, for example, have been rendered unusable by the discontinuation of equipment required to read them.

Given the hardware-dependent characteristics of optical disks, long lifetime estimates do not confer a competitive advantage on dual alloy technology or any other optical recording technology. In a given application, information recorded on particular types of optical disks will need to be transferred to other, newer media to preserve its utility long before the original disks' stability periods have elapsed. As a further complication, all machine-readable information is intended for processing by specific systems software and application programs. Like storage equipment, such software may be updated or otherwise changed in a manner than can render previously recorded information unusable.

Phase-Change Recording. As with the ablative recording technology described above, phase-change optical disks consist of tellurium and/or selenium compounds which are typically alloyed with small quantities of other metals. Initially, these compounds exist in either a crystalline or an amorphous state. A laser records information by heating selected areas of the sensitive layer until its glass-transition temperature is reached. A crystalline-to-amorphous or amorphous-to-crystalline transition occurs in the heated areas, accompanied by a detectable change in their reflectivity characteristics. The amorphous areas typically represent the one bits in digitally coded data, while the crystalline areas represent the zero bits. The technology is described by Chao et al (1990), Gravestein (1987, 1988, 1989), Gravestein et al (1987), Terao (1985, 1985a), Tyan et al (1987), and Van Tongeren and Sens (1987).

In the write-once variant of phase-change recording—the subject of this discussion—the transition is irreversible. In rewritable phase-change recording, to be described below, the altered areas can be returned to their original crystalline or amorphous state, thereby erasing previously recorded information. Phase-change technology is utilized in write-once optical media and drives manufactured by Matsushita. At the time this report was prepared, those products were being sold in the United States by Panasonic, a Matsushita company, and by Reflection Systems, a subsidiary of Plasmon Data Systems. Recording media suitable for use in Matsushita drives is also manufactured by Plasmon Data Systems. Plasmon's write-once media, which features a platinum recording layer, is described by Kalstrom (1988, 1990). In 1991, Eastman Kodak announced a version of its Model 6800 optical disk drive which utilizes phase-change rather than dye-based technology for increased capacity.

Matsushita claims playback stability of fifteen years for its write-once phase-change media. Plasmon claims playback stability of fifty years for its media. Storey et al (1988) report the results of accelerated aging tests performed on Plasmon media.

Thermal Bubble Recording. In the thermal bubble approach to write-once optical recording, heat from a laser evaporates a polymer layer to selectively form bubbles in a thin film composed of precious metals, such as gold or platinum. The bubbles open to form pits which reveal a reflective underlayer. Areas with the exposed underlayer typically represent the one bits in digitally coded data, while unexposed areas represent the zero bits. The technology is described by Chung et al (1984), Cornet (1983), Freese et al (1982), Popoff and Ledieu (1984), Robbins et al (1981), and Schreier (1983).

Although thermal bubble recording was one of the first write-once optical technologies to be successfully commercialized, it has attracted few product developers. At the time this report was prepared, thermal bubble recording was being used exclusively by ATG Gigadisc in a write-once optical disk product line that was originally introduced by Alcatel Thomson Gigadisc. The first Gigadisc drives became commercially available in the early 1980s. In the mid-1980s, thermal bubble recording was briefly supported by the Optimem 1000, a first-generation WORM drive which could also be configured for ablative recording of tellurium thin films. ATG claims a playback life of thirty years for its newest thermal bubble media; it previously claimed a playback life of ten years for its first-generation products. As with other write-once optical disks, the shelf life for unrecorded thermal bubble media is five years.

Other Technologies. As discussed below, current laboratory-based research emphasizes rewritable optical storage technologies. Since the late 1980s, there has been relatively little investigation of write-once recording processes and materials other than those described above. Among examples of published research results dealing with alternative write-once technologies, Tu et al (1981) discuss the optical recording potential of bilayer films that combine silicon with transition metals. Based on experiments conducted by Dai Nippon Printing, Asano et al (1990) discuss the write-once recording potential of copper nitride films. Sella et al (1990) discuss the optical recording properties of gold-chromium films. Gotoh et al (1990) of Fuji Xerox describe a new phase separation recording technique involving binodal decomposition of tellurium oxide thin films. They claim exceptional resistance to degradation when the media are exposed to extreme environmental conditions. Pinsl et al (1987) discuss the advantages of liquid crystalline polysiloxanes. Gambogi et al (1987) discuss an optical recording process in which lasers convert conductive polymers to highly reflective glassy carbon. Hanamura and Itsubo (1988) discuss optical recording via photo-induced structure changes in polydiacetylene crystals. Yoshino et al (1988) discuss the optical recording properties of polymer films containing polyalkylthiophene. Roberts et al (1988) discuss optical recording experiments with a copper-technetium alloy. Ivey et al (1991) discuss the optical storage potential of lead-zirconate-titanate thin films. With any of these experimental processes, the time frame for commercial availability and the likelihood of successful commercialization cannot be determined.

REWRITABLE TECHNOLOGY

Over the past decade, manufacturers of write-once optical disk drives and media have steadily refined their recording technologies and processes to improve equipment performance, product reliability, media capacity, media stability, and other system characteristics. While these continuing refinements have produced the useful and highly varied range of write-once disk drives and media described later in this report, many industry analysts contend that write-once optical storage is an interim technology. While write-once products currently satisfy high-capacity storage requirements which cannot be successfully addressed by magnetics, many observers believe that they will eventually be supplanted by rewritable optical storage systems which offer both high-capacity and erasability.

For purposes of this discussion, rewritability is defined as the ability to delete previously recorded information, typically by overwriting it with new information. As previously noted, rewritable media are reusable. As discussed later in this report, rewritability is seldom required, and may not be desired, in document imaging systems, an important and growing class of applications for write-once optical disks. Among the conventional microfilm products which compete with WORM technology in such applications, only Bell and Howell's Microx system—an updateable microfiche system that employs a proprietary thermoplastic film as its recording medium—can erase previously recorded document images, but that feature is seldom utilized in working installations. In many records management applications, the nonerasable character of write-once optical disks is considered an advantage that facilitates the legal authentication of document images as unaltered copies of the paper records from which they were produced. Turning a potential limitation into a desirable feature, optical storage system vendors further note that write-once media prevent the inadvertent destruction of information and provide a useful audit trail in financial and other data processing applications.

Ultimately, however, computer specialists judge alternative information storage technologies against magnetic media, which are rewritable. They recognize the undeniable advantages of erasability and overwritability in transaction processing, database management, word processing, and other applications where data or text files are updated frequently. To accommodate such updating requirements, write-once optical disk installations must rely on software-based methodologies which employ pointers to indicate the storage locations of replacement data. Yokozeki et al (1989, 1990), for example, describe a software-based "virtual" optical disk system that simulates rewritability on write-once media and provides a complete revision history for all files as a useful byproduct of nonerasable recording. Christodoulakis and Ford (1989), and Lomet and Salzberg (1989) outline access methodologies which utilize rewritable magnetic media for temporary storage of changeable data that will eventually be transferred to WORM disk. Various characteristics of file management software employed in write-once optical recording are discussed by Berg (1989), Dirschedl et al (1987), Garfinkel (1991), Kwok (1989), Levy (1989), MacRae (1989), McDowell (1989), Ooi (1991), and Zwick (1989).

While such techniques may achieve the desired effects in applications where the high storage capacity of WORM disks is required, software-based revision methodologies can increase access times with a resulting unacceptable degradation of system performance. As an additional obvious disadvantage, media space is wastefully consumed by previous versions of files which have been updated. Not so obviously, write-once recording precludes the possibility of erasure should the expungement of particular information become desirable or required. Consequently, as discussed elsewhere in this report, write-once optical disk systems are relegated to data archiving and other applications involving closed files or static information that must be retained and will be recorded on WORM disks in final form.

With their ability to accommodate changing data and text files, rewritable optical disk systems significantly broaden the scope of optical storage applications and offer an alternative, complement, or supplement to conventional magnetic recording technology in a variety of information processing operations. Since the mid-1980s, rewritable optical storage—variously described as erasable or reversible optical storage—has been the focal point of considerable laboratory research and product development. Reflecting these efforts, the number of monographs, journal articles, technical reports, and conference papers dealing with rewritable optical recording technology has grown steadily. Since the late 1980s, such publications have outnumbered their write-once counterparts by a substantial margin, thus buttressing the previously discussed contention that rewritable optical disks will eventually supplant write-once systems.

Various surveys review the characteristics of rewritable optical recording technologies and describe its progress toward commercialization at specific points in time. Examples include Bate (1987), Bell (1986), Bennett (1988), Freese (1988), Funkenbusch (1991), Hecht (1987), Kawabata and Yamamoto (1988), Little (1988), Mansuripur et al (1985), Moeller (1990), Musikant (1990), Ojima and Ohta (1988), Scholte et al (1988), Urrows and Urrows (1988, 1990), and Van Uijen (1985). Rewritable optical disk technologies—including developmental processes as well as those currently available—are described below; commercially available and prototype rewritable optical disk drives will be discussed in a subsequent section.

Magneto-Optical Recording. Since the mid-1980s, magneto-optical (MO) recording—sometimes termed thermo-magneto-optical (TMO) recording—has been the focal point of laboratory research and product development activities pertaining to rewritable optical storage technology. As its name suggests, magneto-optical recording is a hybrid technology; magneto-optical media store information magnetically, but the information is recorded and read by a laser and optical assembly. Magneto-optical disks are actually multilayered magnetic disks which employ vertical recording techniques instead of the horizontal—sometimes described as longitudinal—recording methodologies associated with conventional magnetic media. In vertical recording, magnetic domains are oriented perpendicular to a disk's surface; with longitudinal media, in contrast, the domains are oriented parallel to the recording surface. As its principal advantage, perpendicular recording permits much closer spacing of magnetic domains with a consequent increase in recording density. Perpendicular magnetic recording is also utilized by high-capacity floppy disk systems, particularly those which employ barium-ferrite media. The technology is described in many publications, including Kobayashi et al (1983, 1987), Nakamura and Iwasaki (1984), Suzuki (1984), Ouchi and Iwasaki (1984), Fujiwara (1985), Nakamura (1985), Bolzoni et al (1986), and Katz and Brechtlein (1988).

With unrecorded magneto-optical media, all magnetic domains are initially oriented in a direction—north-pole down, for example—which represents the zero bits in digitally-coded information. The one bits are recorded by reversing the orientation of selected magnetic domains. To accomplish this, a highly focused laser beam heats a spot on the disk to its Curie temperature, the point at which the medium's magnetic orientation is lost. With most magneto-optical recording materials, the Curie temperature ranges between 150 and 200 degrees Celsius. When the required temperature is reached, an electromagnet generates a magnetic field which reorients the domains. The magnetic particles assume the desired orientation as the recording material cools. Data is erased by applying a less powerful laser beam which reverses the magnetization in recorded areas, returning them to the orientation which represents zero bits. Those areas can then be overwritten with new information in a subsequent disk rotation. While the combination of erasure and overwriting currently requires two passes to complete, direct overwriting of magneto-optical media—which will significantly improve operating speeds by eliminating the second pass—is an anticipated future refinement that is under intensive investigation by equipment manufacturers. It is discussed by Fukami et al (1990), Hashimoto et al (1990), Inoue et al (1990), Izumi et al (1990), Lin (1990), Perlov (1991), Tsutsumi and Umesaki (1990), Von den Berg (1990), and Watson and Meystre (1990).

Retrieval of information recorded on magneto-optical media depends on a phenomenon known as the Kerr effect. A magnetic surface rotates the polarization of reflected light in either a clockwise or a counterclockwise direction, depending on the orientation of magnetic particles. When read by a laser and an optical pickup mechanism, light reflected from a spot on a magneto-optical disk's surface will be detected as either a one or a zero bit. A related phenomena, called the Faraday effect, detects the polarization of light transmitted through, rather than reflected from, magnetized materials. While much discussed, it is not currently utilized in magneto-optical systems.

As previously noted, magneto-optical technology currently dominates the field of rewritable optical storage. At the time this report was prepared, magneto-optical disk systems were being manufactured by many companies, including Canon, Hewlett-Packard, Hitachi, IBM, Laser Magnetic Storage International, Literal Corporation, Matsushita, Maxoptix, Mitsubishi, Nakamichi, Pioneer, Ricoh, Sharp, Sony, and Toshiba. Based on work being performed at various research and product development facilities in Asia, Europe, and North America, recent publications on magneto-optical recording outnumber those dealing with all other optical recording processes combined. Technical descriptions of magneto-optical recording processes are provided in hundreds of journal articles and conference papers. Examples include Asano et al (1987), Bartholomeusz (1989), Carey et al (1991), Connell (1986), Crasemann and Hansen (1989, 1990), Crasemann et al (1989), Funkenbusch et al (1987), Gau (1989), Goldmann (1987), Greidanus (1990), Greidanus and Klahn (1989), Grundy (1990), Hansen (1990), Hartmann et al (1984), Haycock et al (1990), Imamura (1988, 1990), Klahn et al (1990), Kryder (1985, 1990), Mansuripur (1987, 1988), Meiklejohn (1986), Mergel et al (1990), Schmitt (1990), Schultz and Kryder (1989), Shieh (1991), Sponheimer (1990, 1991), and Zak et al (1990).

As noted above, magneto-optical disks are multilayered magnetic media. Unlike magnetic disks and tapes, however, they do not employ gamma ferric oxide, chromium dioxide, or other conventional magnetic recording materials. Instead, their active recording layers consist of specially designed thin films which combine iron with selected rare-earths and transition-metals. Rare-earths is the collective name for those chemical elements with atomic numbers twenty-one, thirty-nine, and fifty-seven through seventy-one. Examples employed in magneto-optical recording include terbium, neodymium, dysprosium, and gadolinium. The rare-earths are actually abundant in the earth's crust, but they were initially discovered in very rare minerals, hence their name. The transition metals are a group of elements with atomic numbers twenty-two through twenty-eight, forty through forty-six, and seventy-two through seventy-eight. Examples include cobalt, platinum, titanium, chromium, and zirconium.

Important technical characteristics of specific magneto-optical recording materials have been reviewed by many researchers, including Brandle et al (1990), Buschow (1988, 1989), Carcia et al (1991), Ebert and Akai (1990), Engler (1990), Fujiwara (1989), Greidanus and Zeper (1990), Greidanus et al (1989), Hansen and Heitmann (1989), Hansen et al (1991), Hashimoto et al (1990), Hatwar and Stinson (1991), Iiyori and Takayama (1991), Ishii et al (1989), Kaneko and Yamamoto (1988), Keppler and Goldmann (1988), Kryder et al (1987), Lin and Do (1990), Marinero (1989), McGahan and Woollam (1989), Nakamura and Itoh (1990), Nakamura et al (1990), Niihara et al (1990), Omachi (1988), Reim and Weller (1989), Toki et al (1990), Van Engelen and Buschow (1990), Weller and Reim (1989), and Zeper et al (1990).

For the most part, these sources emphasize the magneto-optic properties of various iron-based rare-earth and/or transition-metal alloys, of which terbium-ferrite-cobalt is currently the combination that is most widely utilized in commercially available products. Other possibilities include ferrite-cobalt, ferrite-terbium, ferrite-silicon, ferrite-terbium-gadolinium, and ferrite-terbium-indium compounds. Abe and Gomi (1990, 1990a), Dillon (1990), Gomi et al (1988, 1988a), Kano et al (1989), Shono et al (1990), and Suzuki (1991) discuss the potential of iron-garnet media as advanced recording materials for the next generation of magneto-optical systems. Ferre (1990) describes magneto-optical experiments with ultrathin cobalt films deposited on gold. Magneto-optical alloys consisting of various combinations of aluminum, maganese, gadolinium, antimony, cobalt, palladium, platinum, and other metals are examined by Attaran and Grundy (1989), Bechevet et al (1991), Gambino et al (1989), Shen et al (1989), Thavendrarajah et al (1989), Yasuda et al (1989), and Zeper et al (1991).

Regardless of the specific compounds employed, magneto-optical recording materials may be vacuum deposited or sputtered onto glass or plastic substrates. Fabrication techniques and substrate characteristics are described by Asari et al (1987, 1989), Brauer et al (1988, 1990), Deschanvres et al (1989), Hellstern et al (1990), Inui et al (1987, 1989), Ohta et al (1989), Schmidgall (1990), and Williams (1991). Moribe et al (1988) analyze the relationship between substrate composition and recording errors. Proponents of glass substrates cite their superior uniformity, optical clarity, mechanical stability, scratch resistance, freedom from warpage, and resistance to moisture absorption. Advocates of plastic substrates cite the economic advantages associated with high-volume production, as well as lighter weight, which facilitates rapid rotation. Siebourg et al (1990) discuss birefringence as a property of polycarbonate substrates.

Numerous research reports document the adverse affects of temperature and humidity on magneto-optical recording materials. Examples include Jacobs et al (1984), Heitman et al (1985), Luborsky et al (1985), Bernstein and Gueugnon (1985), Birecki et al (1985), Tejedor and Fernandez (1986), Arimune et al (1987), Higgins and Oesterreicher (1987), Tokunaga et al (1987), Miller et al (1988, 1989), Maeda et al (1989), Kobayashi et al (1990), Rio et al (1990), and Yardy et al (1990). These sources cite oxidation of rare-earths and transition metals as the principal cause of aging in magneto-optical media. Rare-earths—such as terbium, for example—are readily oxidized, with a resulting adverse impact on magnetic coercivity, recording sensitivity, bit error rates, playback stability, and other media characteristics.

While these degradative effects are time-dependent and inevitable, various experiments have demonstrated the effectiveness of oxidation-resistant alloys and multi-layer barrier coatings in delaying in their onset. Examples are described by Aratani et al (1985, 1987), Tanaka and Imamura (1985), Hartmann et al (1986), Tada et al (1986), Iijima (1987), Iijima and Hatakeyama (1987), Kirino et al (1991), Kobayashi et al (1987, 1987a, 1988), Maeno and Kobayashi (1990), Matsushima et al (1987), Miyazaki et al (1987), Sato et al (1987), Tanaka et al (1987), Wang et al (1987), Watanabe et al (1987), Wright et al (1987), Kobayashi and Kawamura (1988), Hatwar and Majumdar (1988), Kawamoto et al (1988), Niihara et al (1988), McIntire and Hatwar (1989), Majumdar and Hatwar (1989), Misaki et al (1989), Tokushima et al (1989), Abe and Gomi (1990), Gotoh et al (1990), Lee et al (1990), Maeno and Kobayashi (1990), Ohkubo et al (1990), Yan et al (1990), and Horiai et al (1991).

Despite such measures, however, lifetime estimates for magneto-optical disks remain shorter than those for some write-once optical media described above. Manufacturers' technical specifications typically cite a useful life of ten years for reliable recording and playback of information from magneto-optical disks with plastic substrates, although laboratory research suggests the possibility of longer life. Okada et al (1989), for example, provide a lifetime estimate of fifteen years for poly carbonate-based magneto-optical disks produced by NEC Corporation. Several manufacturers claim a longer life, ranging from fifteen to twenty-five years, for magneto-optical disks with glass substrates. Experimental confirmation of such estimates is provided by Katayama et al (1988) and Okazaki et al (1989), among others. Unlike write-once optical disks, manufacturers' lifetime estimates for magneto-optical disks are identical for shelf stability and playback stability. To be useful, rewritable optical media must presumably support both the recording of new information and the retrieval of previously recorded information for equal periods of time.

Phase-Change Recording. With phase-change technology, portions of an optical recording material are selectively converted from a crystalline to an amorphous state, or vice versa. The two states have detectable reflectivity differences which represent the one and zero bits in digitally coded information. As described above, phase-change technology is utilized in write-once optical recording systems in which the phase transformation is permanent. With the technology's rewritable variant, however, the transition between amorphous and crystalline states is reversible, thus permitting the erasure and overwriting of previously recorded information.

The rewritable potential of phase-change recording first attracted the information management community's attention in the early 1980s when Matsushita demonstrated a prototype system employing tellurium suboxide disks. The technology was not commercialized until 1990, however, and Matsushita remains the only manufacturer of reversible phase-change optical disk drives. While not as widely publicized or extensively researched as magneto-optical systems, rewritable phase-change devices and media have been the subject of much recent laboratory experimentation.

In rewritable phase-change recording, a highly focused laser beam heats small areas in a thin layer of crystalline or amorphous material to just above the melting point. Rapid cooling of the heated material transforms the affected areas from the crystalline form to an amorphous state. Because the crystalline form is more stable than the amorphous state, the recording material naturally tends to change back to it when reheated to just below its melting point. The technology is described, in considerable detail, by Chen et al (1985, 1986), Iwasawa et al (1986), Van der Poel et al (1986), Chen and Rubin (1989), Fukushima et al (1990), Gravesteijn (1989), Kimura (1989), Maeda et al (1991), Nishimura et al (1989), Nogami et al (1990), Ohara et al (1990), Ohno et al (1989), Ohta et al (1989), Rubin and Chen (1989), Situ et al (1989), Tanabe et al (1989), Yamada et al (1989), and Sugiyama et al (1990). Ryan (1990) provides a good overview for the general reader.

Reversible phase-change recording, like its write-once counterpart, relies heavily on tellurium thin films alloyed with one or more additional metals, such as selenium, gadolinium, indium, antimony, germanium, tin, and titanium. These alloys are described in a growing number of research reports, including Barton et al (1986), Fujimori et al (1988, 1988a), Hao et al (1989), Jiang and Okuda (1991), Maeda et al (1988, 1989, 1989b), Matsushita et al (1987), Minemura et al (1990), Nishimura et al (1989), Okuda et al (1988), Raychaudhuri (1989), Rhee et al (1987), Sato et al (1989), Suzuki et al (1990), Terao et al (1985, 1985a, 1987, 1989a), Yamazaki et al (1987), and Young et al (1986, 1986a). As discussed by Kimura (1989), Kimura and Ohno (1989), Ohno et al (1989), Ueno (1987), and Yamada et al (1986, 1987, 1989, 1991), Matsushita's rewritable phase change media are tellurium-based. Although they are not currently employed in commerically available products, laboratory experiments have explored the phase change potential of various other alloys, including indium-selenium-lead, indium-selenium-thallium, indium-selenium-cobalt, indium-selenium antimony, gallium antimonide-indium antimonide, silver-zinc, and gold-germanium. These materials are analyzed by Gotoh et al (1989), Holtslag and Scholte (1989), Iijima et al (1989, 1989a), Ikegawa et al (1988), Jiang et al (1989), Koshino et al (1987, 1988), Minemura et al (1988), Nishida et al (1987, 1987a), Terao et al (1986, 1989), Utsumi et al (1988), and Yasuoka et al (1987).

As their principal operational advantage over magneto-optical technology, phase-change optical disk systems support direct overwriting—that is, they can perform erasure and recording in a single pass. The present generation of magneto-optical disk drives, as previously noted, requires separate passes for erasure and overwriting. In theory at least, this advantage should result in faster read/write rates for phase-change drives, but phase-change recording materials themselves have traditionally suffered from slow amorphous-to-crystalline transition times which can limit their practicality in applications where information must be recorded and erased quickly.

Like their magneto-optical counterparts, phase-change optical disks have a stable life of ten years for both recording and playback, although accelerated aging experiments reported by Terao et al (1989b) and Ohta et al (1990) support longer lifetime estimates. In a comparison of magneto-optical and phase-change technologies, Van Uijen (1985) notes that phase-change recording materials are susceptible to accidental erasures at low temperatures, while magneto-optical materials require high temperatures and a surrounding magnetic field for reversibility. On the other hand, phase-change recording materials are largely unaffected by ambient temperatures and relative humidity encountered in most office environments, and they are completely unaffected by magnetic fields.

Other Processes. As described later in this report, magneto-optical and phase-change recording are currently employed by various optical storage products. Other rewritable optical recording technologies exist as laboratory processes only. A considerable number of research reports have examined the characteristics and information storage potential of dye-based—sometimes described as dye-polymer—media for rewritable optical recording. As with phase-change technology, dye-based optical recording exists in write-once and rewritable variants, although only the former has been commercialized. Like their WORM counterparts described above, rewritable dye-based media combine an organic dye with a polymeric binder. The dye absorbs the heat generated by a laser beam to create light-scattering pits, bumps, or bubbles in a thermoplastic layer. Depending on the recording material employed, affected areas of a dye-based optical disk may be melted, blistered, or otherwise deformed. The resulting pits, bumps, or bubbles typically represent the one bits in digitally-coded information; unchanged areas of the recording medium represent the zero bits. When read by a laser, differences between the changed and unchanged areas are optically detectable. To erase previously recorded information, a second laser or one operating at a different wavelength is used to relax the bubbles. The technology is surveyed by Abbott (1985), Gupta and Strome (1986), Kuder (1986, 1988), and Umehara et al (1985).

Although not as well known or as widely investigated as their magneto-optical and phase-change counterparts, rewritable dye-based recording materials have been the subject of laboratory experiments for more than a decade. Reports of research with specific materials are provided by Chung (1987), Eich (1987), Fujimura et al (1987), Gupta and Strome (1985, 1986), Hanna et al (1987), Kobayashi et al (1988), Kowel et al (1987), McIntyre and Soane (1990), Minemura and Andoh (1986), Morinaka and Oikawa (1986), Nishimori et al (1987, 1988), Potember et al (1986), and Sporer (1987). Rewritable dye-based media are compatible with a variety of rigid and flexible substrates. The technology's proponents note that dye-based optical disks can be produced by a thick-film, solvent-coating process that is similar to the well-established manufacturing techniques associated with magnetic media. Compared to magneto-optical and phase-change media, which are produced by vacuum deposition or sputtering of thin films, rewritable dye-based disks should prove simpler and less expensive to manufacture. Because they are composed of inert materials, dye-based optical disks are less vulnerable to oxidation than rewritable media constructed from metallic thin films.

Despite these potential advantages, dye-based rewritable optical disk systems have made no significant progress toward commercialization.

In the late 1980s, Optical Data Incorporated, a small U.S. company, demonstrated prototype dye-based rewritable media in 3.5-inch and 5.25-inch sizes. As described by Hartman et al (1989), Hartman and Lind (1987), Lind and Hartman (1988), and Halter and Iwamoto (1988), Optical Data's technology permitted the production of rewritable media with 100 to 500 megabytes of single-sided storage capacity. In mid-1988, Optical Data gained brief notoriety when Tandy Corporation announced that it would utilize its dye-based media in the Tandy High-Intensity Optical Recorder (THOR), an erasable compact disc system intended for consumer audio applications. That project was subsequently suspended, however. While several companies have since demonstrated recordable compact disc systems for consumer applications, they have employed magneto-optical media. Optical Data itself ceased operation in 1990. Prior to its dissolution, the company had signed non-exclusive licensing agreements with Philips and Du Pont Optical (PDO), a manufacturer of various types of optical storage media, and with Teijin Limited, a Japanese manufacturer of synthetic materials. As of this writing, the technology's status was uncertain; commercialization of rewritable dye-based systems does not appear imminent.

Other rewritable optical recording technologies are at even earlier stages of development. Optex Corporation, for example, is developing an innovative optical storage system based on electron trapping technology. Electron trapping materials are thin crystalline films which are combined with rare-earth elements and sputtered on aluminum or heat-resistant glass substrates. The materials consist of submicron-size areas that are capable of holding energized electrons. To record data, a laser energizes the electrons, trapping them in the recording material. At retrieval time, the trapped electrons are exposed to a laser beam of a different wavelength. Some of the electrons return to a ground energy state, emitting radiation in a characteristic and detectable pattern. Repeated read operations will return a sufficient number of electrons to the ground energy state, thereby erasing the recorded information. The technology process is entirely photonic and does not employ heat. It is explained by Goldsmith (1988), Goldsmith and Lindmayer (1990), Goldsmith et al (1990), Jutamulia et al (1989, 1989a, 1991, 1991a), Lindmayer (1988), Lindmayer and Wrigley (1989), and Lindmayer et al (1989, 1991).

Optex Corporation's Electron Trapping Optical Memory (ETOM) media was originally developed by Quantex Corporation which licensed it to Optex, a Quantex affiliate. Because many bits can be stored in a micron of ETOM, its recording densities compare very favorably with those supported by other optical storage technologies. ETOM recording densities have improved steadily with technological refinements. In late 1991, for example, Optex developed a four-level recording scheme which significantly increases storage density without a corresponding increase in spatial resolution requirements. Compared to magneto-optical and phase-change technologies, ETOM media can be recorded with lower-energy laser beams. Optex recently demonstrated the use of short-wavelength lasers to playback recorded information, thereby permitting further increases in recording density. The company has suggested that such developments could lead to 5.25-inch ETOM disks which can store up to fourteen gigabytes.

Based on early tests, Optex expects that its ETOM media will offer faster recording and retrieval performance than magneto-optical and phase-change materials. Because their recording sensitivity is much greater than rewritable optical storage materials in current use, they should permit much faster data recording rates without the performance degradation associated with thermal cycling. ETOM media can reportedly undergo more than 100 million read, write, and erase cycles without degradation; magneto-optical and phase-change disks, in contrast, are currently engineered for ten million read, write, and erase cycles. Optex further claims that ETOM materials, which are read by spectral emission, are less vulnerable to noise resulting from uneven recording surfaces. At the time this report was prepared, Optex Corporation was demonstrating its electron trapping technology in laboratory prototypes. The company has completed the conceptual design of an optical disk drive compatible with ETOM media, but product availability has not been scheduled.

Among other experimental approaches to rewritable optical storage, frequency domain and wavelength-multiplexed technologies promise very high recording densities but are years away from commercial viability. Employing organic or inorganic photon-gated compounds, frequency domain technology uses two laser sources to record multiple bits within the same focal diameter. A read/write laser beam excites those molecules in the exposed area which are sensitive to the laser's specific frequency. A second beam provides sufficient additional energy to record a bit by bleaching the excited molecules. The presence and absence of such bleached molecules represents the one and zero bits in digitally-coded information. By slightly varying the color of the read/write beam, other groups of molecules can be selectively excited and bleached, thereby recording thousands of bits a given exposed area. Recorded bits can be erased with a separate light source. The technology's history, present status, and future potential are discussed in a sizable and growing number of publications. Examples include Bjorklund et al (1984), Carter et al (1987), Kohler et al (1989), Lenth and Moerner (1986), Lenth et al (1986), Moerner (1985, 1985a, 1988), Moerner and Levenson (1985), Moerner et al (1987), Schellenberg et al (1986), and Yuk and Palais (1991).

In an experiment demonstrating the photon-gating process, IBM scientists recorded one bit by firing a read read/write laser beam and a green gating beam at a spot of photon-gated material measuring one millimeter thick and fifty microns wide (about one-half the width of a typical human hair). Together, the beams bleached a group of molecules in the exposed area. Without moving to another spot, the scientists tuned the read/write laser to a slightly different shade of red. Another group of molecules, representing a second bit, responded to the slightly changed color and were bleached. Using only the red beam, the scientists were able to read the data without detectable degradation. A blue beam was later used to erase the recorded bits. IBM contends that such recording techniques can achieve areal densities approaching 100 billion bits per square inch, but considerable technical and engineering improvements—including narrower hole widths and the ability to opeate at wavelengths associated with semiconductor diode lasers—must be achieved before frequency domain recording can be commercialized.

Various Japanese companies are reportedly researching technologies that utilize multiple laser beams of different wavelengths to irradiate a polymer material, thereby inducing photochemical reactions which record multiple signals in a given spot. Mitsibishi, for example, has demonstrated optical recording at up to 600 times currently attainable densities. Using a laser to burn highly reflective pits into the surface of a cryogenically cooled disk containing dual photochemical layers, Mitsubishi researchers claim recording densities approaching sixty billion bits per square centimeter. The recorded information is erased by extended exposure to high temperatures. Sony has reportedly utilized multi-wavelength technology to record over 100 spectral holes per laser spot. Its experiments with porphyrin-type compounds suggest the possibility of recording 1,000 holes per spot, thereby permitting storage densities which approach 100 billion bits per square centimeter. As a significant impediment to commercialization, however, the recording materials employed in such photochemical hole burning experiments must be cooled with liquid helium at impractically low temperatures. The technology is reviewed by Haarer (1987), Horie and Furusawa (1991), Itoh (1990), Nishimura et al (1989), Rebane (1988, 1990), Rebane et al (1988), Suzuki (1991), Tamura (1990), Tani et al (1987), and Yoshimura et al (1989).

Among other rewritable optical recording technologies which may or may not be successfully commercialized, Stein et al (1990) discuss the use of silver sodalites which exhibit controllable optical absorption and luminescence properties. Hayashi and Ogawa (1991) describe experiments with reflective optical storage materials composed of small silver metallic particles dispersed in a binding agent. Berezhnoy and Popov (1991) describe experimental storage media based on electro-optical crystals. Albin et al (1990) propose a high-capacity rewritable optical storage system based on stimulated electronic transition (SET) concepts for use aboard unmanned orbital space platforms. While its recording materials are composed of oxide and sulfide materials combined with rare-earths, SET technology does not involve localized heating as do magneto-optic and phase-change processes. Babbitt and Mossberg (1988) consider the prospects for optical storage in solid state materials. Shivaraman and Engstrom (1990) describe optical storage experiments with MNMOS materials. Levy et al (1989) discuss optical storage with photochromic materials. Hoffman and Potember (1989) describe experiments with a rewritable organometallic medium, while Kuhnert (1986) describes an optical memory device based on photo-induced phase changes in an oscillating chemical medium. Bowry and Bonnett (1991) examine the potential of liquid crystal polymers for optical recording of digital- and analog-coded information. Mitsunaga (1991) discusses an optical storage methodology based on photon echo technology, which relies on the interference effect of different optical waves. The optical recording potential of holograms, a perennial favorite in surveys of innovative information storage technologies, is reviewed by Berra et al (1989), De Caro et al (1991), Mitsuhashi (1990), Jacobson and Brown (1989), Owechko (1989), Renn et al (1989), Satoh and Kato (1988), Soffer et al (1986), Wai-Hon (1988), Wyrowski and Bryngdahl (1989), and Yariv et al (1986). Researchers at the University of California have patented a cube-shaped data storage device which has a claimed capacity of 6.5 terabytes. Data is recorded at the point where two laser beams intersect. The cube, which is composed of polystrene treated with organic chemicals, changes composition and color on exposure. Data can be erased with infrared radiation or heat. To retain recorded information, however, the cubes must maintained at very low temperatures. The researchers have suggested that a working prototype may be available within a decade; a commercialization date has not been forecasted.

WORM DRIVES AND MEDIA

The journal articles, technical reports, conference papers and other publications cited in preceding sections discuss research and experimentation with specific optical recording processes and materials. Many of them describe prototype optical disk drives, as well as laboratory samples of optical recording media produced in small quantities. As understanding of and experience with optical recording has increased, however, the focus of industry activities has shifted from basic research to product development and the commercialization of existing technologies. As previously noted, optical disk drives and media based on write-once recording technologies became commercially available in the early 1980s. The first such products were introduced in Japan. In the United States, the earliest write-once optical disk drive—the Gigadisc 1000—was introduced by Alcatel-Thomson in 1983. It was joined in the following year by the Optimem 1000 and the OSI LaserDrive 1200 from Optical Storage International, the company which subsequently became Laser Magnetic Storage International. While some of these early WORM devices remain in use, they have since been supplanted by second- and third-generation models with improved performance characteristics.

The number of commercially available write-once optical disk drives has increased steadily and significantly since the mid-1980s. The accompanying tables summarize the most important technical specifications for currently available WORM drives. As the tables indicate, such products are currently being manufactured by more than a dozen companies, including ATG Gigadisc, Eastman Kodak, Fujitsu, Hitachi, Laser Magnetic Storage International, Literal Corporation (formerly Information Storage Incorporated), Maximum Storage, Matsushita (Panasonic), Mitsubishi, Pioneer, Ricoh (which markets its WORM drives in the United States through Maxtor Corporation), Sony, and Toshiba. Several industry pioneers, included in previous reports in this series, are conspicuously absent from the latest listings. Optimem, which was best known for its twelve-inch write-once optical disk drives, ceased operation in 1991. The Optimem 1000, as previously noted, was one of the first WORM drives sold in the North America. The Optimem 2400 and Optimem 4000 were second and third generation products which incorporated successive improvements in media capacity and other performance characteristics. Optotech, one of the first companies to commercialize a 5.25-inch optical disk drive, discontinued its WORM product line in 1988. While the Optotech 5984 was acquired by Shugart, that company never marketed it actively.

The tabulations presented here are limited to write-once optical disk drives actively marketed in North America, although similar or identical models are typically available elsewhere. Historically, Japanese manufacturers have introduced their optical storage products domestically prior to exporting them through their North American, European, or other subsidiaries. Consequently, the number and variety of WORM drives available in Japan have often exceeded their North American counterparts. The tabulations are further restricted to model names designated by the WORM drives' manufacturers. Certain products listed here are also sold under other brand names and model designations by systems integrators, value-added resellers, and other OEM organizations. Such reseller arrangements are particularly common with 5.25-inch optical disk drives.

The tables omit older WORM drives that are no longer being manufactured or actively marketed, although such products may remain in use at installed sites. Readers interested in the technical characteristics of older optical disk equipment should consult specifications provided in previous reports in this series. While the listings indicate the years in which specific WORM drives were introduced in North America, manufacturers have traditionally announced their optical storage products well in advance of general availability. Initial shipments, which may not begin for several months after a given drive is announced, are typically limited to evaluation units. Such devices are purchased in small quantities by prospective resellers or other OEM clients who will ultimately repackage them with interface kits, software, cables, and other components essential to viable end-user configurations. In most cases, one year or more elapses between the announcement of a product and sales to end-users. Thus, 5.25-inch write-once optical disk drives announced by Fujitsu, Hitachi, and Maxtor in late 1986 did not become routinely available until the following year. General commercial availability of several rewritable optical disk drives announced in late 1987 and early 1988 was similarly delayed until late 1988 or early 1989.

Characteristics of write-once optical disk drives as computer peripheral devices have been discussed in various publications, including Apiki and Eglowstein (1989), Rash (1987),

As noted earlier in this report and confirmed by the accompanying tables, various write-once optical drives employ ablative recording of tellurium-based media. Dye-based technology is employed by several vendors. Dual-alloy, phase-change, and thermal-bubble recording remain single-manufacturer technologies.

Most optical disk drive manufacturers also sell blank optical recording media, although such media may actually be produced by a subsidiary or another company. Thus, Maxell, a Hitachi subsidiary, manufactures the tellurium-based optical disks used in drives sold by Hitachi's Computer Sales and Service Division. Similarly, Maxtor's dye-based recording media, like its RXT-800S optical disk drive, are manufactured by Ricoh. To make their products more competitive and meet government requirements for alternative procurement sources, some optical disk drive manufacturers designate a second source for recording media to be used with their equipment. Plasmon, as previously noted, manufactures write-once optical disks for use in Panasonic drives. Philips and Du Pont Optical (PDO) produces write-once optical disks for use in drives manufactured by Laser Magnetic Storage International and Eastman Kodak, while Daicel is a second-source for media utilized by the Literal Corporation's WORM drives. When approved by an equipment manufacturer, such second-source media are said to be "qualified" for use in a particular drive.

Regardless of recording technology or media sources, write-once optical disks intended for computer applications are typically enclosed in plastic cartridges to facilitate handling and to protect them from damage and environmental contaminants. While exact cartridge dimensions may vary, write-once optical disks are currently available in three diameters: fourteen inches, twelve inches, and 5.25-inches. Eight-inch WORM media were briefly available during the 1980s. Although they were employed in several document imaging systems marketed in Japan, eight-inch WORM products attracted very little attention in North America. The Pioneer DD-8100 was typical of eight-inch WORM drives. Employing dye-based optical media with 1.5-gigabytes of double-sided storage capacity, it was offered in a configuration intended for IBM Series/1 minicomputer installations. Matsushita and Sony developed eight-inch optical disk products with similar recording capacities, but they were never actively marketed in North America. As discussed below, eight-inch WORM media have also been utilized by some analog video disc recorders to be described later in this report. Such products fall outside the scope of the present discussion, which is limited to write-once optical disk products intended for digital recording computer applications. Reflecting the state of the art in late 1991, the following sections survey the characteristics and capabilities of commercially available write-once optical disk products in the three media sizes enumerated above.

Fourteen-Inch Systems. At the time this report was prepared, Eastman Kodak was the only manufacturer of fourteen-inch write-once optical disk drives. Fourteen-inch WORM media, as noted above, are produced by Kodak and other approved suppliers. Obviously designed as a magnetic disk complement or replacement for mainframe and large minicomputer installations with very high capacity storage requirements, the Kodak Model 6800 is based on research and development activities that date from the late 1970s. Marketed by Kodak's Mass Memory Division, it was announced in 1986, although product deliveries did not begin until the following year. An earlier fourteen-inch write-once optical disk system, developed by Storage Technology Corporation, was demonstrated in 1984 and installed at several test sites, but it was discontinued prior to commercialization. As discussed below, several companies have demonstrated rewritable optical disk systems based on fourteen-inch media, but such devices were not commercially available at the time this report was prepared.

Kodak's decision to produce a fourteen-inch optical disk system was reportedly influenced by the availability of precision-engineered fourteen-inch aluminum platters which are utilized as substrates in high-capacity magnetic disk drives, although those products are rapidly being replaced by higher-density magnetic disk drives based on ten-to-twelve-inch platters. According to Kodak researchers, the mechanical rigidity of aluminum substrates permits the manufacturing of a larger disk than would be possible with competing technologies based on injection-molded plastic or glass substrates. With their large surface areas, fourteen-inch platters are well suited to applications with large-scale databases, document imaging installations, and other computing applications with high volume data recording requirements.

The Kodak Model 6800 optical disk drive takes its name from the media recording capacity offered by its original configuration—6,800 megabytes (6.8 gigabytes) per double-sided, fourteen-inch WORM cartridge. It features a dye-based recording medium which is coated on a reflective layer and covered with a protective overcoat. In late 1989, Kodak announced its intention to manufacture a fourteen-inch write-once optical disk with a double-sided capacity of 8.2 gigabytes for use in upgraded versions of the Model 6800 drive,

A read/write optical disk drive with recording medium and cartridge. (Courtesy: Pioneer)

Examples of Write-once Optical Disk Drives Available in North America

	Kodak Model 6800	ATG GD 9001	ATG GD 6001	Hitachi OD321	LMSI LD 4100
Year introduced in North America	1986	1991	1989	1991	1990
Recording technology	phase change or dye-based	thermal bubble	thermal bubble	ablative/ tellurium	ablative/ tellurium
Disk size (in inches)	14	12	12	12	12
Storage capacity per recording surface	5.1 or 3.4 GB	4.5 GB	3.2 GB	3.5 GB	2.8 GB
Recording surfaces per cartridge	2	2	2	2	2
ANSI/ISO-compliant cartridge	yes*	no	no	no	no
Heads per drive	1	1	1	1	2
Access time (in milliseconds)	700	90	120	150	130
Transfer rate (per second)	1 MB	1.5 MB	1 MB	1.5 MB	1 MB
Host computer interface	SCSI	SCSI	SCSI	SCSI	SCSI

* Conforms to proposed standard for 14-inch optical disk cartridges

although products with that capacity never became commercially available. In mid-1991, Kodak announced a new version of the Model 6800 drive which supports 10.2 gigabytes of recording capacity per double-sided fourteen-inch WORM platter—the highest media capacity of any optical disk product available at the time this report was prepared. The new version's higher media capacity was achieved by changing from dye-based recording to phase-change technology. Kodak offers field upgrades for the installed base of Model 6800 drives, enabling them to read and record in both the 10.2 gigabyte and 6.8 gigabyte formats.

Kodak's WORM cartridge is the basis for the ISO CD 10085 standard for fourteen-inch write-once optical disk cartridges developed by the International Standardization Organization (ISO). As used in this context, standards are published specifications which provide guidelines for the production and use of particular products, including optical recording media, disk drives, and related hardware and software components. The standardization of optical storage products presumably benefits both manufacturers and users by shortening development cycles, reducing manufacturing costs, and promoting the compatibility and inter-

Examples of Write-once Optical Disk Drives Available in North America

	Sony WDD-600	Toshiba WM-S500	Fujitsu M2505A	Hitachi OD101	ISI 525GB
Year introduced in North America	1989	1987	1986	1986	1988
Recording technology	dual alloy	ablative/ tellurium	ablative/ tellurium	ablative/ tellurium	ablative/ tellurium
Disk size (in inches)	12	12	5.25	5.25	5.25
Storage capacity per recording surface	2.2 GB or 3.3 GB*	2.5 GB	300 MB	300 MB	640 MB
Recording surfaces per cartridge	2	2	2	2	2
ANSI/ISO-compliant cartridge	no	no	yes	yes	no
Heads per drive	1	1	1	1	1
Access time (in milliseconds)	180-500**	210	100	100	100
Transfer rate (per second)	600 KB	500 KB	690 KB	690 KB	2.5 MB
Host computer interface	SCSI	SCSI	SCSI	SCSI	SCSI, PC Bus

* Higher capacity applies to CLV-format cartridges
** Shorter access time applies to CAV-format cartridges

changeability of equipment and media. Standardization encourages competitive purchasing through the availability of alternative procurement sources, facilitates the selection and integration of products appropriate to specific applications, simplifies implementation and training, and generally enhances customers' confidence in and acceptance of optical storage technology.

As with other information processing products, the American National Standards Institute (ANSI) and the International Standardization Organization are the principal organizations responsible for the development of standards for optical storage equipment and media. Their work is accomplished through technical committees and subcommittees which prepare draft standards for review, approval, and eventual publication. The ANSI X3B11 committee on optical digital data disks is specifically concerned with standards for the interchange of optical media. Such standards are designed to enable drives of one manufacturer to be used with conforming media produced by other manufacturers. The committee's work, which began in the mid-1980s, is coordinated with that of the ISO/SC23 committee. Since only one vendor currently manufactures fourteen-inch WORM drives, proposed standards for fourteen-inch write-once optical disk cartridges generated no controversy.

Twelve-Inch Systems. Kodak's enhancements to the Model 6800 WORM drive were necessary to maintain the capacity advantages of fourteen-inch optical disk systems when compared to the latest generation of twelve-inch products, several of which approach or surpass the 6.8-gigabytes of double-sided media capacity offered by the original Model 6800. As previously discussed, twelve-inch WORM drives and media were the first read/write optical disk products to be successfully commercialized. Several models were available for sale by the mid-1980s, and they have been utilized in a variety of mainframe, minicomputer, and microcomputer installations since that time. By the late 1980s, however, twelve-inch WORM drives were being derided as older devices that would soon be replaced by new technology employing smaller, higher-density 5.25-inch media, just as large-format magnetic disk drives have been steadily replaced by products based on smaller formats. Such predictions, which were widely publicized, now seem unlikely for two reasons:

1. During the past several years, several manufacturers of twelve-inch WORM drives have introduced attractive new models with significantly expanded storage capacities and enhanced performance characteristics. Such improved drives have proven particularly popular in document imaging applications which require the high storage capacities provided by twelve-inch platters.

2. The recording capacities of smaller WORM media have not increased as predicted. At the time this report was prepared, the highest 5.25-inch optical disk drive provided 1.28 gigabytes of double-sided recording capacity. That product, the ISi 525GB from Literal Corporation, was introduced in 1988. As discussed below, the majority of 5.25-inch WORM systems offer significantly less than one gigabyte of media capacity.

Introduced between 1983 and 1986, the first generation of twelve-inch write-once optical disk drives could record two to four gigabytes of information per double-sided WORM cartridge. Examples of such products included the ATG Gigadisc 1001 and 1002, the Optimem 1000, and the LaserDrive 1200 and 1250 from Laser Magnetic Storage International, all of which could store two gigabytes per double-sided WORM cartridge; the Hitachi OD301-A1 which supported 2.6 gigabytes of double-sided cartridge capacity; the Optimem 2400 and 4000, two improved versions of the Optimem 1000 which increased cartridge capacity to 2.4 gigabytes and 3.9 gigabytes, respectively; the Sony WDD-3000, which could store 2.2 to 3.2 gigabytes per WORM cartridge, depending on the recording mode employed; and the Toshiba DF-0450, which featured 3.6-gigabyte double-sided media.

By the late 1980s, as noted above, many industry analysts considered twelve-inch write-once optical disk systems to be a mature product group which would not be subject to further innovation. Since that time, however, most manufacturers of twelve-inch WORM drives have introduced higher capacity second and third generation models as replacements for their initial products. Capable of storing 2.4 gigabytes per double-sided WORM cartridge, the Optimem 2400, which was introduced in 1988, provided a modest improvement in media capacity when compared with its predecessor, the Optimem 1000; in the following year, however, Optimem introduced its Model 4000 which increased cartridge capacity to 3.9 gigabytes. The Toshiba WM-S500, introduced in 1987, was the first twelve-inch WORM drive to offer four gigabytes of double-sided media capacity; in a subsequent enhancement, Toshiba increased the recording capacity to five gigabytes.

The LaserDrive 4100, a second-generation twelve-inch WORM drive introduced in 1990 by Laser Magnetic Storage International, can store 5.6 gigabytes per double-sided WORM cartridge—2.8 times the amount supported by its predecessors, the LaserDrive 1200 and 1250. As its

Examples of Write-once Optical Disk Drives Available in North America

	LMSI LD 510	Maxtor RXT-800S	Mitsubishi MW-5D1	Panasonic LF-5012	Pioneer DD-5001
Year introduced in North America	1987	1986	1988	1989	1987
Recording technology	ablative/tellurium	dye-based	ablative/tellurium	phase-change	dye-based
Disk size (in inches)	5.25	5.25	5.25	5.25	5.25
Storage capacity per recording surface	327 MB	400 MB	300 MB	470 MB	327 MB
Recording surfaces per cartridge	2	2	2	2	2
ANSI/ISO-compliant cartridge	yes	no	yes	no	yes
Heads per drive	1	1	1	1	1
Access time (in milliseconds)	75	100	80	90	250
Transfer rate (per second)	600 KB	1 MB	690 KB	2.5 MB	1.5 MB
Host computer interface	SCSI	SCSI	SCSI	SCSI	SCSI

most significant feature, however, the LaserDrive 4100 incorporates separate read/write heads for each recording surface. By making it unnecessary to turn an optical disk cartridge over to access data recorded on the reverse side, dual-headed drives effectively double the online storage capacity of a given cartridge. At the time this report was prepared, the LaserDrive 4100 was the only optical disk drive of any type to be configured with dual read/write heads.

Among other twelve-inch WORM drives with expanded storage capacity, the Gigadisc 6000, introduced by ATG in 1989, can record 6.4 gigabytes per double-sided WORM cartridge. In the same year, Sony introduced its WDD-600 which offers a choice of recording formats and media capacities. In the constant linear velocity (CLV) mode, the WDD-600 can record approximately 6.6 gigabytes per double-sided twelve-inch WORM cartridge; in the constant angular velocity (CAV) mode, however, double-sided media capacity is limited to 4.4 gigabytes. Because CLV format disks rotate at variable speeds, they suffer slower access times than their CAV counterparts;

the customer has the option of trading recording capacity for performance, or vice versa.

In its CLV mode, the WDD-600 approached the recording capacity of Kodak's fourteen-inch WORM drive—prior, that is, to the enhancement described above. The Hitachi OD321-1, introduced in late 1990, was—for a brief time—the highest capacity optical disk drive of any size. Intended to replace Hitachi's OD301-A1, it can store seven gigabytes per double-sided twelve-inch WORM cartridge. As discussed by Arai and Maeda (1990) and Maeda et al (1991), the increased capacity is based on pit-edge recording methods combined with modified CAV recording. In mid-1991, ATG announced the Gigadisc 9001, the company's third generation model which supports a double-sided cartridge capacity of nine gigabytes. At the time this report was prepared, the Gigadisc 9001 was the capacity leader among twelve-inch WORM drives.

As a group, the second and third generation drives described above confirm the position of twelve-inch, write-once optical disk systems as viable information storage products for the foreseeable future. All twelve-inch write-once optical disk systems employ proprietary equipment and media. The ANSI X3B11 committee is developing standards for twelve-inch WORM cartridges, but that work is at an early stage and is not expected to impact product development before the mid-1990s.

5.25-Inch Systems. 5.25-inch optical media are obviously suitable for small computer installations where the 5.25-inch form factor is widely employed by rigid and flexible magnetic disk drives. During the 1980s, as noted above, 5.25-inch devices and media were widely heralded as the write-once optical storage components of choice for future system implementations, but— despite a series of 5.25-inch WORM product announcements in the mid-to-late 1980s— technology improvements have not kept pace with those of larger media. While a number of useful WORM models are available, manufacturers' and customers' interest in 5.25-inch optical storage systems has steadily shifted to the rewritable devices and media described later in this report. The state of the art in 5.25-inch write-once optical storage has changed little since the late 1980s.

The first 5.25-inch WORM drive, the ISi 525WC, was introduced in 1985 by Information Storage Incorporated (ISi), which subsequently merged with LaserDrive Limited to form the Literal Corporation. In its initial configuration, the ISi 525WC employed single-sided optical media with approximately 115 megabytes of storage capacity. Double-sided, 230-megabyte WORM cartridges became available in 1986. Optotech likewise introduced a 5.25-inch WORM drive in 1985. Like its ISi counterpart, it initially employed single-sided media with 204 megabytes of storage capacity; double-sided, 408-megabyte WORM cartridges were subsequently introduced.

A number of interesting 5.25-inch WORM products were introduced during the late 1980s. As with the twelve-inch systems described above, the new models offered greater storage capacities than their predecessors. Maxtor's RXT-800S, which was introduced in 1986 and remains a popular product, uses dye-based technology to record 800 megabytes per double-sided WORM cartridge. Manufactured by Ricoh, it was the capacity leader among 5.25-inch optical disk drives until 1988, when Information Storage Incorporated introduced the ISi 525GB which employs 1.28-gigabyte double-sided media. The Toshiba WM-D070, introduced in 1986, and the Panasonic LF-5010, introduced in 1989, are the only other 5.25-inch WORM drives which approach gigabyte-level media capacities. The Toshiba WM-D070 employs tellurium-alloy media which can store 900 megabytes per double-sided WORM cartridge when information is recorded in the modified constant angular velocity (MCAV) mode; a conventional CAV recording mode permits faster access for recording and playback but reduces media capacity to 600 megabytes. Using the write-once variant of phase-change technology, the Panasonic LF-5010 can store 940 megabytes per double-sided, 5.25-inch optical disk cartridge. It replaced an earlier Panasonic model which employed single-sided WORM cartridges with 200 megabytes of recording capacity. For a brief period of time, that earlier model was also sold by IBM as the 3363 optical disk drive.

The 5.25-inch WORM products described to this point utilize proprietary recording media. In 1987 and 1988, several manufacturers introduced

5.25-inch WORM drives which employ media that conform to the ISO/IEC 9171 standards for 5.25-inch write-once optical disk cartridges. Examples of such drives include the Fujitsu M2505A, the Hitachi OD101, the LaserDrive 510 from Laser Magnetic Storage International, the Mitsubishi MW-5D1, and the Pioneer DD-5001. These drives support media capacities of 600 or 650 megabytes per double-sided WORM cartridge, depending on the recording format selected. As previously noted, optical disk cartridge standards are designed to permit the interchange of optical recording media and equipment of different manufacturers, thereby promoting competitive media procurement from multiple sources. In contrast, the proprietary recording media employed by nonstandard WORM drives must be purchased from the drives' manufacturers or designated, approved suppliers.

The previously cited ISO standards specify the magnetic clamp method, hub diameter, central hole diameter, tracking method, and other characteristics of optical disk cartridges. As a source of potential confusion, however, ISO standards for 5.25-inch write-once optical disk cartridges recognize two different recording formats: continuous composite servo (CCS), sometimes described as Format A, and sampled servo (SS), also known as Format B. The two formats employ different methods of handling the control or servo signals which permit accurate tracking and focus of a drive's optical head during recording and playback. The continuous composite servo format employs pregrooved media, while the sampled servo method uses a series of marks on each side of a track's center. Principals and characteristics of servo control technology are reviewed by Nagasawa (1990).

As its principal advantage, the continuous servo method can be implemented with standard chip sets. As discussed by Ekberg et al (1991a), the sampled servo method is a newer technology which requires customized development. Proponents of the sampled servo method, however, claim the advantages of improved signal-to-noise ratios and the ability to increase track density as shorter wavelength lasers become available. While both formats are permitted by ISO standards for 5.25-inch WORM cartridges, they are incompatible with one another. Each requires its own media; continuous servo and sampled servo cartridges are not interchangeable, even though both are advertised as ISO-compliant. When evaluating standard 5.25-inch WORM drives, prospective purchasers must consequently determine the particular format supported by a given product. At the time this report was prepared, the continuous servo format was utilized in 5.25-inch WORM drives manufactured by Hitachi, Fujitsu, and Mitsubishi. The sampled servo format was utilized in 5.25-inch WORM drives manufactured by Pioneer and Laser Magnetic Storage International.

Cherokee Data Systems occupies a unique market niche among optical disk drive manufacturers; it produces ruggedized 5.25-inch WORM systems for military, avionic, industrial, and other applications associated with harsh environments. Like other ruggedized information processing products, the Cherokee drives are manufactured to withstand severe vibration, shock, temperatures, and rough handling. They feature temperature sensing components, gold-plated pin and post connectors, heavy duty base plates, and air filters.

Drive Characteristics. Regardless of media size, all write-once optical disk drives use lasers to record information as pits, bubbles, or spots of altered reflectivity. Kume et al (1987), Nakane et al (1987), Niina and Hamada (1986), and Suzuki (1987) survey the characteristics of lasers employed in optical disk equipment. While the earliest WORM drives utilized gas lasers, new products feature semiconductor diode lasers which are more easily modulated, more compact, and potentially less expensive than their gas counterparts. Kozlovsky et al (1990) discusses the potential of short-wavelength blue lasers in optical storage configurations. Some researchers contend that such devices will permit significant improvements in recording density.

While write-once optical disk drives support very high media capacities, their access times and other performance characteristics suffer in comparisons with fixed magnetic disk drives. As direct access storage devices, all write-once optical disk drives write data onto, and retrieve data from particular tracks within a platter-shaped recording surface. The individual tracks are divided into sectors. Typically measured in milliseconds, a given drive's average access time is a combination of the average seek time—the time required to move the read/write head to the proper track for recording or retrieval—and the average latency—the time required for the desired sector to revolve under the read/write head. Seek time is measured from the receipt of a motion command until a ready command is sent to the drive's controller. The average latency is one half of the time required for one disk revolution.

Performance characteristics of write-once optical disk drives are discussed by Kaneko (1987), Lange (1987), Ranade (1989), and Ranade and Ng (1990). With average access times ranging from about 100 milliseconds to over 400 millisecons, write-once optical disk drives operate at about the same speeds as many floppy disk drives. They are considerably slower than fixed hard disk drives. Average access times for such devices range from less than twenty milliseconds for high-performance models to about sixty-five milliseconds for the least expensive devices encountered in entry-level microcomputer configurations. Like floppy disk drives, the slow access times associated with write-once optical disk drives are partly attributable to long latencies resulting from slow disk rotation rates, but WORM drives are also burdened by slow read/write head movements.

Through various design refinements, however, newer WORM drives are typically faster than earlier models, and ongoing research and development activities suggest that continuing improvements are likely. Tsunoda and Ojima (1987) contend that performance characteristics of future optical disk drives will compare more favorably with magnetic disk systems. Kasai et al (1987) describe Hitachi's experiments with a rapid access method based on cross-track counting techniques. Reporting on research performed at Nippon Telegraph and Telephone, Itao et al (1987) describe an experimental write-once optical disk drive with an average access time of sixty-five milliseconds. Similarly fast WORM drives are described by Ito et al (1987) and Ogawa et al (1987). Komura et al (1989) discuss the use of a split optical head and linear actuator mechanism to significantly reduce seek time in a prototype optical disk drive developed by NEC Corporation.

In addition to hardware advances, various software-based techniques can yield significant improvements in access times for information recorded on WORM disks. As an example, write-once optical disk drives are sometimes implemented in caching configurations which utilize a fixed magnetic disk drive for temporary storage of frequently reference data, thereby reducing the time required to access or re-access such information. Typically, such cache-oriented WORM systems employ a "read ahead" approach which transfers to a magnetic disk drive the contents of those optical disk sectors which immediately follow the data requested by a given retrieval operation. Where successive retrieval operations will access sectors sequentially such anticipatory reading can effectively reduce access time. When an access command is received, the magnetic disk cache is first checked to determine whether it contains the desired data. If the data is present, it is accessed at magnetic disk speeds; otherwise, the optical disk drive is consulted. As the cache becomes full, infrequently referenced data is automatically deleted from it.

To improve recording speed by minimizing head movements, some write-once optical disk systems also use magnetic disk storage to consolidate data to be recorded in a given track. In such configurations, data is only transferred to an optical disk drive when the magnetic disk cache fills to a specified level. While such caching techniques can improve access times, they do not necessarily give optical disk drives parity with their magnetic disk counterparts, since magnetic disk access times can be improved by utilizing random-access memory as a cache for frequently reference data.

Once a desired data area on an optical disk is located, information must be transferred between a WORM drive and its host computer. Data transfer rates supported by write-once optical disk drives range from as low as 250 kilobytes per second for certain early models to about one megabyte per second for the newest devices. With a given WORM drive, data rates for recording are typically lower than those for reading. For both reading and recording, optical disk transfer rates are typically lower than those supported by fixed magnetic disk drives. To address this limitation, Beshore (1989) proposes sector striping techniques which distribute consecutive logical sectors across two or more physical drives.

REWRITABLE DRIVES AND MEDIA

The end product of the significant research and development activities discussed in preceding sections of this report, rewritable optical disk drives based on magneto-optical technology became commercially available in the United States in 1988, although several models were introduced in Japan in late 1987. A magneto-optical disk drive developed by Canon attracted considerable attention when it was selected as the principal storage peripheral for the initial configuration of the widely publicized NeXT computer; subsequent implementations of the NeXT system dropped the magneto-optical drive as a standard feature, however, replacing it with a fixed magnetic disk drive. The Sony SMO-D501, the most widely utilized magneto-optical disk drive, received its first public demonstratin at the 1988 conference and exhibition of the Association for Information and Image Management. Similar models were subsequently announced by Ricoh, Hitachi, Maxoptix, Sharp, and other companies. Such products are described by Ai et al (1990), Hosokawa et al (1989), Kushizaki and Shigematsu (1989), Murikami et al (1989), Ojima et al (1990), Tanaka and Sugawara (1989), Tanaka et al (1990), and Yamaoka (1989). Panasonic introduced the first rewritable optical disk drive based on phase-change technology in 1990.

The most important characteristics of typical rewritable optical disk drives are summarized in the accompanying tables. As with the WORM drives described in preceding sections, the table is limited to models that were available for sale in North America at the time this report was prepared. Additional rewritable drives may be available elsewhere. The tabulations are further limited to the drive manufacturers' U.S. model designations. Some of the listed products are marketed under different model names by value-added resellers and systems integrators. Like their WORM counterparts, most manufacturers of rewritable optical disk drives sell their products to OEM clients rather than end-users. The OEM clients repackage the drives with interface kits, cables, software, and other components appropriate to specific computer configurations.

Most of the rewritable drives listed in the accompanying tables employ magneto-optical recording technology. A special group of rewritable optical disk drives—termed multifunctional drives—can operate in either the rewritable or write-once mode. The earliest multifunctional devices were introduced in 1990. Additional product announcements are expected, but it is uncertain whether multifunctional devices will eventually supplant WORM-only and rewritable-only equipment configurations. Terry (1990) and Wingert (1991) provide a product group overview. Specific problems associated with multifunctional implementations are reviewed by Berg (1990), Dundon (1986), Hara et al (1988), Itao et al (1988), Stevens (1991), Wtabe et al (1988), and Yazawa (1991).

Specific approaches to multifunctionality vary from manufacturer to manufacturer. Most combine a specific write-once recording technology with a specific rewritable recording technology. The LaserDrive 520 from Laser Magnetic Storage International, for example, combines ablative recording of tellurium-based write-once media with magneto-optical technology for rewritable recording. It is discussed by Hoy (1991). As described by Furuhata et al (1989) and Ekberg et al (1991), the Pioneer DE-7001 employs magneto-optical recording in its rewritable mode, but dye-based media for write-once recording. Jasionowski (1991) describes Panasonic's LF-7010 drive, which combines write-once and rewritable phase-change technologies.

The majority of multifunctional drives employ different media for write-once and rewritable recording. The drive detects the type of media inserted into it and automatically activates the appropriate recording mode. In the write-once mode, the multifunctional drive's command set does not support file deletions, media reformatting, or other destructive operations. Taking a completely different approach described by Roby (1991), Hewlett-Packard offers a multifunctional optical disk drive which employs magneto-optical media for both write-once and rewritable recording, although different disks are required for each operating mode. Write-once and rewritable media are identified by factory-inscribed codes which are detected by the multifunctional drive when a given optical disk cartridge is loaded. The drive automatically invokes the recording mode appropriate to the loaded cartridge. As noted above, the multifunctional drive's write-once command set does not support deletion or overwriting. Accidental erasure is consequently impossible. Additional coding prevents recording in data blocks which have already been utilized. Write-once and rewritable media are also color-coded and labelled for visual identification.

Whether implemented as single-purpose or multifunctional devices, rewritable optical disk drives available at the time this report was prepared were primarily intended for microcomputer and desktop workstation installations. Most models employ 5.25-inch media, although 3.5-inch magneto-optical drives—which were introduced in the United States in 1990—are expected to proliferate. Several companies have demonstrated magneto-optical disk drives with larger media, but such products have not been commercialized. Cinelli (1988) and Levene (1988, 1989) describe a prototypical fourteen-inch magneto-optical disk drive intended for military applications. Edwards et al (1990) discuss media requirements for such a drive. In early 1990, Fujitsu announced the F6443D, a multi-platter, multi-spindle magneto-optical disk system for its Japanese mainframe and supercomputer installations. As described by Kudou et al (1990), it can store thirty-six gigabytes of data. As discussed by Tanaka and Suzuki (1988), Pioneer and Kokusai Denshin Denwa (KDD) have jointly developed a twelve-inch magneto-optical disk system designed for analog video recording rather than digitally-coded, computer-generated data. Such products will be described in a later discussion of video disc recorders.

5.25-Inch Systems. The same size as many rigid and flexible magnetic disk devices, 5.25-inch

3.5 inch rewritable drives with media. (Courtesy M.O.S.T.)

Examples of Rewritable Optical Disk Drives Available in North America

	Canon M-O	Hitachi OD 112-1	Maxtor Tahiti	Panasonic LF-9000
Year introduced in North America	1988	1989	1989	1990
Recording technology	magneto-optical	magneto-optical	magneto-optical	magneto-optical
Disk size (in inches)	5.25	5.25	5.25	5.25
Storage capacity per recording surface	256 MB	300 or 325 MB	300 - 512 MB*	300 or 325 MB
Recording surfaces per cartridge	1 or 2	2	2	2
ANSI/ISO-compliant cartridge	no	yes	yes	yes
Heads per drive	1	1	1	1
Access time (in milliseconds)	90	75	60	85
Transfer rate (per second)	1.1 MB	925 KB	700 KB- 1.1 MB	900 KB
Host computer interface	SCSI	SCSI	SCSI	SCSI

* Higher capacity in proprietary ZCAV format

rewritable optical disk drives are well suited to desktop computer installations. Like their WORM counterparts, 5.25-inch rewritable recording media are encapsulated in plastic cartridges. Depending on the system selected, double-sided cartridge capacities range from 512 megabytes to one gigabyte. Magneto-optical media employed by the most widely utilized rewritable drives conform to the ISO 10089 standard for 5.25-inch rewritable optical disk cartridges. Examples of such drives include the Sony SMO-D501, Ricoh RO-5031E and RO-5030EII, Hitachi OD112-1, Sharp JY-700, Hewlett-Packard HP C1711A and HP1716A, and Panasonic LF-9000. ISO-compliant media are also utilized by those multifunctional optical disk drives which employ magnet-optical recording as their rewritable technology.

Avoiding the multi-format confusion associated with standards for 5.25-inch WORM disks, ISO-compliant rewritable media employ the con-

Examples of Rewritable Optical Disk Drives Available in North America

	Ricoh Hyper-Space	Ricoh RO-5030E-II	Sharp JY-700	Sony SMO-D501
Year introduced in North America	1991	1988	1989	1988
Recording technology	magneto-optical	magneto-optical	magneto-optical	magneto-optical
Disk size (in inches)	5.25	5.25	5.25	5.25
Storage capacity per recording surface	300 or 325 MB	300 or 325 MB	300 or 325 MB	300 or 325 MB
Recording surfaces per cartridge	2	2	2	2
ANSI/ISO-compliant cartridge	yes	yes	yes	yes
Heads per drive	1	1	1	1
Access time (in milliseconds)	37	67	70	104
Transfer rate (per second)	1 MB	1.4 MB	925 KB	925 KB
Host computer interface	SCSI	SCSI	SCSI	SCSI

tinuous composite servo (CCS) format only. Their double-sided recording capacities are 600 megabytes for disks formatted with 512 bytes per sector and 650 megabytes for disks formatted with 1,024 bytes per sector. Unrecorded media are purchased in versions which support one or the other format.

Among rewritable optical disk systems which employ proprietary media, the Canon M-O drive has the lowest recording capacity. In its original configuration, it employed single-sided media with just 256 megabytes of storage capacity, but double-sided 512-megabyte cartridges are now available. Industry analysts have observed that optical disk standards sacrifice capacity to obtain compatibility.

With 5.25-inch write-once optical disks, for example, standardized media offer considerably less storage capacity than some proprietary products. Among nonstandard approaches to rewritable optical recording, however, the Tahiti I drive from Maxoptix supports a modified zoned constant angular velocity (ZCAV) format which can store one gigabyte per double-sided magneto-optical cartridge. With standard format magneto-optical disks, each track contains the same number of sectors, regardless of the track's circumference. The relatively short inner tracks are more densely recorded than the longer outer tracks. In contrast, the outer tracks of a ZCAV disk contain more sectors and more data

Examples of Rewritable Optical Disk Drives Available in North America

	IBM PS/2	MOST RMD 5100S	MOST MD-5200-S	Ricoh Transporter	Sony SMO-D301
Year introduced in North America	1991	1990	1991	1991	1991
Recording technology	magneto-optical	magneto-optical	magneto-optical	magneto-optical	magneto-optical
Disk size (in inches)	3.5	3.5	3.5	3.5	3.5
Storage capacity per recording surface	128 MB	128 MB	128 or 256 MB	128 MB	128 MB
Recording surfaces per cartridge	1	1	1	1	1
ANSI/ISO-compliant cartridge	yes	yes	yes*	yes	yes
Heads per drive	1	1	1	1	1
Access time (in milliseconds)	82	50	50	45	50
Transfer rate (per second)	540 KB	512 KB	1.2 MB	640 KB	625 KB
Host computer interface	SCSI	SCSI	SCSI	SCSI	SCSI

* In the 128 MB mode only

than the inner tracks. In July 1990, the ZCAV recording format was endorsed by a group of optical disk equipment and media manufacturers, including Maxoptix, Hewlett-Packard, Phillips and Du Pont Optical, Optical Storage Corporation, Mitsui Petrochemical Industries, and Mitsubishi Kasei Corporation. Such endorsements are expected to bolster efforts to establish a rewritable optical disk standard based on the ZCAV format. As discussed by Freeman (1991), however, any standardization efforts will probably follow the implementation of a two-gigabyte ZCAV format. In addition to ZCAV recording, the Maxoptix Tahiti I drive can read and write onto ANSI/ISO-compliant magneto-optical disk cartridges.

At the time this report was prepared, the Panasonic LF-5010 and the multifunctional LF-7010 were the only rewritable optical disk drives employing phase-change media. As previously noted, Panasonic's optical disk drives are also sold by

Examples of Multifunctional Optical Disk Drives Available in North America

	Hewlett-Packard HP C1716C	LMSI LD 520	Panasonic LF-7010	Pioneer DE-7001
Year introduced in North America	1991	1990	1990	1990
Write-once recording technology	magneto-optical*	ablative/tellurium	phase-change	dye-based
Rewritable recording technology	magneto-optical	magneto-optical	phase-change	magneto-optical
Disk size (in inches)	5.25	5.25	5.25	5.25
Storage capacity per recording surface	327 MB	327 MB	500 MB	327 MB
Recording surfaces per cartridge	2	2	2	2
ANSI/ISO-compliant cartridge	yes	yes	no	yes
Heads per drive	1	1	1	1
Access time (in milliseconds)	90	70	70	90
Transfer rate (per second)	1 MB	1.5 MB	1.3 MB	1.5 MB
Host interface	SCSI	SCSI	SCSI	SCSI

* With rewritability inhibited

Reflection Systems. Panasonic's 5.25-inch rewritable optical disk cartridges offer one gigabyte of double-sided recording capacity. The recording format is proprietary.

3.5-Inch Drives. 3.5-inch rewritable optical disk drives were demonstrated in prototype versions in the mid-to-late 1980s, but early research and development activities failed to produce commercially viable systems. Verbatim Corporation, for example, exhibited a magneto-optical unit at the 1985 National Computer Conference. It is described by Sander and Slovenkai (1987) and Cheriyan (1988). The company distributed descriptive

Comparison of Write-once and Rewritable Optical Disk Drives

	Write-Once	Rewritable
Year Introduced in North America	1983	1988
Number of recording technologies in use	5	2
Media sizes (disk diameter in inches)	14, 12, 5.25	5.25, 3.5
Media capacity (range for all sizes)*	230 MB - 10.2 GB	128 MB - 1 GB
Media capacity (range for 5.25-inch disks)*	230 MB - 1.28 GB	512 MB - 1 GB
Media standardization (sizes affected, in inches)**	14, 5.25	5.25, 3.5
Average access times (all drives in milliseconds)	100-700	37-110
Average access times (5.25-in drives in milliseconds)	100-300	60-104
Equipment costs (all drives)	$2,200 - $30,000+	$2,000 - $8,000
Equipment costs (5.25-inch drives)	$2,200 - $6,000	$4,500 - $8,000
Media cost (per megabyte for all sizes)	$0.08-$0.30	$0.30-$0.40
Media cost (per megabyte for 5.25-inch disks)	$0.20-$0.30	$0.30-$0.40
Autochanger capacities (all media sizes)	6 GB - 1.6 TB	6 GB - 90 GB
Autochanger capacities (5.25-inch media)	6 GB - 90 GB	6 GB - 90 GB
Media playback life (in years)	10 - 100	10 - 25

* Single-sided for 3.5-inch rewritables; double-sided for others; includes some discontinued models

** Approved or proposed ANSI/ISO standards for WORM and rewritable cartridges

product literature and preliminary specifications for the drive through the late 1980s, but its development was eventually discontinued. In 1988, Maxtor announced its Fiji I, a 3.5-inch magneto-optical disk drive to be developed jointly with Seiko Epson but that project was ultimately suspended.

3.5-inch rewritable optical disk drives and media finally became commercially available in 1990. Such products invariably employ magneto-optical recording technology. The cartridges resemble 3.5-inch floppy disks but are thicker. Given their compact external dimensions, 3.5-inch rewritable optical disk drives are particularly well suited to laptop and notebook computer configurations, as well as to desktop computers with small footprints. At the time this report was prepared, 3.5-inch rewritable drives were being manufactured by several companies, including Sony, IBM, and Mass Optical Storage Technologies (MOST), a subsidiary of Nakamichi Peripherals Corporation. Other manufacturers of computer storage equipment have announced their intention to offer 3.5-inch magneto-optical drives, and a variety of reseller arrangements can be expected. Anticipating a significant market for such drives an increasing number of magneto-optical media manufacturers are adding 3.5-inch cartridges to their product lines.

3.5-inch magneto-optical systems are the first optical storage products to post-date ISO standards for interchangeability of optical disk cartridges. All available products are consequently affected by and conform to the ISO 10090 standard, which specifies a nominal recording capacity of 130 megabytes per single-sided magneto-optical disk cartridge. The actual capacity is 128 megabytes for media formatted with 512 bytes per sector and 132 megabytes for media formatted with 1,024 bytes per sector. At the time this report was prepared, however, only the 128-megabyte media were in use. In late 1991, Mass Optical Storage Technologies (MOST) introduced a 3.5-inch magneto-optical disk drive which supports a proprietary recording format to store 256 megabytes per single-sided cartridge. The MOST drive also supports the 128-megabyte ISO standard. The dual-format capability is media dependent; different cartridges are required for each mode. While all 3.5-inch rewritable optical disk systems currently employ the continuous composite servo (CCS) recording format, ISO standards also provide for a Discrete Block Format (DBF) which may be utilized by future 3.5-inch products. It is similar to the sampled servo (SS) format employed by some 5.25-inch write-once optical disk cartridges.

The recording capacities of 3.5-inch rewritable media are much greater than those of 3.5-inch diskettes but low when compared to other optical disks. This is attributable to their smaller surface areas and lower areal recording densities. The low areal recording densities of 3.5-inch rewritable optical disks are the result of lower linear recording densities than their 5.25-inch counterparts. The linear recording density of 3.5-inch rewritable media is 15,875 bits per inch; in contrast, linear recording densities of 5.25-inch magneto-optical disks typically exceeds 24,000 bits per inch. The storage capacities and areal recording densities of 3.5-inch rewritable optical disks does compare very favorably, however, with those of removable magnetic disk systems manufactured by such companies as Syquest and Iomega. Syquest's 5.25-inch hard disk cartridges store approximately forty-two megabytes of data. In their highest capacity configuration, the 5.25-inch cartridges utilized by Iomega's Bernoulli Box drives can store up to forty-four megabytes. Among 3.5-inch removable magnetic disk products, the much publicized "floptical" disk drives, developed by Insite Peripherals, employ 3.5-inch magnetic media with twenty-one megabytes of recording capacity—approximately one-sixth that of 3.5-inch rewritable optical disks. Floptical disks, which are flexible, feature barium ferrite as their recording material. As described by Godwin (1989), Phillips (1988), Satchell (1990), and Williams and Adkisson (1989), they combine magnetic recording with optically-encoded control signals which support increased track densities when compared to conventional floppy disks.

As a group, rewritable optical media capacities are lower than those of certain write-once optical disks. This is partly attributable to the larger recording surfaces provided by twelve- and fourteen-inch WORM media; as discussed above, rewritable optical disks are currently available in smaller sizes. Ongoing research and development activities suggest, however, that continued technological refinements will ultimately permit multi-gigabyte storage capacities with 3.5- and 5.25-inch media. Sony, for example, is developing its Iris Thermal Eclipse Reading (IRISTER) technology, which reduces the size of signals recorded on magneto-optical disks, thereby permitting shorter intervals between signals with a resulting increase in storage density. Based on laboratory experiments, Sony claims that IRISTER technology can store four gigabytes of data per double-sided, 5.25-inch magneto-optical disk cartridge. Aratani et al (1991) discuss super resolution techniques which can significantly increase the linear recording density of magneto-optical media by reducing the spot size of focused beams. Ito and Kojima (1991) likewise discuss the potential for increased recording densities through reductions in beam spots and track pitch. Takeda et al (1991) contend that narrower tracks will permit recording capacities exceeding 300 megabytes per 3.5-inch magneto-optical disk cartridge, an amount that is almost triple current levels. Sukeda et al (1990) discuss the impact of pit-edge recording on media capacity. As discussed by Therrien (1991), the current generation of rewritable optical disk drives employs semiconductor lasers which operate at wavelengths of 780 to 830 nanometers. When 660-nanometer ruby lasers are commercialized, media capacities are expected to double. When short-wavelength blue lasers become available, media capacities may increase by as much as nine-fold from current levels; some researchers have suggested that such lasers will permit recording capacities approaching twelve gigabytes per 5.25-inch magneto-optical disk cartridge. Takahashi et al (1991) discuss the impact of short-wavelength lasers on magneto-optical recording.

As an interesting feature, the ANSI/ISO standard for 3.5-inch rewritable optical disks supports partial and full read-only formats in addition to or instead of read/write operation. Described as Optical Read-Only Memory (OROM), these formats are intended for distribution of databases, software, or other prerecorded information. In a partial OROM application, for example, a software vendor might provide 3.5-inch rewritable optical disks which contain programs plus unrecorded space for user files. Full OROM disks offer an alternative to CD-ROM and other electronic publishing media. Compared to CD-ROM, the OROM format provides less storage capacity but supports much faster access. It also permits direct recording; most CD-ROM media are produced by a mastering process, although recordable CD-ROM systems have recently become available. Within a given 3.5-inch rewritable cartridge, the ANSI/ISO standard provides for a Disk Definition Structure which identifies the location and length of recordable and read-only areas. The possibility of 3.5-inch optical disks based on write-once media has been discussed, but such products are not addressed by ANSI/ISO standards.

Drive Characteristics. As a group, rewritable optical disk drives support faster access times than their write-once counterparts, but they are slower than most fixed magnetic disk drives. Average access times less than 100 milliseconds are typical of 5.25-inch rewritable optical disk drives. With average access times of sixty to seventy milliseconds, several 5.25-inch models approach the performance levels of the slowest hard disk drives. With 3.5-inch drives, average access times range from fifty to seventy milliseconds. The fastest models feature split-optics systems which minimize the number of components on the drive's actuator, thereby reducing its mass and speeding its movement. Such configurations are described by Katayama et al (1989) and Psaltis et al (1989). As reviewed by Nishihara (1990), designers of optical disk pickup mechanisms are currently exploring various improvements, including further miniaturization of components, the substitution of laser/photodiode chips for conventional focus servo systems, the substitution of holographic optical elements for discrete components, and the use of waveguide pickups which will integrate multiple optical components on a single chip. Ng (1991) discusses possible improvements in drive performance through reductions in rotational latency. Average access times are expected to improve in future models. Takahashi et al (1990), for example, describe a prototype 3.5-inch rewritable optical disk drive which employs direct track-seeking techniques and lightweight moving parts to reduce access times below twenty milliseconds. Ogawa and Maeda (1990) discuss potential improvements in magneto-optical drive performance through reductions in the flying height of optical heads. Other drive characteristics and improvements are described by Eguchi et al (1990), Ikeda et al (1990), and Nakashima et al (1990). At 700 kilobytes to 1.5 megabytes per second, data transfer rates supported by rewritable optical disk drives are comparable to those of medium-performance magnetic disk drives. These transfer rates can be expected to improve as rewritable drive technologies are refined and enhanced. Sharp et al (1990), for example, describe a pre-erase feature which can significantly improve transfer rates during magneto-optical recording.

AUTOCHANGERS

While the write-once and rewritable optical media described in the preceding sections offer substantial recording capacity, high-volume data and document storage applications can require frequent interchanges of optical disk cartridges in order to bring desired data online. In the simplest optical storage equipment configurations, such interchanges are performed manually; specific cartridges are removed from drives and replaced with different ones as required. When not in use, optical disk cartridges are maintained offline on shelves, on storage racks, or in cabinets in the manner of magnetic tapes and floppy disks.

With the exception of 3.5-inch rewritable systems, double-sided optical disk cartridges have largely supplanted single-sided media. Such cartridges provide two recording surfaces and twice the storage capacity of their single-sided counterparts, but they must usually be turned over to access information recorded on their opposite sides. Their online capacity is consequently one-half their total recording capacity; they are, in effect, two optical disks packaged in the same enclosure. As a notable exception, dual-head optical disk drives can access both sides of a cartridge without manual removal and reinsertion. Such devices, which effectively double the amount of information available online, were introduced in 1990. Industry analysts have predicted that dual-head models would eventually supplant single-head drives—just as dual-head floppy disk drives replaced their single-head counterparts in microcomputer installations—but single-head WORM and rewritable drives continue to dominate new product announcements. At the time this report was prepared, only one dual-head drive—the Laser-Drive 4100, a twelve-inch WORM device manufactured by Laser Magnetic Storage International—was commercially available.

Whether single- or dual-head drives are utilized, multi-drive equipment configurations can minimize disk handling. Several optical storage equipment manufacturers offer preconfigured models with twin drives housed in a single chassis. The Ricoh RS-8200HH, for example, is a dual-drive optical storage subsystem that provides online access to 800 megabytes of data recorded on WORM cartridges. The dual drives, which are available in either horizontal or vertical casings, accept Ricoh's dye-based, 5.25-inch WORM media which can store 400 megabytes per recording surface. As discussed by Berg (1988, 1990), Tewell (1989), and Wright (1988), most write-once and rewritable optical disk drives are equipped with a Small Computer Systems Interface (SCSI) that can support up to eight optical disk drives or other peripheral devices. Depending on the storage capacity of the optical media employed, such multi-drive configurations can provide convenient online access to dozens of gigabytes of data, albeit at the relatively high cost of purchasing two or more optical disk drives. Available in rack-mounted configurations, multiple optical disk drives may be intermixed with hard disk drives, magnetic tape units, and other storage devices for use in file server installations and similar applications to be described later in this report.

Where very large amounts of computer-processable information must be conveniently and continuously available, an optical disk autochanger—variously termed an optical disk jukebox or an optical disk library—is often the preferred equipment configuration. Broadly defined, an optical disk autochanger is a mass storage peripheral which provides unattended access to gigabytes or even terabytes of data recorded on multiple optical disk cartridges. The typical optical disk autochanger is a floor-standing computer peripheral; several vendors, however, offer tabletop models which are primarily intended for microcomputer-based file server implementations in local area network installations. Regardless of size, an autochanger contains one or more optical disk drives and a collec-

READ/WRITE OPTICAL DISKS 37

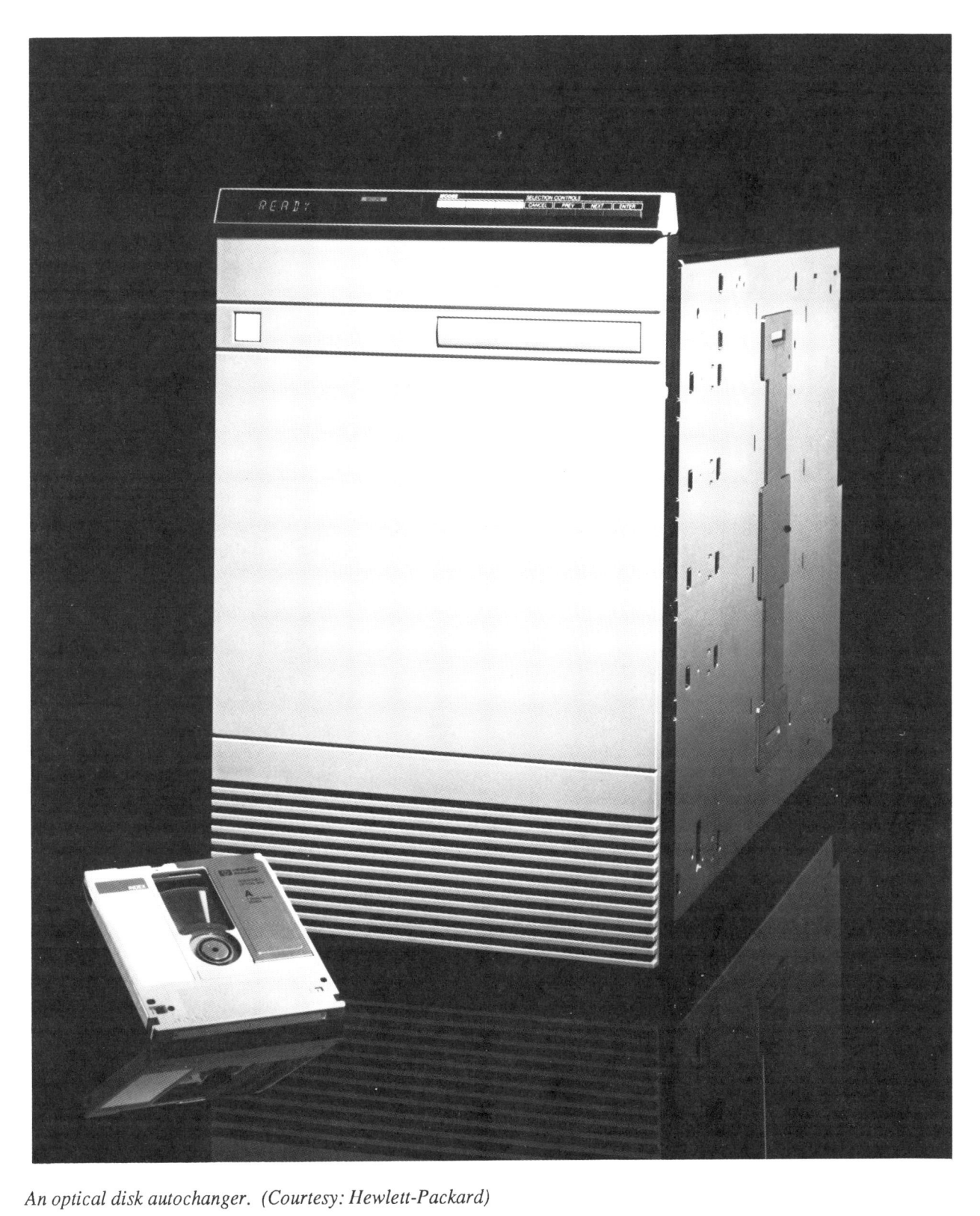

An optical disk autochanger. (Courtesy: Hewlett-Packard)

A desktop autochanger. (Courtesy: Bell and Howell)

tion of optical disk cartridges arranged in stacks or bins. On instructions received from a host computer, a microprocessor-based controller directs a robotic mechanism to extract a designated cartridge from its stack or bin location and mount it in an optical disk drive. The robotic mechanism also removes previously mounted cartridges and returns to them to their storage areas.

While they operate as online peripheral devices, optical disk autochangers are best described as providing "nearline" access to stored information, since information recorded on specific optical disk cartridges is not brought online until the cartridges are requested and mounted. Access times are consequently measured in seconds rather than the milliseconds associated with true online access. Interchange times for optical disk cartridges range from six to twenty seconds, with newer models being generally faster than older ones. Some autochangers also include an import/export slot for the manual addition and removal of cartridges. To improve cartridge interchange time, some autochangers are configured with two optical disk drives as standard equipment, thereby allowing a previously mounted cartridge to be removed from one drive while a specified cartridge is being inserted into the other. In other cases, a given autochanger can be optionally configured with multiple drives. Depending on the model, two to five drives may be supported. Because they occupy space that would otherwise be utilized for optical disk cartridges, additional drives invariably reduce an autochanger's storage capacity.

The first optical disk autochangers were custom-engineered for specific computer installations in the early 1980s. Altman et al (1986), Ammon (1983), Ammon and Siryj (1983), Bessette and Sullivan (1984), Bonini et al (1985), and Levene (1985) describe such a device developed by RCA for the National Aeronautics and Space Adminis-

A multi-disk changer intended as an alternative to conventional jukebox devices. (Courtesy: Laser Magnetic Storage International)

tration. Bessette and Thomas (1990) discuss that installation's latest optical storage configuration which includes two autochangers totalling 2.5 terabytes of storage capacity. Several autochangers were available for general sale by the mid-1980s; the commercial introduction of optical disk drives in 1983 and 1984 was, of course, a necessary precondition for autochanger implementations. The number of available models has increased steadily and significantly since that time. Equipment configurations, operating capabilities, performance characteristics, and product selection parameters are described and compared in numerous publications. Examples include Balafas (1990), Behara (1991), Bessette and Thomas (1990), Daigle et al (1990), Dauner et al (1990), Donsbach (1988), Holberger (1990), Holmes (1989), Hoover (1986), Ichiyama et al (1985), Kato (1990), Kelly (1989), Levene (1988, 1989), Marsh (1988), Miyazaki and Nishi (1985), Moritsugu et al (1989), Oliver and Bianchi (1990), Ranade (1990), Ranade and Yee (1989), Reichardt (1985), Schewe (1989), Shin (1986), Stavely et al (1990), Stolte et al (1990), Trapp (1988), Urrows and Urrows (1990a), Wilkins (1990), Yochum (1988), and Zelinger (1987).

At the time this report was prepared, autochangers were available for fourteen-inch, twelve-inch, and 5.25-inch optical disk drives and media. Depending on the model, 5.25-inch autochangers may be configured with write-once or rewritable

Characteristics of Selected Optical Disk Autochangers

Manufacturer	Model Name	Maximum Disks	Jukebox Capacity*	Drives Supported	Media Size	Drive Type
Cygnet	1800	141	1270 GB	1-5	12"	WORM
Cygnet	1602	29	261 GB	1-5	12"	WORM
Cygnet	5250	25	16.25 GB	1-2	5.25"	WORM
Eastman Kodak	560 ADL	60	75 GB	1-5	5.25"	WORM or RW
Eastman Kodak	6800 ADL-A	50	510 GB	1	14"	WORM
Eastman Kodak	6800 ADL-AB	100	1020 GB	2	14"	WORM
FileNet	OSAR-48	48	28.8 GB	1-4	5.25"	WORM
FileNet	OSAR-64	64	166 GB	1-4	12"	WORM
FileNet	OSAR-64GT	64	128 GB	1-4	12"	WORM
FileNet	OSAR-79GT	79	205 GB	1-2	12"	WORM
FileNet	OSAR-90	90	234 GB	2-4	12"	WORM
FileNet	OSAR-111	111	289 GB	2	12"	WORM
FileNet	OSAR-200	200	520 GB	1-4	12"	WORM
FileNet	OSAR-204	204	530 GB	1-4	12"	WORM
FileNet	OSAR-288	288	720 GB	1-4	12"	WORM
Hewlett-Packard	HP C1710A	32	16.25 GB	2	5.25"	RW
Hitachi	OL321-22	47	329 GB	1-4	12"	WORM
Hitachi	OL321-32	64	448 GB	1-2	12"	WORM
Hitachi	OL101	48	28.8 GB	1-4	5.25"	WORM
IBM	3995-042	32	19.5 GB	2	5.25"	WORM
IBM	3995-112	144	87.8 GB	4	5.25"	WORM
IBM	3995-131	144	87.8 GB	4	5.25"	RW
IBM	3995-132	144	87.8 GB	4	5.25"	WORM
Literal	Personal Library	10	12.8 GB	1	5.25"	WORM
LMSI	LF-500	32	20.8 GB	1-2	5.25"	WORM or RW
Mitsubishi	MS-5G1-A	56	34 GB	1-2	5.25"	WORM
Mitsubishi	MW-5G1-B	152	90 GB	1-4	5.25"	WORM
NKK Electronics	N-556MP	56	36 GB	2	5.25"	WORM
Panasonic	LFJ5000	50	47 GB	2	5.25"	WORM or RW
Reflection Systems	RF-10J	11	10.34 GB	1	5.25"	WORM
Ricoh	RJ-5160	20	16 GB	1	5.25	WORM
Ricoh	Shuttle	5	3.25 GB	1	5.25	RW
Ricoh	RJ-5330E	56	36 GB	2	5.25"	RW
Sony	WDA-610	50	327.5 GB	2	12"	WORM
Sony	WDA-3000-10	50	164 GB	2	12"	WORM
Summus	OPTS 505-600	10	6 GB	1	5.25"	RW

* Maximum capacity; may be lower in some configurations

drives and media. Several 5.25-inch optical disk autochangers are equipped with multifunctional drives or with a combination of write-once and rewritable drives. Described as multifunctional jukeboxes, such devices can store both WORM and rewritable cartridges. When a given cartridge is requested, the robotic mechanism will automatically load it into the appropriate drive.

Most optical disk autochangers include a Small Computer Systems Interface and appropriate supporting software. Cygnet Systems, for example, offers its 1800 Series Expandable Jukebox as a fully integrated, transparent file management subsystem which includes a file server engine based on the Motorola 68020 microprocessor, the Unix operating system, and file server software which supports file management, network communications, and other capabilities. To simplify integration with application software running on host computers, the Cygnet Jukebox Interface Management System keeps track of robotic operations and cartridge locations, thereby eliminating the need for customized programming.

Some optical disk drive manufacturers—including Eastman Kodak, Hitachi, Mitsubishi, Panasonic, Ricoh, and Sony—offer autochangers as extensions to their product lines. Other autochangers, developed by systems integrators, incorporate optical disk drives obtained on an OEM basis from other sources. Such autochangers may incorporate a specific optical disk drive; the Cygnet Model 5250, for example, is based on the LaserDrive 510, a 5.25-inch WORM drive manufactured by Laser Magnetic Storage International. Some autochangers can be configured with the optical disk drives of several different manufacturers. Cygnet's 1800 Series Expandable Jukebox, for example, supports twelve-inch WORM drives from ATG, Hitachi, and Laser Magnetic Storage International. Similarly, Eastman Kodak's Model 560 Automated Disk Library can be configured with the 5.25-inch optical disk drives of various manufacturers. In most cases, optical disk drive manufacturers provide specially engineered versions of their products for autochanger installations. As discussed by Saldanha and Howe (1990), such drives must be able to operate efficiently and reliably over hundreds of thousands of cycles of media insertion and removal. Media housings must similarly be able to withstand such repeated handling.

As summarized in the accompanying table, autochangers are a diverse product group. Available models range from limited-capacity desktop units to large-scale mass storage systems which provide unattended access to terabytes of data. The ISi Personal Library from Literal Corporation is typical of desktop autochangers. Measuring twelve inches wide by twelve inches high by 18.75 inches deep, it incorporates one ISi 525GB optical disk drive and provides nearline access to 12.8 gigabytes of data recorded on ten write-once optical disk cartridges, each with 1.28 gigabytes of double-sided storage capacity. Nearline storage requirements in the twenty to forty gigabyte range are addressed by the growing group of autochangers which can accommodate twenty to fifty 5.25-inch WORM or rewritable cartridges. Several 5.25-inch autochangers support higher capacities, however; the Mitsubishi MW-5G1-B, for example, provides unattended access to ninety gigabytes stored on 152 WORM disks.

As might be expected, the highest capacity autochangers incorporate twelve- and fourteen-inch write-once optical disk drives and media. Typical nearline capacities of first generation models ranged from approximately 166 to 300 megabytes. FileNet's popular OSAR 64 unit, for example, provided unattended access to 166.4 gigabytes recorded on sixty-four WORM cartridges, each with 2.6 gigabytes of double-sided capacity. A Cygnet 1800 Series jukebox configured with one Optimem 1000 WORM drive could store 141 optical disk cartridges containing 282 gigabytes of information. Other Cygnet 1800 Series configurations offered more or less storage capacity, depending on the number and type of WORM drives and media installed in them.

Very high-capacity autochangers were introduced in the late 1980s. FileNet's OSAR-288, for example, offers a nearline storage capacity of 720 gigabytes when configured with 2.6-gigabyte, double-sided WORM cartridges. Recent increases in the recording capacities of twelve-inch WORM cartridges, described earlier in this report, have raised autochanger capacities to very high gigabyte and low terabyte levels while employing fewer media than would have been required to attain such capacities in the past. When configured with the WDD-600 WORM drive and CLV-format media, for example, Sony's WDA-610 autochanger provides unattended access to 328 gigabytes of information recorded on fifty twelve-inch optical disk cartridges. Its predecessor, the WDA-3000-10 autochanger configured with Sony's WDD-3000 drive, stored 164 gigabytes on fifty WORM cartridges. Similarly, Hitachi's OL321 autochanger provides unattended access to 448 gigabytes recorded on sixty-four WORM cartridges, each with seven gigabytes of double-sided capacity. An earlier Hitachi autochanger, the OL301S, provided a nearline storage capacity of eighty-four gigabytes on thirty-two disks.

Cygnet Systems has continually modified its Series 1800 Series Expandable Jukebox to accommodate the newest twelve-inch WORM drives. When configured with the ATG Gigadisc 9001, for example, it provides unattended access to 1.269 terabytes stored on 141 optical disk cartridges, each with nine gigabytes of double-sided recording capacity. When configured with the LaserDrive 4100 from Laser Magnetic Storage International, the Cygnet Series 1800 autochanger offers a nearline storage capacity of 789 gigabytes stored on 141 WORM cartridges, each with a double-sided recording capacity of 5.6 gigabytes. These examples assume that the Cygnet jukebox will contain one optical disk drives. Additional drives, as noted above, will reduce the space available for cartridge storage with a corresponding reduction in nearline capacity. Eastman Kodak offers two jukeboxes for use with its fourteen-inch Model 6800 write-once optical disk drive. The higher capacity model incorporates two WORM drives and one hundred optical disk cartridges. When filled with Kodak's recently announced 10.2-gigabyte WORM media, it provides unattended access to 1.02 terabytes of informaton.

As a simpler, potentially less expensive alternative to a conventional autochanger, Laser Magnetic Storage International offers the LF 4500 RapidChanger, a twelve-inch write-once optical disk drive which accepts five WORM cartridges loaded into a specially designed magazine. On instructions from a host computer, the LF 4500 RapidChanger automatically selects and mounts a designated cartridge. The cartridge interchange time is approximately three seconds. The LF 4500 RapidChanger provides nearline access to twenty-eight gigabytes of information. Each cartridge provides 5.6 gigabytes of double-sided recording capacity. As a convenient feature, the LF 4500 RapidChanger uses the dual-head read/write mechanism employed in the previously discussed LaserDrive 4100. Up to four LF 4500 RapidChanger units, installed in a nineteen-inch rack, can be combined in a given computer installation. Together, they provide unattended access to 112 gigabytes of information. Optical disk cartridges can be individually inserted into and removed from the magazine as application requirements dictate. Magazines can be locked in the RapidChanger or stored offline when not in use. In late 1991, Ricoh introduced a similar cartridge autoloader which stores five 5.25-inch magneto-optical disks in a specially designed magazine. It provides nearline access to 3.5 gigabytes of information.

DATA STORAGE APPLICATIONS

When optical disk systems were first introduced—and even prior to their commercial availability—they were widely heralded as a dramatic and important advance in the evolution of computer storage products. Market researchers, information management consultants, and other industry analysts predicted that optical disk systems would soon account for a significant percentage of the installed base of computer storage peripherals, eventually supplanting magnetic recording devices and media in many data processing applications. Published market forecasts which predicted multibillion-dollar revenue levels for optical storage products have been widely cited by equipment and media manufacturers, systems integrators, value-added resellers, and others with obvious interests in promoting an optimistic view of the technology's prospects. As discussed by Saffady (1991), however, such predictions have invariably overestimated the market for optical storage devices and media in terms of both unit sales and total revenues. To the disappointment of hardware and media manufacturers, the optical disk market has developed much more slowly than anticipated. This disappointment is reflected in papers presented, as well as comments expressed privately or overheard, at professional meetings; in various publications, including interviews with industry participants; in revised market assessments which present downward adjustments of previous sales forecasts; and in individual vendors' often expressed hope that sales will "take off" soon.

For this to occur, optical storage products must win market share from a well established competitor. Magnetic recording equipment and media have dominated computer storage technology since the 1950s. While semiconductor materials have long since supplanted magnetic cores as main memory components, magnetic storage peripherals remain essential hardware components in computer systems of all types and sizes. Fixed magnetic disk drives—so-called hard disk systems—are the storage peripherals of choice in online, interactive computing applications requiring direct access to machine-readable data. Steady and continuing improvements in their cost/performance characteristics have reinforced their position as indispensible components in such applications. Magnetic tape systems—and, to a lesser extent, removable magnetic disk systems—are utilized for backup operations and data archiving, as well as for offline storage of data files intended for batch processing. Magnetic tapes and diskettes are also used for software and data distribution.

The competitive relationship between optical and magnetic storage technologies is discussed in many publications, including Allin (1989), Bate (1989), Behara and Singh (1990), Bloom (1989), Cowan (1990), Harvey and Reinhardt (1990), Hecht (1987a), Perlman (1988), Simpson (1989), and Steinbrecher (1987). Saffady (1990) provides a detailed survey of the principle competitive issues. Any computer-processible information that can be recorded on magnetic media can be recorded on optical disks. Optical disk equipment and media manufacturers consequently hope to replace, complement, or supplement magnetic disk drives and magnetic tape units in applications where the distinctive advantages of optical storage technology can be effectively utilized. Those advantages include very high areal recording densities and media capacities, nearline access to large quantities of data through autochanger implementations, removability of media for data distribution or offline storage, and longer media lifetimes when compared to magnetic disks and tapes.

The most important characteristics and capabilities of selected optical and magnetic storage devices are summarized and compared in the accompanying table. High media capacity—which approaches or exceeds gigabyte levels, as discussed in preceding sections—is the most distinctive characteristic of optical disk technology and the one on which its competitive aspirations are typically based. The high recording capacities of write-once and rewritable optical disks are obviously attractive to computer system administrators, records managers, office automation specialists, archivists, and others responsible for the storage of increasingly voluminous quantities of machine-readable information. Where frequent reference to stored information is required, optical disk autochangers can provide unattended access to formidable amounts of data. While the storage capacities of fixed magnetic disk drives have increased steadily and significantly over the past three decades, they typically require multiple platters to store the contents of a single optical disk surface. Among other storage peripherals, magnetic tape systems based on helical scan technology—half-inch VHS-type data recorders, 8mm data recorders, and 4mm digital audio tape (DAT) devices—support gigabyte-level media capacities and, in the case of 8mm and DAT cartridges, can be configured with autochangers. The serial access characteristics associated with all tape formats, however, render such media unsuitable for applications requiring rapid, random retrieval of recorded information. Only optical disks combine very high media capacities and autochanger implementations with direct access to recorded data.

As a further advantage, optical disk drives combine high storage capacity with removable media. As noted above, such media are suitable for data archiving, hard disk backup, and other applications involving offline storage. Removable media can also be used for data and/or software distribution. Historically, such applications have relied on magnetic tapes and, more recently, removable magnetic disks. The role of optical disks as alternatives to magnetic tape for offline data storage is discussed below. As a group, removable magnetic disks—including floppy disk in various sizes and densities, Bernoulli cartridges, and hard disk cartridges—offer much lower recording capacities than optical disk cartridges. Most removable magnetic disk systems provide less media capacity than their fixed disk counterparts.

Compared to magnetic media, optical disks offer greater stability for recorded information. The Joint Technical Commission on Permanence of Optical and Magnetic Systems, which is sponsored by the American National Standards Institute and the Audio Engineering Society, has been formed to develop standards and recommended practices for the stability of magnetic and optical media, but their work will not be completed for some time. As discussed earlier in this report, media lifetime estimates cited in manufacturers' product specifications range from fifteen to 100 years for write-once optical disks and ten to twenty-five years for rewritable optical disks. Saffady (1991a) surveys published literature and manufacturers' claims dealing with the stability of removable magnetic media. (Media stability is not a meaningful consideration in fixed magnetic disk installations, since fixed disks—being inextricably connected to the drives which read and record information on them—are vulnerable to damage from head crashes or other hardware malfunctions; in any case, media life is limited by the utility of the equipment which incorporates such media). Several studies, and considerable anecdotal evidence, suggest that nine-track magnetic tapes based on gamma ferric oxide recording materials can retain their utility for a period of ten to twenty years when stored under tightly controlled temperature and humidity conditions, rewound at predetermined intervals, and handled carefully. The stability of many write-once and rewritable optical disks, as noted above, exceeds twenty years when such media are stored in an office rather than a controlled environment; periodic media rewinding is, of course, unnecessary. There is relatively little published information about the stability of other removable magnetic media, particular those based on recording materials other than gamma ferric oxide. Generally, however, such materials—which include chromium dioxide, barium ferrite, and iron particles—are considered less stable than gamma ferric oxide. As additional advantages, write-once and rewritable optical disks are not susceptible to head crashes, abrasive or adhesive wear, and print-through effects associated with magnetic media.

While the advantages described above are substantial, certain characteristics of optical disk systems limit the range of information management applications which they can successfully address. Write-once optical disk drives, for example, are generally unsuitable for information that will be updated frequently. Because previously recorded information cannot be overwritten, write-once optical disks must store each of the successively updated versions of a given record or file —an approach that can quickly squander available storage space and fill WORM cartridges with obsolete data. Consequently, write-once optical disks cannot replace magnetic media in the broad spectrum of active transaction processing, word processing, database management, or other computer operations, although they can prove useful in applications where an audit trail is desired or a nonerasable final version of a given file will be archived.

Rewritable optical disk systems do not share these constraints, but their relatively slow access times—as discussed earlier in this report—can pose problems in high-volume transaction processing and other interactive computing applications where high performance is a paramount consideration. While some new rewritable drives support faster access times than their predecessors, fixed magnetic disk systems are likely to remain the most appropriate storage devices in high performance applications for the foreseeable future. Rewritable optical disk drives are very well suited, however, to applications where storage capacity is more important than access time. In autochanger configurations, for example, rewritable optical disk systems can provide nearline access to dozens of gigabytes of data. With their removable media, rewritable optical disk systems—like their write-once counterparts—can also be used to archive data files for offline storage.

While available WORM and rewritable optical disk drives can be purchased by corporations, government agencies, hospitals, schools, research institutions, and other organizations for use in locally designed data storage systems, the development of hardware and software interfaces for such end-user implementations can require considerable engineering and programming expertise. Although optical disk manufacturers sometimes provide de-

Comparison of Selected Magnetic and Optical Storage Technologies

	Media Capacity	Access Time	Removable Media	Rewritable Media	Equipment Cost*	Media Cost	Autochanger Available
Fixed Magnetic Disks	20 MB - 2 GB+	12-65 ms	no	yes	$400-$3,000	included	no
Removable Hard Disks	45 MB	25-30 ms	yes	yes	$1,300-$1,500	$140	no
Bernoulli Box Systems	20-90 MB	65 ms	yes	yes	$1,500-$1,800	$80-$125	no
Floppy Disk Systems	360 KB-20 MB	160-350 ms	yes	yes	$70-$300	$1-$4	no
Quarter-Inch Magnetic Tape	20 MB-1.3 GB	minutes	yes	yes	$250-$1,000	$25-$40	no
8mm Magnetic Tape	2 GB	minutes	yes	yes	$6000-$7,000	$40	yes
4mm Digital Audio Tape	1.3 GB - 2 GB	minutes	yes	yes	$7,000-$7,500	$20	yes
VHS-type Data Recorders	2.5 GB-10 GB	minutes	yes	yes	$5,000-$7,000	$10-$20	no
5.25 WORM Disks	230 MB-1.28 GB	100-300 ms	yes	no	$2,200-$7,000	$70-$250	yes
5.25 Rewritable Optical Disks	256 MB - 1 GB	60-110 ms	yes	yes	$5,000-$6,000	$250-$350	yes

* Typical price for plug-and-play configuration suitable for microcomputer installation; costs for larger computer configurations will be higher

velopmental "toolkits" which include file management systems, programming language interfaces, low-level access routines, and other components, the successful integration of optical disk drives into specific computer configurations can prove difficult and time-consuming. As a result, optical disk drive manufacturers typically sell their equipment to systems integrators, value-added resellers, and other OEM clients who incorporate them into products developed for specific applications, such as magnetic tape replacement and file server implementations. Examples of such products and their applications are discussed in the following subsections.

Magnetic Tape Replacement. One of the earliest and most important applications of optical disk technology involves the emulation of magnetic tape systems for hard disk backup, data archiving, and other offline storage applications. In such "optical archiving" applications, files are recorded on optical disks in the straightforward sequential fashion associated with magnetic tape. During the 1980s, several dozen vendors introduced turnkey equipment configurations which can replace magnetic tape drives without modifying a customer's existing computer hardware or software environment. Such systems respond to conventional tape drive commands. Operating characteristics and capabilities of typical implementations are described by Bostwick et al (1988), Carringer (1988), Davis (1987), Devoy et al (1988), Donsbach (1988), Ferebee and Kibler (1989), Francis (1988), Gibson and Cross (1987), Green (1988), Halper (1988), Hume (1988), Keele (1988), Laskodi et al (1988), Lowenthal (1987), MacRae (1989), Moran (1988), Osterlund (1987), Owen (1988), Ramsay (1988), Slicker (1988), Williams (1987), and Yamashita et al (1987).

Turnkey magnetic tape replacement systems have been developed for various computer environments, including IBM mainframe and AS/400 systems, VAX and MicroVAX processors, Data General Eclipse and MV series models, Hewlett-Packard HP 1000 and HP 3000 systems, Prime computers, Tandem computers, and Wang VS systems. Such systems are offered by the computer manufacturers themselves or from independent peripheral equipment suppliers. Examples of the latter include the Optical Archiving System (OAS) from Aquidneck Systems International, the LX400 Series Laser Optical Subsystem from Emulex, the LaserSystem from Perceptics, the OPCA-11 system from C. Itoh Electronics, the TEC OAS/1 system from TECEX, the Virtual Optical Storage (VOS) system from U.S. Design, the OPTIFILE II system from KOM Incorporated, the Archiver Optical Option from Strategic Information, the LRS-10 system from Zetaco, the Archeion system from EMC Corporation, the SMS 0109 system from Scientific Micro Systems, the Opto-QUBE system from Unbound Incorporated, the DW34800 Mainframe Optical Storage Transport (MOST) from Data/Ware Development, and the QLC-5000 system from Qualogy Incorporated.

While their specific features differ, turnkey magnetic tape replacement systems typically combine optical disk drives with host adapters, cables, and interface software. The earliest models employed twelve-inch write-once drives, the only optical storage devices available prior to 1988; most systems now support rewritable optical disk drives as alternatives to or replacements for their original WORM configurations. Because files are transferred to optical disks in their entirety for recording in sequential fashion, write-once media are not penalized for their inability to overwrite specific blocks of data. Like magnetic tape systems, however, rewritable drives permit the reuse of media in applications where backup files will be replaced on a regular schedule, thereby reducing media costs and eliminating the full platters encountered in write-once configurations. As a potential disadvantage, the storage capacities of 5.25-inch rewritable media may be too limited for some applications; as discussed below, twelve-inch WORM cartridges are often preferred for their high capacities. Autochanger implementatons, based on WORM or rewritable media, are offered by some vendors. Some systems also support a standard nine-track magnetic drive as an adjunct to optical storage. Data may be transferred from the host computer to an optical disk, from the host computer to a magnetic tape, or between a magnetic tape and an optical disk.

Specific hardware configurations aside, turnkey magnetic tape replacement systems include software which makes an optical disk drive appear to a host computer as a magnetic tape formatter and drive. Such software is typically loaded like a device driver. It responds to input/output commands generated by the host computer's operating system and interacts with the computer through conventional application programs. Some software packages can also emulate magnetic disk drives, an approach that permits direct access for faster retrieval of recorded information.

As their principal advantage, optical archiving systems permit dramatic consolidations of magnetic tape collections with correspondingly significant savings in storage space. As an example, a two-gigabyte WORM cartridge of the type used by certain first-generation twelve-inch optical disk drives can store the equivalent of ninety-five reels of nine-track magnetic tape recorded at 800 bits per inch, fifty reels of magnetic tape recorded at 1,600 bits per inch, and twelve reels of magnetic tape recorded at 6,250 bits per inch. The same WORM cartridge can store the equivalent of ten IBM 3480-type magnetic tape cartridges. Newer WORM media provide greater opportunities for tape consolidation. A seven-gigabyte, twelve-inch WORM cartridge, for example, can store the equivalent of 330 reels of nine-track magnetic tape recorded at 800 bits per inch, 175 reels of magnetic tape recorded at 1,600 bits per inch, forty-two reels of magnetic tape recorded at 6,250 bits per inch, or thirty-five IBM 3480-type magnetic tape cartridges. Such consolidation is particularly important where magnetic tapes are stored in environmentally controlled vaults or similarly expensive facilities. As additional advantages, a single optical disk cartridge is much easier to handle than multiple magnetic tapes, and—with their direct access capabilities—optical disks can simplify and speed the transfer of recorded information to magnetic disks when required.

As their principal disadvantage, magnetic tape replacement systems record information on optical disk cartridges that are considerably more expensive than an equivalent quantity of magnetic tapes. In many applications, of course, the higher media costs may be favorably offset by reductions in storage space requirements. Where commercial storage facilities, which charge by the amount of space consumed, are utilized, the conversion of backup and data archiving operations from magnetic tape to optical disks can yield substantial savings, despite high media costs. Since the late 1980s, however, optical archiving systems have experienced formidable competition from the high-capacity, helical-scan magnetic tape systems mentioned above. With their gigabyte-level storage capacities, such systems are as effective as optical disks in consolidating large collections of magnetic tape reels, but their media costs are a small fraction of optical disk cartridge prices.

Workstations and Servers. Write-once and rewritable optical storage subsystems are increasingly available for microcomputer and workstation installations. Characterized as "plug and play" products because they require no hardware modifications or reprogramming on the customer's part, such optical storage subsystems typically include a write-once or rewritable optical disk drive, a host computer adapter, cables, software, and documentation. Useful products are offered by dozens of systems integrators and value-added resellers, including Accell Computer Corporation, Advanced Graphics Applications, Advanced Storage Concepts, Alphatronix, Ambertek Systems, American Digital Systems, Applied Programming Technologies, Apunix Computer Services, Arix Computer Corporation, Artecon Incorporated, Automated Solutions Incorporated, Bay MicroSystems, Bering Industries, Consan Incorporated, Corel Systems Corporation, Deltaic Systems, DocuFile Incorporated, Dolphin Systems Technology, DynaTek Automation Systems, FWB Incorporated, Image Management Technologies, Jasmine, LaCie Limited, MASS Microsystems, Micro Design International, MicroNet Technology Incorporated, Microtech International, Mirror Technologies, N/Hance Systems, OCEAN Microsystems, Online Computer Systems, Optima Technology Corporation, Peripheral Land Incorporated, Pinnacle Micro, Procom Technology, Relax Technology, Storage Dimensions, Summus Computer Systems, Tecmar, Ten X Technology, and Xyxis Corporation.

Most of these systems employ 5.25-inch WORM and rewritable drives which function as high-capacity supplements or complements to magnetic disk drives. They also offer an alternative to magnetic tape units and removable magnetic disk systems for data backup and archiving. While available products differ in their specific capabilities, they all include software which transparently supports operating system commands, allowing unmodified application programs to access a write-once or rewritable optical disk drive as if it were a conventional magnetic disk system, albeit one with high-capacity, removable media. In an IBM-compatible microcomputer that includes a floppy disk drive identified as device "A" and a hard disk drive identified as device "C," an optical disk drive may be identified as device "D." The MS-DOS operating system and associated application programs can record files on that drive, copy files from magnetic to optical disks or vice versa, view a directory of files recorded on a mounted optical disk cartridge, or delete previously recorded files. With write-once media, of course, file deletion involves a revision of directory listings, since previously recorded data cannot be erased.

The rapid proliferation of local area networks that interconnect an organization's computing equipment has stimulated considerable interest in optical disk drives and autochangers as high-capacity data storage devices in file server installations. For purposes of this discussion, a file server is a computer that provides data storage resources to other computers which operate on a telecommunications network; while file servers are most closely associated with local area networks, wide area network implementations are also possible. A file server may be a microcomputer, a minicomputer, or a mainframe; a given network installation may include all three types. Network computers configured with optical disk drives are sometimes described as optical file servers.

Specific computer configurations aside, storage devices attached to a file server can be accessed by other network nodes for data recording and retrieval. As previously discussed, write-once optical disks can store large, relatively static databases, word processing documents, and spreadsheet files. Rewritable optical disks, like conventional magnetic disks, can be used for information that is subject to change. Ranade (1991) provides a detailed examination of server-based implementations of optical storage technology. Gladney and Mantey (1990) review design issues for a server-based library of electronic documents. Ishii et al (1990) contend that optical disks are more effective than magnetic disks for low-traffic, random-access in local area network installations. Gomez and Demetriades (1990) discuss the role of a microcomputer-based optical file server in a prototype online archiving system based on WORM media. Turtur et al (1990) and Fantini et al (1990) describe an optical file server which stores digitized color images. Balafas (1991) examines the potential of optical disks in Unix networks. Arai and Itao (1990) discuss the potential of optical file servers for the high-volume storage requirements of integrated services digital network (ISDN) implementations.

In theory, any optical disk drive can be attached to a network file server, provided, of course, that the drive is compatible with the server's hardware configuration and operating system. In local area network installations, however, optical storage devices must also be compatible with the network's operating system, interface cards, and other components. Recognizing the enormous potential of file server applications, an increasing number of systems integrators and value-added resellers are certifying their optical storage subsystems for use with specific combinations of local area network hardware and software. Such certification indicates that particular products have been tested for compatibility with a given local area network configuration.

In file server installations, WORM and rewritable optical disks are typically combined with magnetic disk and tape drives. Several vendors offer "mix and match" components that can be configured to address specific application requirements and take advantage of the special capabilities of different technologies. Such devices typically consist of component racks with 5.25-inch slots for the installation of desired peripherals. In addition to WORM and rewritable drives, the choices may include CD-ROM readers, fixed magnetic disk drives in various capacities, hard disk cartridge drives, conventional or high-capacity floppy disk drives, quarter-inch magnetic tape units, 8mm data cartridge drives, and digital audio tape units.

Taking a more sophisticated and complex approach to file server implementations, several vendors offer combinations of magnetic and optical storage devices that are based on hierarchical storage concepts. Briefly defined, hierarchical storage configurations combine and rank two or more storage technologies in order to take advantage of the unique strengths of different devices and media. Hierarchical storage concepts are discussed in various publications, many of which predate the commercial availability of optical disk products. Examples include Ramamoorthy and Chandy (1970), Christodoulakis (1985), Cohen et al (1989), Gelb (1989), Langendorfer et al (1986), Matick (1977), Mattson (1974), Matson et al (1970), Peskin (1985), Ramakrishnan and Emer (1989), Satyanarayanan (1986), and Smith (1981, 1986). A given device's position in a storage hierarchy is determined by various factors, including media capacity, access time, and cost:

1. At the apex of a typical computer storage hierarchy, semiconductor-based main memory—the fastest and most expensive storage component—is reserved for data and programs which are under immediate execution by the central processor.

2. Fixed magnetic disk drives, the hierarchy's principal online peripheral devices, are utilized for information which will be referenced frequently and which must be accessed quickly. Standalone WORM and rewritable drives may also provide such online access, but their relatively slow access times place them at a disadvantage when compared to fixed magnetic disk drives.

3. Optical disk autochangers and automated tape retrievers provide high-capacity storage for information which may be referenced at any time and which must consequently be conveniently but not necessarily instantaneously available.

4. Standalone WORM and rewritable drives, removable magnetic disk drives, and magnetic tape units may be used for backup operations and archiving of inactive information. In such applications, access times are relatively unimportant, and information recorded on optical disk cartridges, floppy disks, magnetic disk cartridges, or magnetic tapes can be stored offline until needed.

Hierarchical concepts are implicitly implemented in any computer configuration that incorporates two or more storage technologies. When different magnetic and optical storage devices are combined in a given file server installation, a system manager or authorized user can employ operating system commands or utility programs to transfer infrequently referenced files between fixed magnetic disks and removable magnetic disks, optical disks, or magnetic tapes. Such file transfer procedures require manual intervention, however; the system manager or user must keep track of the storage locations of particular information and specify the desired device when a given file is required by an application program. As an alternative, several vendors offer fully automated hierarchical storage systems which support the unattended migration of data between magnetic and optical storage components.

In a fully automated storage hierarchy, file transfers are performed without operator involvement. Fully automated hierarchical configurations give users the impression that an unlimited amount of magnetic disk storage is at their disposal. All files are assumed to reside on fixed magnetic disk drives, regardless of their actual locations. The user's logical view of the system's data storage facilities consequently differs from its physical organization. Employing file migration algorithms, hierarchical storage software automatically transfers selected data files from magnetic disks to optical disks or magnetic tape for storage in autochangers and/or offline locations. Such automatic transfers are typically based on a file's reference history, but additional factors—such as the need to free magnetic disk space for other purposes—may also be considered. Files transferred to autochangers or offline media are similarly returned to magnetic disks, without operator intervention, when requested by users.

Fully automated hierarchical configurations utilizing magnetic and optical storage components have been implemented on a customized basis in a variety of applications. Choy and O'Lear (1983), O'Lear and Kitts (1985), and Thanhardt and Harano (1988), for example, discuss the role of hierarchical storage components, including magnetic and optical disks, at the National Center for Atmospheric Research. Guru Prasad (1984), De Valk et al (1985), Mankovich et al (1986), Dallas et al (1987), and Reijns et al (1988) describe systems that combine magnetic and optical storage components for digital radiographs and other medical imagery. Narayan (1988) describes a system that combines magnetic and optical disk storage at the U.S. Patent and Trademark Office.

As an alternative to such customized installations, several systems integrators have developed preconfigured hierarchical storage systems based on combinations of magnetic and optical technologies. As an example, the Storage Machine from FileTek Incorporated is a specialized database processing system that provides high-capacity, hierarchical facilities for mainframe and minicomputer installations. As described by Burgess (1985, 1987), Burgess and Ramsey (1988), and Owen (1988), the FileTek Storage Machine can support a variety of peripheral devices, including fixed magnetic disk drives, write-once and rewritable optical disk drives, optical disk autochangers, and magnetic tape units. Following the typical hierarchical pattern outlined above, fixed magnetic disk drives are the Storage Machine's principal direct access storage devices for frequently referenced information. One or more optical disk autochangers provide unattended access to files that are referenced less frequently. Inactive data files can be stored offline on optical disk cartridges or magnetic tapes. An integral processor controls access to data files, file transfers, and other processing operations. The Storage Machine's software automatically migrates data through the hierarchy of available devices, based on access requirements, reference patterns, and available storage space. Ramsay (1990) describes the integration of FileTek's Storage Machine with a database computer manufactured by Teradata Corporation.

Designed specifically for file server applications in local area network installations, the Infinite-Server product line from Epoch Systems likewise combines magnetic and optical storage components in a hierarchical configuration. As described by Lieberman (1988), Olsen (1988), and Olsen and Kenley (1989), Epoch's Infinite Storage Architecture employs high-capacity optical disks as application-transparent staging media for data transferred from high-performance magnetic disk drives. Files are automatically moved between magnetic and optical storage based on their activity levels. Aged files are transferred to optical disks when they have not been referenced for a specified period of time or when magnetic disks reach a predetermined level of capacity. The physical storage locations of individual files are transparent to users. The Epoch InfiniteServer—which can be configured with magnetic disk drives and optical disk autochanger units totalling almost one terabyte of storage—appears to the user as a magnetic disk system that never becomes full. When a data file stored on an optical disk is requested by an application program, it is automatically returned to magnetic disk storage.

Scientific Applications. The preceding subsection briefly noted the use of optical storage components in hierarchical configurations implemented in scientific applications. With their high storage capacities, optical disks are obviously well suited to meteorological, geological, aerospace, and other applications where large amounts of scientific and technical data are routinely collected and processed. Among published descriptions of such applications, Thomas (1985) describes the advantages of write-once optical disks for the storage of very large aeronautical databases at the Marshall Space Flight Center. Benjamin (1990), Ravner and Shull (1990), and Schull et al (1988) discuss optical disks as a storage alternative for data generated by the National Aeronautics and Space Administration's Space Station Program, while Chen and Livingston (1988) describe a simulation model for such spaceborne optical disk applications. Levene (1990) describes a high-capacity rewritable optical recording system for spaceflight installations. Albrecht et al (1990), McGlynn et al (1988), and Rushton et al (1989, 1990) discuss an optical disk archive implemented at the Space Telescope Scientific Institute to store the gigabytes of data generated daily by the Hubble Space Telescope. Hamana et al (1990) describe an optical disk storage system for spectral images at the Norikura Solar Observatory.

Kraus and French (1990) a WORM-based archiving system for spectroscopic data. Anderson (1989) advocates the use of optical disks in scientific imaging applications. Waggener (1987) and Davis (1987) discuss the advantages and limitations of optical storage in image sensing applications. Wallgren (1986) and Wallgren and Michael (1988) contend that high-capacity, high-performance optical storage systems must be developed for supercomputer installations. Thompson et al (1987) describe a two-terabyte optical storage unit utilized with a cluster of minicomputers at the Physical Sciences Laboratory of the University of Wisconsin.

Various optical disk subsystems have been implemented to store the voluminous amounts of data generated by accelerometers, thermocouples, and other scientific instrumentation. Onsite Instruments Incorporated, for example, offers an optical disk option for its portable data acquisition and signal analysis system, while Quantel Limited offers a digital image microscopy system with an optical disk subsystem. Mouton (1986) describes the advantages of optical disks for interactive seismic interpretation in petroleum engineering applications. Kohsaka et al (1989) discuss an optical storage system for chromatograms. Kutt and Balamuth (1989, 1989a) describe the use of WORM disks in an event-recording system for nuclear physics data. Stamulis and Shevenell (1988) describe the use of WORM disks for nonvolatile storage of oceanographic data. Kaehler and Theissing (1989), Light (1986, 1986a), Okazaki et al (1990), and Waruszewski (1987) discuss an optical disk installation for cartographic information systems.

As outlined by Stewart (1986), Hoffos (1986), Huntting (1986), Dayhoff (1988), Kohn (1991, 1991a), and others, health science applications have represented an important vertical market for optical storage technology since the mid-1980s. Medical training and health promotion programs are among the most widely encountered applications of interactive optical video disc technology, while CD-ROM implementations of MEDLINE and other biomedical databases are offered by various publishers. More directly relevant to this discussion, the potential of write-once and rewritable optical disks as data storage media in so-called Picture Archiving and Communication Systems (PACS) has attracted the attention of medical records specialists, radiologists, researchers, hospital administrators, and others responsible for the creation and management of patient information as an important component in health-care delivery and research systems.

Briefly defined, a Picture Archiving and Communication System is a special-purpose computer network which can store, retrieve, transmit, and display medical image data, including digitized versions of conventional x-rays, computerized tomographic (CT) scans, and images generated by magnetic resonance, nuclear medicine, digital radiographic, and other devices. In many cases, these images are produced by medical instruments which generate digital data, and the use of such digital modalities is an increasingly common feature of radiological practice. A PACS substitutes electronic images for conventional photographic films. Rather than working with lightboxes to make their interpretations, radiologists and other physicians retrieve and view electronic images at specially designed video display stations.

Because radiological devices that employ digital modalities can generate many images per procedure, they require high-capacity storage facilities. Based on typical radiological workloads in the 614-bed Massachusetts General Hospital, for example, Goodsitt et al (1986) estimated daily storage requirements at 1.3 gigabytes for conventional radiography, PET, and MRI workloads. The conversion of film-based radiographic studies to digitized form would require an additional 11.3 gigabytes, bringing the total daily storage requirement to 12.6 gigabytes. The annual data storage requirement would be 4.225 terabytes. Witt et al (1986) of the Veterans Administration Medical Center and the Indiana University Medical Center in Indianapolis reported that digital images generated by their nuclear medicine facility required between 32 megabytes and 75 megabytes of storage per day. One month's data requires five to seven 2,400-foot reels of magnetic tape. They further noted that the implementation of a PACS usually increases a hospital's data storage requirements.

As discussed by Arink (1982), Blom (1982a), Marceau (1982), Meyer-Ebrecht et al (1982), Drexler (1983), Duerinckx et al (1983), and Lehr (1983), awareness of the capacity of optical storage for medical picture archiving predated the commercial availability of optical disk devices. Numerous publications have since reported the use of optical storage components in specific PACS installations and applications. Among systems implemented during the 1980s, Mankovich et al (1986a, 1988, 1988a), Kangarloo et al (1987), and Madachy et al (1988) discuss the integration of an optical storage subsystem with VAX minicomputers and desktop workstations at UCLA's Medical Imaging Division. Dayhoff (1987) describes a radiological imaging system which uses the MUMPS programming language to integrate image processing equipment, optical disks, and database management software. Hack et al (1986) describe a filing, indexing, and optical storage system for radiological images at the Albany Medical College. Jaggi et al (1987) describe an optical disk storage system for image cytometry. Nicolosi et al (1988) discuss a hybrid system that uses optical disks for image storage and magnetic media for clinical summary data at the Ospedale Civile in Pordenone, Italy. Komori et al (1987) describe the use of an optical disk autochanger linked to a CT scanner in a pilot PACS implementation at Kyoto University Hospital. Wiltgen et al (1990) discuss the use of optical disks to store CT images at the University Clinic for Radiology in Graz, Germany. While many optical disk-based PACS installations have preferred twelve-inch WORM media for their high storage capacity, Inamura et al (1990) discuss an implementation based on rewritable optical disks. Glenn and Marx (1990) and Parkin et al (1990) describe microcomputer-based diagnostic imaging installations with optical storage components. Seshadri et al (1990) describe an optical disk autochanger which functions as a image archive in a radiological installation at the University of Pennsylvania.

A number of medical instrumentation vendors—including Philips Medical Systems, AT&T, General Electric Medical Systems Group, Hewlett-Packard, Del Mar Avionics, and various Japanese manufacturers—have developed turnkey picture archiving systems that employ optical disks for image storage. Such systems—which typically accept digital input from CT scanners, ultrasound devices, and other medical instruments—feature specially-designed single- or multi-screen radiological consoles for image retrieval and display. Published descriptions of available products and operational installations include Cohen et al (1988), Hedge et al (1986), Heshiki et al (1988), Heu (1986), Hindel (1986, 1990), Mun et al (1988) O'Malley and List (1987), Stockbridge and Ravin (1986, and Tobes et al (1987).

COLD for COM Replacement. Since the mid-1980s, there has been much discussion of the potential impact of optical storage technology on computer-output microfilm (COM) systems. As its name suggests, COM technology converts machine-readable, computer-processible data to miniaturized, human-readable textual or graphic information recorded as microfilm images. COM-generated images look as if they were created by microfilming computer-printed reports or similar paper documents, but no paper is generated at any step in the recording process. Instead, the page images are recorded directly on microfilm, using CRT photography or laser-beam recording techniques. Saffady (1990a) provides an overview of the technology and its data processing applications.

Computer-output microfilmers, typically called COM recorders, are a variant form of computer printer. While 16mm and 35mm roll microfilms can be produced, most models record information on microfiche, the most widely encountered formats containing the equivalent of 270 B4-size (eleven-by-fourteen-inch) pages per fiche. The simplest and most widely installed COM recorders are limited to textual output. More sophisticated devices, often described as COM plotters, have graphic as well as alphanumeric output capabilities. They are intended for computer-aided design, computer-assisted mapping, complex micropublishing, and similar applications. A special group of COM plotters can record images of engineering drawings on aperture cards.

COM offers a potentially cost-effective alternative to conventional paper output in batch processing applications involving computer-generated reports and similar documents. Since the early 1970s, however, computer systems analysts and data processing specialists have emphasized the implementation of online information systems as high-performance alternatives to batch processing. Such systems rely on direct access storage devices, especially magnetic disk drives. Terminal inquiries provide interactive access to stored data; if reports are printed, they typically serve as a backup reference in the event of computer failure. Some computer installations, however, lack the disk storage space required for pervasive online implementations involving very large quantities of machine-readable information. As a result, batch processing applications—especially those initially implemented during the 1960s—persist. Even applications which primarily operate in the online mode, rely on batch processed reports for historical information which has been transferred to offline storage.

With their high storage capacities, optical disks allow large quantities of data to be retained online for long periods of time. Optical storage technology consequently promotes the implementation of online systems, and—by minimizing or eliminating the need for printed reports associated with batch processing—they indirectly threaten COM installations. A relatively new group of optical storage products, however, directly attacks COM technology by recording computer-generated reports on read/write optical disks. Sometimes termed Computer Output onto Laser Disk (COLD) systems, such products feature retrieval software which provides online access to the stored reports. Retrieved information is displayed on video monitors as page images, much as it would appear on microfilm or in paper printouts. While they are collectively marketed as COM replacement systems, COLD products offer an alternative to any report production methodology, including paper printouts as well as computer-output microfilm.

Some COLD products are implemented as self-contained, microcomputer-based turnkey systems. Examples include the COM-Squared Alternative from Com Squared-Systems Incorporated, the Optical Fiche System (OFS) from Computron Technologies Corporation, the Computer Output Information System (COINS) from IMTECH Optical Systems Inforporated, and the Computer Output Retrieval Environment (CORE) system from FileMark Corporation. Typically, an IBM-compatible microcomputer serves as the system's central processor. Most models run under the MS-DOS operating system, but multi-terminal systems have been implemented on Unix-based workstations. Other COLD products are implemented as subsystems intended for mainframe or minicomputer installations. A COM replacement system from LaserAccess Corporation, for example, is designed for IBM and plug-compatible mainframe installations running under the MVS operating system. It attaches to the same mainframe channel as a COM recorder and permits access to stored data by 3270-compatible terminals. The Total Solution DW34800 Optical Storage Subsystem from Data/Ware Development, the Gigapage System from Aquidneck Systems International, and the SYS-OUT Archival and Retrieval (SAR) system from Goal Systems International are other examples of COLD products for IBM mainframes.

Regardless of configuration, COLD systems accept information generated by batch-oriented application programs operating on mainframes or minicomputers. The information is ASCII-coded and formatted as report pages, just as it would be transmitted to a COM recorder or paper printer. Some systems can also store images of business forms or organizational logos. Such images will be superimposed on report data at the time specific pages are retrieved. In the case of microcomputer-based turnkey COLD systems, page-formatted input may be transferred from mainframes or minicomputers via downloading, floppy disks, or magnetic tapes.

COLD systems include software which indexes the input in a manner specified by particular customers. Once indexed, the report pages are recorded on write-once or rewritable optical disks. Because information is stored as ASCII-coded text rather than as digitized images, many pages can be recorded on a single optical disk cartridge. Assuming a typical computer printout format of 60 lines per page (six lines per vertical inch) with a maximum of 132 characters per line (ten characters per horizontal inch), a twelve-inch WORM cartridge with two gigabytes of double-sided recording capacity can store at least 250,000 report pages — the equivalent of over 930 microfiche. Some systems use data compression algorithms to achieve even greater media capacities. Autochanger units, typically offered as an optional accessory, can provide unattended access to millions of report pages.

The most flexible COLD systems include powerful retrieval software which permits an unlimited number of index fields, supports relational expressions and Boolean operators, offers wildcard searching capabilities, and provide other useful features. Most systems include a wide-screen video monitor capable of displaying 132 columns of data. Once a given report page is retrieved and displayed, commands can be used to browse through preceding and following pages in a given report or series of reports. To produce reference copies, specified pages can be printed. Retrieved data can also be exported to other application programs.

Data Distribution. As removable storage media, write-once and rewritable optical disk cartridges can be used to distribute data and/or software in applications which require greater recording capacity than floppy disks can provide but where the number of distribution copies is too small to justify the mastering charges associated with CD-ROM discs.

Most 5.25-inch write-once and rewritable optical disk cartridges provide double-sided storage capacities that are comparable to or greater than the capacities of CD-ROM discs. Depending on the model selected, twelve-inch WORM cartridges can store data equivalent to more than a dozen CD-ROM discs. As previously noted, the ISO standard for 3.5-inch magneto-optical disks includes an OROM option which is designed specifically for data or software distribution.

DOCUMENT IMAGING APPLICATIONS

As discussed in the preceding section, read/write optical disk systems can provide useful, high-capacity storage facilities for the voluminous quantities of character-coded text and data produced by computers and scientific instrumentation. Write-once and rewritable optical disks can also store digitized images generated by document scanners, making them a potentially effective alternative to microfilm technology and conventional paper filing systems in records management applications. Computer configurations that generate, store, display, retrieve, print, disseminate, and otherwise manipulate digitized document images are variously described as electronic document imaging systems, document image processing systems, digital document processing systems, digital document automation systems, electronic image management systems, and electronic document filing systems. Such systems may utilize magnetic or optical media for document image storage. The large number of bits associated with digitized document images necessitates a high-capacity storage medium. While some configurations utilize high-density magnetic tapes, such as 8mm data cartridges and digital audio tape, optical disks are the storage media of choice for most installations. When configured with optical disk components, electronic document imaging systems are sometimes described as optical filing systems to distinguish them from equipment configurations that utilize magnetic storage components.

As one of the oldest and most widely publicized applications of optical storage technology, optical filing systems offer a completely computerized approach to document storage and retrieval.

Most optical filing systems employ write-once optical disks as their recording media. This is, in part, attributable to the earlier commercial availability of WORM systems when compared to rewritable optical disk drives and media, but write-once storage components also offer certain functional advantages. While data storage applications have traditionally relied on rewritable magnetic media to accommodate changing files, erasability—as previously noted—is seldom required and may not be desired in document imaging installations. Write-once characteristics are consequently not a liability; on the contrary, an unalterable recording medium promotes file integrity and facilitates the legal authentication of document images. Several vendors, however, have implemented optical filing systems which employ rewritable optical disks. Such systems are typically intended for applications where document images will be deleted after a brief period of time, thereby permitting the reuse of optical disk cartridges with resulting savings in media costs. Rewritable optical disks can also be used to store document images while they are subject to frequent reference. In such applications, documents may also be microfilmed. The microfilm versions will satisfy long-term retention requirements; the optical disk images are deleted when reference activity diminishes.

As a product designation, the phrase "optical filing" is a misnomer, since such systems do not "file" information in the traditional sense of placing logically-related documents in close physical proximity to one another. Instead, like the computer-assisted microfilm retrieval (CAR) products with which they compete in certain applications, optical filing systems rely on computer-based indexes that contain pointers to the optical disk locations of specific document images. The images' actual physical locations are transparent—that is, unknown and of no significance—to the user; related images may be scattered across multiple optical disk cartridges. As in microfilm-based CAR installations, the indexes are created and maintained by database management software. They are typically stored, in character-coded form, on magnetic disks where they can be searched to identify document images pertinent to specific retrieval requirements. Once identified, the document images are retrieved from their optical disk storage locations

An electronic document imaging installation. (Courtesy: IBM)

and displayed at a special workstation which is typically equipped with a high-resolution video monitor. A laser printer can be used to produce reference copies.

Optical filing concepts, technology, and applications have been widely discussed at professional information management conferences and are treated, in varying levels of detail, in a sizable and growing published literature which analyzes the advantages and limitations of electronic imaging and optical disk technology for automated document storage and retrieval. Recent examples include Attinger (1990), Cinnamon (1988), Cooper (1989), Cullen (1991), D'Alleyrand (1989), Fisher and Gilbert (1987), Fruscione (1988), George and Harden (1990), Gingras (1991), Hall (1990), Harrington and Braunschweig (1990), Ishigame (1990), Kalb and Schmit (1990), Kalthoff (1990), Kane (1991), Lace and Lee (1988), Lau (1990), Lunin (1990), Moller (1990), Morgan (1989), Moore (1990), Saffady (1989), Skelton et al (1989), Skupsky (1991), Takeda and Isomura (1990), Tas (1991), Walker and Thoma (1989, 1990), Walter (1990), and Wiggins (1990). Among published descriptions of specific optical filing implementations and system configurations, Jacobson (1990) and Kurtenbach (1988) discuss the Automated Patent System, which will eventually support over 1,000 workstations and thirty terabytes of optical storage at the U.S. Patent and

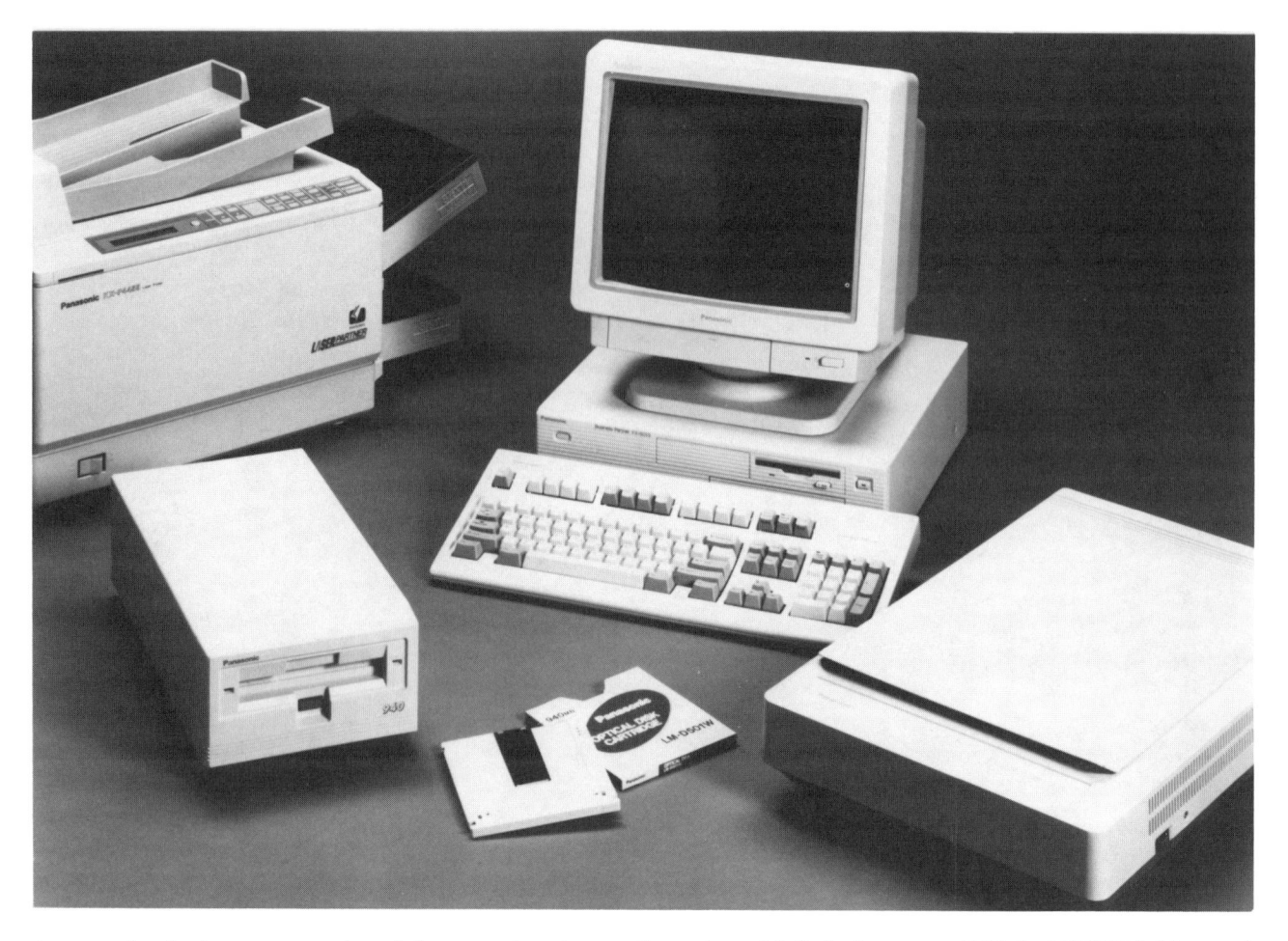

An entry-level microcomputer-based document imaging configuration with flatbed scanner, 5.25-inch WORM drive, and laser printer. (Courtesy: Panasonic)

Trademark Office. Matsuda et al (1990) describe an imaging implementation at the Japanese Patent Office. Gazdar (1991), Karcher (1990), McCready (1989), Plesums (1989), Plesums and Bartels (1990), Reynolds (1990), and Trammell (1989) discuss optical filing installations in insurance companies. Fulton (1990, 1990a) describes a retrieval system for newspaper clippings at Aberdeen City Libraries. Castle (1989) describes an optical filing installation involving personnel and payroll records in the U.S. House of Representatives. Brown (1991) describes a similar system to manage member records at the Public Employees Retirement Association of Colorado. Prokupets and Somers (1990) and Sypherd (1990) discuss the potential of document imaging and optical storage for law enforcement applications. The following subsections survey the state-of-the-art in optical filing technology, emphasizing product characteristics and recent hardware and software developments of significance for office-oriented records management applications.

Document Digitization. Optical filing installations include specially designed input workstations which convert documents to the electronic form suitable for computer processing and storage on optical disks. Such input workstations typically include a document scanner, a video display unit with keyboard, and access to magnetic and optical storage facilities. The document scanner—variously called a document digitizer or an image digitizer—is a computer input peripheral which converts paper documents—or, in some applica-

Bit-mapped imaging workstations. (Courtesy: LaserData)

tions, microfilm images—to digitally-coded, electronic images suitable for computer processing and storage on optical media. Marks (1989) presents a useful survey of scanner technology and applications. Clark (1991) provides a briefer, less technical presentation.

The scanning process, which is properly termed document digitization, divides a subject document into a series of horizontal lines which are themselves subdivided into small scannable areas called picture elements or, simply, pixels. The resulting grid of picture elements is described as a raster, and the process itself is sometimes termed raster scanning. Using photosensitive components, the scanner measures the amount of light reflected by successively encountered pixels and transmits a corresponding electrical signal to an image processing unit which performs the digital coding and image compression required for computer storage. In some cases, the image processing circuitry is built into the scanner itself. In others, image processing is performed by an external controller or by the computer to which the scanner is attached. Most document scanners incorporate solid-state, charge-coupled device (CCD) arrays as their photo-sensitive elements. Designed to scan an entire line at a time, such arrays contain one light-sensitive component for each pixel.

In the simplest and most widely encountered digitization technique, picture elements which reflect light in excess of some specified amount are considered white and are encoded as either a one or a zero bit. With most textual documents, such white pixels constitute the background areas of a page. Where the amount of reflected light is lower than the predetermined threshold amount, the scanned pixels are considered black and are represented by the opposite bit value. Black pixels usually represent the textual areas of a page. In most cases, the voltage threshold is set midway between black and white. Gray or colored pixels are treated as either black or white, depending on their relative lightness or darkness. To digitize photographs and other pictorial documents, more complex scanners use multi-bit coding schemes to represent gray or color pixels. A four-bit coding scheme, for example, can represent sixteen shades of gray, while an eight-bit coding scheme can represent 256 gray levels. Color scanners typically utilize twenty-four bits to encode each pixel.

The exact raster pattern—that is, the number of horizontal scan lines and pixels per line—supported by a given scanner is an important determinant of image quality, since the resolution, or amount of detail in digitized document images, varies directly with the density of pixels. Scanning resolution is typically expressed in pixels or dots per inch or millimeter applied to both the horizontal and vertical dimensions of a document. Available scanners support resolutions which range from less than seventy-five to more than 600 pixels per horizontal and vertical inch. In most optical filing installations, 200 pixels per inch is considered the minimum scanning resolution required for consistently legible digitization of typewritten business documents and much printed material. At 200 pixels per inch, a letter-size page will be divided into 2,200 horizontal scan lines (eleven inches times 200 pixels per inch); each line will be subdivided into 1,700 pixels (8.5 inches times 200 pixels per inch). The quality of the resulting images is comparable to that of copies produced by facsimile transceivers conforming to the CCITT Group 3 standard protocol which supports approximately 200 pixels per inch (actually 196 by 203 pixels per inch) as its highest resolution setting. Bagg (1987) discusses the relationship between resolution and image quality in specific situations.

Where higher image quality is desired or required, many document scanners support operator-selectable resolutions of 300 or even 400 pixels per inch. The quality of images digitized at 300 pixels per inch is comparable to that of the most popular laser printers and approaches office copier quality. Images digitized at 400 pixels per inch closely resemble original documents. While they will unquestionably enhance the appearance and readability of any document, such higher scanning resolutions can prove particularly advantageous in records management and library applications involving journal articles, contracts, preprinted forms, and other documents which contain footnotes or other text segments printed in very small type sizes. As a potentially significant disadvantage, however, higher scanning resolutions generate a greater number of pixels per page. They can significantly increase storage requirements for digitized images and will correspondingly reduce a given optical disk's document storage capacity. As a further constraint, few video monitors are available for resolutions exceeding 200 pixels per inch. Higher resolution images must consequently be scaled down for display purposes, with their quality being effectively reduced in the process. Laser printers, however, can routinely produce hardcopy output at 300 pixels per inch, and some models support output resolutions up to 400 pixels per inch.

Resolution aside, document scanners can be subdivided, by mode of operation, into flatbed and sheetfed varieties. Flatbed models, as their name indicates, feature a flat surface on which pages are individually positioned for scanning. Because they can accommodate books, technical reports, and other bound volumes, flatbed scanners are particularly suitable for library-type applications. Most flatbed scanners, like the photocopiers they closely resemble, feature a glass platen on which pages are positioned face down. During scanning, a CCD array and lens system, located beneath the glass, are transported by a mechanical assembly across an illuminated page. As notable exceptions, several companies offer overhead scanners which resemble planetary-type microfilmers. With such devices, individual pages are positioned face up on a flat copyboard for scanning by components positioned above the copyboard.

Sheetfed digitizers—sometimes described as pass-through or pull-through scanners—resemble facsimile transceivers in appearance and operation. The page to be scanned is inserted into a narrow opening where it is grabbed by rollers which transport it across a stationary optical head assembly and light source. Depending on equipment design, the scanned page will be ejected at the back or bottom of the machine. Because they are mechanically simpler than their flatbed counterparts, sheetfed scanners are often less expensive, although direct price/performance comparisons between flatbed and sheetfed models are typically complicated by the varying capabilities of different products. As a potentially significant disadvantage, sheetfed scanners cannot accommodate bound materials. Such documents must either be unbound or the individual pages photocopied for scanning.

Regardless of design, all document scanners intended for office-oriented optical filing applications must be able to accommodate U.S. letter-size (8.5-by-eleven-inch) pages as well as international

A4-size (210-by-297mm) documents. Most models can also accommodate U.S. legal-size (8.5-by-fourteen-inch) pages, computer printout (eleven-by-fourteen-inch) pages, and international B4-size (297-by-364mm) documents. Some scanners can accommodate A3-size (297-by-420mm) documents, the international counterpart of U.S. ledger-size (eleven-by-seventeen-inch) pages. As described below, large-document scanners, designed primarily for engineering applications, are also available.

Specific equipment configurations aside, the commercial availability of appropriate scanners is both a precondition for the successful implementation of document-oriented optical disk systems and a stimulus to their continued development. Optical filing system developers variously utilize scanners manufactured by Fujitsu, Ricoh, Canon, Improvision, Hewlett-Packard, Pentax, Panasonic, Hitachi, Bell and Howell, Terminal Data Corporation, and other companies. Operating speed depends on various factors, including page size and scanning resolution. Typical speeds—measured from the time a page is inserted into a scanner until digitization is completed—range from three to six seconds per letter-size page at a resolution of 200 pixels per horizontal and vertical inch. Some high-volume devices can operate at faster rates; certain models in Terminal Data Corporation's DocuScan product line, for example, can scan over 3,000 letter-size pages per hour. In contrast, some relatively inexpensive, entry-level scanners may require twenty seconds or longer to digitize a letter-size page. Several manufacturers—including Terminal Data Corporative, Hitachi, and Improvision—offer scanners that are capable of simultaneously digitizing both sides of two-sided documents. With conventional scanners, two-sided pages must be digitized on one side, then removed from the scanner and reinserted to digitize the other side.

As noted above, special scanners are available for engineering drawings and other large documents. Such products can typically accommodate E-size (thirty-six-by-forty-eight-inch) drawings. The most versatile devices can accept bond paper, mylar, vellum, blueline copies, and sepia copies in thicknesses from onion skin to cardboard. Special features include image and contrast enhancement for poor-quality documents, light normalization for uniform distribution of illumination across scan lines, and dynamic thresholding with multiple gray levels. Resolutions may range from less than 200 to more than 1,000 pixels per horizontal and vertical inch.

Several companies manufacture scanners which can digitize document images recorded on roll microfilm, microfiche, aperture cards, or other microforms. Such devices are typically utilized by service bureaus which specialize in large-scale backlog conversions for customers who are replacing long-established microfilm systems with electronic document imaging systems. As an alternative method of integrating microfilm and electronic imaging technologies, Eastman Kodak, Bell and Howell, and other companies have demonstrated scanner/microfilmers which simultaneously produce digitized and microform images. Such devices produce digitized images for recording on optical disks to satisfy active reference requirements and microfilm images for backup copies or long-term retention.

Whether they accept paper documents or microfilm images, scanners require attachment to a host computer. As input peripherals, they produce machine-readable, digital signals suitable for computer processing and, ultimately, optical disk recording. Rather than being directly connected to a scanner, the optical recording medium itself resides in a disk drive which usually operates online to the same host computer to which the scanner is attached. In some optical filing installations, digitized document images are routed to the host computer and immediately displayed on a video monitor for operator inspection and the entry of index data. Improperly scanned documents can be rescanned to obtain a satisfactory image. Images are not recorded on optical disks until inspection is completed. Alternatively, documents may be scanned in batches for inspection and indexing at some later time. In such cases, scanned images may be stored temporarily on magnetic disks; once inspected and approved, they are transferred to optical disks. Rejected images are deleted and the documents rescanned, either immediately or in subsequent batches.

Disk Capacities. As discussed earlier in this report, optical disk storage capacities, like those of magnetic media, are measured in bytes, a practice that is appropriate for the character-coded numeric and textual information generated by data and word processing activities but which provides little information about the number of digitized document images that can be recorded on write-once or rewritable optical disk cartridges. To estimate the document storage capacity of a given optical disk cartridge, the cartridge's total byte capacity must be divided by the number of bytes required to store a digitized image of a typical page. Such page storage requirements will depend on the size and other characteristics of documents being recorded, the scanning resolution employed in a given application, and the effectiveness of compression algorithms used to reduce the amount of information to be stored about each image.

The following formula will calculate the number of bytes required to store a single page of a given size digitized at a specified scanning resolution:

$$S = \frac{(H \times R) \times (W \times R)}{8} \times \frac{1}{C}$$

where:

S = the storage requirement per page in bytes;
H = the height of a typical subject document in inches or millimeters;
W = the width of a typical subject document in inches or millimeters;
R = the scanning resolution in, pixels per inch or millimeter, along the document's horizontal and vertical dimensions; and
C = an image compression factor.

Most optical filing systems employ computer-based compression algorithms to reduce the amount of disk space required to store digitized document images, thereby conserving optical disk capacity and minimizing the number of cartridges required to store a given quantity of pages. Applied before document images are recorded on optical disks, the most popular image compression techniques utilize run-length encoding methodologies—so-called because they produce coded messages which indicate the number of successively encountered pixels of a given tonality. Many typewritten and printed documents contain relatively long stretches of light or dark areas. Instead of generating a string of bits representing the tonal values of successively encountered pixels, run-length encoding records the line positions of alternating tonal values. As noted above, a given optical disk's storage capacity will vary with the characteristics of documents encountered in a given application. Documents with large amounts of contiguous light or dark space, such as typewritten pages with wide margins or other large blank areas, are well-suited to run-length encoding and will yield high compression factors. On the other hand, densely printed documents with more frequently light-to-dark transitions offer much less compression potential.

Image compression methodologies employed by most optical filing systems are based on standard algorithms, the two most widely encountered examples being the CCITT Group Three and Group Four algorithms developed for facsimile transmission by the Consultative Committee on International Telephony and Telegraphy. The CCITT Group Three algorithm employs the one-dimensional Modified Huffman (MH) compression technique which applies run-length encoding to a single horizontal line at a time. It yields typical compression ratios of ten to one for office documents and fifteen to one for engineering drawings. The CCITT Group Four algorithm recognizes that black or white pixels on a given line are often surrounded by pixels of identical tonality on adjacent lines. It consequently employs the two-dimensional Modified Modified READ (MMR) technique which compresses digitized images both horizontally and vertically. It yields typical compression ratios of fifteen to one for office documents and twenty to one for engineering drawings. Many optical filing systems support both Group Three and Group Four compression. To make the most effective use of optical disk capacity, Group Four compression is preferred.

It is important to note that specific compression ratios attainable in a given application depend on the tonal characteristics of documents being scanned and may be higher or lower than those stated here. Pages with large amounts of contiguous light and dark space will yield higher compression ratios than densely printed documents with

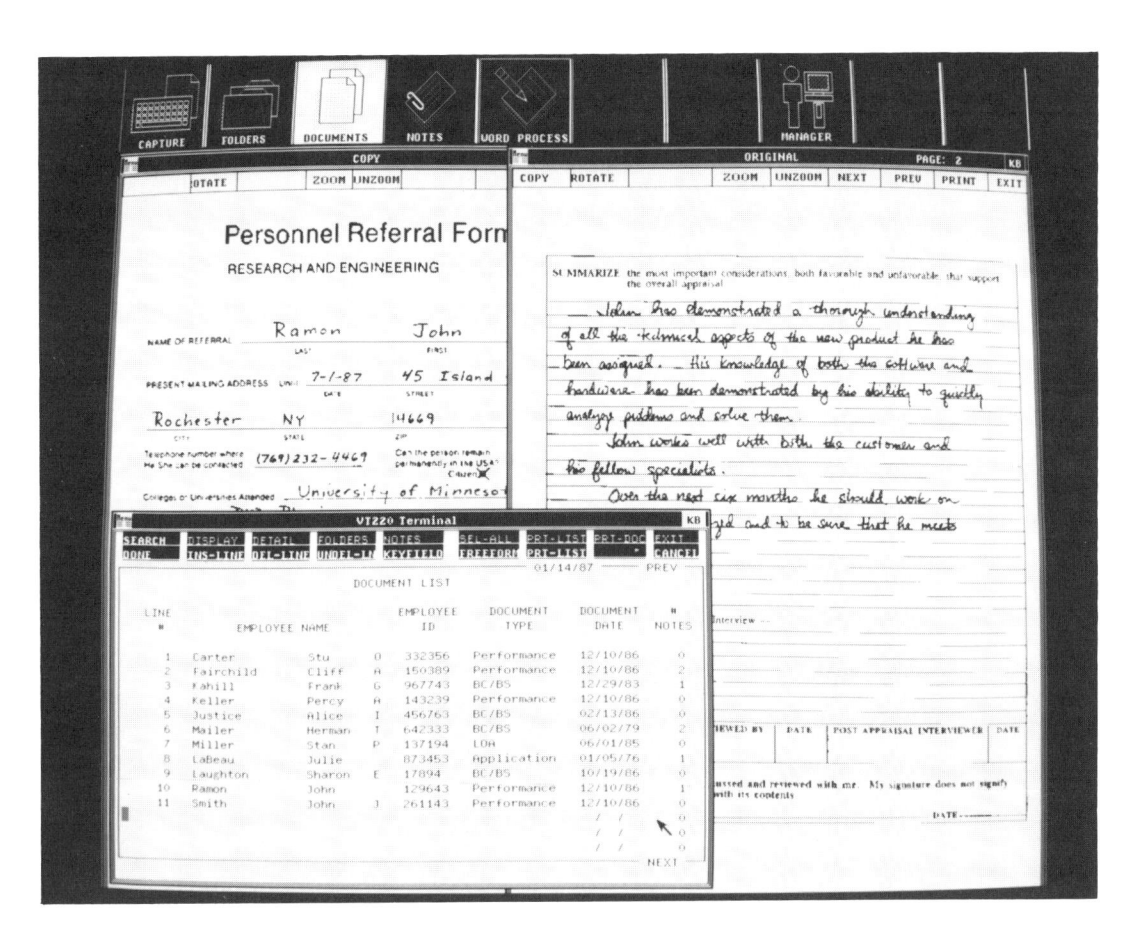

Digitized document images (backround) with data from mainframe session displayed in a separate window. (Courtesy: Eastman Kodak)

frequent light-to-dark transitions. Partial page business memoranda, for example, may be compressed by a factor of twenty to one or higher, while densely printed journal articles, technical reports, or business forms may offer little compression potential. Although it is a relatively rare occurence, images of certain densely printed documents can actually require more storage space when compression algorithms are applied.

Applying the foregoing formula, the accompanying tables calculate storage requirements for documents of various sizes digitized at common scanning resolutions, as well as estimated page storage capacities for commonly encountered write-once and rewritable optical disk cartridges. It is important to note that the formula and the tabular estimates based on it are only valid for applications involving black and white documents. In such applications, as discussed above, each pixel in a scanned page is encoded as a single bit, and the calculation $((H \times R) \times (W \times R))$ consequently yields the uncompressed page storage requirement in bits. Division by eight converts the uncompressed page storage requirement to bytes. The resulting quotient is then multiplied by the reciprocal of the compression factor.

Index Data Entry. As noted above, an optical filing system maintains a computer-processible database that serves as an index to digitized document images recorded on optical disks. The database typically contains one record for each indexable item in a given collection of documents. The records are divided into fields that correspond to user-specified index categories. Saffady (1988) reviews the most important conceptual and practical issues pertinent to document indexing in optical filing systems.

Index data entry involves the entry of values associated with specific fields. It may be performed immediately following scanning or at some later time. Depending on application characteristics and the capabilities of hardware and software employed in a given installation, field values may be key-entered, downloaded from existing computer databases, or extracted from scanned documents via optical recognition methodologies. Of these, key-entry is the most widely utilized. It is typically integrated with image inspection. Digitized document images are individually displayed on a video monitor for operator examination; once satisfactory image quality is confirmed, the document's assigned index values are typed at the monitor's keyboard in a manner prescribed by the database management software employed in a particular application. Many programs support specially formatted screens, with labelled fields accompanied by adjacent blank spaces, to facilitate the key-entry of specified index values.

Some electronic document imaging applications employ barcode or optical character recognition (OCR) technologies to minimize or eliminate the key-entry of index data. Such approaches are sometimes described as "auto-indexing" methodologies because they involve the automatic extraction of index values from specified portions of input documents. In a typical auto-indexing implementation, input documents are scanned to create digitized images which are stored in temporary files on magnetic disks. The digitized images are then processed by barcode or optical character recognition software. In some cases, barcode or optical character recognition are performed during the scanning process itself, simultaneously with document digitization.

In barcode recognition, document identifiers or other numeric values are encoded by predetermined patterns of closely spaced lines of varying widths. The barcodes may be printed directly on input documents or on labels which are affixed to the documents. OCR uses reflected light to identify the individual characters contained in input documents. The recognized characters are converted to ASCII-coded form for transfer to a computer-maintained database, just as if they had been key-entered. While barcodes are typically restricted to numeric values, OCR technology can recognize letters of the alphabet, numeric digits, punctuation marks, and other symbols encountered in text.

The simplest OCR devices impose significant restrictions on type fonts, page formats, and other characteristics of input documents. More sophisticated products, however, can recognize many different type fonts in various styles and sizes. Such devices, which are sometimes described as Intelligent Character Recognition (ICR) machines, combine sophisticated feature extraction algorithms with spelling dictionaries and other techniques to accommodate a broad range of input documents. Feature extraction algorithms recognize characters by their distinctive shapes, an approach which transcends ornamental differences associated with specific type fonts. As an example, the upper-case letter "A" is recognized as a character with two diagonal lines, joined at the top and bisected by a horizontal crossbar, while an uppercase "D" is recognized as having one vertical line joined at the ends by a loop. Presumably, those characters will have the indicated features regardless of the type font in which they are printed.

The Compound Document Processor (CDP), manufactured by Calera Recognition Systems, is perhaps the most widely encountered example of an ICR scanner. As described by Fruchterman (1988), Greenblatt (1988), Pritchard (1989), and Schein (1989), it uses multiple microprocessors, a pipelined architecture, and proprietary algorithms to recognize a wide variety of typewritten, typeset, laser printer, and dot matrix fonts, whether monospaced or proportionally-spaced, in many different sizes. Operating at scanning resolutions up to 400 pixels per horizontal and vertical inch, the CDP can both recognize text and digitize documents in a single operation. Its character recognition capabilities are based on feature extraction techniques. If feature extraction fails to conclusively identify a given character, additional tests—based on word placement, spelling relationships, frequency of appearance, and other criteria—are applied. Wang Laboratories, Plexus Computers, AT&T, Genesis Imaging Technologies, Micro Dynamics Limited, and other systems integrators have utilized the Compound Document Processor in optical filing installations implemented for corporations and government agencies.

As discussed by Natraj (1990, 1990a) and

Approximate Storage Requirements (uncompressed) in Bytes for Documents of Various Sizes

Page Size (in inches)	Scanning Resolution 200 pixels/inch	300 pixels/inch	400 pixels/inch
8.5 x 11	467,500	1,051,900	1,870,000
8.5 x 14	595,000	1,338,750	2,380,000
11 x 14	770,000	1,732,500	3,080,000
11 x 17	935,000	2,103,750	3,740,000
18 x 24	2,160,000	4,860,000	8,640,000
24 x 36	4,320,000	9,720,000	17,280,000
34 x 44	7,480,000	16,830,000	29,920,000

Wetzler (1990), OCR-based auto-indexing will perform most reliably in optical filing applications where field values can be extracted from designated areas of specially formatted documents, such as purchase orders, invoices, and other standardized business forms. OCR also permits full-text indexing of correspondence, memoranda, reports, and other unformatted documents. Such applications do not employ conventional field-oriented databases; instead, index entries are created for every word in the text of input documents. Characteristics of full text storage and retrieval technology are surveyed by Saffady (1989a). The potential of full text indexing as an alternative or complement to document images in optical filing applications is discussed by Allen (1989), Bender (1987, 1988), and Cherry and Waldstein (1989).

Retrieval Capabilities. An optical filing system's retrieval workstation includes a video monitor for image display and, optionally, a laser printer for hard copy output. The video monitor—which is configured with a typewriter-style keyboard and, in some cases, a mouse—is typically a bit-mapped graphics-type device designed specifically for high-resolution document display. Such monitors store the bit patterns for a given document image in internal memory circuits and selectively illuminate or darken portions of the video screen in accordance with the light and dark picture elements in the original document. Many of the bit-mapped video monitors employed in optical filing systems support a display resolution of 200 pixels per horizontal or vertical inch, although some models support display resolutions as low as 72 pixels per inch. As previously noted, displayed images are often scaled to accommodate discrepancies between the scanning resolutions and display resolutions supported in a given optical filing installation. Safdie (1988) provides a useful discussion of display resolution for document imaging applications. Black (1990) explains the relationship between display resolution and scanning resolution.

Regardless of display characteristics, retrieval operations begin with a search of an optical filing system's index database to determine the existence and location of document images meeting specified parameters. The simplest search statements typically include a field name, a relational expression, and a field value. To address more complex application requirements, most optical filing systems permit retrieval specifications containing combinations of search terms linked by the Boolean AND, OR, and NOT operators. Some programs also support search term truncation and wildcard symbols.

While specific responses to an index search command will vary from implementation to implementation, most optical filing systems identify a set of document images which satisfy a particular retrieval specification. The system then responds with an indication of the number of retrievable items identified by the index search, thus giving the operator an opportunity to broaden or narrow the retrieval specification. Once an appropriately sized set of items is identified, database records are displayed for operator perusal. With some systems, users can specify the fields to be included in such displays, as well as the sort sequence for retrieved records. When full document images corresponding to specific database records are requested, the system prompts the operator to locate and load a particular optical disk cartridge—assuming, of course, that the required documents are recorded on a cartridge other than the one already loaded in the drive at the time the search was performed. Multidrive configurations and autochanger devices, as previously noted, will minimize or eliminate manual cartridge loading.

Retrieved document images are typically transferred to a magnetic disk drive which serves as a staging area and permits browsing and reexamination without repetitive and potentially time-consuming optical disk accesses. Depending on the capabilities supported by a given optical filing system, displayed images may be enlarged, reduced, rotated, or otherwise manipulated. To support electronic publishing activities, some systems permit the transfer of retrieved document images to page layout programs. If the retrieval workstation includes a laser printer, reference copies can be produced.

Implementation Alternatives. The commercial availability of document scanners, optical disk drives, bit-mapped video monitors, laser printers, database management programs, and other information processing hardware and software does not guarantee their successful implementation in optical filing configurations. As with the data-oriented optical disk systems described in a preceding section, considerable hardware customization and software development may be required to incorporate specific components in effective document storage and retrieval systems. While this work might conceivably be performed by end-users, most of the document-oriented optical filing systems installed to date were either customized for specific applications by so-called systems integrators or purchased as turnkey configurations of hardware and software.

Operating as contractors to businesses, government agencies, and other organizations, systems integrators develop the hardware and software interfaces required to combine the computer, telecommunications, and optical disk components of various manufacturers in custom-developed document storage and retrieval installations. While their most recent activities have emphasized electronic imaging and optical disk technology, systems integrators are not tied to any particular document or data storage methodology. Some of them developed their reputations and client base in the 1970s by implementing sophisticated microfilm applications involving computer-assisted retrieval and microimage transmission to remote workstations. Others, however, are relatively new companies formed specifically to implement optical disk technology. Corporate origins aside, systems integrators typically implement optical filing capabilities in complex applications with special recording, indexing, or other requirements. In some installations in the financial services industry, for example, imaging capabilities and optical storage components are integrated with high-volume transaction processing operations.

Examples of systems integrators with experience in optical disk-based electronic imaging implementations include Advanced Data Management Incorporated, Advanced Projects International, Advanced Systems Development Incorporated, Advanced Technology Incorporated, Alpaharel Incorporated, American Management Systems, Amitech Corporation, Andersen Consulting, Applied Computer Technology, Arthur Young and Company, BDM International, CACI Image Support Services, Capital Software Incorporated, Centel Federal Systems, Computer Horizons Corporation, Computer Sciences Corporation, Coopers and Lybrand, CSSI, DataImage Incorporated, Data Management Design Incorporated, Document Imaging Systems Corporation, EDS Corporation, Ernst and Young, FORMTEK, Genesis Imaging Technologies, Grumman InfoConversion, GTX Corporation, Image Business Systems Corporation, Image Conversion Technologies, Image

Approximate Storage Requirements in Bytes For Pages of Various Sizes With CCITT Group 3 Compression

Page Size (in inches)	200 pixels/inch	Scanning Resolution 300 pixels/inch	400 pixels/inch
8.5 x 11	46,750	105,200	187,000
8.5 x 14	59,500	133,900	238,000
11 x 14	77,000	173,250	308,000
11 x 17	93,500	210,400	374,000
18 x 24	216,000	486,000	864,000
24 x 36	432,000	972,000	1,728,000
34 x 44	748,000	1,683,000	2,992,000

Approximate Storage Requirements in Bytes For Pages of Various Sizes With CCITT Group 4 Compression

Page Size (in inches)	200 pixels/inch	Scanning Resolution 300 pixels/inch	400 pixels/inch
8.5 x 11	31,200	70,150	124,700
8.5 x 14	39,700	89,250	158,700
11 x 14	51,350	115,500	205,350
11 x 17	62,350	140,250	249,350
18 x 24	144,000	324,000	576,000
24 x 36	288,000	648,000	1,152,000
34 x 44	498,700	1,122,000	1,994,700

Data Corporation, Image Data Systems, IMNET Corporation, Laser Recording Systems, Litton Industries, Metafile Information Systems, OGDEN/ERC Government Systems, Optical Storage Solutions, Plexus Software, Recognition Equipment Incorporated, Science Applications International Corporation, Sigma Imaging Systems, ST Systems Corporation, System Development Corporation, Systemhouse Incorporated, Trident Systems, TRW, TSC, ViewStar Corporation, Vision Three, West Coast Information Systems, and Xerox Corporation.

Since the late 1980s, most mainframe and minicomputer manufacturers have incorporated some form of electronic document imaging system or service in their product offerings. Examples include Digital Equipment Corporation, Unisys, NCR, Bull Worldwide Information Systems, Hewlett-Packard, Wang, Nixdorf, Data General, and, of course, IBM. Some industry analysts contend that IBM's entry into the document image processing field will legitimize optical storage technology in the minds of many prospective users. IBM's imaging strategy is discussed by Glavitsch (1989), Myers (1988), Liddell (1990), and Steen (1989). IBM's ImagePlus system, which was introduced in mid-1988, is a combination of hardware and software for document image processing with optical storage components. It supports the document scanning, indexing, optical disk recording, retrieval, display and printing capabilities outlined above. The initial implementation, intended for IBM mainframes, was subsequently joined by a version for AS/400 systems. Those versions are described by Addink and Mullen (1990), Anderson et al (1990), Avers and Probst (1990), Dinan et al (1990, and Harding et al (1990). In late 1991, IBM announced ImagePlus/2 which runs on IBM PS/2 microcomputers under OS/2 Extended Edition in standalone or networked configurations. Jointly developed by IBM and Eastman Kodak, it is intended for small to medium-size businesses as well as departmental installations within large organizations. Employing the multitasking capabilities of the OS/2 operating system, ImagePlus/2 can run several different programs while executing an imaging application.

A number of systems integrators and consulting firms are reportedly developing industry-specific applications, ranging from mortgage loan processing to building code enforcement, for ImagePlus installations in banks, insurance companies, investment firms, local governments, and other organizations. In mid-1990, IBM announced an implementation of ImagePlus designed specifically for check-processing applications in banks. The ImagePlus High-Performance Transaction System (HPTS) combines image processing and amount recognition technologies. The system, which runs on IBM mainframe computers under the MVS/ESA operating system, digitizes bank checks for storage on optical or magnetic disks. Once digitized and stored, specific check images can be retrieved for display on IBM PS/2 workstations. As its most distinctive feature, the HPTS can recognize machine-printed and handwritten amounts of checks, thereby minimizing or eliminating the need to keystroke such amounts and offering significant potential for labor reductions in check-processing installations. Electronic image processing systems for check-processing applications are also offered by other companies, including Unisys and Recognition Equipment Incorporated. In its initial configuration which was announced in late 1989, the Unisys system differed from ImagePlus HPTS in its use of magnetic rather than optical disks for image storage. The potential of imaging technology in banking applications is examined by Costanzo (1991).

Among other computer manufacturers, Digital Equipment Corporation offers a variety of products designed to support the development and implementation of imaging applications in VAX installations. To promote imaging capabilities throughout an organization's computing environment, Digital emphasizes implementation within the context of its Network Application Support (NAS) services. In early 1991, Digital announced DECimage EXpress, a line of preconfigured document imaging systems that utilize standard hardware and software combined with imaging components. Initial DECimage EXpress offerings are designed for the VAX/VMS computing environment. The Compound Document Architecture component of NAS allows DECimage EXpress applications to share images and other data types with applications running on MS-DOS, Unix, OS/2, and Macintosh systems. Document images can

Approximate A4-page Image Capacities of Selected Optical Disk Cartridges
Assuming Group 3 Compression

Disk Size (in inches)	Disk Capacity	200 pixels/inch	300 pixels/inch	400 pixels/inch
3.5	128 MB	2,750	1,200	700
5.25	600 MB	12,800	5,700	3,200
5.25	650 MB	13,900	6,200	3,500
5.25	800 MB	17,100	7,600	4,300
5.25	940 MB	20,100	8,900	5,000
5.25	1.2 GB	25,700	11,400	6,400
12	2 GB	42,800	19,000	10,700
12	2.6 GB	55,600	24,700	13,900
12	5 GB	107,000	47,500	26,700
12	6.6 GB	141,200	62,700	35,300
12	7 GB	149,700	66,500	37,400
12	9 GB	192,500	85,500	48,100
14	6.8 GB	145,500	64,600	36,400
14	10.2 GB	218,200	100,000	54,500

Approximate A4-page Image Capacities of Selected Optical Disk Cartridges
Assuming Group 4 Compression

Disk Size (in inches)	Disk Capacity	200 pixels/inch	300 pixels/inch	400 pixels/inch
3.5	128 MB	4,100	1,800	1,000
5.25	600 MB	19,200	8,600	4,800
5.25	650 MB	20,800	9,300	5,200
5.25	800 MB	25,600	11,400	6,400
5.25	940 MB	30,100	13,400	7,500
5.25	1.2 GB	38,500	17,100	9,600
12	2 GB	64,100	28,500	16,000
12	2.6 GB	83,300	37,100	20,900
12	5 GB	160,300	71,300	40,100
12	6.6 GB	211,500	94,100	52,900
12	7 GB	224,400	99,800	56,100
12	9 GB	288,500	128,300	72,200
14	6.8 GB	217,900	96,900	54,500
14	10.2 GB	326,900	145,400	81,200

be stored on optical or magnetic disks; as noted in the preceding discussion of data storage applications, Digital offers both write-once optical disk drives and autochangers for VAX installations. To promote its imaging activities, Digital has announced business alliances with Eastman Kodak, LaserData, and other optical storage systems vendors. Digital plans to integrate those vendors' offerings into its imaging product lines.

The NCR Document Management System (DMS) is similarly designed as an enterprise-wide approach to imaging applications. It is based on the NCR System 3000, which employs client/server architecture, relational database management, and open systems standards. Scanning and retrieval workstations consist of NCR personal computers running under the MS-DOS or OS/2 operating systems. Special features include NCR's Workflow Manager, which graphically depicts the work flow associated with specific document processing activities, and an OCR module for hand-printed numeric characters. Hewlett-Packard, which markets read/write optical disk subsystems and CD-ROM drives for data storage applications, has added a document imaging system to its product line. The HP Advanced Image Management System (AIMS) runs on HP 9000 series minicomputers under the HP-UX operating system. The HP 9000 operates as an image and data server for microcomputer-based client workstations linked in an Ethernet local area network.

Wang Laboratories' principal document imaging activities are embodied in the much publicized Wang Integrated Information System (WIIS). Prime Computer added imaging capabilities to its product line in mid-1991. Its IMAGE WAY system is an expandable series of modular components for Prime computer servers running under the PRIMOS or Unix operating systems. Tandem's NonStop Image product line was likewise introduced in 1991. It combines two image management products: the Tandem Image Processing System (TIPS), an image management software package for high-volume transaction-oriented applications, and Product and Process Document Management (PPDM), which permits the implementation of process-oriented imaging applications. Bull HN Information Systems has added imaging capabilities to its computerized Public Safety Management System which runs on Bull DPS 6 PLUS computers. The imaging module permits the integration of digitized suspect photos with crime reports and other law enforcement records.

Offering undeniably impressive capabilities, the customized optical filing configurations developed by systems integrators and computer manufacturers may be the preferred implementation approach in large-scale document storage installations with unusual retrieval requirements, but the straightforward characteristics of many applications can be successfully addressed by less expensive, turnkey optical filing systems. As discussed here, a turnkey optical filing system is a preconfigured combination of optical disk and computer components, including both hardware and software, which are designed for self-contained operation, usually in an office environment. Intended for a broad spectrum of records management applications, the turnkey approach offers rapid, convenient implementation of optical disk technology with simplified procurement and single-vendor responsibility for all system components. Narrowly defined, turnkey systems limit customization to the selection of hardware components from a range of available options. Most systems, however, include flexible data management software which can be tailored to specific application requirements. In actual practice, turnkey system vendors may undertake considerable customization, including some original programming and hardware integration, for specific applications. At the extreme, such configurations may incorporate so many customized components that their original turnkey characteristics are barely discernible.

The turnkey approach to document storage and retrieval is not unique to optical filing systems. It has been successfully implemented in microfilm-based CAR systems since the early 1970s, and such systems remain an important and growing segment of the document storage and retrieval marketplace. Although they utilize different recording media, turnkey optical filing systems resemble their microfilm-based CAR counterparts in both concept and operation. With both technologies, a dedicated computer maintains an index to document images. To identify documents relevant to particular information needs, CAR and optical filing system users consult the computer-based index to determine the existence and location of potentially relevant documents. Depending on the system, the actual retrieval and display of document images may be performed automatically or require modest manual intervention.

The first turnkey optical filing systems were introduced in Japan and Europe in the early 1980s. Some vendors—including Hitachi, Toshiba, Matsushita, Ricoh, NEC, and Philips —are now marketing second and third-generation products. During the mid-1980s, several Japanese optical filing systems were exported to the United States where they were marketed by such American vendors as Tab Products and the 3M Company. Since the late 1980s, however, American companies have developed their own turnkey optical filing systems, albeit with Japanese optical disk drives, scanners, laser printers, and other hardware components. By the early 1990s, at least one hundred companies were offering some type of turnkey optical filing system. While a comprehensive examination and evaluation of such products is beyond the scope of this report, the following discussion will survey the most important characteristics and capabilities of turnkey optical filing systems, delineating their distinctive attributes and emphasizing features of greatest significance for records management applications.

Turnkey optical filing systems are often categorized by the type of computer configuration on which they are based. As with CAR systems, the earliest turnkey optical filing systems featured minicomputers as their central processors. Examples included the previously cited Tab Laser-Optic 2500 and 3M Docutron 2000 systems, the Wang Integrated Information System (WIIS), and the KIMS 3000 System from Eastman Kodak. While such minicomputer-based configurations are well suited to many document storage and retrieval applications, the fastest growing group of turnkey optical filing systems utilize IBM-compatible microcomputers as their central processors. Such optical filing implementations usually incorporate an Intel 80386 or 80486 microprocessor and run under the MS-DOS operating system, possibly in conjunction with Microsoft Windows. The first microcomputer-based optical filing product, the DISCUS 1000 System, was introduced by Advanced Graphics Applications (AGA) in 1985. Other examples of this increasingly popular approach to turnkey system implementation are offered by Adaptive Information Systems, Bell and Howell, Canon, COM Squared, Document Technologies Incorporated, DocuPoint, Eastern Computers Incorporated, Eastman Kodak, Executive Technologies, Eye-COM, Filequest, IMNET Corporation, LaserData, Minolta, Summit Software, ViewStar Corporation, and Tab Products, among many others. Examples of turnkey optical filing systems based on Macintosh computers include the MARS system from Micro Dynamics Limited and the CD*STAR system from Conversion Dynamics Incorporated. Wang Laboratories offers software which allows Macintosh computers to be used as image display stations in its WIIS configurations.

Microcomputer-based optical filing systems are entry-level products designed for low-to-medium-volume records management applications. Minicomputer-based products are typically intended for medium-to-high volume installations. As a potential advantage that permits sharing of an optical filing system by several offices or departments, most minicomputer-based implementations can support multiple workstations and multiple applications, although a basic configuration typically includes a single workstation as standard equipment. In their least expensive configurations, most microcomputer-based turnkey optical filing systems are single-workstation products, although most vendors optionally offer local area network implementations that permit multi-workstation access to microcomputer functioning as an optical file server.

Regardless of the particular central processor utilized, turnkey optical filing systems include document scanners, magnetic disk storage for index data, video display terminals, printers, and data management software which supports document indexing and retrieval. All turnkey optical filing systems include copier-like, desktop scanners which convert source documents to digitized images suitable for recording on optical disks. As one component in a document entry station, the scanner is typically configured with a video terminal for image review, a keyboard for the entry of index data, and a controller which performs image compression and other functions prior to recording. Operating speeds of three to six seconds per letter-size page are common for scanners supplied with minicomputer-based turnkey optical filing systems. To minimize costs, some entry-level microcomputer-based systems include slower scanners which can take twenty or more seconds to digitize a single letter-size page. All turnkey optical filing systems support document scanning and optical disk recording at 200 pixels per horizontal and vertical inch—as discussed above, the current de facto standard resolution in optical filing applications. Where higher image quality is desired, most systems support scanning resolutions of 300 or 400 pixels per horizontal and vertical inch, although the video terminals included with most equipment configurations typically display 200 or fewer pixels per inch. To reduce costs, however, an increasing number of turnkey optical filing systems incorporate lower resolution monitors with displays limited to 100 or 150 pixels per horizontal and vertical inch. For high-quality hardcopy output, some systems are equipped with high resolution laser printers which can operate at 400 pixels per inch. While they are not currently displayable, such higher resolution images may be supported by future developments in video display technology, although—as previously noted—they consume twice the disk space of images recorded at 200 pixels per inch and significantly reduce the number of documents which can be recorded on a given optical disk.

With their high storage capacities, twelve-inch write-once optical disks are the dominant document recording media employed by minicomputer-based turnkey optical filing systems. Assuming a scanning resolution of 200 pixels per horizontal and vertical inch and an average image compression ratio of ten to one, a double-sided, twelve-inch optical disk with two gigabytes of recording capacity can store about 43,000 letter-size pages; higher capacity media and greater amounts of image compression will significantly increase that amount. While some microcomputer-based systems employ twelve-inch media, others feature less expensive 5.25-inch optical disk subsystems. The most popular 5.25-inch WORM configurations, as described earlier this report, provide 600 megabytes to 1.2 gigabytes of recording capacity per double-sided cartridges. A few systems, as previously noted, employ rewritable optical media.

The number of such configurations may increase as the price/performance characteristics of magneto-optical technology improve.

In their standard configurations, most turnkey optical filing systems are equipped with a single optical disk drive. In such installations, only one disk can be online at a time, the remainder being stored in an offline cabinet. In a manner similar to most CAR systems, software may instruct the operator to mount or turn a specific disk to retrieve desired document images. To increase online storage capacity and minimize disk handling, some turnkey systems can be configured with one to eight additional optical disk drives. However, as discussed earlier, an optical disk autochanger is the preferred method of expanding online document storage capacity. Most turnkey optical filing systems consequently support an autochanger as optional equipment. In networked configurations, autochangers provide the only effective approach to multi-workstation access to document images recorded on optical disks.

Turnkey optical filing systems increasingly support optional capabilities that permit communication with other information systems. Some systems, for example, can emulate specific computer terminals—such as IBM 3270 or DEC VT100 models—for purposes of accessing a database of other information stored on a mainframe or minicomputer. When equipped with a facsimile option, a turnkey optical fiing system can transmit document images over telephone lines to any CCITT Group Three facsimile machine. With some systems, facsimile machines can also function as document scanners for remote input.

VIDEO AND AUDIO RECORDING

The preceding sections have surveyed applications of read/write optical disk systems for data and document storage in computer installations. While such computer-based applications attract the most attention, read/write optical disk equipment and media can also be used for audio and video recording. Kurahashi et al (1985) is typical of early research reports which describe prototype optical disks systems for audio recording. In 1988, as noted above, Tandy announced plans to develop and commercialize an audio compact disc recorder based on rewritable dye-polymer optical storage technology, but that project was subsequently discontinued. Croll (1990) discusses the potential of optical disks for audio recording in the broadcasting industry. In 1990, Thomson Consumer Electronics demonstrated a prototype magneto-optical compact disc system for digital audio recording applications. As discussed by Schroeder and Uhde (1990) and Van Geider (1990), Thomson claims a potential playback time of four hours with audio signal quality comparable to that of compact discs. In 1991, Sony proposed a Mini Disc (MD) system which will utilize 2.5-inch magneto-optical media and data compression technology to record over seventy minutes of digitally-encoded stereo audio. Commercial availability is planned for late 1992. The Mini Disc system will also be able to play prerecorded media which will be based on compact disc technology and produced in existing compact disc manufacturing facilities.

Primarily intended for entertainment applications, such audio recording systems fall outside the scope of this report, which emphasizes optical storage technology for business-oriented information management applications. As noted earlier in this report, several companies offer optical disk recorders for analog video signals and accompanying audio. Properly described as video disc recorders, such systems can accept input from video cameras, video tapes, read-only video discs, or other video sources. Developed by Matsushita, the various models in the Panasonic TQ product line are the best known and most widely utilized examples of such devices. In its original configuration, the TQ series Optical Memory Disc Recorder (OMDR) could record 24,000 still video frames or 13.5 minutes of full-motion video images, accompanied by stereo audio signals, on an eight-inch, write-once optical disk composed of a tellurium-based thin film. It has been commercially available since the early 1980s. In 1988, Panasonic introduced TQ series models which can record up to 54,000 analog still frames or 30 minutes of full-motion video on each side of a twelve-inch, write-once optical disk. Similar products have been developed by Sony, Hitachi, and Teac.

In 1990, Panasonic introduced the LQ-4000, a video disc recorder that employs rewritable optical disks. It can record video images in the NTSC composite, RGB, and Super VHS formats. A high-resolution recording mode generates images with 450 scan lines. The LQ-4000 is bundled with software that supports the creation of video databases. In late 1989, Pioneer and KDD announced the joint development of a video disc recorder which can store up to one hour of full-motion analog video images on a twelve-inch magneto-optical disk, but the system's commercial availability has yet to be announced. Streets and Tugwell (1990) discuss the Asaca AAM-800 which uses magneto-optical disks to store analog video signals as well as digitally-coded data. Itoh et al (1988), Kawabe et al (1990), and Ohtani et al (1990) describe a magneto-optical video disc recorder developed by Sharp. Okada et al (1990) and Yoshihara et al (1990) discuss a similar device developed by NEC. Tanaka et al (1990) and Yoshikawa et al (1990) report on video recording research conducted by KDD and Pioneer, respectively. Other Japanese manufacturers are reportedly working on similar products.

Analog video disc recorders offer an alternative to videocassette recorders and read-only video disc systems in a variety of applications, including interactive training, point of sale operations, and the preparation of graphic presentations. Compared to read-only video discs, they eliminate the delay and cost associated with mastering and permit the use of video disc technology in applications where only one copy of a disk is required. More pertinent to this discussion of optical filing systems, analog video disc recorders can also be used by archives, museums, libraries, newspapers, publishing companies, and other organizations to store photographs and other pictorial documents. Among reported applications, Hawkins and Skriba (1986) describe the use of a Panasonic OMDR recorder as an alternative to slides, videocassettes, and microfilm in various medical applications at the University of Cincinnati. Similarly, the International Sculpture Center has used a Panasonic OMDR system to transfer images of 3,000 contemporary sculptures from color slides to write-once video discs. The art images are supplemented by a textual database which can be searched for works by particular sculptors, about specific subjects, installed in particular geographic locations, constructed of designated media, or representing a given style. Designed by the Information Technology Group Incorporated, the system is microcomputer-based and includes a color video printer. At its factory in Orlando, Martin Marietta Corporation has installed Panasonic OMDR recorders to store engineering change documents.

Because they record video signals which conform to conventional broadcast television standards, the analog video disc recorders discussed above do not provide sufficient resolution for consistently legible reproduction of textual documents, a limitation which they share with read-only analog optical video disc systems. The development of video disc recorders based on high-definition television (HDTV) technology has been widely discussed, and several Japanese companies have demonstrated prototype models. Examples are described by Fujino et al (1987), Hioki et al (1988), Horstman (1988), Mano et al (1988), Saeki et al (1990), Satoh et al (1990), Streets (1990), Shiotani et al (1990), Takahashi (1988), Toyama et al (1986, 1987), and Tsuchiya et al (1991).

Part Two:
CD-ROM and Related Media

CD-ROM TECHNOLOGY

Read-only optical discs are publishing media for electronically recorded information. Unlike write-once and rewritable optical media, which are purchased blank and permit direct recording of information by end-users, read-only optical discs lack recordable properties. As their distinguishing characteristic, they are produced in "editions" of multiple copies that contain prerecorded information. The individual copies are created by a mastering process. The information they are to contain is sent to a factory where a specially prepared mold or matrix is used to produce multiple read-only copies for distribution to users. As their name indicates, the prerecorded contents of the read-only copies can be read—that is, retrieved—but not modified, added to, or deleted. The purchaser is principally interested in the information that the read-only copies contain; other media characteristics, as well as the capabilities of associated hardware and software, are only significant to the extent that they support the distribution and retrieval of such information.

The most important read-only optical disc formats are enumerated and briefly described in the accompanying table. The following sections will survey their characteristics and capabilities beginning with Compact Disc-Read Only Memory (CD-ROM), the most important read-only optical disc technology for computer applications. The discussion intentionally emphasizes those formats that are suitable for information storage and retrieval in computer applications involving data, text, or images; other types of read-only optical discs, designed for playback of audio and video recordings in consumer applications, will be covered only as they relate to such computer applications.

Compact disc is the generic designation for a group of optical storage formats and products that are based on technology developed jointly by Sony and Philips during the 1970s and 1980s. Introduced in 1980, the most widely encountered type of compact disc is a rigid plastic platter that measures twelve centimeters (approximately 4.75 inches) in diameter and is 1.2 millimeters thick. A nine-centimeter (approximately 3.5-inch) version was introduced in 1987. While the term compact disc is sometimes loosely applied to 3.5- and 5.25-inch read/write optical disks, which are compact in size, such usage is improper. Compact disc is a precisely defined product designation for specific information storage media; 3.5- and 5.25-inch write-once and rewritable optical media do not conform to Sony/Philips specifications for physical characteristics and recording formats of compact discs. As explained later in this report, however, Sony and Philips have developed recordable compact disc formats that are utilized by certain commercially available products.

As discussed by Pohlmann (1988, 1989), the various compact disc formats are typically categorized by the type of information they contain. In addition to computer-processable data, the possibilities include audio, graphics, and video signals. The technology's earliest and most widely publicized implementation—properly termed, Compact Disc-Digital Audio (CD-DA) but popularly and simply described as a "CD"—offers a super high-fidelity alternative to conventional long-playing phonograph records and prerecorded magnetic tape cassettes in consumer audio applications. Most published descriptions of the CD-DA format date from the 1980s, when the technology was new and required explanation. Nakajima (1989) of Sony Corporation explains the characteristics and advantages of digital audio recording in general and the compact disc format in particular. Carosso *et al.* (1982) provide an excellent overview from the standpoint of Philips engineers.

As an audio recording product, CD-DA technology falls outside the scope of this report; its widespread consumer acceptance, however, has had an impact on the development of computer-oriented compact disc products. The availability of CD-DA media and equipment has heightened awareness of the potential of optical storage technology, while economies of scale resulting from a strong market for CD-DA systems have reduced equipment prices and stimulated product research and development. While magnetic tape cassettes are still the dominant consumer audio recording medium, CD-DA sales have surpassed those of long-playing phonograph records. As record collectors are aware, an increasing number of albums are being issued in CD-DA and magnetic tape cassette formats only.

As originally conceived, the CD-DA standard provided some storage space for computer-processible, character-coded information to identify the individual musical selections on a given compact disc, although such character-coded data is used sparingly as an adjunct to the audio signals which occupy the majority of disc space. CD-ROM, the subject of this discussion, is an implementation of compact disc technology designed specifically for machine-readable, computer-processible data. Like their CD-DA counterparts, CD-ROM discs typically measure twelve centimeters in diameter, although nine-centimeter versions are also available. Regardless of size, CD-ROM discs feature a reflective metal layer covered with a protective coating. Their rugged polycarbonate base material is well suited to a wide range of use environments and permits relatively casual handling, although scratches can render a given disc unusable. The following subsections describe the technology's characteristics and production methodologies. Subsequent sections will discuss CD-ROM equipment, information products, and the relationship of CD-ROM to other information processing technologies.

Storage Characteristics. As with Compact Disc-Digital Audio, many published discussions of CD-ROM technology date from the 1980s, although new publications continue to appear at a rapid rate. A number of monographs, reports, and journal articles provide useful tutorial treatments of varying depth and technical detail. Examples include Bagg (1989), Buddine and Young (1987), Chen (1986), Davies (1988), Davies and Clark (1991), Desmarais (1989), Eaton et al.. (1989), Einberger (1987), Elshami (1990), Hendley (1987), Holtz (1988), Lampton (1987), McCormick (1990), Myers (1987), Oppenheim (1988), Oren and Kildall (1986), Roth (1986, 1988), and Sherman (1988). Like other types of compact discs, CD-ROMs contain digitally coded information recorded as a series of microscopic pits and adjoining spaces arranged in spiralling tracks. With 16,000 tracks per inch, CD-ROM recording densities compare favorably with those of the highest capacity read/write optical disks and far exceed densities supported by magnetic media. Track densities of most fixed magnetic disks, for example, range from 500 to 2,000 tracks per inch, and the most widely encountered models contain less than 150 tracks per inch.

With both CD-ROM and CD-DA discs, recorded information is organized into 270,000 blocks, each of which can store 2,344 bytes. While the nominal storage capacity of a 4.75-inch compact disc exceeds 600 megabytes, the actual capacity attainable in a specific application will vary with the type of information being recorded. If a given block contains audio signals, for example, 2,336 bytes are available for user data, the remainder being utilized for error correction codes. If an entire 4.75-inch compact disc contains digital audio information, its capacity is 630 megabytes—the equivalent of about seventy minutes of continuous playback time. Computer-processible data, however, requires more elaborate error correction and detection coding than audio information. As a result, CD-ROM blocks typically contain 2,048 bytes of user data. The resulting overall storage capacity is 553 megabytes per 4.75-inch disc, but technical specification sheets and other product descriptions often simplify individual block capacities to 2,000 bytes, yielding the 540 megabytes that is customarily cited as the CD-ROM's overall storage capacity.

Several companies have demonstrated that CD-ROM recording formats can double or quadruple a disc's capacity, but such innovations have not been incorporated into commercially available products. Nimbus Records, for example, has announced a CD4X format that increases CD-ROM

Summary of Read-Only Optical Disc Formats

Format	Media Size	Commercial Availability	Encoding Methods	Information Storage Applications
— COMPACT DISC FORMATS —				
CD-DA	3.5", 4.75"	1982	digital	super high-fidelity audio recording; 20 or 70 minutes of digital audio, depending on media size; single-sided media only
CD-ROM	3.5", 4.75"	1985	digital	the compact disc format for data: 540 megabytes per 4.75-inch medium; digital audio also possible; single-sided media only
CD-V	4.75"	1987	digital and analog	6 minutes of full-motion analog video with analog stereo audio; 20 additional minutes of digital audio; single-sided media only
CD+G	4.75"	1989	digital and analog	digital audio accompanied by still-frame graphics intended for television display; an enhancement to CD-DA format; single-sided media only
CD-I	4.75"	1991	digital and analog	combination of digital audio, computer-processible data, computer graphics, still-frame video, full-motion video; single-sided media only
— OTHER FORMATS —				
Videodisc	8", 12"	1978	analog	full-motion or still-frame video; 54,000 video frames per side (12" inch media); 30-60 minutes of full-motion video per side with stereo; single- or double-sided media available
Videodisc	8", 12"	1982	digital	data storage; 800 megabyte to 1 gigabyte of per side; digital audio also possible; single- or double-sided media available; increasingly supplanted by CD-ROM
DVI	4.75"	*	digital	60 minutes of full-motion video with audio; single-sided media only

* Prototype applications have been implemented; full commercial availability not yet announced

capacity to 2.4 gigabytes by packing bits more closely together. Double-sided media offer an obvious approach to increased storage capacity; all CD-ROM discs currently contain information on one side only. There is little interest in double-sided recording for CD-DA, however, because few audio compact discs utilize the full seventy minutes that is currently available. For those CD-ROM information products that require more than 540 megabytes, data compression provides a potentially effective means of increasing disc capacity. Compression methodologies appropriate to CD-ROM applications are discussed by Anderson (1990) and Beltrami and Kulkarni *et al.* (1989). Klein *et al.* (1989) discuss a CD-ROM implementation of the Tresor de la Langue Francaise, a 700-megabyte database that when compressed can be recorded on a single disc.

The storage capacities cited above apply to compact discs in the 4.75-inch form factor. With its smaller surface area, the 3.5-inch compact disc offers less recording capacity. In its CD-DA implementation, the 3.5-inch disc provides approximately twenty minutes of digital audio recording capability. When fitted with an inexpensive adapter, the 3.5-inch compact disc can be played on devices intended for 4.75-inch media. Sometimes termed the CD-Single (CD-S) or CD-3 format, it is marketed as an alternative to forty-five-rpm phonograph records in consumer applications, although its recording capacity is more directly comparable to that of the defunct extended play (EP) record format.

In CD-ROM implementations, the 3.5-inch compact disc format can store approximately 180 megabytes of computer-processible data. Sony is utilizing 3.5-inch CD-ROMs in its Data DiscMan, a portable electronic reference book system introduced in Japan in 1989. The Data DiscMan became available in the United States in 1991. Several other vendors have proposed 3.5-inch CD-ROM drives for notebook computer configurations, but such products were not commercially available at the time this report was prepared.

Disc Production. As noted in the introduction to this discussion, most CD-ROM discs are produced by a mastering process. Like other read-only optical storage products, CD-ROM is essentially an electronic publishing technology. It is intended for applications requiring multiple copies of a database or other computer-processible information. As outlined by Andrews (1991), Belani (1991), Celestre (1990), Hallgren (1990), Lee and O'Connor (1991), Pahwa and Rudd (1991), Rodgers (1990), and Thiel *et al.* (1990), CD-ROM production involves a combination of premastering, mastering, replication, packaging, and distribution. Each of these operations requires special equipment or system design expertise. Computer-processible data, prepared in a specified format, is typically sent to a CD-ROM manufacturing facility where a master disc is prepared as a mold or matrix for the production of individual distribution copies. As the first step in this production cycle, premastering procedures organize, index, and otherwise prepare databases for eventual CD-ROM recording.

Database producers, reference book publishers, and other information providers interested in implementing a CD-ROM product often utilize a premastering service company to prepare their information for publication on CD-ROM. As discussed by Robinson *et al.* (1990) and O'Connor (1991), most premastering companies offer a combination of database design, file conversion services, data reformatting, indexing, software support, and general consultation services for CD-ROM implementations. They typically accept customer-supplied databases, text files, or other information on magnetic tapes, floppy disks, or other machine-readable media. CD-ROM origination software, operating on the premastering company's own computers, prepares files for compact disc recording in a particular format. The formatted information is then sent to a CD-ROM factory that produces a test disc for evaluation by the premastering service and customer. If the test disc's performance characteristics are satisfactory, a production run is initiated. In addition to database preparation, most premastering companies provide disc layout assistance, art work for package and label design, documentation preparation, and other support services. CD-ROM packaging and labelling are discussed by Pemberton (1991).

As described by Adkins (1987), Han and Nicholls (1990), Hinds (1990), Kosmin (1990), Meyer (1990), Tally (1987), and Tamura *et al.* (1987), microcomputer-based in-house origination systems are playing an increasingly important role in data preparation for CD-ROM production. As an alternative to the external origination services offered by premastering companies, microcomputer-based origination systems allow information providers to perform their own premastering. They are also utilized by some premastering services, however. Examples of such systems include VR Publisher from Meridian Data, TOPIX from Optical Media International, ReferenceSet from Reference Technology, CD-Image-Build from Nimbus Information Systems, and CD-Formatter from Crowninshield Software. Most in-house origination systems operate on IBM-compatible microcomputers equipped with 80386 or more powerful microprocessors. Macintosh implementations are also available. As an alternative to microcomputer implementations, several vendors offer in-house origination software for mainframes and minicomputers.

As their principal advantages, in-house origination systems give the customer more direct control over data preparation and generally shorten the development cycle for CD-ROM information products. They include software that will format and index data or text files for CD-ROM production. Most systems also utilize a magnetic disk drive for real-time simulation of CD-ROM operation prior to mastering, thereby minimizing the need for test discs and providing an immediate indication of how a given CD-ROM information product will appear to end-users. The application designer can then adjust the disc layout, indexing, or other parameters that influence system performance. When data preparation and indexing are completed, the in-house origination system produces output in a format acceptable to a CD-ROM mastering facility. Depending on the system's capabilities and the mastering facility's requirements, the output may be recorded on nine-track magnetic tape, quarter-inch magnetic tape, eight-millimeter data cartridges, digital audio tape cartridges, or read/write optical disks. Acceptable media formats are discussed by Arps (1991).

With their high recording capacities, read/write optical disks and helical-scan tapes, such as eight-millimeter data cartridges, are well suited to CD-ROM data delivery. With forty to 160 megabytes per reel depending on recording density, the premastered contents of a 540-megabyte CD-ROM disc may require as many as fourteen reels of nine-track magnetic tape, each of which must be correctly labelled and loaded in the proper sequence. With double-sided recording capacities ranging from 600 megabytes to 1.28 gigabytes, 5.25-inch write-once and rewritable optical disks can easily accommodate premastered input for CD-ROM discs. Eight-millimeter data cartridges and digital audio tapes likewise offer gigabyte-level recording capacities.

The CD-ROM mastering process itself is described by Anders and Hardt (1987) Armstrong (1987), Crawford (1988), Eichlseder and Eusemann (1987), Honma (1987), Kaempf (1987), Kobayashi *et al.* (1989), Legierse (1987), Mayr (1987), McCrary (1988), Reynolds and Halliday (1987), and Urrows and Urrows (1988). CD-ROM mastering is performed in a clean-room environment. In the typical production sequence, laser beam recorders encode data contained in customer-supplied input by burning microscopic pits into a thin glass master disc. The one and zero bits in digitally coded data are represented by the presence or absence of pits that can be detected by a laser beam in a specially designed player. The master disc is then used to create one or more intermediate metal matrices from which individual copies are produced, usually by an injection molding process using polycarbonate materials. A reflective aluminum layer is applied by thermal evaporation or sputtering techniques. A protective transparent coating keeps dust and surface damage outside of the playback laser's focal plane.

Marshall and Voedisch (1990), Machovec (1991), and others have raised questions about the playback stability and continued retrievability of information recorded on CD-ROM. The degradative effects of temperature and moisture on the polycarbonate substrates utilized in compact disc production are well documented. Potential manifestations of deterioration include internal cracking, swelling, shrinkage, changes in tensile strength, and the formation of water-filled pockets, any of which can alter the substrate's optical characteristics with a resulting adverse impact on media performance. Injection-molded media may also contain stresses and strains which can distort their shape. As noted by Day (1989), certain inks used for compact disc labels can penetrate protective coatings, oxidizing the aluminum layer. While lifetime estimates vary, most manufacturers claim that their compact discs will be playable for at least twenty-five years. Concerned about the long-term stability of their products, several compact disc manufacturers have experimented with gold, silver, platinum, and other alternatives to aluminum coatings in order to reduce their media's vulnerability to oxidation. Digipress, for example, offers its Century Disc CD-ROM, which is constructed of hard-tempered glass layered with gold and coated with a non-organic protective layer. The company claims that Century Discs offer greater resistance to corrosion and other forms of chemical deterioration, as well as more reliable operation in a broad range of environments, when compared to conventional CD-ROM media. Among CD-DA producers, Mobile Fidelity Sound Lab likewise uses twenty-four-karat gold for its reflective layers.

Long-term media stability is of little significance for those CD-ROM databases that are updated by replacement on a subscription basis at relatively frequent intervals; such information products are more directly affected by manufacturing defects that may render discs unusable. Media longevity is a concern, however, for purchasers of so-called "archival" discs, which contain database backfiles or other closed files that will not be updated. The use of CD-ROM as a storage medium for long-term retention of computer-processible information transferred from magnetic disks and tapes has also been suggested, but the advantages and limitations of such applications have not been fully explored. Compact disc longevity is an obvious concern for CD-DA collectors and for organizations, such as libraries, which maintain large numbers of audio recordings on compact discs.

As anticipated, compact disc mastering costs have declined steadily since the mid-1980s. Mastering and replication rates typically vary with the amount of data to be recorded and the number of copies required. Some production facilities quote a single price for each copy, including a prorated portion of mastering charges; others cite separate prices for mastering and replication. The typical mastering time cycle—from submission of appropriate formatted data to receipt of the specified number of disc copies—is about two weeks, although some compact disc manufacturers offer five-day, three-day, and overnight turnaround times at premium prices.

In late 1987, Sony and Philips announced a recordable compact disc format, based on read/write optical recording technology. It is described by Yamamoto and Mons (1988). When write-once optical media are utilized, the recordable format is variously described as CD-Write Once (abbreviated as either CD-WO or CD-W) or CD-WORM. The CD-Recordable (CD-R) designation recognizes the future potential of rewritable media for compact disc recording; rewritable compact disc systems, while demonstrated in prototype for both audio and data recording, were not commercially available at the time this report was prepared. As their principal advantage, recordable compact disc systems eliminate mastering requirements, thereby dramatically reducing the turnaround time required to produce a usable CD-ROM. Typically implemented as a back-end component in an in-house CD-ROM origination system, they can produce test discs of information products for trial use and evaluation before multiple copies are ordered from a mastering facility. In the absence of such test discs, magnetic disks and specially developed software must be used to simulate CD-ROM implementations prior to mastering. Recordable compact disc systems also permit the use of CD-ROM in applications where a limited number of required copies does not justify the cost of mastering. Because recordable compact discs are produced one at a time, however, they are unsuitable—from the standpoint of both time and cost—for applications that require many distribution copies.

Media produced by recordable CD-ROM systems should not be confused with 5.25-inch write-once and rewritable optical disks, which have been commercially available since the 1980s. While such media can be configured for read-only operation and—as previously noted—are sometimes loosely described as "compact," they are somewhat larger than compact discs, do not utilize the CD-ROM recording format, and cannot be read by CD-ROM drives. Conventional write-once and rewritable optical disks permit the recording of information in increments, as it is generated by application programs; with recordable CD-ROM discs, in contrast, all information is recorded in a single session. Current compact disc standards

A microcomputer-based CD-ROM development system. (Courtesy: Meridian Data)

support a fixed table of contents that is generated at the end of a recording session and cannot be updated. Sony and Philips are reportedly developing specifications for recordable compact discs that will permit dynamic tables of contents, but those specifications—sometimes referred to as the "Orange Book"—had not been finalized at the time this report was prepared.

In late 1988, Yamaha Corporation became the first vendor to commercialize a CD-ROM recording system. At the time this report was prepared, it had been incorporated into several microcomputer-based, in-house CD-ROM origination systems. The Yamaha Programmable Disc System employs proprietary optical recording media supplied by Fuji. As discussed by Takahashi *et al.* (1990), it features a recording layer of indium alloyed with germanium sulfide. Sony Corporation and Taiyo Yuden Company have formed Start Labs, a joint venture to commercialize a CD-Write Once system based on optical recording media developed by Taiyo Yuden. The medium consists of a polycarbonate substrate coated with an organic dye recording layer, a gold reflective surface, and a protective resin. The system is described by Hamada et al. (1989). Ashikaga *et al.* (1990) and Naitoh *et al.* (1990) describe a CD-ROM premastering and recording system developed by Fujitsu. Kenwood U.S.A. Corporation demonstrated a recordable compact disc system for audio and CD-ROM applications in late 1990, but that product was not commercially available at the time this report was prepared. In 1991, Ricoh announced a hybrid CD-ROM format with read-only and write-once segments; it is scheduled for commercialization in 1992. Several companies have announced plans to develop recordable CD-ROM systems based on rewritable optical media. Maeda *et al.* (1991), for example, describe a prototype implementation by Sharp. Given their potential for audio and multimedia applications as well as computer-based information management, such recordable compact disc systems are expected to increase in both availability and popularity. The Frankfort Consortium, a group of CD-ROM product developers, was formed in 1991 to promote the standardization and future compatibility of recordable compact discs. Its members include Philips, Sony, Taiyo Yuden, Ricoh, Teac, Sun Microsystems, Eastman Kodak, and Meridian Data.

CD-ROM DRIVES

CD-ROM drives—variously described as CD-ROM players or CD-ROM readers—are computer peripheral devices designed primarily for microcomputer and desktop workstation installations. Produced and sold by many of the same companies that manufacture and market other computer storage peripherals, a CD-ROM drive is essentially a modified CD-DA player with more elaborate error detection and correction capabilities. The earliest models were introduced by Hitachi, Sony, and Laser Magnetic Storage International (formerly Philips Subsystems and Peripherals) in 1985. Panasonic, Denon, Toshiba, Sanyo, and others announced similar products in the following year. By late 1987, a variety of CD-ROM drives were routinely available, and several vendors had introduced second-generation models. Availability has increased significantly since the late 1980s as the previously mentioned manufacturers have expanded their product lines. New vendors include Chinon America, Goldstar, Mitsumi, Tandy, and Texel.

A CD-ROM drive is just one hardware component in a CD-ROM workstation; a computer is also required. Historically, CD-ROM drive manufacturers have emphasized models for IBM-compatible microcomputers running under the MS-DOS operating system, largely because that computer platform is so widely installed and so many CD-ROM information products are intended for it. While specific workstation requirements are determined by software suppliers, an 80386-based or more powerful central processor configured with several megabytes of random-access memory and at least sixty megabytes of hard disk storage will accommodate the majority of CD-ROM information products and minimize the need for hardware upgrades as new information products are acquired. 80286-based systems may prove acceptable in some cases, but their continued utility is suspect; future CD-ROM information products may increasingly run under Microsoft Windows and require an 80386-based system. CD-ROM drives are also selectively available for Macintosh computers, NeXT systems, the Commodore Amiga, Sun workstations, Hewlett-Packard, and Digital Equipment Corporation minicomputers, and other computer platforms. As in IBM-compatible microcomputer installations, specific configuration requirements vary with the CD-ROM information products to be utilized, but fast processors, several megabytes of random-access memory, and high-capacity hard disk drives are generally recommended.

Some CD-ROM drive manufacturers sell their products primarily to systems integrators, value-added resellers, and other OEM clients who repackage them for sale to end-users; others market their CD-ROM drives directly to end-users, although they may also sell them to OEM clients. Features and capabilities of CD-ROM drives and workstations are reviewed in various publications, including Adams (1990), Alberico (1988), Baycroft (1990), Brueggeman (1990) Falk (1990), Gielda (1989), Harvey (1991), Hughes (1989), Hutchison (1991, 1991a), Jacso (1989, 1990), Meyer (1990), Nickerson (1991), Nosaka et al. (1990), Shiller (1990), and Sponheimer and Santon (1990). The following discussion summarizes the most important characteristics of available products, emphasizing those features and capabilities that can influence the evaluation and selection of CD-ROM drives for particular applications.

Equipment Configurations. CD-ROM drives are available in internal and external equipment configurations. As their name suggests, internal CD-ROM drives are designed for direct installation in a microcomputer's system unit. They typically reside in a 5.25-inch installation slot, which might otherwise hold a floppy disk drive, hard disk drive, magnetic tape cartridge system, or other peripheral device. While older internal CD-ROM drives required a full-height installation slot, most newer models are half-height units. Their smaller dimensions permits the installation of two or more drives in a single microcomputer chassis.

Recognizing the potential of CD-ROM as an information management technology, several mi-

An internal CD-ROM drive. (Courtesy: Laser Magnetic Storage International)

crocomputer vendors have introduced business- and consumer-oriented systems that are preconfigured with internal CD-ROM drives. As an example, Sun Moon Star—a Taiwanese microcomputer manufacturer—offers an 80386SX-based system with an internal CD-ROM drive, two megabytes of random-access memory, a forty-megabyte hard disk drive, and a Super VGA monitor for less than $3,000. Prices for other CD-based configurations from Sun Moon Star range from $2,600 for an 80286-based model to $8,400 for an 80486-based system. Similarly equipped microcomputer systems are offered by other companies, including Tandy, Magnavox Consumer Electronics, and GRiD Systems. While this type of microcomputer configuration is relatively new in the United States, Japanese microcomputer manufacturers have supplied internal CD-ROM drives as standard or optional peripheral equipment since the late 1980s. Fujitsu, for example, offers an internal CD-ROM option for its FACOM series of workstations, while Matsushita provides internal CD-ROM drives for its OPERATE series of microcomputers. As described by Kimura *et al.* (1988), Sony's NEWS line of engineering workstations supports a CD-ROM option, while NEC offers an internal CD-ROM drive with its microcomputer products.

Internal CD-ROM drives are sometimes incorporated into retrieval workstations that are intended for use with specific CD-ROM information products, such as library catalogs or databases of proprietary information intended for closed user groups in government agencies or corporations. As a potential advantage, internal CD-ROM drives require no additional installation space in offices where an increasing number of machines must compete for already crowded work surfaces. As a convenience in older buildings where electrical outlets are often in short supply, an internal CD-ROM drive draws its power from the microcomputer in which it is installed.

As its name indicates, an external CD-ROM drive—sometimes described as a stand-alone drive—is housed in a self-contained chassis that is equipped with its own power supply. Unlike its internal counterpart, an external CD-ROM drive requires attachment to an electrical outlet. It is usually installed on a desktop next to the computer to which it is attached. Most external drives occupy about ninety square inches of desk space, although some "zero footprint" models can be installed between a microcomputer's system unit and video monitor. As discussed by Raitt (1990), several manufacturers offer portable CD-ROM drives, which are primarily intended for laptop and notebook computer configurations. The popular NEC Intersect CDR-35 is typical of such products. Styled much like a portable CD-DA player, it weighs three pounds and can operate with an AC adapter or battery pack. Fletcher (1990) describes its use with a Commodore C286-LT notebook computer and a parallel to SCSI adapter. Among competing models, the CM 50 portable CD-ROM drive from Laser Magnetic Storage International weighs just 1.87 pounds and draws electrical power through its interface cable. As CD-ROM information products address an increasingly broad range of applications, portability requirements may intensify. Wright and Friend (1991), for example, describe an application for a mobile CD-ROM workstation to be used for staff training in a library installation.

The earliest CD-ROM disc drives were external devices. While most vendors now offer internal units as well, stand-alone models remain very popular. They can be easily connected to existing computer configurations, including those for which internal drives are unavailable or impractical. A vendor-prescribed interface and cable permits attachment to a host computer. In IBM-compatible microcomputer installations, the external CD-ROM drive is often connected to a proprietary adapter card installed in an expansion slot within the microcomputer's system unit. Depending on the CD-ROM drive selected, such adapter cards may be available for Industry Standard Architecture (ISA) or Micro Channel Architecture (MCA) data buses, the latter being intended for certain IBM PS/2 microcomputers and compatible devices. As is the case with other PS/2 peripheral products, CD-ROM drives configured with MCA-type adapter cards are typically more expensive than their ISA counterparts.

For other computer configurations, most CD-ROM drive manufacturers offer at least one model equipped with a Small Computer Systems Interface (SCSI), an industry-standard bus design that is utilized with an increasing number of computer peripherals. Macintosh computers, Sun workstations, and various other processors feature SCSI ports as standard equipment, and SCSI adapters are widely available for IBM-compatible microcomputers as well. As discussed by Warren (1986), SCSI-compatibility greatly simplifies the implementation of CD-ROM configurations by product developers, systems integrators and value-added resellers, and it is the only practical CD-ROM interface for microcomputers with closed architectures. As a further advantage which can conserve expansion slots in IBM-compatible microcomputer installations, a single SCSI controller can support as many as eight CD-ROM drives and other peripheral devices. Such multi-drive configurations can minimize or eliminate time-consuming and inconvenient media handling in applications where very large databases are recorded on multiple discs. Multi-drive support is not unique to SCSI configurations, however; some proprietary adapter cards can likewise control two or more CD-ROM drives.

Operating Characteristics. Among the first commercially available products, the LMSI CM-100 and CM-110, and their private-label counterparts sold by Digital Equipment Corporation and other companies, were the only desktop CD-ROM drives with top-loading mechanisms. While those devices are no longer manufactured, some of them remain in use. Top-loading is also employed by portable CD-ROM drives. Although they required slightly more installation space, most early CD-ROM drives—like their CD-DA counterparts—were front-loading devices equipped with an extendable drawer for the insertion of a compact disc. New models, however, have replaced the extendable drawer with a removable caddy or cartridge which facilitates disc handling and protects it from scratches, dirt, or other damage. Such compact disc caddies were originally developed to simplify the insertion of discs in automotive CD-DA players. As an additional advantage, caddies permit the vertical installation of internal CD-ROM disc drives. As a complication, caddies of incompatible design are employed by the CD-ROM drives of various manufacturers.

Loading methods aside, all CD-ROM drives employ a laser beam to read the microscopic pits and spaces which represent digitally-coded information. As described by Lavender (1986), the laser beam is focused through an objective lens, which measures changes in the intensity of light reflected from pits and spaces, interpreting them as either one or zero bits. The reading mechanism, sometimes described as a read head, is mounted on a movable sled that must be positioned over those areas of the disc's surface which contain the desired data. The difficulty of rapidly and accurately moving the read head to the appropriate disc area can lead to disappointly slow retrieval times in CD-ROM installations. This is especially the case where users' performance are based on experience with rigid magnetic disk drives.

These performance difficulties are compounded by significant differences in the recording characteristics of CD-ROM discs and their magnetic counterparts. Magnetic disks store data in concentric tracks which are divided into sectors in pie-like fashion. Sectors near the center of a magnetic disk are physically smaller than those at the outer edges, but—with most magnetic disk drives—all sectors have the same data storage capacity. This approach wastes some space within the larger sectors, but—because each track has the same number of sectors —any given sector can be located quickly and easily. In contrast, data is recorded on a CD-ROM disc in a continuous spiralling track which is divided into sectors of identical size. This approach makes very efficient use of the compact disc's recording surface and is well-suited to the sequential access requirements of CD-DA recordings, but it leads to time-consuming retrieval operations in CD-ROM applications where data recorded on widely separated areas of a disc's surface will be accessed in random sequence.

The high-performance rigid magnetic disk drives used for online storage and retrieval in computer equipment configurations routinely support access times below twenty milliseconds. In contrast, access times with older CD-ROM drives and some less expensive newer ones range from 500 milliseconds to one second. The newest and fastest CD-ROM drives support access times of 350 to 400 milliseconds; their performance is comparable to that of the slowest floppy disk drives. Future improvements should result from continuing refinements in drive design, however. Yak *et al.* (1991), for example, propose the use of a three-beam optical reading head mounted on a swing arm which might ultimately reduce CD-ROM access times to the twenty millisecond range, making them competitive with hard disk drives.

In the meantime, software designers and application developers typically compensate for the limited performance characteristics of CD-ROM hardware by minimizing physical distances between related parts of a database, thus reducing the distance which the read head must travel to access related data. Some drives also include random-access memory circuits which provide cache storage for directory information, thereby improving performance by speeding access to frequently referenced data. Cache memory also permits continuous read-

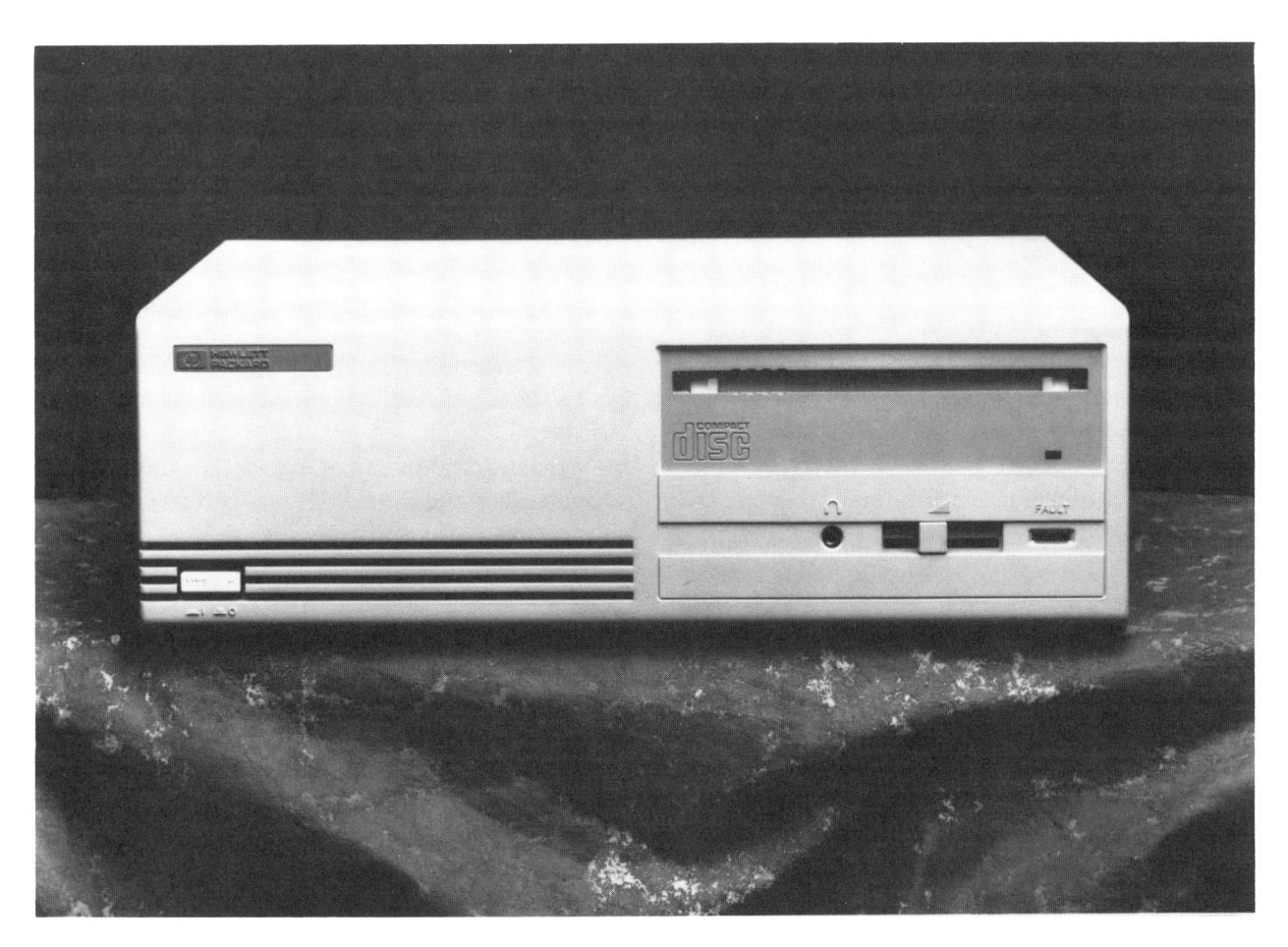

An external CD-ROM drive. (Courtesy: Hewlett-Packard)

ing, which promotes an even flow of data from the CD-ROM drive to the central processor, an especially important consideration in the multimedia applications. While older CD-ROM drives provided two to eight kilobytes of cache memory, some newer models are configured with sixty-four kilobytes of random-access memory for cache operations.

Access times aside, the performance and reliability of newer CD-ROM drives are enhanced by other improvements in equipment design and construction. To prevent the infiltration of dust and other contaminants which can obscure data, for example, an increasing number of CD-ROM drives feature sealed cabinets and double-door mechanisms. Self-cleaning lenses are also provided.

Some CD-ROM drives can be optionally equipped with digital audio boards, which enable them to play CD-DA discs when configured with an appropriate stereo amplifier, speakers, and other audio system components. Such audio-adaptible CD-ROM players are believed to be particularly attractive to consumers who want to purchase a single compact disc player for audio and data applications. To accommodate the multimedia CD-ROM products described elsewhere in this report, audio capability is increasingly a standard feature of newer CD-ROM drives. Most models are now equipped with audio headphone jacks and volume control knobs on their front panels. Among the most unusual equipment configurations, Megasys has announced a multi-technology drive that can accommodate CD-ROM as well as write-once and rewritable optical media. While CD-ROM is supported in the read-only mode, the Megasys drive permits both reading and recording of write-once and rewritable media.

Prices. At the time this report was prepared, single-quantity prices for CD-ROM drives ranged from less than $400 to more than $1,500, depending on the model purchased, its operating capabilities, the optional features selected, and the procurement source. Because they require a separate power supply and more elaborate packaging, external models are typically more expensive than internal drives, although pricing patterns vary from vendor to vendor. While some CD-ROM drives can be purchased directly from their manufacturers, attractive prices can often be obtained from CD-ROM publishers who want to propogate an installed base of equipment for use with their current and future products. In some cases, CD-ROM drives are bundled with specific information products at prices that are lower than the cost of the information products purchased separately. CD-ROM drives are also available at substantial discounts from mail-order computer equipment suppliers.

The recent introduction of several relatively inexpensive CD-ROM drives in reflects the industry's increasing attempts to broaden the market for CD-ROM equipment and information products. Typically, however, such devices sacrifice performance for economy. With access times approaching one second, for example, the Tandy CDR-1000 is significantly slower than most new CD-ROM drives, but it is readily available through Radio Shack stores for less than $400, including interface adapter, cables, and software. Industry analysts expect further declines in CD-ROM drive prices as the market develops, production quantities increase, and competition among suppliers intensifies. Reflecting a common computer industry trend, however, retail prices for some new CD-ROM drives are actually higher than those of older models because the new devices provide added value in the form of audio adapters, headphone jacks, faster access times, and other features discussed above.

Compatibility. The compatibility of CD-ROM equipment and media is an important consideration for libraries, corporations, government agencies, and other organizations where CD-ROM databases and other information products may be purchased from a variety of sources. Such information products typically include software utilities, in the form of low-level interface code or driver files, which can communicate with specific CD-ROM equipment. Such utilities, which are analogous to the printer driver files supplied with many word processing programs, translate requests for stored information resulting from retrieval operations into the commands required by a CD-ROM drive.

The earliest CD-ROM information products included device drivers for one or more designated CD-ROM drives, such as the Hitachi CER-1502S or the LMSI CM-100. In some cases, different versions of a given information product were required for use with different equipment configurations. This approach, while limiting, posed no immediate problem for organizations acquiring their first CD-ROM information product; such organizations simply purchased one of the drives designated as compatible with that product. During the mid-1980s, a few CD-ROM drives dominated the market; CD-ROM publishers could consequently produce versions of their information products for the two or three most popular models. Today, however, a greater variety of CD-ROM drives are readily available, and CD-ROM information products are increasingly marketed to organizations that already own a satisfactory CD-ROM drive and do not want to purchase another.

Since the late 1980s, the compatibility of CD-ROM drives and information products intend-

A portable CD-ROM drive. (Courtesy: NEC)

A CD-ROM minichanger with six-disc cartridge. (Courtesy: Pioneer)

ed for IBM-compatible microcomputer installations has been greatly facilitated by widespread support for Microsoft's CD-ROM Extensions. Designed for CD-ROM equipment manufacturers, product developers, and other OEM clients, Microsoft Extensions includes specifications for a device driver to control CD-ROM equipment and a program module which provides an interface between the device driver and the MS-DOS operating system. Introduced in 1986, Microsoft Extensions are typically supplied with CD-ROM drives from licensed manufacturers; the drive manufacturer also provides the required device-specific drivers. When advertised as compatible with Microsoft Extensions, a given CD-ROM information product will presumably operate correctly with any drive that supports the Extensions, regardless of the drive's manufacturer. Like any software product, however, Microsoft Extensions is subject to revision; organizations must be sure that they have installed the version appropriate to a particular information product. To ensure product utility and avoid potentially costly procurement errors, users should conclusively determine equipment requirements and compatibility before purchasing any CD-ROM information product.

CD-ROM Networks. As noted above, some CD-ROM adapters can support multiple drives, a capability that can minimize or eliminate media handling where information products are recorded on multiple discs. Several companies offer rack-type enclosures for such multi-drive configurations. As an example, the MultiDrive system from CD Plus can hold up to four CD-ROM drives in a stacked enclosure. A single controller can support two MultiDrive units containing up to eight drives. The units can be locked to prevent removal of the drives, an important consideration in libraries and other public-use CD-ROM installations. Recognizing that computer users must increasingly rely on a variety of peripherals to satisfy their information storage requirements, several manufacturers offer rack-type cabinets that can house mix-and-match combinations of magnetic disk, magnetic tape, and optical disk drives. NCR's 6091 series of stackable data storage subsystems, for example, can combine one or more CD-ROM drive, 5.25-inch write-once or rewritable optical disk drives, hard disk drives in capacities up to 760 megabytes, quarter-inch magnetic tape units, and eight-millimeter data cartridge drives in a single cabinet. Similarly, the HP Series 6000 from Hewlett-Packard combines a hard disk drive with a the customer's choice of two additional devices selected from CD-ROM drives, magneto-optical disk drives, and digital audio tape units.

Multi-drive configurations address a practical problem encountered in CD-ROM networks where the manual loading of individual discs requested by particular workstations is impractical or impossible. Broadly defined, a CD-ROM network is a

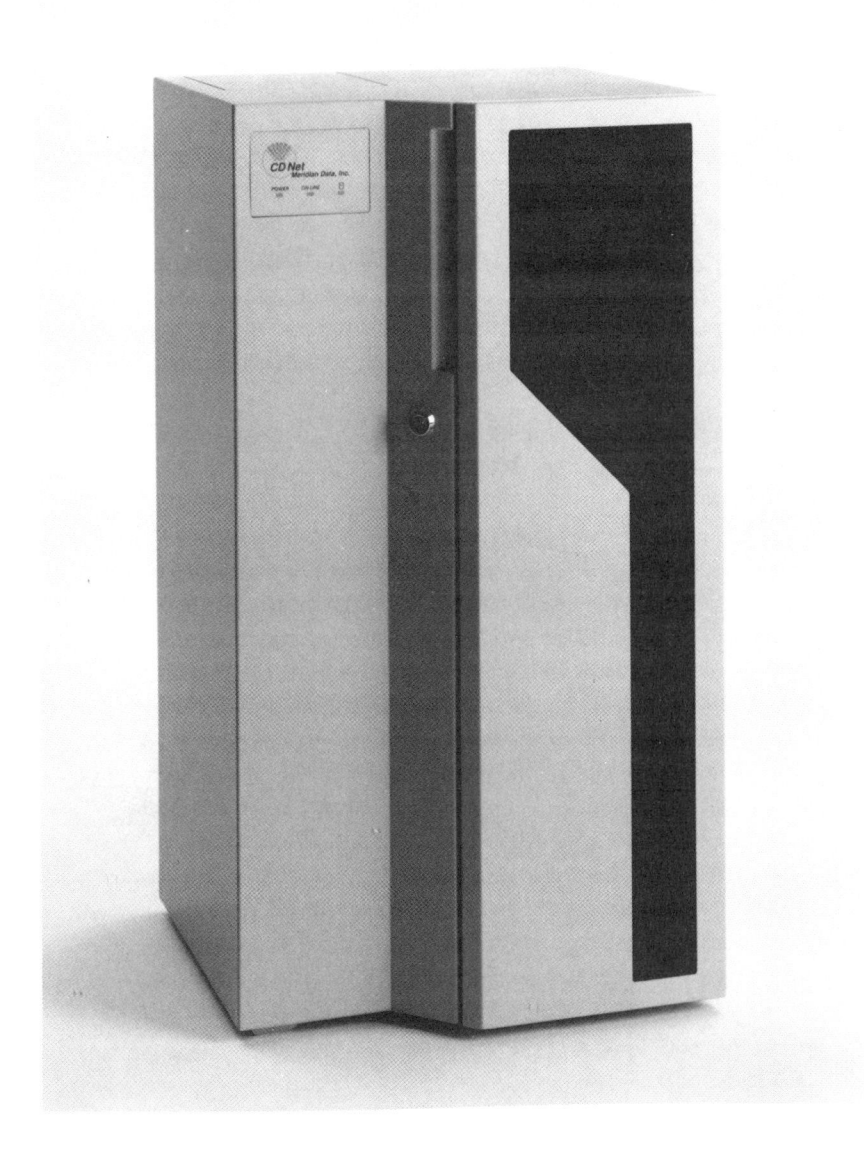

A multi-drive CD-ROM system for local area networks. (Courtesy: Meridian Data)

computer network that provides multi-workstation access to CD-ROM drives and the information products mounted on them. A CD-ROM network may be based on conventional timesharing principles with one or more CD-ROM drives attached to a minicomputer or other central processor which individual workstations can access through local or remote communication facilities. More commonly, however, a local area network of autonomous microcomputers accesses CD-ROM drives connected to one or more file servers; used in this context, a file server is a computer that provides network access to stored information. Regardless of approach, such installations fulfill two of the principal objectives of computer networks: information sharing and more effective utilization of specific hardware and software resources.

Reflecting intense interest in both local area networks and CD-ROM technology, library installations of CD-ROM networks are described in a rapidly growing number of journal articles and conference papers. Basic concepts, advantages, and limitations of such installations are discussed by Akeroyd (1991), Au (1989), Bell (1990), Brueggeman (1991), Coe (1990), Flanders (1990), Gielda (1989a), Lowe (1987), Kittle (1989), Matsuda (1989), McQueen (1990, 1990a), Metz (1991), Meyer (1988), Nagano (1990), Neubauer (1989), Noordzij and Van De Pol (1990), Pearson and MacKinnon (1988), Perry (1990), Pesch (1990), Propps (1990), Prussian (1989), Rosen (1990), Simon (1990), Sloan (1990, 1990a, 1991), and Ventress (1989). LaGuardia et al. (1991) report the results of a survey of networked CD-ROM installations in research libraries. Kratzert (1991) discusses systems design and policy issues pertaining to a CD-ROM network at California State University at Fullerton. Kriz et al. (1991) describe an installation at Virginia Polytechnic Institute. Butcher (1990) provides a detailed description of a local area network implementation at Oregon State University. Rutherford (1990) discusses a CD-ROM LAN at Central Connecticut State Univeristy. Blackwelder et al. (1990), Garnham and Brodie (1990), Gomez et al. (1991), Harris (1991), Lee and Balthazar (1991), Miller and Backus (1991), Rhine (1990), and Wu et al. (1990), describe installations in medical libraries. Folmsbee et al. (1990) discuss a simple configuration for multi-workstation access to CD-ROMs in a law school library. Polly (1989) describes a Macintosh-based CD-ROM network at the Liverpool (New York) Public Library. Brown and Coleman (1991) discuss the development and testing of a system for remote access to CD-ROM databases at the Pacific Regional Aquaculture Information Service. Among reported installations outside of the United States, Wachter et al. (1991) discuss a CD-ROM network at Dauphine University, while Ovens (1990) describes an implementation at the University of the Orange Free State. Pollack (1990) describes remote access via an asynchronous dialup network at the Weizmann Institute of Sciences in Israel.

Some local area networks support shared access to CD-ROM drives without additional hardware or software resources. This is the case, for example, with LANtastic, an inexpensive, straightforward local area network operating system from Artisoft; its advantages for CD-ROM implementations are discussed by Brunnel (1990), Morrow (1990), and Paul et al. (1991). In other network configurations, however, additional components must be purchased. As discussed by Rietdyk (1990), the MultiPlatter system from Silver-Platter Information Incorporated provides multi-workstation access to multiple CD-ROM drives housed in a tower-like enclosure attached to a network file server. MultiPlatter installations are described by Grant and Stalker (1989), Grant and Weinschenk (1990),, Massey-Burzio (1990), and Teger (1991). Other LAN products for CD-ROM implementations include CD NET from Meridian Data, OPTI-NET from Online Computer Systems, PlusNet from CD Plus, CD-Connection from CBIS, AGANET from Advanced Graphic Applications, and HP OfficeShare from Hewlett-Packard. Thompson and Maxwell (1990) and Van Name and Catching (1990) provide informative reviews of selected products and implementation issues.

Autochangers. While high-capacity autochangers for read/write optical disks have been available since the early 1980s, comparable jukebox-type retrieval devices for CD-ROM discs have only recently been introduced. Next Technology—a British company not to be confused with the

U.S. computer manufacturer, NeXT—introduced the first CD-ROM autochanger in 1989. As described by Nelson (1989), it provides unattended access to 270 compact discs containing 145 gigabytes of data. A robotic mechanism locates a desired disc, extracts it from its position in a storage column, and mounts it in a CD-ROM drive. The Voyager autochanger can be configured with up to eight CD-ROM drives. At the British Library, it is used by the ADONIS Project which provides automated access to the contents of biomedical journals recorded on CD-ROM discs. That project is discussed in many publications, including Braid (1989), Cawkell (1991), Line (1989), Pozza (1990), Stern (1986, 1990), Stern and Campbell (1989), and Stern and Compier (1990).

INCOM of Bonn, Germany, announced a 100-disc CD-ROM autochanger in 1991. It stores discs in two magazines which can be easily loaded and changed. At the time this report was prepared, University Microfilms International (UMI) was testing a 240-disc CD-ROM autochanger manufactured by Kubik Enterprises. One such unit has been installed at the University of Michigan's Kresge library where it stores UMI's Business Periodicals Ondisc product, a CD-ROM collection of digitized images produced from magazine articles and other publications. Each CD-ROM disc holds 5,000 to 7,000 digitized page images. The autochanger's total capacity is equivalent to about 100,000 books. Library users, working at microcomputers attached to the autochanger search a computer-maintained index for articles about specified topics. They can review brief abstracts at their workstations and, if desired, print digitized images of desired publications.

While these high-capacity robotic units offer impressive capabilities, the best known CD-ROM autochanger is a much simpler device. Employing an equipment design originally developed for audio applications, the Pioneer DRM-6000 CD-ROM minichanger is loaded with interchangeable cartridges containing six discs each. A single cartridge provides unattended access to approximately 3.2 gigabytes of information. Up to seven minichangers can be attached to a single controller for a total nearline capacity of 22.4 gigabytes per configuration. The DRM-6000 is described by Ekberg *et al.* (1990), Ferelli (1991), and Pournelle (1991).

APPLICATIONS

As previously defined, CD-ROM and other read-only optical discs are electronic publishing media. More specifically, they permit a form of electronic publishing that is often described as optical publishing—a phrase that denotes the recording and dissemination of machine-readable information on optical storage media. Other forms of electronic publishing employ different dissemination methodologies, including the distribution of information on floppy disks or time-shared access to information recorded on hard disk drives. With their high storage capacities, read-only characteristics, and economical replication through mastering techniques, CD-ROM discs are particularly well-suited to the distribution of large collections of computer-processable data, text, or images. The present role and future potential of CD-ROM for electronic publishing has been widely discussed in journal articles, conference papers, and other publications since the mid-1980s. Examples include Abt (1989), Bowers (1987), Curtis (1987), Hendley (1987), Hensel (1986), Jones (1990), Klausmeier (1986), Paisley and Butler (1987), Richards (1989), Richman (1987), Spigai (1987), and Williams (1986). As discussed later in this report, CD-ROM offers a potentially attractive and cost-effective alternative to timesharing systems which provide remote access to databases maintained by minicomputers and mainframes. In certain situations, CD-ROM can also replace computer-output microfilm (COM) systems for the distribution of computer-generated reports and lists.

In terms of their intended audiences, CD-ROM applications can be divided into two broad categories: (1) private implementations intended for controlled release to closed user groups; and (2) databases, reference publications, and other information products designed for public sale to any interested parties. Examples of both types of applications are described in the following subsections.

Private Implementations. A growing number of CD-ROM applications are intended for closed user groups—that is, for controlled release to a predefined population within a corporation, government agency, or other organization. Excellent candidates for such implementations include proprietary databases of technical or bibliographic information, policy directives, regulations, system and product specifications, standard operating procedures, technical manuals, internal publications, and business forms. With its high capacity, a single CD-ROM disc can contain a large computer-processible database or the equivalent of many linear feet of hardcopy documentation stored as either character-coded text or digitized document images. Organizations which convert in-house databases and publishing applications for distribution on CD-ROM can anticipate one or more of the following benefits.

- Reduced dependence on main frame or minicomputer-based systems that provide time-shared access to information;

- Elimination of costly telecommunication links between remote computer sites and desktop workstations;

- Lower costs when CD-ROM mastering and replication charges are compared with production, binding, and other charges associated with printed documentation;

- Reduced handling, mailing, and other distribution costs for printed documentation replaced by CD-ROM;

- Simplified filing and reduced storage space requirements at sites that previously received printed documentation; and

- More effective and varied retrieval capabilities.

The general characteristics and requirements of private CD-ROM implementations are discussed by McCauley (1987), Jordahl (1989), and Ralphs (1990). Reporting the results of a survey of data processing professionals, however, Fisher (1988) found that few executives were aware of the potential benefits of CD-ROM technology.

As is often the case with innovative technologies, U.S. federal government agencies have been among the first organizations to implement CD-ROM systems to support specific information management activities. The Social Security Administration, for example, has produced a CD-ROM disc containing the contents of its procedures and operations manuals for benefit claims. In paper form, the manuals—which are distributed to all Social Security Administration offices—consist of thirty volumes that occupy seven linear feet of shelf space. The Social Security Administration is reportedly considering future CD-ROM implementations of personnel and administrative manuals, a supervisor's guide, and the agency's telephone directory. In an application described by Luettgen et al. (1991), Los Alamos National Laboratory is using CD-ROM as the delivery medium for a computer-based training course for radiation protection technicians. As discussed by Fluty (1988), the U.S. Postal Service has replaced a mainframe-based zip code retrieval system with similar information recorded on CD-ROM discs. Called ZIP+4, the CD-ROM system is installed in selected post offices. The Canadian Post Corporation has implemented a similar CD-ROM database of addresses in its customer enquiry centres. Campbell (1989) describes the Postcode Address File, which contains the postcode of every address in Great Britain.

U.S. military agencies have been active implementors of CD-ROM systems. In a pilot project described by Kercheval (1989), for example, the Army Corps of Engineers published CD-ROM editions of various engineering manuals, regulations, and specifications. Schankin (1989) describes a project to distribute U.S. Air Force regulations, pamphlets, and forms on CD-ROM discs. The Defense Technical Information Center has utilized CD-ROM to distribute its proprietary bibliographic database to authorized sites. The U.S. Army Health Facility Planning Agency uses CD-ROM discs to distribute construction manuals and related documentation for selected medical facilities. The U.S. Marine Corps has developed the Warchest CD-ROM which contains information on demographics, U.S. embassies, and strategic terrain in Persian Gulf countries. The Marine Corps is also experimenting with CD-ROM for distribution of directives and technical publications. The U.S. Navy employs CD-ROM for storage and dissemination of its Compressed Aeronautical Chart database, which is a mission requirement for many Navy and Marine Corps flights. It is described by Lohrenz and Ryan (1990). A tactical mission support system, to be installed on every aircraft carrier in the U.S. fleet, includes MicroVAX workstations configured with CD-ROM drives. The Navy has also implemented CD-ROM systems to reduce shipboard storage requirements for technical manuals, operational directives, and other voluminous documentation.

In the private sector, several automotive manufacturers—including Ford, Chrysler, Honda, and Nissan—have utilized CD-ROM to distribute parts catalogs to dealers, an application which previously relied on computer-output microfilm. Ford also distributes its repair manuals on CD-ROM. The CD-ROM edition of the Pirelli Tire Catalog is designed for the company's authorized dealers. As discussed by Williams (1991), British Airways has implemented a CD-ROM system to replace its microfilm parts lists and maintenance manuals. Updates are provided on floppy disks. Japan Airlines, in cooperation with Sony, has announced plans to develop a similar CD-ROM system for parts catalogs and maintenance manuals. CD-ROM catalogs have likewise replaced printed and microfilm publications in applications ranging from bookstores to real estate offices. Arthur Andersen and Company equips its auditors with a CD-ROM library of government regulations, internal procudural documents, and other technical information equivalent to over 250,000 printed pages. Arthur Young and Company similarly produces CD-ROM discs that contain tax code information, SEC regulations, and various internal publications. Price (1989, 1990) outlines the advantages of CD-ROM in such applications.

Exxon's research and engineering division has developed a CD-ROM edition of oil refinery construction practices. The DoveSystem is a CD-ROM directory of florists who participate in Teleflora's worldwide ordering and delivery service. A number government agencies, corporations, and other organizations are reportedly considering CD-ROM for electronic storage of business forms, thereby eliminating the need to warehouse multiple copies of blank forms; paper copies or specific forms, retrieved from a CD-ROM disc, can produced by a laser printer on demand. Using a computer program, information can be entered on the form prior to printing.

Hewlett-Packard, Sun Microsystems, IBM, Digital Equipment Corporation, Lotus Development and other computer manufacturers and software developers are utilizing or considering CD-ROM as a publishing medium for user manuals, product specification sheets, application notes, and other hardware and software documentation. The characteristics and advantages of such CD-ROM-based documentation systems are discussed by Beltrami and Ramana (1989), Brown (1989), Cathell *et al.* (1987, 1989), DePompa (1991), Herther (1990), Hoffman (1989), Martin (1990), and Weisenfeld (1987). Spitz (1991) describes a CD-ROM system for self-paced customer training developed by Hewlett-Packard. As discussed below, CD-ROM discs are also utilized by computer manufacturers for the distribution of system and application software.

Library catalogs constitute one of the most important groups of private CD-ROM implementations. Such CD-ROM catalogs are steadily replacing computer-output microfilm catalogs implemented during the 1970s and early 1980s; they also offer an alternative to mainframe- and minicomputer-based systems that provide timeshared access to library catalogs. Designed to promote interlibrary lending and other forms of resource sharing, CD-ROM catalogs typically include information about the holdings of two or more libraries joined in a consortium or other cooperative arrangement. They are accompanied by software that supports the retrieval, display, and printing of records meeting specified search requirements. The general characteristics of such systems are discussed by Beiser and Nelson (1989), Hildreth (1987) and Bills and Helgerson (1988, 1988a). Desmarais (1989a) provides a bibliography on the subject.

Complete CD-ROM systems, designed specifically for library catalog management applications are available from a number of vendors. Examples include the Auto-Graphics IMPACT system, described by Morrow (1989); Brodart's LePac, described by Soy (1987) and Weide (1990); the Library Corporation's Intelligent Catalog, described by Landrum (1988); the WLN LaserCAT system, described by Eckwright and Bolin (1990); General Research Corporation's LaserGuide, described by Smorch (1990); and Marcive/PAC, described by Masters (1988) and Gomez (1990). Such products are typically designed for IBM-compatible microcomputers equipped with one or more CD-ROM disc drives. While libraries have the option of supplying their own hardware components, some vendors offer catalog-access workstations equipped with internal CD-ROM drives and specially-designed keyboards. Most vendors offer stand-alone and local area network implementations of their products.

CD-ROM catalog installations in U.S. libraries are discussed by Beiser (1987), Cassel (1987), Crane (1990), Hegarty (1988), Neary (1990), Sertic and Mann (1989), Stasek and Sperry (1989), Uricchio *et al*. (1990), Warner (1990), Watson and Golden (1987), and Wismer (1988). Nixon (1990) and Pearson (1989) describe an implementation at the University of Guelph. German installations are described by Binder (1989), Binder *et al*. (1988), Lobeck (1989), and Neubauer (1988). Dalto (1989) discusses a CD-ROM union catalog for the holdings of science libraries in Milan. Hallgren (1990a) describes the CD-Kat project for Swedish public libraries. Australian installations are discussed by Parkes and Wade (1989) and Wood (1989). Tamura (1988) discusses the conversion of JAPAN/MARC records to CD-ROM discs.

Reference Products. While closed user group implementations of the type described above can improve access to information and make a significant contribution to an organization's operating efficiency and effectiveness, CD-ROM editions of databases, reference books, and other information products intended for public sale have been the focal point of optical publishing activity since the technology's inception. The earliest such products were announced in 1985, although some titles were initially implemented as demonstration discs rather than as complete versions. Confused by premature product announcements, some overly enthusiastic industry analysts and CD-ROM directories cited forty to sixty titles as commercially available in 1986, but the actual total was closer to two dozen. Product availability increased rapidly in the late 1980s, however. A discography prepared by Tiampo (1987) listed eighty-two CD-ROM publications from seventy-two information providers, with an additional forty titles available as demonstration discs or planned for future availability. In a revised version prepared in the third quarter of the year, Tiampo (1987a) listed 156 CD-ROM publications—including thirty-five prototypes, demonstration discs, and products in controlled release—from ninety information providers. The first edition of *CD-ROMs in Print* (Westport, CT: Meckler Corporation, 1987) listed almost 200 titles, including some prototype products and demonstration discs; the second edition, published in 1988, listed 239 titles. Nicholls and Van Den Elshout (1990) summarize the characteristics of 496 CD-ROM information products available for sale in late 1989. Nicholls (1991) reported that the number of publicly available titles had more than doubled by mid-1990. Recent estimates place the total at approximately 1,500 commercially available titles with continued growth anticipated through the mid-1990s. Nicholls (1990) surveys CD-ROM product directories and related information sources. Nicholls (1991a) describes the TFPL CD-ROM Directory, which is available in both CD-ROM and printed editions. In addition to listing information products, the CD-ROM version includes information about equipment, conferences, and publications about CD-ROM. The Disc of Discs from Euro-CD Management is a catalog, with demonstrations, of CD-ROM titles distributed by Euro-CD.

Available CD-ROM information products include hundreds of reference- and research-oriented databases intended primarily for libraries and information centers, the principal purchasers of the printed indexing and abstracting journals, encyclopedias, and other reference books on which such CD-ROM information products are based. Reports by Chen (1987), Fox (1988), Herther (1988), Kurdyla (1988), and others have confirmed the expansion of library-based CD-ROM installations during the late 1980s. As summarized by Herther (1990a), an OCLC study indicated that library ownership of CD-ROM information products increased from six percent in 1986 to sixty-six percent in 1989. CD-ROM products were being utilized by ninety-four percent of academic research libraries, seventy-six percent of other academic libraries, and sixty percent of public libraries.

Aimed at the large and potentially lucrative public and school library markets, several CD-ROM publications index and/or abstract articles contained in general-interest periodicals. Examples include the InfoTrac Magazine Index Plus, General Periodicals Index: Public Library, and TOM databases from Information Access Company; EBSCO's Magazine Article Summaries; the WilsonDisc implementation of the Reader's Guide to Periodical Literature and Reader's Guide Abstracts; and Periodical Abstracts Ondisc from University Microfilms International. Their characteristics are described by Bogage (1991), Gonzalez (1991), Sullivan (1991), and Tenopir and Smith (1990). University Microfilms International also offers the General Periodicals Ondisc, which combines indexing and abstracting information contained in the Periodical Abstracts database with digitized images of selected articles. It is described by Flanders (1991).

CD-ROM versions of general reference works, such as encyclopedias and dictionaries, likewise appeal to public and school libraries. As outlined by Weyer and Borning (1985), the concept of an electronic encyclopedia predates CD-ROM technology; its advantages were discussed by Vannevar Bush and Arthur C. Clarke, among others. Grolier's CD-ROM implementation of the Academic American Encyclopedia, now known as Grolier's New Electronic Encyclopedia, was one of the earliest CD-ROM information products. Other examples include World Book's Information Finder, Compton's MultiMedia Encyclopedia, and the Hutchinson Electronic Encyclopedia. They are described and discussed by Becker (1991), Dickinson (1990), Hollens and Rible (1991), Urrows and Urrows (1991, 1991a), and Van Brakel (1987). The Information Finder and Compton's MultiMedia Encyclopedia include dictionaries. A CD-ROM edition of Merriam-Webster's Ninth New Collegiate Dictionary, which includes pronunciations, is available for Macintosh computers. The FindIt Webster CD-ROM from Innotech Incorporated contains 85,000 English-language entries derived from citations in *The New York Times*. The Amazing Moby CD-ROM contains entries for more than one million English words and phrases. Mardeusz (1988) and Bowers (1989) describe the much publicized CD-ROM edition of the Oxford English Dictionary.

Encyclopedias and dictionaries are examples of CD-ROM information products with potentially broad appeal; others include Microsoft Corporation's Bookshelf, a much publicized collection of useful reference books designed for integration with word processing software and other computer applications; the Guinness Disc of World Records, produced by Pergamon Compact Solutions; and the various CD-ROM implementations of the Bible produced by Ellis Enterprises, Innotech, Tri Star Publishing, the Foundation for Advanced Biblical Studies, Deutsche Bibelgesellschaft, and other companies. Many CD-ROM reference products, however, are designed to support specialized research in particular subject areas. As discussed by Helsel (1989) and Myers (1989), the medical profession has been one of the most receptive audiences for interactive optical storage technologies, and a number of CD-ROM reference products address the information requirements of biomedical researchers and healthcare professionals. The best known examples, of course, are the various CD-ROM implementations of the MEDLINE database offered by CD Plus, Compact Cambridge, Dialog, Digital Diagnostics, SilverPlatter, and others. Characteristics of specific versions are discussed by Backus (1989), Bakker *et al.* (1989), Capodagli et al. (1988), Glitz (1988), Hewison (1989), Kemp (1987), Kittle (1988), Ladner and Barnett (1990), Nesbit (1990), Schultz (1989), Tennenhouse (1987), and York (1990). The machine-readable counterpart of the printed *Index Medicus,* the MEDLINE database is also available through various online search services. As an alternative to the complete MEDLINE database, which occupies multiple discs, several CD-ROM publishers offer subsets which correspond to the *Abridged Index Medicus*. Examples include the MEDLINE Clinical Collection from Dialog, MEDLINE Professional from SilverPlatter, BiblioMed from Healthcare Information Services, and the MEDLINE Knowledge Finder from Aries Systems Corporation.

Fryer *et al.* (1989) survey other CD-ROM information products of interest to biomedical professionals. Elsevier Science Publishers and SilverPlatter offer a CD-ROM implementation of

EMBASE, the machine-readable counterpart of the printed *Excerpta Medica*. Subsets are available for selected medical specialties, including cardiology, gastroenterology, obstetrics and gynecology, pathology, and radiology. Specialized CD-ROM products containing information about specific diseases include implementations of the CANCERLIT database from SilverPlatter, Compact Cambridge, and J.B. Lippincott; the Pediatric Infectuous Disease Journal from CMC ReSearch Incorporated; the Compact Library: AIDS and Compact Library: Viral Hepatitis discs from the Massachusetts Medical Society; and the Computer Clinical Information System, a database of poisons and their emergency treatments produced by Micromedex. CD-ROM editions are available of standard medical reference books and journals; examples include the *Physician's Desk Reference*, which also includes the *Merck Manual*, the *Oxford Textbook of Medicine*, *Renal Tumors of Children*, the *Journal of the American Medical Association*, and the *New England Journal of Medicine*. As discussed by Miller and Backus (1991a), the MAXX CD-ROM contains the full-texts of nine medical manuals published by Little, Brown and Company. SilverPlatter offers CINAHL-CD, a CD-ROM implementation of the Cumulative Index to Nursing and Allied Health Literature database. Intended for a lay audience rather than biomedical professionals, the Family Doctor on CD-ROM from CMC ReSearch provides diagnostic and anatomical information plus a guide to prescription drugs.

Scientific and technical databases, the historical mainstay of online search services, are increasingly available in CD-ROM implementations. Colborne and Nicholls (1990), Condic (1991), Gordon and Suer (1990), Mullan and Blick (1987), and Whittall (1989) examine CD-ROM databases of biological and botanical information. Examples include SilverPlatter's implementation of Biological Abstracts, the Biological and Agricultural Index from H.W. Wilson, and the Life Sciences Collection from Compact Cambridge. As discussed by Harrington (1990), the CD-ROM edition of the ASFA database (Aquatic Sciences and Fisheries Abstracts), produced by Compact Cambridge, is a principal reference source for aquatic biology. Available agricultural databases include AGRIS, AGRICOLA, CAB Abstracts, FSTA (Food Science and Technology Abstracts), and TROPAG, all of which are produced by SilverPlatter.

Among general scientific and technical databases, the Applied Science and Technology Index and the General Science Index are available in CD-ROM implementations from H.W. Wilson. The McGraw-Hill CD-ROM Science and Technical Reference Set combines the contents of two printed publications: the *Concise Encyclopedia of Science and Technology* and the *Dictionary of Scientific and Technical Terms;* it provides broad coverage of biology, the physical sciences, and engineering. The SCI-TECH REFERENCE PLUS CD-ROM from R.R. Bowker includes scientific and technical citations from the Books in Print and Ulrich's databases, biolgraphic entries from the American Men and Women of Science database, laboratory information from the Directory of American Research and Technology, and corporated data from the Corptech database. The CD-ROM edition of the SCISEARCH database (the machine-readable counterpart of the printed *Science Citation Index)* is discussed by Burke (1990), Cawkell (1989), Nagy-Teti (1990), Taylor (1989), and Wagner and Little (1989). Dialog's CD-ROM implementation of the COMPENDEX PLUS database is also available in subsets covering chemical, electrical, and environmental engineering. University Microfilms International offers a CD-ROM implementation of the INSPEC database that covers technical literature from 1989 to the present. Holland describes a test of a CD-ROM database produced by the Institute of Electrical and Electronics Engineers (IEEE) and the Institute of Electrical Engineers (IEE). Covering the literature of metallurgy and materials science, the METADEX COLLECTION CD-ROM from Dialog contains citations to publications on metals, polymers, and ceramics. John Wiley and Sons offers CD-ROM implementations of the Kirk-Othmer Encyclopedia of Chemical Technology and the Mark Encyclopedia of Polymer Science and Engineering. O'Donnell and Derksen (1990) survey CD-ROM information products for the earth sciences; the GeoRef and Geophysics of America databases are examples. Various U.S. government agencies are utilizing CD-ROM as a publishing medium for large scientific databases; Motley (1990), for example, describes a CD-ROM edition of datasets collected by the Airborne Antarctic Ozone Experiment. As noted by Jackson (1990), however, some government-produced CD-ROMs are accompanied by minimal software. Jackson (1990), Lawson (1989), and Lobeck (1990), review CD-ROM implementations of patent databases. Examples include the CASSIS CD-ROM, an implementation of the U.S. Patent Office database; ESPACE, a CD-ROM version of the European Patent Office database; the Automated Patent Searching (APS) system from Chadwyck-Healey; the CLAIMS/ Patent CD from SilverPlatter; and the full-text patent database from MicroPatent.

A growing number of CD-ROM information products contain business-oriented databases. Designed for financial analysts, researchers, business librarians, and others who need access to information about publicly held companies, Compact Disclosure was one of the earliest CD-ROM information products. Berry (1991) describes its use to download financial data for manipulation by spreadsheet software. Other CD-ROM sources of company information include the CD/Corporate, CD/Corptech, CD/Private+, CD/Banking, and CD/ International databases from Lotus Development; the Spectrum Ownership and Corporate Snapshots databases from Disclosure; Corporate Industry Research Reports (CIRR) from Bowker Business Research; Compustat PC Plus and S&P Corporations from Standard and Poor; the Million Dollar Directory from Dun's Marketing Service; OTC Plus on CD-ROM from Moody's Investors Service; and the WorldScope database from Wright Investors' Service. These products are reviewed by Fowler and Loomis (1988), Karp (1990), Kellough (1989), Littlejohn and Janousek (1991), Matthew (1990), and Weide (1991), among others. Useful company information can also be found in bibliographic databases, such as Business Periodicals OnDisc and the CD-ROM implementation of ABI/ Inform, both produced by University Microfilms International; the F&S Index plus Text, produced by Predicasts and SilverPlatter; and SilverPlatter's implementation of the COMLINE News Service database, which covers Japanese-language newspapers, trade journals, and other publications. Clark (1990) describes the CD-ROM edition of the popular Thomas Register of American Manufacturers. Hardin (1990) reviews the American Business Disc, which contains the yellow pages sections from 4,800 U.S. telephone directories. The QuickRef+ CD-ROM from PhoneDisc USA Corporation contains the nation's most frequently called telephone numbers; it also includes directory listings of businesses, manufacturers, government agencies, associations, schools, libraries, and toll-free numbers accessible from the United States. The PhoneDisc Business Reference Disc provides addresses and telephone numbers for U.S. corporations and other business organizations. Other PhoneDisc USA publications include a national telephone directory, which features ninety million residential listings on two CD-ROM discs. The FAST TRACK Digital Directory from NYNEX Information Resources Company combines 300 telephone directories from six northeastern states; customized versions are available for law enforcement and library use.

With their high capacities, CD-ROM discs are well suited to the publication of voluminous statistical and demongraphic databases produced by government agencies and other organizations. Examples of business-oriented statistical information products include the various collections of federal, state, and county statistics produced by Slater Hall Information Products; the AGRI/ STATS, CONSU/STATS, ECON/STATS, FOOD/ STATS, and LABOR/STATS discs from Hopkins Technology; the Citibase, International Financial Statistics, and Main Economic Indicators databases from DSI-Data Service and Information; the Statistical Masterfile from Congressional Information Service; Fedstat and Fedstat Zip-Industry from U.S. Statistics Incorporated; and the National Trade Data Bank, Monthly Import Data, and Monthly Export Data discs published by the U.S. Department of Commerce. Sheets (1991) describes a CD-ROM disc that contains the National Longitudinal Survey of Labor Market Experience. The Census Bureau has announced plans to distribute portions of the 1990 Census of Population on multiple CD-ROM discs, although it will reportedly leave the development of sophisticated analytical software to private sector firms. National Decision Systems offers a CD-ROM version of its Infomark Laser PC System, a demographic analysis and decision support system that was originally implemented on digital video discs.

As discussed by Chester (1989), Griffith (1990, 1990a), Kauffman (1988), and Urrows and Urrows (1991b), a growing number of legal and legislative databases and publications are available in CD-ROM implementations. Griffith (1989) reviews West Publishing's CD-ROM editions of legal databases. Binwal and Rao (1989) describe LegalTrac, a CD-ROM implementation of the *Legal Resources Index*. H.W. Wilson offers a CD-ROM edition of the *Index to Legal Periodicals*. Shumaker (1990) discusses the Search Master Tax Library, a CD-ROM database of federal and state tax codes produced by Matthew Bender and Company. Various state legal codes are available in CD-ROM implementations. Examples include the Nebraska Statutes disc, produced by CD Media and Reference Technology; New Mexico Law on Disc, the Delaware Code Annotated, and the Virginia State Legal Code, published by The Michie Company; Colorado Revised Statutes, published by Oster and Associates; and the California Practice Library from Matthew Bender. FD Incorporated offers FDA-on CD-ROM, a compilation of FDA-related federal statutes and government regulations, FDA manuals, and judicial decisions. The same company's HCFA-ON CD-ROM provides similar coverage of health care laws and regulations. Martindale-Hubble offers a CD-ROM edition of its seventeen-volume directory of attorneys, law firms, and legal services. The PAIS database that provides bibliographic coverage of many legal and public affairs publications and has been available on CD-ROM for several years. The Congressional Record has been produced in a pilot CD-ROM edition. McCormick (1991) discusses the CD-ROM implementation of the Federal Register. Kellough and Gomez (1990) review the Congressional Masterfile, a CD-ROM collection of committee prints, unpublished hearings, and other Congressional documents.

As is the case with databases offered by online search services, researchers in the social sciences and humanities are served by a smaller number of CD-ROM products than their scientific, business, and professional counterparts. PsycLit (Psychological Abstracts) and the ERIC database, however, were among the earliest and most widely publicized CD-ROM products. Other CD-ROM databases of interest to social scientists include the Social Sciences Citation Index from the Institute for Scientific Information; the Social Sciences Index from H.W. Wilson; SocioFile (Sociological Abstracts); the Cross-Cultural CD, a series of textual extracts from sociological and anthropological publications; and Psyndex, which provides bibliographic coverage of German-language publications on psychology. ABC-CLIO offers CD-ROM editions of its Historical Abstracts and America: History and Life databases. The U.S. History on CD-ROM collection, described by Desmarais (1991), contains the full text of over 100 American history books. U.S. Presidents on CD-ROM, produced by Quanta Press, contains biographical and historical information about America's chief executives. The first three titles in the USA Wars series from Quanta Press cover the U.S. Civil War, the Korean War, and the Vietnam War. Future releases are planned for World War I, World War II, the Spanish-American War, and Operation Desert Storm.

Intended for general readers as well as scholars, various CD-ROM publishers have issued machine-readable compilations—the equivalent of huge anthologies—of literary works. Examples include Shakespeare on Disc and Sherlock Holmes on Disc collections from CMC ReSearch. The Greatest Books Ever Written is a CD-ROM collection of literary classics from ancient times to the present. The Library of the Future Series, from World Library Incorporated, contains the complete texts of over 450 literary, historical, philosophical, and religious works. DiscLit: American Authors, produced by G.K. Hall and OCLC Electronic Publishing, contains the texts of 143 volumes from Twayne's United States Author Series. Chadwyck-Healey's English Poetry Full-Text Database contains the works of 1,350 poets from 600 A.D. to the early twentieth century. In a joint venture with Harmonie Park Press, Chadwyck-Healey also offers the Music Index on CD-ROM. A CD-ROM implementation of the RILM database of music literature is available from National Information Services Corporation. Bibliographic coverage of religious publications is provided by H.W. Wilson's Religion Indexes, which are described by Womack (1990), and R&TA on CD-ROM, which is produced by Religious & Theological Abstracts Incorporated.

While the majority of CD-ROM information products originate in the United States, the technology is attracting considerable interest in other countries. Fox (1991) reports the results of a survey of CD-ROM use in Canadian libraries conducted under the auspices of the Canadian Library Association. In a previous survey, discussed by Fox (1988), only 25.7 percent of responding libraries had installed a CD-ROM system. By 1990, penetration of the Canadian library market had increased to 30.4 percent, and 207 different CD-ROM titles were reported to be in use. Campbell (1989) had earlier noted the reluctance of Canadian publishers to undertake CD-ROM projects because of uncertain customer demand, although researchers would presumably like to obtain Canadian information in the CD-ROM format. The 1990 survey of Canadian library use indicated that five of the twenty most widely utilized CD-ROM titles were Canadian in origin: the CCINFO Chemical Information disc, produced by the Canadian Center for Occupational Health and Safety; the CCINFO Occupational Health and Safety Information disc; the Canadian Business and Current Affairs Index; CD-CATSS, a cataloging support tool derived from the Utlas database; and the BiblioDisc, a source of book ordering and cataloging information produced by the National Library of Canada and the Canadian Telebook Agency. The BiblioDisc development project is described by Beaumont and Campbell (1990). Several French-language CD-ROM products have been developed for the Canadian library market; examples include Termium, a bilingual dictionary produced by the Canadian Secretary of State, and the CHOIX and DAVID databases produced by Services Documentaires Multimedia Incorporated. Abeytunga (1990) emphasizes the role of Canadian government agencies as users and producers of CD-ROM information products; the CANSIM discs produced by Statistics Canada are good examples. Dysart (1990) suggests a need for a Canadian encyclopedia intended for the school library market and for databases of information about Canadian companies.

As discussed by Daum (1989), Raitt and Chen (1989), and David (1990), the Western European market for CD-ROM information products lags behind its U.S. counterpart. Nelson (1990) cites various reasons, including the relatively high cost of CD-ROM products, the absence of a significant installed base of CD-ROM drives, the small number of indigenous European databases available in the CD-ROM format, and the Europeans' traditionally more conservative response to new information processing technologies. Moore (1989) presents a survey of CD-ROM installations in the United Kingdom. Raitt and Chen (1990) discuss CD-ROM use in West German libraries. Guerts and Borman (1989) describe a CD-ROM feasibility study involving libraries in the Netherlands. Nieuwenhuysen (1990, 1990a) surveys CD-ROM implementations in Belgium. Heimburger (1991) and Storleer (1989) discuss CD-ROM applications in Scandinavian countries.

While the majority of CD-ROM information products originate in the United States, a number of European publishers and database producers have introduced CD-ROM titles, and—evidently anticipating future market expansion—others have announced products for future availability. Like their U.S. counterparts, most of the European CD-ROM titles are reference and research databases intended for library installations; breadth of subject coverage compares favorably with that of U.S. products, but—since fewer European titles are available—the depth of coverage in specific subject areas is not as great. Hanson (1990) surveys bibliographic and nonbibliographic databases produced by the European Community, including those available on CD-ROM. Lehmann and Sledge (1988) present a report on CD-ROM prepared by a committee of European librarians and publishers. Mastroddi (1987) outlines the European Commission's plans for CD-ROM and other electronic publishing formats. Under the Commission's auspices, the British Library, Bibliotheque Nationale, Deutsche Bibliothek, and other national libraries have announced a collaborative CD-ROM initiative designed to promote the exchange of bibliographic records and the improvement of database structures and software. It is discussed by Buckley (1990), Smith (1989a, 1990), and Van Halm and Danczak (1990).

Several European libraries have separately implemented CD-ROM projects based on their own bibliographic activities. Chadwyck-Healey (1989) and Lealand (1989), for example, discuss the CD-ROM version of the British Library's Catalog of Printed Books to 1975. The planning and production of a CD-ROM edition of the British National Bibliography (BNB) are described by Haynes (1989), Smith (1989), and Smith and McSean (1989). The BNB backfile contains over one million records for imprints dated between 1950 and 1985; publications since 1986 are listed on a current disc. Chadwyck-Healey Incorporated offers an implementation of the BNB with multilingual menus. Chadwyck-Healey also offers CD-ROM editions of the Bibliographie Nationale Francaise from 1975 to the present and the Deutsche Bibliographie Aktuell from 1986 to the present; the latter is described by Buchbinder (1988), Marloth (1989), and Nowak (1989).

A number of European CD-ROM titles are the counterparts of printed reference works and online databases. LISA (Library and Information Science Abstracts), which is produced in the United Kingdom by the Library Association, was among the first CD-ROM database to be offered by SilverPlatter. It is described by Moore (1988). BookBank, from J. Whitaker and Sons, is the CD-ROM edition of *British Books in Print*. Le Robert Electronique, produced by Dictionnaires Le Robert and Bureau Marcel van Dijk, is a CD-ROM implementation of the Grand Robert de la Langue Francaise. The Documentacion De Medios CD-ROM, produced by Micronet S.A., provides indexing information and abstracts for articles published in Spanish and international newspapers and magazines. In the United States, CD-ROM editions are available of various newspapers, including the *New York Times, Wall Street Journal, Boston Globe,* and *Chicago Tribune.* While Arundale (1991) raises European concerns about the relationship of such products to printed publications and online implementations, several companies offer CD-ROM editions of European newspapers. Examples of this include the Independent on CD-ROM, produced by K.G. Saur and the Guardian on CD-ROM, produced by Guardian Newspapers Limited. Given the delays inherent in CD-ROM mastering and distribution, such products are necessarily limited to newspaper backfiles.

Among European CD-ROM titles for specific subject areas, Vidal Sur Disque contains the *Dictionnaire Vidal,* a standard reference to pharmaceutical products. The ESPACE CD-ROM, produced by the European Patent Office, was mentioned above. The PATOS CD-ROM, produced by Wila Verlag, contains patent information intended for distribution in East Germany. Caniglia (1989) describes the CD-ROM implementation of Kompass Europe, a database of directory information for 210,000 European companies; a version for United Kingdom companies is also available. Other business-oriented CD-ROM databases include Compact Disclosure Europe, which contains financial information for 2,000 European public companies; Review and Analysis of Companies in Holland, which provides financial information about 5,000 Dutch companies; FINN-COIN, a compendium of financial information about West German companies prepared by Verband der Vereine Creditreform; and the Hoppenstedt CD-ROM, produced by Verlag Hoppenstedt, which contains detailed descriptions of 36,000 German companies. The CD-ROM implementation of The Wer Liefert Was? database contains information about more than one million products sold by 90,000 suppliers in Germany and Austria. Helecon on CD-ROM, produced by the Helsinki School of Economics and Business, is a compilation of European management databases.

CD-ROM address and telephone directories have proven popular with European publishers. Phone Base, produced by British Telecom, contains residential addresses and telephone numbers as listed in printed directories. Compact Deutschland, from Tele-Info Verlag, is a five-disc set that contains twenty-three million residential telephone listings for West Germany. Postreklame GmbH offers a CD-ROM version of the German Postcode Address File. TEI of Kozani KIIA offers the Greek Telephone Book on CD-ROM. The Italian Yellow Pages for the U.S.A., produced by SEAT, contains listings for over 20,000 Italian companies that export products to the United States. The CommDisc Telefax from Telex-Verlag Jaeger & Waldman, contains addresses, telex and fax numbers for international companies.

The Lawbase CD-ROM, which contains decisions of the Swiss Federal Court, is typical of European titles for the legal market. It is published by IBIS Service AG. Other examples include the Repertorio del Foro Italiano, which contains excerpts from Italian case law and bibliographic citations pertaining to legal questions; Rechtsprechung des Bundesfinanzhofs, the CD-ROM counterpart of the online Juris Datanbanken; and the CD-ROM edition of Legal Databank produced by Kluwer Datalex.

A survey by Langerman (1990) of installations in Israel indicated that CD-ROM information products were being utilized in fifty-six organizations, thirty-five of them libraries and the remainder consisting of hospitals, physicians, and information brokers. MEDLINE, the most popular title, was utilized in 68.5 percent of the installations. Miura (1990) reports that the Japanese market for CD-ROM products is growing rapidly. While more than three-quarters of the reference-oriented CD-ROM information products originate in the United States, Japanese-produced titles are increasingly encountered. Examples include J-DISC, a bibliographic disc produced by the National Diet Library; CD-FOREX, a collection of historical data for foreign exchange rates produced by Toppan Printing Company and Tokyo Economic Press; the JETRO ACE database of company information produced by the Japan External Trade Organization; Wraptop Kojien, a CD-ROM edition of a widely utilized Japanese dictionary published by Iwanami Shotem; Saishin Igaku Daijiten, a dictionary of medical terms produced by Ishiyaku Shuppan; and NTT's Town-Page Map, which contains a yellow-pages directory for Tokyo. Elsewhere in Asia, Yan and Lin (1990) discuss the implications of CD-ROM for Chinese libraries. Chou (1990) describes a CD-ROM database of Chinese MARC records produced by the National Central Library. Chamchuklin (1990) discusses CD-ROM MEDLINE use in Thailand. Pagell (1990) found that many librarians in southeast Asian countries were unfamiliar with CD-ROM. Crawford (1990) and Stocks (1989, 1989a) survey CD-ROM usage in Australian libraries; Traub (1990) estimated that at least fifteen CD-ROM information products were being produced domestically in 1990.

CD-ROM's potential for libraries and other information agencies in developing countries is discussed by Abid (1989), Ali (1990), Brito (1989), Carino (1989), Kinney (1989), Ritzler (1989), Samarajiva (1989), and Sever (1989). Such countries are particularly interested in CD-ROM implementations of medical and agricultural databases. Brito (1989a) describes plans by the Pan American Health Organization to use CD-ROM for the dissemination of healthcare information in Latin America. Castro *et al.* (1989) discuss the CD-ROM implementation of the LILACS database of Latin American and Caribbean health sciences literature. Butler (1990), Frierson (1989), and Prierson and Zoellick (1990) describe the Compact International Agricultural Research Library, a CD-ROM compendium of books, technical reports, and other publications on agricultural topics. Developed by the Consultative Group on International Agricultural Research, it will be distributed in developing countries.

Library Support Products. An interesting and widely utilized group of CD-ROM information products is specifically designed to support cataloging, acquisitions, serials control, and other technical service activities in libraries of various types and sizes. Bibliofile, introduced by the Library Corporation in 1985, was the first CD-ROM-based cataloging support system and one of the earliest CD-ROM information products of any type. It has since been joined by a number of conceptually similar products, including CDMARC Bibliographic from the Library of Congress, CAT CD450 from OCLC, CD-CATSS from Utlas International, LaserCat from the Western Library Network, LaserQuest from General Research Corporation, SuperCat from Gaylord Informtion Systems, Alliance Plus from Follett Software, and Precision One Disc from Brodart Automation. These CD-ROM cataloging support systems have proven particularly popular with medium-size and smaller public, academic, and school libraries and library-related agencies. Their characteristics, capabilities, and applications are described in many publications, including Allan (1990), Barrett (1990), Bibi (1990), Bills and Helgerson (1989), Brennan (1989), Burton and Cheng (1989), Colgazer (1988), Cormouls and Gaudin (1988), Ferrell and Parkhurst (1987), Gartshore (1987), Giesbrecht (1988), Guttuso (1989), Hooten (1990), Irwin (1991), Jacso (1989), Johnson (1988, 1989), Khurshid (1991), Latham (1989), Machovec (1987), McKnight (1987), Morrow (1988, 1989), and Stock (1989).

CD-ROM cataloging support systems combine bibliographic data with software that supports the retrieval of specific records, the production of catalog card sets, and/or the creation of a machine-readable catalog file. While they share conceptual similarities, available products differ in the size, source, and scope of their cataloging data bases. CDMARC Bibliographic and SuperCat, for example, rely exclusively on the LC MARC data base as a source of cataloging records. Updated weekly by the Library of Congress, the LC MARC data base contains approximately three million records for books, serials, and other library materials. In addition to CDMARC Bibliographic, the Library of Congress CDMARC series includes compact disc implementations of the LC Subject Headings and LC Name Authority data bases. They are described by Joy and Keane (1989) and Turner (1991). CAT CD450 and the CD-CATSS system augment the LC MARC data base with bibliographic records contributed by subscribers to the online cataloging services operated by OCLC and Utlas International, respectively. LaserQuest similarly supplements the LC MARC data base with cataloging records obtained from General Research Corporation's customers. Primarily intended for school libraries, the cataloging records in Follett's Alliance Plus system contain Sears and Library of Congress children's subject headings. The Library Corporation also offers Sears subject headings in its Bibliofile data base. Brodart's Precision One Disc includes a selection of one million LC MARC records considered appropriate to school and public libraries.

Regardless of scope, CD-ROM cataloging support systems are marketed as potentially cost-effective alternatives to other cataloging methodologies for the retrospective conversion of library shelflists as well as for the ongoing cataloging of newly acquired titles—subject, of course, to limitations on currency that are inherent in CD-ROM discs produced and distributed at predetermined intervals. While most products are updated monthly or quarterly, they do contain Cataloging-In-Publication (CIP) records for forthcoming books. Chao (1989), Saffady (1989), and Co (1990) discuss costs associated with CD-ROM-based cataloging systems and analyze their competitive relationship to other other computer-based cataloging support products and services. Characterized by high fixed costs but negligible variable costs, CD-ROM cataloging support products can offer an attractively economical alternative to the timeshared data bases offered by bibliographic utilities in high-volume current cataloging and retrospective conversion applications—assuming, of course, that the data base provided by a given CD-ROM information product contains bibliographic records appropriate to the items being cataloged. Data base updates which rely on periodic supplements or replacement of CD-ROM discs at predetermined intervals can, as noted above, pose potential problems for current cataloging, while the relatively small size and chronological span of some CD-ROM cataloging support data bases may limit their utility for retrospective conversion.

Intended for procurement support in libraries and bookstores, Bowker's Books in Print Plus (BIP Plus) is an attractive menu-driven CD-ROM implementation of the United States' best known trade bibliography. It is described by Desmarais (1987), Hagan (1987), Holloway (1987), Mead (1988), Nisonger (1990), and Pollack (1990). Available in versions for IBM-compatible and Macintosh microcomputers, BIP Plus contains essential bibliographic and ordering information for more than 800,000 titles on a single CD-ROM disc. Once the record for a desired title is retrieved, the operator can add information in a form suitable for transmission to electronic ordering systems operated by Baker and Taylor, Blackwell North America, Brodart, Ingram, and other distributors. Rioux (1988) describes the transfer of ASCII text output from BIP Plus to a microcomputer-based library acquisition system. A variant version, Ingram-Books In Print Plus, contains the Books In Print data base augmented by Ingram's inventory information for books and audio-visual titles. It is described by Brooks (1989). Books In Print with Book Reviews Plus includes the full texts of reviews from various publications. Designed for rapid bibliographic verification, Bowker's Books Out of Print Plus contains information about 300,000 titles declared out of print or out of stock by their publishers since 1979.

In the United Kingdom, J. Whitaker and Sons Limited offers BookBank, a CD-ROM version of British Books In Print. It contains information about English language titles published in Western Europe. Modelled on Books In Print Plus,

Online Computer Systems and Buchhandler Vereinigung have produced a CD-ROM version of the Verzeichnis Lieferbarer Bucher data base. It is discussed by Wolf (1989).

For bibliographic control of periodicals and other serial publications in libraries, information centers, and related work environments, Bowker offers Ulrich's Plus, a CD-ROM version of the popular data base and printed directory of serials and annuals. It is described by Desmarais (1988), Ferraro (1987, 1988), and Karch (1990). As discussed by Walters (1989), the Serials Directory CD-ROM from EBSCO Electronic Information provides information about 118,000 serials. Jacso (1991) compares the EBSCO product with the CD-ROM implementation of Ulrich's.

CD-ROM Maps. While bibliographic, financial, and statistical data bases acocunt for the majority of available CD-ROM information products, considerable attention has been given to the use of CD-ROM in such geographic information systems as computer-based surveying, military command and control, and property management, all of which involve voluminous mapping data. Cooke (1987) and Ochmann (1991) provide informative overviews of CD-ROM's potential in such applications. Since the late 1980s, several publishers have introduced CD-ROM implementations of atlases and other mapping products. Armento et al (1990) review examples for IBM-compatible and Macintosh microcomputers. Weide (1990) describes the Electromap World Atlas which contains over 230 topographical, political, and thematic maps of countries and regions of the world. The maps are stored on CD-ROM as bit-mapped color images which can be exported to other software packages in various graphic formats. To examine a specific region or country in detail, the user selects the desired location from a global map. Textual information—dealing with such topics as geography, government, regional economy, and travel—is accessible through pulldown menus, making the World Atlas a potentially valuable reference tool for a broad range of applications. In its latest version, the World Atlas disc includes a U.S. Atlas which contains reference maps of the fifty states and the District of Columbia. Klimley (1988) evaluates the GEOdisc U.S. Atlas, which provides topographic maps on CD-ROM, as an alternative to conventional paper maps. Produced by GEOVISION Incorporated, it includes political boundaries, roads, waterways, railroads, federal land areas, and hydrological districts, as well as one million place names. Mapping information is stored in a vector format. Other titles in the GEOdisc series provide similar cartographic coverage for specific parts of the United States. The GEOdisc Georgia Atlas CD-ROM, for example, includes all place names and landmark features in that state. Designed for Macintosh computers, the Electronic Map Cabinet from Highlighted Data Incorporated can generate customized maps of any area of the continental United States in various scales.

Leeuwenburg (1987) describes an implementation of the much-publicized Supermap CD-ROM system at Melbourne University. Produced by Space-Time Research of Australia and distributed by Chadwyck-Healey Incorporated, Supermap is available with U.S. and Australian census data which can be retrieved, manipulated, tabulated, and mapped in multiple colors and in various ways. It is intended for urban planning, market research, and similar applications involving demographic analysis. Chadwyck-Healey (1989, 1989a) compares the Supermap series with Mundocart/CD, a CD-ROM disc containing world maps produced by Petroconsultants CES Limited from U.S. Operational Navigation Charts and the Russian Karta series. It references over half a million place names and geographic features. As discussed by Tobe and Kawabe (1990), Japanese companies are exploring linkages between maps and telephone directories recorded on CD-ROM. Dainihon Computer Systems and Nippon Columbia offer the CD-MAP, which combines maps of metropolitan Tokyo with over three million residents names and addresses. An early version is described by Yokomizo (1987). The Town-Page Map, published by NTT, contains information about Tokyo businesses. As described by Miyazaki (1987), Hitachi has demonstrated several CD-ROM mapping products, including a system which features color maps indicating government boundaries, roads, railways, and buildings. Among institutional publishers, the Defense Mapping Agency produces a variety of CD-ROMs containing topographic maps, tactical operations maps, and navigation charts.

Many of the CD-ROM map products described above are intended for library reference and research applications. As an entirely different application of optical map publishing, various Japanese, European, and North American companies are deeply involved in the development of vehicle navigation systems which utilize CD-ROM discs to store mapping data. As outlined by Frank (1989), on-board automobile information systems—based on such technologies as CD-ROM, cellular telephony, and satellite communications—offer potentially attractive solutions to various motoring problems, including route determination and rerouting necessitated by traffic congestion. While specific implementations differ in details, vehicle navigation systems consult a map data base to determine the best route between a specified origination point and destination. Depending on the system, turning instructions and other driving directions may be displayed on a screen or synthesized as speech. Dead-reckoning methodologies or satellite tracking are utilized to determine a vehicle's location at a given moment.

Target markets for CD-ROM-based vehicle navigation systems include package and message delivery companies, the trucking and transport industry, taxicab companies, and police and fire departments. Such systems have been demonstrated in prototype since the mid-1980s; early published discussions of their characteristics and potential include Cooke (1986) and Honey and White (1986). Fushiki (1987) discusses a standard for CD-ROM map data bases proposed by the Navigation System Research Society, an organization composed of major Japanese electronics equipment manufacturers and software companies. Tsujimura et al (1990) describe a CD-ROM software format intended specifically for vehicle information display systems.

Among other published discussions of this rapidly developing application of CD-ROM technology, Asami et al (1987) and Koide and Kitoh (1989) survey experimental vehicle navigation systems developed by Japanese electronics equipment and automobile manufacturers in the late 1980s. Japanese research development activities are reported in a growing number of technical articles and conference papers. Kobayashi et al (1990) and Nawaoka et al (1990), for example, describe a system developed for Nissan automobiles by Sumitomo Electric. Kakihara (1989) discusses the Mazda Car Communication System. As discussed by Hirata and Yokouchi (1987), Mitsuibishi's automobile navigation system employs the satellite tracking to determine vehicle locations. Intended for police-managed traffic control in Japanese cities, the Advanced Mobile Traffic Information and Communication System (AMTICS) includes an automobile navigation component that relies on CD-ROM for map storage. As described by Kanayama and Kaizu (1990), Kawabata et al (1990), Kawashima (1991), Miyauchi (1988), Mizuno (1989), Okamoto (1989), Okamoto and Nakahara (1988), Terasaki et al (1991), and Tsuzawa and Okamoto (1989), AMTICS uses a combination of dead-reckoning and radiowave navigation to determine a vehicle's location and coordinate it with mapping information retrieved from CD-ROM. Ueno et al (1989) describe an emergency information system gas-line maintenance vehicles which combines CD-ROM map storage with data base updates accessed via cellular telephone. As discussed by Ohe et al (1988) and Ono et al (1988), NEC Home Electronics has developed a CD-ROM-based automobile navigation system which employs satellite technology to determine a vehicle's location and voice synthesis to give directions to a designated destination, a feature that is also employed by Philips' CARIN system described below.

Radke (1986), Schips (1988), and Smith (1989) survey European interest in vehicle navigation technology. Neukirchner (1991) discusses automobile navigation requirements and problems, using Bosch's TravelPilot system—which incorporates CD-ROM for map storage—as an example. As discussed by Buxton et al (1991), TravelPilot is based on technology developed by Etak Corporation. It relies on dead-reckoning and map-matching. Houze (1991) describes the Audio Visual Information Communication (AVIC) system which uses CD-ROM to store color map images. Fernhout (1987), Pungel (1988), Royce (1986), Thoone (1987), and Thoone and Breukers (1984) describe the CAR Information and Navigation (CARIN) system developed by Philips. Employing a dead-reckoning system, a map data base, and voice synthesis, it informs the vehicle's driver when turns are required. CARIN concepts predated but envisioned CD-ROM's commercial availability.

Other implementations are discussed by Alegiani et al (1989), Hunter (1989), and Hirata (1989). While North American activity lags behind its Japanese and European counterpart, vehicle navigation technology is attracting increasing attention in the United States. In mid-1991, for example, the U.S. Department of Transportation, the state of Illinois, a group of Illinois universities, and Motorola Incorporated announced joint funding of a project to equip 5,000 automobiles with vehicle navigation systems consisting of computers, CD-ROM drives, dashboard displays, and radio transmitters. The systems will be manufactured by Motorola.

Software Distribution. With its high capacity, faster production time, and potentially lower production and shipping costs, CD-ROM offers an attractive and cost-effective alternative to floppy disks and magnetic tapes for software distribution. High recording capacity makes CD-ROM a particularly useful medium for the distribution of large collections of public domain software and customer-supported shareware programs, a type of application that is surveyed by Reese (1989). Among examples of available products, the PC-SIG Library from PC-SIG Incorporated contains over 10,000 programs—incuding a number of well-known word processing, spreadsheet, and data base management packages, as well as compilers, interpreters, assemblers, and other system programs—for IBM-compatible microcomputers. The programs were previously distributed on over 1,400 floppy disks. Likewise intended for IBM-compatible microcomputers, the PC-Blue and Super Blue discs, produced by Alde Publishing, contain public domain and shareware programs from members of the New York Amateur Computer Club. The Shareware Gold CD-ROM from Quanta Press contains programs from such well known shareware providers as ButtonWare, Medlin Accounting, PKware, and Quicksoft. Many of the programs are business-oriented. Alde Publishing's Shareware Grab Bag contains a more diverse group of programs from a broader range of suppliers. The First Canadian Shareware Disc from BETACORP Technologies contains several hundred programs, emphasizing Canadian software.

CD-ROM software collections for Macintosh computers include the Macademic Disc and Mega-ROM from QLTech, the Club Mac disc from Quantum Access Incorporated, Mac Guide USA from Mac Guide Magazine, the Public Domain Shareware Hypercard Stack from Laser Optical Technology, the CD-ROM Public Domain Library from Educorp Computer Services, and the BCS-Mac Software Exchange Library from the Boston Computer Society. The Public Domain Software on File disc, produced by Facts on File, contains programs for Apple II computers. Other CD-ROM-based software collections support specialized computing activities. Alde Publishing, for example, offers several CD-ROM discs of interest to ADA programmers. Taken from the ADA software repository at White Sands Missile Range, they include application programs, utilities, tutorials, and reference manuals. Alde's C CD-ROM disc provides similar coverage for the C programming language. The various DECUS discs, produced by the Digital Equipment Corporation Users Group, contain public domain programs and shareware for VAX computers.

As previously noted, a growing number of computer manufacturers and commercial software developers are using CD-ROM for software publishing and documentation distribution. Sun Microsystems, for example, has distributed new releases of its operating systems and other systems software on CD-ROM for several years. The MacApp disc and Macintosh Programmer's Workshop from Apple Computer provide systems software, utility programs, documentation, and other materials of interest to Macintosh programmers. The Programmer's Library, produced by Microsoft Corporation, contains books, technical manuals, and sample programs pertaining to Microsoft's operating systems, programming languages, and hardware devices. The Microsoft Office, one of the most innovative and comprehensive applications of CD-ROM for software distribution, includes the Macintosh versions of four Microsoft software packages—Word, Excel, Powerpoint, and Mail—accompanied by fully searchable electronic documentation, audio-visual program demonstrations, and selected third-party software. The ability to distribute machine-readable manuals, help files, template files, and other supporting materials along with program object code allows software publishers to add value to the CD-ROM editions of the products.

CD-ROM is an increasingly popular publishing medium for computer-processible graphic images—so-called "clip art"—employed in desktop publishing applications. Intended for IBM-compatible or Macintosh microcomputers, most CD-ROM clip-art collections contain drawings and photographs in industry-standard graphic image formats, such as TIF and PCX, which can be imported by image processing and desktop publishing programs. Examples of such CD-ROM products include the Full Spectrum Clip-Art disc from Dover Clip-Art, the Artroom and Darkroom discs from Image Club Graphics, the Image Gallery and Photo Gallery discs from NEC Home Electronics, the Publique Arte collection of shareware images from Quanta Press, the Comstock Desktop Photography disc, the Laser Art CD-ROM from Somak Software, the Wheeler Quick Art CD-ROM from Wheeler Arts, and the Kwickee In-House Graphic System and ProArt discs from Multi-Ad Services. Some products combine clip art images with image processing software. Corel Systems, for example, offers a CD-ROM version of its CorelDraw graphics program accompanied by 10,000 clip-art images. Similarly, the PixelPaint Art CD-ROM from SuperMac Technology contains PixelPaint Professional, a color graphics program for Macintosh computers, plus a variety of color images. Also intended for desktop publishing applications, several companies offer CD-ROM collections of type fonts. Examples include the Type Gallery product line from NEC Home Electronics and the LetterPress CD-ROM from Image Club Graphics. Type fonts are also included in some of the CD-ROM shareware collections listed above.

Various CD-ROM products contain directory listings or descriptive information about computer hardware and software. As an example, the Data-World Infodisk, MicroData Infodisk, and Communications Infodisk from Faulkner Techical Reports Incorporated contain product specifications, evaluations, and prices as well as news abstracts from major industry publications. The Datapro Software Finder from Datapro Research Group provides system requirements, functional descriptions, prices, and other information about 18,000 software packages for computers of all types and sizes. The Software-CD from Silver Platter and the ICP Software Information Directory are described by Jackson (1989) and Salomon (1990). The SelectWare Systems disc from SelectWare Technologies is representative of CD-ROM products which contain demonstration versions of software, together with electronic brochures, specification sheets, and other useful information.

STANDARDS AND SOFTWARE

Like their magnetic media counterparts, CD-ROM discs feature a logical format superimposed on a physical structure. From the physical standpoint, a CD-ROM disc provides a circular storage surface divided into spiralling tracks, each of which is subdivided into sectors. From the logical standpoint, the same disc contains a volume table of contents, a directory structure, and one or more data files which can be accessed by appropriate application programs. The physical characteristics of CD-ROM discs were standardized in 1985 by a Sony/Philips document that is popularly described as the "Yellow Book." It is the CD-ROM counterpart of the Sony/Philips "Red Book" which specifies the physical characteristics of CD-DA discs. The Yellow Book standardizes the CD-ROM discs's external dimensions, prescribes its organization into tracks and sectors, and defines the recording modes which determine the allocatio of bytes for user data, error correction, and control information. In mid-1987, Philips released the Yellow Book to the European Computer Manufacturers Association (ECMA), thereby placing its specifications in the public domain and permitting the development of a corresponding ECMA standard which would subsequently be submitted to the International Standardization Organization (ISO).

Standardized Logical Formats. A logical format specifies the characteristics of volume tables of contents and directories to be recorded on CD-ROM discs. A volume table of contents provides general information—such as the publisher's name, copyright holder, and publication date—

about a given disc. It indicates the volume sequence number for multi-disc sets, indentifies the type of information being recorded, and gives the locations of directories, boot blocks, and other disc components. Boot blocks cause the host computer's operating system to load information into memory, thereby allowing users to start an application directly from a CD-ROM disc.

Directories indicate the physical disc locations of specific data files. Compared to lower-capacity magnetic media, CD-ROM discs can store very large numbers of data files, each of which may contain many records. In applications intended for IBM-compatible microcomputers, the CD-ROM logical format must override file-size limitations associated with certain early versions of the MS-DOS operating system. Because CD-ROM drives access data more slowly than magnetic disk drives, directory structures must avoid complicated hierarchical paths.

The Sony/Philips Yellow Book does not provide logical format specifications which mandate specific file management procedures. File management schemes developed for magnetic disks are poorly suited to a high-capacity read-only medium. To support their own product development efforts, the earliest CD-ROM publishers consequently developed proprietary logical formats and file management systems which were tailored to the special characteristics and limitations of CD-ROM technology. Examples of such proprietary file management systems included the STA/F FILE system from Reference Technology, LASERDOS from TMS Incorporated, LASERFILE from LaserData, and UNI-FILE from Digital Equipment Corporation.

While they offer similar capabilities and address the same types of tasks, proprietary CD-ROM file management systems are necessarily incompatible with one another. Although proprietary file management techniques may be acceptable for CD-ROM applications intended for closed user groups, the importance of standardization was quickly recognized by industry analysts, information providers, and customers. In late 1985, the CD-ROM standards subcommittee of the Information Industry Association urged the adoption of logical format standards as critical to the continued development and widespread acceptance of CD-ROM technology in a broad spectrum of information management applications. As discussed by Befeler and Einberger (1988), Rosie (1989), Shimbori (1987), and Zoellick (1988), among others, it was hoped that such standards would broaden the CD-ROM market, increase customer confidence in the technology's viability, and simplify the work of equipment manufacturers, software developers, application designers, and service bureaus.

As discussed by Roth (1986), it initially appeared that one of the proprietary CD-ROM formats discussed above might emerge as a de facto standard. For a time, Digital Equipment Corporation actively promoted its UNI-FILE format as a CD-ROM standard, and it was endorsed by various industry participants, including Xerox, Lotus Development, Tecmar, and the 3M Company. In 1985, however, the focal point of CD-ROM standardization activities shifted to an informal committee of equipment manufacturers, software developers, and information providers known as the High Sierra Group (HSG). Composed of representatives from Apple Computer, Digital Equipment Corporation, Hitachi, IBM, Meridian Data, Microsoft, Philips, Reference Technology, Sony, 3M, TMS, Xebec, and other companies, the High Sierra Group developed a standard logical file format that specified a directory structure and basic layout for information recorded on CD-ROM discs. Described in detail by Einberger and Zoellick (1987), the HSG file format specifications were published in mid-1986 by the National Information Standards Organization as *The Working Paper for Information Processing, Volume and File Structure of Compact Read Only Optical Discs for Information Interchange.*

The HSG file format was specifically designed for high performance in CD-ROM applications involving many large files. It compensated for the slow access times of CD-ROM drives and facilitated product implementation under a variety of operating systems. The HSG file format was immediately but informally adopted by most CD-ROM product developers, although some early CD-ROM information products continued to employ the proprietary file management systems on which their original implementations were based. It became the basis for the American National Standard for CD-ROM Volume and File Structure

(ANSI Z39.60). Its international counterpart, *Information Processing—Volume and File Structure of CD-ROM for Information Interchange* (ISO-9660) was approved in 1988.

The High Sierra Group format was developed as a proposal for an international CD-ROM standard. With the approval of the ISO 9660 standard, its purpose was fulfilled. While some publishers continue to produce CD-ROM discs in the HSG format, new information products increasingly conform to the ISO 9660 standard. As discussed by Kovarick (1989), the ISO 9660 standard incorporates some features —including file interleaving and extended record attributes—that were not supported by the High Sierra Group format, although relatively few CD-ROM information products currently employ such special capabilities. Minor differences between the two formats can pose problems, however, in libraries and other installations where HSG format and ISO 9660 discs may be used interchangeably.

Both HSG and ISO 9660 discs are intended for CD-ROM drives equipped with Microsoft Extensions, the device-driver software described earlier in this report. High Sierra Group discs can be read by CD-ROM drives equipped with any version of Microsoft Extensions; ISO 9660 discs, however, require version 2.0 or higher. Organizations equipped with CD-ROM drives purchased in the 1980s may need to upgrade their versions of Microsoft Extensions in order to utilize ISO 9660 discs.

It is important to note that the High Sierra Group format and the ISO 9660 standard provides rules and mechanisms for naming and finding files. They do not specify file contents which may include character-coded text, digitized document images, compressed speech, or other information. Work continues on related CD-ROM standards which will define application-specific data elements and formats, including publishers information, data preparer information, copyright information, bibliographic data, and abstract file information. In 1991, the Rock Ridge Group—a consortium of sixteen companies involved in CD-ROM production—submitted two preliminary proposals to the National Institute of Standards and Technology for consideration as federal standards for CD-ROM technology. The Rock Ridge Group's proposed System Use Sharing Protocol (SUSP) is an extension to the ISO 9660 standard which allows multiple file system extensions to coexist within a given CD-ROM. It will permit the development of CD-ROM information products which contain multiple applications or a single application intended for different computing platforms. The Rock Ridge Interchange Protocol (RRIP) proposal is designed to facilitate the execution of CD-ROM-based Unix applications by allowing POSIX files and directories to be recorded on CD-ROM discs without modifications to file and directory names.

Retrieval Software. The standardization of physical and logical formats for CD-ROM discs is of critical concern to information providers, software developers, disc producers, and equipment manufacturers. End users, however, interact with CD-ROM information products through retrieval software, the characteristics of which may vary considerably from one product to another. As noted by Goodwin (1989), Heacox (1991), Kahn (1988), and Rosen (1990), this variety forces users to master different retrieval procedures for CD-ROM information products obtained from different sources. This is a particularly troublesome disadvantage in libraries and other public-use installations where diverse CD-ROM products are widely encountered. The standardization of retrieval software, while of potential benefit to users, is unlikely to occur, since the special features of specific programs add value to otherwise similar products and enhance their competitive positions. This is especially the case where popular data bases, such as Medline and ERIC, are offered by multiple CD-ROM publishers.

As used in this context, the phrase "CD-ROM software" denotes the programs which permit retrieval or other manipulation of information recorded on CD-ROM discs. It is important to distinguish CD-ROM software from the information with which the software will operate; the latter may be confusingly described as software, but that usage is incorrect. While a few CD-ROM information products consist of data or text files to be utilized with customer-provided software, most combine retrieval software and information in a single package. The general characteristics of CD-ROM retrieval software are discussed, in varying levels of detail, by Andrews (1990), Beheshti (1991), Cichocki and Ziemer (1988), Helgerson and Martens (1988), Jackson and Kinyon (1989), Nicholls et al (1990), Price (1991), Robinson et al (1990), Schwartz (1989), Tiampo (1988), Van der Walt (1989), and Zink (1991). Product history varies. Some retrieval programs were expressly developed for specific CD-ROM information products. Examples include the retrieval programs furnished with Bibliofile, Le Pac, and the Lotus Development product line; H.W. Wilson's WilsonDisc software; the Silver Platter Information Retrieval System (SIRS); Search CD450 from OCLC; Searcher from Slater Hall Information Products; and Search Master from Matthew Bender. A number of retrieval programs were designed expressly for CD-ROM applications but may be utilized with the information products of different vendors. Examples include the Knowledge Retrieval System (KRS) from KnowledgeSet Corporation, FindIt from Reteaco, the KAWare 2 Retrieval System from Knowledge Access International, COBRA from Bertelsmann Computer Beratungsdienst, the Plus System from Online Computer Systems, CD-Answer from DataWare Technologies, MediaBase from CrowninShield Software, I-Search from I-Mode Retrieval Systems, Knowledge Finder from Aries Systems Corporation, Questar from Publishers Data Service Corporation, and Quantum Leap from Quantum Access.

A small group of CD-ROM retrieval programs, like STA/F TEXT from Reference Technology, Laser Key from LaserData, and Research from TMS, were derived from software developed for digital videodisc applications and subsequently adapted for CD-ROM. Others are based on programs originally developed for magnetic media. As an example, MicroBASIS is the CD-ROM version of a famous data base management and information retrieval program which is available for a variety of minicomputers and mainframes. Similarly, Dialog Information Services and BRS Information Technologies have implemented CD-ROM versions of their online retrieval software. An important category of CD-ROM retrieval programs consists of personal computer software packages which were originally developed for relatively small data bases maintained on magnetic disks. Examples includes ZyIndex from Zylab Corporation, Textware from Unibase Systems, FulText from Fulcrum Technologies, Textbank/PC from Group L Corporation, Search Express from Executive Technologies, Word Cruncher from Electronic Text Corporation, and HyperCard from Claris Corporation.

Regardless of product history, the typical CD-ROM retrieval program is a search-only product which runs on a microcomputer-based workstation equipped with a CD-ROM disc drive. Typical hardware specifications mandate an IBM-compatible device configured with at least 640 kilobytes of random-access memory, a hard disk drive, and a specific version of the MS-DOS operating system. For effective performance, an 80386SX-based or more powerful system is recommended. CD-ROM information products and retrieval software designed for IBM-compatible microcomputers running under the OS/2 operating system have not developed as predicted, principally because of the slow market acceptance of OS/2. As previously noted, a growing number of CD-ROM products are available in Macintosh implementations. Some retrieval programs can also operate on Unix-based systems, on MicroVAX workstations running under VMS, or on other computer platforms.

With their high storage capacities, CD-ROM discs are well suited to records which contain lengthy abstracts or even the entire text of documents. As discussed by King (1991), full-text information products have been among the most popular CD-ROM implementations. Many CD-ROM information products utilize text retrieval software, an interesting goup of programs which permit retrieval by individual words or phrases, regardless of their locations within records. As discussed by Saffady (1989a), text retrieval programs accomplish this through a combination of data and index files. The latter typically employ an inverted structure consisting of alphabetical lists of words with pointers to their locations in associated data files. All words, except those contained in user-specified stoplists, are included. As described by Blumer et al (1987), Jones and Bell (1984), Colvin (1987), Cooper and Tharp (1989), Du et al (1987), and Fand (1987), the considerable storage space required by such inverted indexes often exceeds the available capacities of magnetic disks, but CD-

ROM discs provide ample space for most applications. Where very large data bases are involved, data compression can be applied to files and their associated indexes, but such applications may ultimately require multiple discs. The use of data compression algorithms in CD-ROM applications is discussed by Klein et al (1988) and Beltrami and Kulkarni (1989).

Text retrieval programs are sometimes contrasted with conventional data management software which operates on records that are organized into fields. The distinction is often artificial, since many data management programs can retrieve records containing specified words or phrases in any or all fields. Similarly, some text retrieval programs can operate on structured records and allow users to limit searches to specified fields. As a more meaningful distinction between text retrieval and conventional data management programs, the former typically impose fewer restrictions on record and field lengths. The complete text of a document may simply be treated as a very long data field.

Unlike online systems which often require formal training for effective searching, most CD-ROM retrieval programs are designed for casual users who will receive little or no instruction. As such, they make extensive use of menus, function keys, prompts, and help screens to simplify retrieval operations. Recognizing that elaborate menu systems intended for novice users can prove tedious to experienced searchers, many retrieval programs also provide command-oriented shortcuts for specific operations. Most programs also make use of function keys to minimize typing. Graphical user interfaces which feature pulldown menus, dialog boxes, and multi-window displays are increasingly common and are likely to proliferate as CD-ROM products are developed for the Microsoft Windows environment.

Although CD-ROM technology is new, users have well-defined retrieval expectations that are based on two decades of experience with the online information services with which many CD-ROM products compete. Most CD-ROM retrieval programs consequently provide capabilities similar to those of their online competitors. When known, a specific record can usually be retrieved by an accession number or some other unique identifier, such as a Library of Congress Card Number (LCCN), an International Standard Book Number (ISBN), or a Chemical Abstracts Service (CAS) registry number. More often, however, a user will enter a character string—typically, a word or phrase—to be matched in a specific field or an entire record, although some retrieval programs restrict the fields on which such character string matches can be performed. The most powerful programs support multiple search terms and parenthetical retrieval statements linked by Boolean operators that can broaden or narrow a retrieval specification.

As a distinctive and useful alternative or complement to Boolean operators, many CD-ROM retrieval programs support commands which can locate two or more words in a specified proximity relationship. Depending on the program, such commands may be able to retrieve documents containing two words in the same record, in the same paragraph, in the same field, in the same sentence, or within a specified number of words of one another. Right truncation of search terms may be implicit or activated by a special command. With some programs, the user types the first few characters of a search term to display a specified alphabetical section of an index which can then be browsed to locate the desired term.

Some CD-ROM retrieval programs offer special features which online search services may not routinely support. As an exmple, wild card symbols can be used to match any combination of characters in specified locations within search strings. Depending on the program, data base or textual records identified by an index search may be displayed in their entirety for browsing, printing, or other manipulation. Alternatively, display information may be initially limited to fields, sentences, paragraphs, or other parts of retrieved records that contain specified search terms. Such terms are typically highlighted for display purposes. Some CD-ROM retrieval programs allow words in previously retrieved text segments to be utilized as search terms. The Research program from TMS Incorporated, for example, offers a "sideways browsing" feature in which retrieved records may contain cross references to related items. The operator can view the related items and return to the original record afterwards. The Research program also supports a "sideways search" feature which allows an operator to quickly initiate a search by positioning the cursor on any term in a displayed record. When the search is completed, the operator can return to the original record. SilverPlatter's CD-ROM retrieval software offers similar lateral search capabilities. Several CD-ROM retrieval programs offer an "electronic bookmarking" feature which allows an operator to return to previously marked locations within a data base.

With most CD-ROM retrieval programs, an operator can save search statements on magnetic media for repeated execution. For later editing by a word processing program, retrieved records can usually be transferred to ASCII text files. As discussed by Foulds and Foulds (1990), Jackson (1988), Jacso (1991a), Keen (1990), and Sieverts (1989), downloading capabilities vary from program to program; their suitability for specific information processing applications should consequently be confirmed by a demonstration in advance of purchase. Some CD-ROM retrieval programs can also convert retrieved records to formats required by specific spreadsheet and data management software packages, such as Lotus 1-2-3 or the dBASE product line.

USER EXPERIENCES

As CD-ROM technology becomes increasingly commonplace, prospective purchasers are less concerned about the availability of appropriate products than about the ability of those products to support particular information retrieval requirements in a usable, cost-effective manner. As noted above, most CD-ROM information products are intended for direct searching by end users, as opposed to mediated searches which are performed by a librarian or other trained professional on a user's behalf. Confirming the technology's utility, a growing number of publications report heavy utilization and favorable experiences with CD-ROM information products in library installations. Examples, reflecting a variety of use environments, include Allen (1990), Belanger and Hoffman (1990), Bernal (1991), Browning and Haas (1991), Crawley and Adams (1991), Dalrymple (1990), De Smet (1989), Ensor and Hardin (1991), Erkkila et al (1991), Gilliam and Sluzenski (1990), Goldfinch (1990), Jewell (1989), King et al (1990), Lam and Lam (1990), Neame (1990), Pedemonte et al (1991), Pendlebury and Lewis (1989), Rapp et al (1990), Reifsnyder (1990), Richardson (1991), Schultz and Salomon (1990), and Silver and Dennis (1990).

Brahmi and Tyler (1990) found that the introduction of CD-ROM caused a drastic reduction in mediated online searches at the Indiana University School of Medicine Library. They also reported increased use of CD-ROM by librarians as an alternative to online information services for mediated searches. Bernal and Renner (1990) likewise noted a reduction in mediated searches via online information services following the introduction of CD-ROM but found that the decrease was temporary. They reported, however, that CD-ROM use continued to rise, despite the availability of free mediated searches.

Some studies, however, report difficulties with CD-ROM implementations. Puttapithakporn (1990), for example, identifies problems encountered in searches of a CD-ROM implementation of ERIC by undergraduate students. Tonosaki (1990) reports problems with CD-ROM editions of Medline at the Nippon Medical School Library in Tokyo. A survey by Kaltenborn (1991) found that clinicians and scientists preferred direct searching of Medline on CD-ROM without a librarian's assistance to mediated searches of the Medline data base via online information services. Most users were satisfied with their search results, but analysis revealed that their search strategies were often inadequate and failed to retrieve available citations. The least experienced users were typically the most satisfied. Charles and Clark (1990) describe an online updating system which addresses currency limitations inherent in the CD-ROM edition of the Agricola data base. Bonta (1990), Ensor (1990), Moore (1990) discusses the impact of CD-ROM's availability on other library services, including reference staffing patterns and interlibrary loan activity. Giesbrecht and McCarthy (1991) discuss staff resistance to CD-ROM.

Finding that many users require professional assistance with CD-ROM searching, Yamazaki (1990) recommends that reference librarians shift their focus from mediated online searching to training for effective end-user searching. Bibliographic instruction for CD-ROM searching is discussed by Allen (1990a), Earl and Hamberg (1991), Nash and Wilson (1991), Nickerson (1991), Nipp (1991), and Richwine and Switzer (1990). Sabler (1991) describes a program to train reference librarians to assist users in CD-ROM searching.

The competitive relationship between CD-ROM information products and online information services which provide timeshared access to data bases maintained by minicomputers and mainframes was noted in the preceding section. Widely discussed at professional meetings, the advantages, limitations, and competitive cost/performance characteristics of online information services and CD-ROM systems have been reviewed in various publications, including Cohen and Young (1986), Erkkila (1990, 1991), Halperin and Renfro (1988), Landrum (1989), Litman (1987), Nicholls (1989), Peters (1987), Schnelling (1989), and Van Hartevelt (1989). Leaving the issue of equivalent performance temporarily aside, CD-ROM systems are widely advertised as potentially cost-effective replacements for online information services. Economic comparisons of the two technologies are of obvious and considerable interst to library administrators, information center managers, and others responsible for the procurement of computer-based information services.

The competitive economic relationship between CD-ROM and online information services depends on the volume and characteristics of searches performed in a particular application. Any cost advantage enjoyed by one or the other technology is largely determined by the different role of fixed and variable charges in CD-ROM and online information services. Fixed costs associated with online information services are limited to the procurement of required equipment and communications software, site modifications, searcher training, and search aids, such as thesauri associated with particular data bases. Some online information services also impose sign-up fees and password charges. These fixed costs are usually incurred as initial start-up expenses, although some additional fixed costs—including equipment maintenance, ongoing searcher training, and password renewal charges—will be incurred annually.

Because online information services sell access to individual data bases on an as-needed basis, their most significant costs vary with the nature and duration of individual searches. In most cases, customers must pay connect time, communications, online display, and offline printing charges associated with individual data bases, although no charges are incurred until searches are actually performed. Depending on the service and data base selected, connect time rates range from twenty-five dollars to more than three hundred dollars per hour. Communication charges generally range between eight and fifteen dollars per hour. Typical display and printing charges range from ten cents to several dollars per record, although significantly higher charges may be encountered with certain data bases.

As with online information services, CD-ROM users will incur fixed costs associated with equipment procurement, site preparation, training, the procurement of search aids, and annual maintenance charges. Such costs are typically comparable to their online counterparts. In a marked departure, however, from the variable, usage-based charges associated with online information services, CD-ROM data bases are sold by subscription. The customer pays a fixed annual fee which permits unlimited searching without additional charges for connect time, display, or printing. Given this difference, the potential economic advantage of CD-ROM over online information services is clear: a CD-ROM data base will prove less expensive than its online counterpart when, and if, the total variable charges for searching a given data base in a particular year exceed the annual cost of a CD-ROM subscription to that data base. From the cost standpoint, CD-ROM is best suited to data bases which are searched frequently; online information services remain the preferred approach for data bases which are searched occasionally. The break-even point for justification of a CD-ROM subscription varies with search characterstics and can only be determined in the context of specific applications. For some data bases, CD-ROM can prove less expensive than online information services for data bases that are searched just three or four times per month.

Such cost comparisons necessarily ignore non-economic factors which can limit CD-ROM's utility as an alternative to online information services in certain situations. As a potentially significant constraint, the number of CD-ROM information products—while increasing steadily—remains smaller than the number of data bases available through online information services. As a further limitation, many CD-ROM data bases are updated by replacement at specified intervals, usually quarterly but occasionally semiannually or annually. In most cases, however, data base creators issue new records at monthly or more frequent intervals, and online information services may add such new records to their data bases soon after receipt. Delays inherent in CD-ROM production typically prohibit such frequent updating. Since many tasks require information that is as current as possible, CD-ROM systems cannot entirely replace online services, even where cost comparisons indicate that CD-ROM subscriptions are more economical. On the other hand, many CD-ROM data bases contain less backfile information than their online counterparts. Consequently, they are poorly suited to applications requiring exhaustive retrospective searches.

While CD-ROM can offer economic advantages over online information services for long searches which retrieve large numbers of records for online display or printing, several reports suggest that CD-ROM searches can take longer to complete than their online counterparts. Based on experience with OCLC's CD-ROM implementation of the ERIC data base, for example, Reese (1987, 1987a) indicates that searches involving broad subject terms can prove especially time consuming. Following an experimental comparison of search speed for typical retrieval operations, Crane (1987) concludes that Dialog's OnDisc edition of the ERIC data base offers faster execution than the SilverPlatter version, but both CD-ROM implementations are significantly slower than online Dialog searching during off-peak hours. In a comparison of WLN's LaserCat CD-ROM system with timeshared searching of the online WLN data base, Force (1987) found the online service to be significantly faster for exact author/title and ISBN searches. Analyzing a survey of user reactions to CD-ROM information products, Perry (1990) reported slow response time as the most frequently cited complaint. As an additional complication, the time-consuming local printing of large numbers of retrieved citations can monopolize CD-ROM workstations, necessitating additional equipment and subscriptions which can significantly increase CD-ROM costs. Online information services address this problem by permitting offline printing of citations, although that approach is unacceptable in applications where retrieval results are needed immediately. To minimze this problem, some libraries limit CD-ROM users to a specified amount of search time and/or printing activity.

MULTIMEDIA TECHNOLOGIES

As described in preceding sections, the most numerous group of CD-ROM products consists of computer-processible data bases which contain character-coded text and/or quantitative values—the historical mainstays of computer-based information systems. As general-purpose computer storage media, however, CD-ROM discs can contain any information which can be represented in computer-processible form. Reflecting the increasingly diverse scope of computer applications, a growing number of CD-ROM discs incorporate digitized visual images, either alone or as supplements to textual or quantitative data bases.

The large amounts of space required for image storage can overwhelm some magnetic media, even when compression methodologies are employed; with their high capacities, however, CD-ROM discs can accommodate such requirements. The images, which may be monochrome or color, are displayed at workstations equipped with appropriate graphic capabilities. Most image-oriented CD-ROM information products are intended for use with a Macintosh system or with an IBM-compatible microcomputer configured with a VGA adapter and monitor, although higher-resolution display devices are sometimes required.

Davies and Clark (1990) review CD-ROM's potential in image-based applications. Clip art discs designed for desktop publishing and CD-ROM-based map collections are obvious examples of image-oriented products. Others include the Urban Phytonarian Handbook which, as described by Cheney (1990), features color images of plants; the National Portrait Gallery CD-ROM, from Abt Books Incorporated, which contains images of

3,093 portraits of notable Americans from the Smithsonian Institution's National Portrait Gallery, accompanied by descriptive information in textual form; and Coate's Art Review: Impressionism, the first in a series of art-oriented discs to be published by Quanta Press. Perhaps the most widely publicized example of image-oriented CD-ROM technology is Eastman Kodak's Photo CD system which has attracted considerable attention among amateur and professional photographers. Developed jointly with Philips, it will utilize compact discs to store photographic images converted by designated service bureaus from user-supplied thirty-five-millimeter films. As discussed by Stepnes (1991) and Urrows and Urrows (1991a), a single CD-ROM disc will store up to 100 images in a compressed format. Recordable write-once media will be utilized, thereby allowing new images to be added to a previously created CD-ROM. Commercial availability is scheduled for 1992.

As discussed by Befeler (1988), CD-ROM can be also be used as a publishing medium for digitized document images, thereby offering an alternative to microform publications. As is the case with systems which employ write-once or rewritable optical media for document storage, the digitized images are typically generated by document scanners. With 540 megabytes of capacity, a single CD-ROM can store the equivalent of at least 11,000 letter-size pages scanned at 200 pixels per inch and recorded with an average compression ratio of ten to one. Actual media capacities are affected by various factors, including page sizes, scanning resolutions, compression algorithms, and page layouts. Carpenter and Mitz (1989) and Fody (1990) describe the LaserDisclosure system which uses CD-ROM to distribute image of documents submitted to the Securities and Exchange Commission by public companies. University Microfilms International has similarly demonstrated a CD-ROM system which stores images of journal articles and other documents indexed in various data bases. A prototype implementation, installed in 1991, employed networked workstations linked to a CD-ROM jukebox. Because CD-ROM discs are created by a mastering process, the technology is principally suited to applications where multiple copies of a document image data base are desired and immediate turnaround time is not required. It has been suggested that recordable CD-ROM systems can be used for document image storage where a single copy and immediate availability are required, but such applications have not been reported.

Multimedia CD-ROM. As noted earlier in this report, many CD-ROM drives incorporate audio adapters and headphone jacks as standard or optional components. CD-ROM was, of course, derived from a technology that was originally developed for audio recording, and such accessories are designed for information management applications that combine data, text, and/or images with digitized audio signals. Such applications are collectively described as "multimedia" or "mixed mode" CD-ROMs. They are one facet of the widely publicized but vaguely defined field of multimedia computing which combines data, text, visual, and audio components to broaden the scope of computer technology and create innovative information presentations which are not possible with conventional data processing methodologies. CD-ROM and multimedia technologies are closely associated; with their high capacities, CD-ROM discs are viewed as an attractive medium for the publication and distribution of voluminous multimedia information products.

The characteristics of multimedia CD-ROM are discussed by Apperson and Doherty (1987), Bonomi (1991), Desmarais (1990), Fox (1989), Gale (1990), Garofolo and Pallett (1989), Mathisen (1991), Menasce and Ierusalimschy (1988), Schipma (1989), Traub (1989), Williams (1989), and Yu et al (1989). Like the image-oriented CD-ROM products described above, multimedia CD-ROMs require a computer system with graphic display capabilities. In the North American market, most multimedia CD-ROM applications are intended for Macintosh installations or IBM-compatible microcomputers equipped with VGA display components. The Commodore Dynamic Total Vision (CDTV) product line, announced in 1990, offers attractive multimedia capabilities but has been slow to develop. Primarily intended for consumer installations, it combines CD-ROM technology with Commodore's Amiga line of microcomputers. Accessories include a joystick, a trackball, memory cards, a modem, and MIDI input/output capabilities for muscial devices. While approximately three dozen CDTV-compatible multimedia information products have been developed, marketing has been limited to selected U.S. cities.

In Japan, where multimedia computer products predate their North American counterparts, Fujitsu's FM TOWNS is a microcomputer-based system which supports a variety of multimedia CD-ROMs. Introduced in 1989, it is described by Fukuda et al (1990), Munakata and Urano (1989), Nakamura (1989), Nishiuchi et al (1990), Okuno and Ohtsuka (1989), Tamai et al (1990), and Ueda (1990). Available information products emphasize recreational and educational programming and data bases for consumer rather than business applications. Examples include the Oshare Cooking disc, a collection of recipes from Misawa Home Research Laboratory; the Super Odyssey collection of entertainment software from Wavetrain; the Invitation adventure game from Datawest; the Airwave Adventure disc, a mystery/adventure game from Tiger Media; and the ENKAIOH disc from Dennoh Shokai which contains speeches, songs, and sound effects for parties. Nakamura (1989) describes the use of FM TOWNS in a multimedia presentation support system developed by Suntory Limited for installation in liquor stores.

While currently less numerous than conventional CD-ROM information products, multimedia discs have attracted considerable attention as a vehicle for broadening the scope and appeal of CD-ROM applications. Several CD-ROM editions of reference books, for example, use digitized images and/or audio to augment textual information. One of the earliest examples, the Visual Dictionary developed jointly by Facts on File and Editions Quebec/ Amerique Incorporated, is designed for language instruction. It uses a CD-ROM disc to store digitized images of objects accompanied by text and audio in multiple languages. The CD-ROM edition of Webster's Ninth New Collegiate Dictionary, produced for Macintosh computers by Highlighted Data, uses digitized audio for pronunciation. Compton's Multimedia Encyclopedia, a CD-ROM publication co-developed by Encyclopedia Brittanica and Josten's Learning Corporation, includes sixty minutes of audio recording for speeches and music associated with specific entries. It is described by Steffey (1991) and Urrows and Urrows (1991). As discussed by Flanders (1991), the latest edition of the New Grolier Electronic Encyclopedia similarly incorporates audio capabilities, as well as full-color maps and other visual images. The Guiness Disc of Records likewise features visual images as well as audio for music and sound affects.

The Multi-Media Birds of America and Multi-Media Audubon's Mammals discs from CMC ReSearch Incorporated contain the full texts of works by John James Audubon enhanced by full-color images and audio recordings of animal and avian vocalizations. Similar material is provided in Mammals: a Multimedia Encyclopedia, a CD-ROM published by the National Geographic Society. Among the most innovative and comprehensive demonstrations of the potential of multimedia CD-ROM products, the Voyager Company's CD Companion Series combines CD-DA recordings of important musical compositions with supporting textual and graphic information recorded on CD-ROM discs. As discussed by Holzberg (1990), the supporting materials provide biographical information about the composer and interprets the composition from musical, historical, and sociological perspectives. As an example of a multimedia CD-ROM application with potentially broad appeal, Layton (1991) describes a CD-RM school yearbook which combines text, audio, and visual images. Among multimedia projects undertaken by government agencies, Fleischhauer (1990) describes the American Memory Project, which uses CD-ROM as the publishing medium for textual materials, photographs, and sound recordings pertaining to American history and culture from the collections of the Library of Congress. Mason (1991) discusses the development of a multimedia CD-ROM on ornamental horticulture at the National Agricultural Library. Spitz (1991) describes the use of multimedia CD-ROM in a computer-based training system developed by Hewlett-Packard.

While multimedia CD-ROM information products offer unquestionably attractive capabilities, their widespread acceptance has been impeded by several factors, including the absence of standards for CD-ROMs which combine data, text, images, and audio; relatively complicated production procedures and resulting higher costs when compared to conventional CD-ROM information products; and the still small installed base of CD-ROM workstations which can accommodate multimedia discs. The CD-ROM Extended Architecture (CD-ROM XA) format—announced in late 1988 by Philips, Sony, and Microsoft—addresses the first of these limitations. Designed as a standard format for information processing applications requiring multimedia capabilities, CD-ROM XA combines character-coded data and text with graphics and audio information. Designed for VGA-format video displays, CD-ROM XA records images at a resolution of 640 by 480 pixels with eight-bit color capability. Adaptive Differential Pulse Code Modulation (ADPCM) is used to encode up to four hours of FM stereo audio information, up to eight hours of AM steoreo audio information, up to eight hours of FM monoraul audio information, or up to sixteen hours of AM monoraul audio information in a compressed format interleaved with data, text, and graphics. In contrast, digitized audio signals stored on conventional CD-ROM discs are separated from other information, thus posing significant synchronization problems.

The CD-ROM XA format employs volume and file structures specified in the ISO 9660 standard discussed above. Ghislandi and Campana (1989) provide an overview of CD-ROM XA technology. Demonstration discs are described by Saito and Nomura (1989) and Hattori (1990). CD-ROM XA products have been announced by various companies since the late 1980s. Sony, for example, has introduced several CD-ROM XA hardware components and developers' kits, including a drive, an interface card, an audio encoder card, and a mastering card. CD-ROM XA drives have also been announced by Hitachi. As discussed by Nairn (1991), the proposed Disk Description Protocol (DDP) is designed to simplify the production of multimedia CD-ROMs. It establishes standards for the submission of multimedia information to CD-ROM mastering facilities. In the absence of such standards, individual mastering facilities have established proprietary guidelines for the submission of multimedia information, a situation which promotes confusion and production errors.

As previously noted, newer CD-ROM drives are typically equipped with audio capabilities which support multimedia information products. Various companies have announced microcomputer workstations designed specifically for CD-ROM-based multimedia applications. the Multimedia Personal Computer (MPC) specification, announced by the Interactive Multimedia Association (IMA) in 1991, establishes minimum hardware and system software requirements for multimedia applications. It specifies IBM-compatible microcomputers equipped with 80286 or more powerful microprocessors, CD-ROM XA-compatible drives, VGA display displays, and the Microsoft Windows graphical operating environment with multimedia extensions. A number of computer manufacturers—including AT&T Computer Systems, CompuAdd Corporation, Fujitsu, NEC, Olivetti, Philips, Tandy, and Zenith Data Systems—have announced plans to produce MPC-compatible systems as well as MPC upgrade kits. Such products wil be identified by the MPC trademark to ensure compatibility with multimedia information products which bear the same logo. Although it does not bear the MPC trademark, the IBM PS/2 Ultimedia product line—which was introduced in late 1991—likewise combines IBM-compatible microcomputers with a CD-ROM XA drive and other components suitable for multimedia applications. Philips and Nintendo have announced plans to develop a modified implementation of the CD-ROM XA format for use with the Super Nintendo Entertainment System. Sega and JVC have similarly announced plans to develop multimedia CD-ROM capabilities for Sega's Genesis game system.

CD-I. Some industry analysts view the CD-ROM XA format as a bridge between CD-ROM technology and the widely publicized Compact Disc-Interactive (CD-I) format. CD-I is a self-contained, interactive, multimedia compact disc format for computer-processable data, character-coded text, audio signals, and images, including computer-generated graphics, still-frame video, and full-motion video. Designed primarily for consumer and educational markets rather than business applications, CD-I has been depicted as both a logical evolution of the CD-ROM format and a multimedia extension of CD-DA technology. Enthusiastic industry analysts depict it as a "hypermedium", the "ultimate" CD format, and the focal point for future developments in compact disc technology. CD-I technology, applications, and market potential have been the topic of considerable discussion at professional and trade meetings and educational seminars as well as in a various publications, many of which date from the 1980s when CD-I was still in the planning stages. Examples include Bardes (1986), Bonime (1991), Brandt (1991), Bruno (1987), Bruno and Mizushima (1986), Chen (1991), DeBloois (1987), Edmead (1987), Frenkel (1989), Gall (1987), Herther (1988), Isbouts (1987), Ismael (1989), Lloyd (1990), Lowe (1986), Megarry (1989), Miller and Miller (1991), Minar (1988), Moes (1986), Pelz (1991), Robinson (1990), Ruppert and Gilbertson (1988), Sharpless (1987), Sijstermans and Van der Meer (1991), Tomisawa et al (1991), Valk (1987), and Van Luyt and Zegers (1989, 1990).

As defined by Sony and Philips, CD-I is a specific application of CD-ROM technology with a rigidly defined implementation similar to CD-DA systems. CD-I specifications, as outlined in the "Green Book" published by Sony and Philips in 1987, are based on the CD-ROM physical format. Like their data-oriented counterparts, CD-I discs are divided into tracks which are subdivided into sectors with 2,352 bytes of storage capacity each. As with CD-ROM, the amount of sector capacity available for user information depends on the recording mode. For the audio and video information which will dominate many CD-I applications, Mode Two recording provides 2,336 bytes of user information per sector, with the remaining bytes being utilized for control inforamtion and error correction coding. The basic compact disc error correction codes utilized by CD-DA systems should prove adequate for audio and video information which degrades "gracefully" and can be corrected by interpolation techniques. CD-I specifications also support Mode One recording which provides additional error detection and correction codes but limits user information to 2,048 bytes per sector. Mode One is the standard recording mode for CD-ROM discs, and it is appropriate for CD-I sectors which contain computer-processible data or text.

With respect to logical layout, Green Book specifications reserve the first track of each CD-I disc for a descriptor record and optional boot information. The descriptor record includes product identification information, a copyright statement, the disc's root directory, and local character-set identifiers. If a CD-I disc contains CD-DA tracks, they must be located after the first CD-I track. To address a broad range of application requirements while making the most efficient use of available disc space, CD-I specifications recognize four levels of audio quality:

1. The Super HiFi music level uses the same sixteen-bit pulse code modulation (PCM) techniques employed by CD-DA discs. It provides one channel of stereo recording, where a channel is the equivalent of seventy-two minutes of continuous playing time. As its name implies, the Super HiFi level provides audio quality equivalent to CD-DA discs, but the resulting signal occupies all or most of the available CD-I disc space.

2. The HiFi music level uses eight-bit adaptive dynamic pulse code modulation (ADPCM) techniques to provide two stereo channels or four monoraul channels. In the stereo mode, audio quality is comparable to the best long-playing phonograph records. When the HiFi music level is used, audio signals occupy about fifty percent of available disc space, leaving the remainder free for visual information and data.

3. The MidFi music level uses four-bit ADPCM techniques to provide four stereo channels or eight monoraul channels with quality that is comparable to FM radio broadcasts. When Mid-Fi recording is used, audio signals occupy about twenty-five percent of available disc space.

4. The Speech level uses four-bit ADPCM techniques with a fifty percent reduction in the sampling rate to provide eight stereo channels and sixteen monoraul channels. These channels can be used for audio information of different content or in different languages. Speech level quality is comparable to that of AM radio broadcasts, and the resulting audio signals occupy as little as six percent of available disc space. In a related development, Sanyo has announced a Background Music (BGM) system which can record eight hours of monoraul audio on a CD-I disc.

The ability to store video information distinguishes CD-I from the CD-DA and CD-ROM formats. CD-I discs can contain video images and graphics. Primarily designed as an affordable product for consumer markets, CD-I's video recording specifications are compatible with American and European television standards. The normal video resolution is 360 by 240 pixels when used with NTSC television systems and 384 by 280 pixels when used with PAL television systems. In the manner of some home computer systems, textual information, which can be represented by either bit-mapping or character-coding techniques, is displayed in a twenty-line by forty-character screen format. Designed for use with color video monitors and digital color television receivers, a double resolution mode supports 720 by 240 pixels when used with NTSC television systems and 768 by 280 pixels when used with PAL television systems. It can display textual information in the eighty-character lines familiar to business computer users. A high resolution mode provides 720 by 480 pixels in NTSC television installations and 768 by 560 pixels in PAL television installations. To ensure compatibility with inexpensive CD-I players and video display devices, high resolution images must also contain normal resolution images.

In the graphics mode, CD-I technology uses absolute RGB coding and stores full color, uncompressed images which can be manipulated by users when appropriate software is available. The animated mode supports full-motion graphics, using a color lookup table and image compression. The still video mode likewise uses image compression to conserve storage space, improve loading time, reduce memory requirements, and attain updating speeds appropriate to interactive applications. Full-motion video images can be displayed at approximately one-tenth of full-screen size with ten frame changes per second. In 1991, Philips announced a planned extension to CD-I specifications to accommodate full-screen, full-motion video images based on image compression methodologies developed by the Motion Picture Experts Group (MPEG). Philips expects full-motion video capabilities to be incorporated into CD-I players and software in late 1992 or early 1993.

Unlike a CD-ROM drive which is a storage peripheral designed for attachment to a customer-supplied computer, a CD-I player is a computer-based device equipped with a microprocessor, internal memory, and a compact disc drive that is compatible with both CD-I and CD-DA media. Its operating system, called CD-RTOS (Compact Disc-Real Time Operating System), is based on Microware's OS-9 operating system enhanced by a file manager designed specifically for CD-I media. Additional computer components are not required; the purchaser attaches the CD-I player to a television set and stereo system. Possible peripherals include a floppy disk drive, keyboard, printer, modem, MIDI audio interface, and SCSI interface.

Compatibility with CD-DA media allows CD-I systems to be marketed as upscale compact disc players. Conventional CD-DA devices can play the audio portions of CD-I discs. Philips has also indicated that CD-I systems will be compatible with the Photo CD discs mentioned above. While CD-I players can technically be connected to external computers for data-oriented applications, CD-ROM is the preferred compact disc technology for such situations. CD-I systems are compatible with CD-ROM discs recorded in Mode Two, but CD-ROM drives cannot read CD-I discs. Some CD-ROM publishers and software developers, viewing CD-I as a potential competitor in multimedia applications, criticize its dependence on a specific computer configuration, noting that CD-I is vulnerable to obsolescence resulting from inevitable hardware advances. CD-I proponents, however, insist that CD-ROM technology is the foundation for, rather than a competitor of, the new format. They emphasize CD-I's potential in consumer and educational markets which CD-ROM, as a more expensive and complex computer peripheral technology, cannot cost-effectively address. At the other extreme, CD-I must compete with video game systems, which—as previously noted—increasingly incorporate CD-ROM components. Effective product positioning is critical to CD-I's success, and some prospective purchasers will doubtless be confused by the rapid emergence of similar multimedia technologies.

CD-I equipment and information products, which have been expected every year since 1987, became commercially available in late 1991 when

Philips introduced a CD-I player and more than thirty software titles, including children's programs, an interactive golf game, and a tour of the Smithsonian museums. It is expected that many companies will obtain licenses to manufacture and market CD-I players, and that innovative equipment configurations will be developed. Pioneer, for example, has demonstrated a multi-format device which can accept CD-DA discs, CD-I discs, and analog videodiscs. Sony has announced a portable CD-I player for availability in 1992. Additional software titles from a variety of sources are expected to emphasize the so-called "edutainment" market for leisure time and self-improvement products. Examples of anticipated CD-I information products—some of which will be adapted from other media, such as multimedia CD-ROM and videodiscs—include talking books, reference books, and encyclopedic collections of art and music which take advantage of the technology's audio and visual capabilities; how-to manuals and similar task-specific training materials; interactive fiction and viewer-guided films; action and strategy games; interactive travel discs and other activity simulations; and automobile navigation aids. American Interactive Media (AIM) and European Interactive Media (EIM) were formed in 1986 to promote the development of CD-I products. They have announced joint software development agreements with various publishers and other organizations, including Grolier, Harcourt Brace Jovanovich, Rand McNally, WNET-TV, and Time-Life Incorporated. Microware, mentioned above as the original developer of the operating system employed by CD-I players, has formed a publishing group to promote the joint development of CD-I products with companies owning the rights to previously published books or other intellectual properties. With partial funding from Microware, MicroMall Incorporated is developing point-of-sale information kiosks based on CD-I technology, an application that has historically relied on the videodisc systems described below. Japan Interactive Media (JIM) was formed in 1988 to develop CD-I products for Japanese consumer and educational markets. PolyGram has announced a line of "CD-I Ready" discs which contain up to one hour of recorded music plus interactive audio and video materials, including interviews, song lyrics, and album liner notes. The musical selections are compatible with conventional CD-DA players, but the supplemental interactive materials are only accessible through CD-I devices.

DVI. Digital Video Interactive (DVI) is a multimedia technology which uses proprietary data compression algorithms to store one hour of full-motion digitally-encoded video images on a 4.75-inch optical disc. Taking a digital video image which normally requires 600 kilobytes of storage space, DVI compresses both resolution and color depth, reducing the storage requirement to approximately five kilobytes per image and permitting full-motion video applications which are not possible with conventional compact disc technologies. DVI can combine full-motion video images with foreground video objects, text, graphics, and stereo audio signals. DVI implementations are based on customized video, audio, and computer components designed for installation in an IBM-compatible microcomputer equipped with a color monitor and a CD-ROM disc drive. The technology is described by Alesandrini (1989), Berthreaux (1991), Bunzel and Morris (1992), Dixon (1987, 1989), Glass (1989), Hurst (1988), Hurst and Luther (1988, 1991), Kaiman (1988), Korenjak (1987), Loveria and Kinstler (1990), Luther (1987), Luther and Chaney (1987), Morris (1987, 1987a, 1988, 1988a, 1991), Priestley (1991), Ripley (1988, 1989), Tinker (1989), and Zimmerman (1988).

The DVI format was developed in the 1980s at RCA Corporation's David Sarnoff Research Center. General Electric, which acquired RCA, sold DVI technology to Intel Corporation which has been completing development of initial DVI products and promoting application development by strategic business partners. Microsoft, IBM, Lotus Development, and other companies have announced plans to utilize DVI in multimedia computing applications. DVI components and prototype applications have been demonstrated at various professional meetings and on other occasions since 1987. A variety of DVI adapter boards, software, and developers' kits are currently available. Among published reports of DVI implementations, Carey et al (1991) discuss an engineering-oriented expert system for lithography troubleshooting developed by Intel. Silber (1989) describes a DVI-based truck driver safety training program developed by Applied Optical Media Corportion for Du Pont Safety Services. Wilson (1988) describes a prototype DVI application developed by the Bank Street College for children and their families.

Videodiscs. The availability of multimedia CD-ROM systems and the development of CD-I and DVI technologies raises questions about the present status and future viability of read-only optical videodiscs, the historically dominant technology for interactive multimedia applications involving full motion video images. Introduced in 1978, the read-only optical videodisc—variously called a laser disc, a laser videodisc, a Laservision disc, or, simply, an LV disc—was the first commercially available type of optical disc. It is a platter-shaped storage medium designed specifically for analog video images and accompanying analog stereo audio signals. Read-only optical videodiscs feature a thin reflective metal layer and protective coating which rests on a polymethyl methacrylate (PMMA) substrate. Recorded information is represented by microscopic pits of varying sizes and spacings. Read-only optical videodiscs are typically dual-sided media constructed, in effect, of two platters bonded together. They should not be confused with the Capacitance Electronic Disk (CED) videodisc system, which—as discussed by Graham (1986)—was introduced in the 1980s by RCA and subsequently removed from the market, or with the Video High Density (VHD) videodisc system, which is available in Japan but was never marketed in the United States. As non-optical products, CED and VHD videodiscs are outside the scope of this discusson.

Produced by mastering techniques, read-only optical videodiscs enjoy the often-cited advantages of high storage capacity, rapid image retrieval, durability, attractive workstation components, and low unit cost in applications where mastering charges and related preparation costs can be spread over multiple disc copies. A twelve-inch videodisc—the original and still most widely encountered size —can store 54,000 still video images or sixty minutes of continuous, full-motion video accompanied by stereo audio signals on each of two sides. An eight-inch optical videodisc, introduced by Pioneer in 1985, can store 24,000 still video images or 13.5 minutes of continuous full-motion video plus stereo audio signals per side. The technology is surveyed by Clemens (1982), Isailovic (1985), Kloosterboer and Lippits (1986), Lippits and Melis (1986), Marsh (1982), Roth and Galloway (1983), Troeltzsch (1983, 1984), and Van Rijsewijk et al (1982), among others.

Read-only optical videodiscs are read by relatively inexpensive players sold by Pioneer, Philips, Sony, Hitachi, and other companies. Deisgned for industrial and institutional applications, the most versatile models can retrieve and display specified video frames in as little as three seconds. Designed to operate under computer control, such devices support still-frame displays with sound, variable playback speeds, and instant track jumping for seamless branching between images. Integral character generators can overlay video signals with one or more lines of text in various fonts, sizes, and colors. The newest models can read information from both sides of a mounted disc; with older players a previously mounted had to be manually removed and turned over to access the reverse side. For computer-assisted instruction and other training applications, several companies offer special videodisc workstations which combine a microcomputer, videodisc player, and graphics overlay system in a single chassis, thereby eliminating integration problems and simplifying implementation.

Originally developed and promoted as an economical, high-performance alternative to video tape for feature films and other entertainment programming, read-only optical videodisc systems could not compete with video cassette recorders in the North American consumer market for which they were originally intended, although they have proven successful in the Japanese consumer market. In the United States and elsewhere, videodiscs have been ingeniously and successfully utilized in a variety of business, government, and educational installations. They are currently the information storage media of choice for interactive training applications involving full-motion video images. Miller (1986) provides an informative overview of interactive videodisc installations. Specific training applications and experiences are described in various journal articles and conference papers, many of which date from the mid-to-late 1980s. Examples include Burwell (1991), Carlson and Falk (1991), Carnine et al (1987), El-Bibany and Paulson (1991), Fraser et al (1991), Gartshore et al (1991), Gerstein and Sasnett (1987), Gist et al (1989), Hammack et al (1985), Haukom and Malone (1986), Helsel (1987, 1988), Henderson and Landesman (1989), Holder and Daynes (1986), Hon (1986), Hughes (1989), Kearsley and Frost (1985), Kelly et al (1986), Leonard (1989), McWhinnie (1992), Rees (1986), Ross (1991), Rubin et al (1991), Schitai (1989), Schroeder (1984), Singarella et al (1991), Stroot et al (1991), and Thorkildsen et al (1986). Videodiscs have also been utilized widely and successfully in point of purchase applications and information kiosks.

Because they contain analog video images which conform to prevailing broadcast television standards, read-only optical videodiscs do not provide sufficient resolution for consistently legible reproduction of the textual information contained in most typewritten or printed documents. With the NTSC broadcast standards used in North America, for example, each video image is composed of just 525 scan lines. By way of contrast, electronic document imaging systems which utilize read/write optical disks as storage media routinely provide 2,000 scan lines per page, and some devices record twice that number. Since the late 1980s, various Japanese companies have demonstrated videodisc systems based on high definition television (HDTV) technology. Examples are described by Hibino et al (1990), Hioki et al (1988), Horstman (1988), Itoga (1987), Mano et al (1988), Ohno and Sugiura (1986), Saeki et al (1990), Shimada and Kato (1985), Tachibana and Takahashi (1990), Tachibana et al (1989), Terasaki et al (1991), Toyama et al (1987), and Tsuchiya et al (1991). While such devices can conceivably be in such as information applications as electronic document imaging and high-resolution computer graphics, their utility for such purposes has not been established, and—in any case—they are not generally available.

While they are poorly suited to the recording of textual documents, the current resolution capabilities of conventional read-only optical videodiscs are appropriate for the storage and publication of visual data bases—an application that is of considerable interest to records managers, museum curators, librarians, and othrs responsible for photographic archives and other large collections of pictorial materials. Well publicized examples of applications which use videodisc systems to store pictorial documents include the Videodisc Catalogue produced by the National Gallery of Art and the videodisc edition of photographs from the collections of the National Air and Space Museum. Chen (1985), who organized a project to store Chinese visual materials on optical videodiscs, discusses the medium's potential for the storage of visual documents in microcomputer-based equipment configurations. Parker (1985) discusses the use of videodiscs in the Non-Print Pilot Project at the Library of Congress, while Kamisher (1986) describes a videodisc application involving 30,000 images of Islamic architecture. Lamielle and De Heaulme (1986) describe the use of videodiscs as an alternative to 35mm photographic slides, transparencies, and other media in biomedical applications, a traditional videodisc stronghold. Binder (1988) surveys videodisc applications in museums. Since the mid-1980s, various companies have introduced microcomputer software to index, retrieve, and otherwise manage still images stored on read-only optical videodiscs. Such visual data base applications are increasingly being addressed, as discussed above, by multimedia CD-ROM and CD-I systems.

Even if conventional video recording standards are eventually replaced by high-definition formats suitable for the legible representation of textual documents, information storage applications of read-only optical videodiscs will still be limited by their use of analog recording techniques in which the characteristics of individual picture elements are represented by variations in the size and spacing of microscopic pits. While analog recording is adequate for video images, it is inappropriate for the character-coded data and text generated by computers and word processors. Such information requires digital recording capabilities, but—because manufacturing processes introduce irregularities and imperfections into their recording surfaces—conventional optical videodiscs are poorly suited to reliable data storage. In conventional video recording, where entire scan lines may be omitted from an analog image, videodisc players can compensate by substituting adjacent lines. With computer-processible data and text, however, the slightest defect in a recording surface can alter the meaning of individual characters or numbers, thereby rendering text files and data bases unusable.

Addressing this problem, such companies as LaserData, Reference Technology, and TMS Incorporated have developed special premastering products and services which convert customer-supplied digital information—consisting of character-coded text, files of quantitative data, or digitized document images—to a form suitable for reliable recording on optical videodiscs within the constraints of prevailing recording standards and media manufacturing processes. Proprietary error-correction codes are applied to counteract disc defects. The resulting media, which are described as digital optical videodiscs to distinguish them from their more common analog counterparts, offer impressive data storage capacities. With twelve-inch videodiscs, for example, usable recording capacities range from 800 megabytes to one gigabyte per side after error correction codes are applied. The recorded data is read by a special converter unit attached to a conventional videodisc player in a microcomputer-based workstation. Multi-player controllers can support online access to very large amounts of data.

Digital optical videodiscs are principally intended for data base publishing, an application for which CD-ROM is now the optical medium of choice. When digital optical videodiscs were introduced in the early 1980s, however, CD-ROM was unavailable, and various impressive applications—involving large data bases —were implemented. Examples included the Infomark Laser PC System developed by National Decision Systems for demographic analysis and similar applications; the Info Trac data base, the digital videodisc implementation of the magazine Index and related data bases produced by the Information Access Company; and the National Agricultural Library's videodisc edition of the Pork Industry Handbook. An interesting variant of the digital videodisc, intended for multimedia applications, combines computer-generated data with video images and accompanying audio signals. The LV-ROM format—which was used in the Domesday Book Project implemented by Philips for the British Broadcasting Company and United Kingdom Department of Trade and Industry—can store 54,000 analog video images, each accompanied by up to six kilobytes of digital data. The total data storage capacity is 324 megabytes. Designed as an educational resource, a reference tool, and a political, economic, social, and cultural archive of the British Isles in the late twentieth century, the Domesday Book Project is described by Armstrong (1987), Atkins (1985), Bales (1987), Blizzard (1989), Dewe (1987), Forer (1987), Geensen (1986), Gove (1988), Grimshaw and Williams (1987), Holmes (1988), Kelly et al (1986), Lee (1987), Maguire (1989), Slater (1988), Tapper (1986, 1987), Tibbetts (1987, 1988), Turley (1989), and Van Kervel (1988). The Domesday discs' analog video images store photographs, maps, and full-motion video segments. Digital data is used for textual and statistical information. The Domesday Project workstation includes a microcomputer, a color monitor, a trackball, and a specially designed videodisc player. At retrieval time, the videodisc player extracts digital data from the recorded signals and sends it to the microcomputer which either overlays it on its associated video image or displays it on a separate monitor. In addition to the original Domexday discs, Philips has used LV-ROM technology in the ECODISC, which supports environmental studies through the use of still photographs, film sequences, graphics, and data.

Similar multimedia capabilities are offered by the LD-ROM format. Announced by Pioneer in the late 1980s, LD-ROM components became commercially available in 1991. As with LV-ROM media, LD-ROM discs combine computer-generated digital data with analog video images and audio signals. The video and audio components are compatible with the Laservision format employed by conventional analog videodiscs; the computer-generated data conforms to the ISO 9660 standard for CD-ROM, a feature which can facilitate the addition of full-motion video images to existing CD-ROM information products. An LD-ROM disc's capacity totals 54,000 video images, 2.5 hours of analog audio, and 270 megabytes of computer-generated digital data. Each video image can be accompanied by up to five kilobytes of computer-generated data. In addition to data, the digital signal can record audio information in the compact disc format. The digitally recorded information is decoded by a LD-ROM adapter which installs between a host computer and a videodisc player. With the adapter in place, the computer views the LD-ROM player as a CD-ROM drive. Device drivers are available for IBM-compatible microcomputers and Macintosh systems.

Part Three:
Optical Cards and Optical Tape

OPTICAL CARDS

While optical disks have attracted the majority of attention from information specialists interested in high-capacity storage technologies, they are just one—though, admittedly, the most important and fully developed—member of a product group that also includes optical cards and optical tape. As their name suggests, optical cards—sometimes termed optical memory cards or optical digital data cards—are wallet-size media coated with optical recording materials. Their general characteristics are described by Cory (1990), Hosaka (1988), Lunin (1988), and Urrows and Urrows (1989). Compared to most optical disks, optical cards are smaller and perhaps better suited to portable computer configurations; currently available products offer much less storage capacity than optical disks, however, and their portability advantage is challenged by the recent introduction of 3.5-inch magneto-optical disk cartridges. As an additional advantage, optical cards which feature a single recording surface—can be annotated on the reverse side. As non-rotating media, optical cards have potential advantages over magnetic and optical disks in military, automotive, and other applications where vibration or other stress is likely to be encountered. As discussed below, however, they can also be utilized as alternatives to other optical and magnetic storage media in a variety of general business applications.

The best known and most widely demonstrated example of an optical card is the LaserCard developed by Drexler Technology Corporation. Introduced in the early 1980s, it has been described in many publications and conference presentations, including Barnes (1984, 1984a, 1986, 1987), Barnes and Field (1987), Barnes and Kilty (1986), Barnes and Sukernick (1985, 1986, 1986a, 1986b), Field (1985), Kilty (1988), Schwerin (1985), and Shaw (1988). The LaserCard measures approximately 2.1 inches high by 3.4 inches wide by .03 inches thick, the size of a credit card. It is based on a proprietary, patented optical recording material called Drexon which Drexler Technology Corporation introduced in the late 1970s. As described by Brody (1981), Drexler (1979, 1981, 1982, 1983, 1983a), LaBudde et al (1985), Lichtenstein (1983), Mcleod (1985), and Mendez (1986), Drexon features metallic silver filaments dispersed in a gelatin matrix that is coated on glass, plastic, or other substrates. It is produced by chemical conversion of high-resolution photographic emulsions using proprietary processes. A Drexon-coated surface has reflectivity characteristics similar to a low-quality mirror. A protective overcoating is optional. Like the silver gelatin materials utilized in conventional photography, Drexon features a low melting point that permits recording by a low-power laser.

Drexon recording materials can be coated on disks and tapes; cards, however, are the only format that is commercially available. LaserCards contain a Drexon strip or stripe encapsulated between protective layers. A single Drexon stripe measuring thirty-five millimeters wide by seventy-five millimeters long can store 2.86 megabytes of computer-processable information when error-correction coding is utilized or 4.11 megabytes without error-correction coding. A narrower Drexon stripe measuring sixteen millimeters wide by seventy-five millimeters long can store approximately 850 kilobytes of data with error-correction coding. In contrast, the magnetic stripes commonly coated on credit cards store about 1,700 bits (approximately 200 bytes). LaserCards offer greater storage capacities than the most commonly encountered 3.5- and 5.25-inch floppy disks, but higher-density diskettes —which are available but not yet widely utilized—equal or exceed the LaserCard's capacity.

Like optical disks, LaserCards are available in read-only and read/write configurations. The read/write variety, the more common type, is designed for direct recording in a variety of information management applications. Read/write LaserCards are purchased blank and can accept any machine-readable information that might be recorded on other optical or magnetic media. Operating as a computer peripheral device, a LaserCard reader/writer—sometimes called a LaserCard drive or optical card drive—uses a low-power semiconductor diode laser to record data through the card's clear plastic cover layer. Direct-read-after-write (DRAW) techniques are utilized for error detection and correction. The recorded information is immediately usable without further processing. Like the materials utilized in many read/write optical disks, Drexon is a write-once recording medium; read/write LaserCards are not erasable.

Read-only memory (ROM) LaserCards, which contain prerecorded information, are produced by photolithographic techniques. An optical photomask master of the data is used to prepare a master film loop from which long reels of photographic film are replicated. Chemical conversion and physical development then convert the film into Drexon which is subsequently coated onto LaserCards. In late 1986, Drexler Technology Corporation announced a patented "quad density" recording technique that increases the capacity of read-only LaserCards to the current total of four megabytes. Operating as peripheral devices in microcomputer workstations, optical card readers support the use of read-only LaserCards.

Drexler Technology Corporation has manufactured LaserCards since the early 1980s. Several million LaserCards have been produced for marketing, testing, and other purposes. To create a worldwide optical card industry that will generate commercial demand for LaserCards, Drexler has sold non-exclusive licenses to more than two dozen North American, European, and Asian companies. Most Drexler licensees are authorized to distribute LaserCards and to produce compatible reading and recording equipment for use in optical card installations. Until 1989, Drexler Technology Corporation was the only source for the LaserCards themselves. In that year, however, it sold a LaserCard manufacturing license to Canon; a second card manufacturing license was sold in 1991 to Optical Card Business Company Limited, a Japanese joint venture formed by Dai Nippon Printing, Omron Corporation, Nippon Conlux, and Olympus Optical. Under the terms of that license, LaserCards will be manufactured by Dai Nippon Printing; the other three companies will manufacture optical card reader/writers. In 1989, a working group of the Drexler European Licensees Association (DELA) developed a European optical memory card standard based on LaserCard technology. The standard, which is available as a public document to interested parties, is designed to encourage manufacturers and customers to adopt a common approach to optical card systems. It specifies data formatting and physical characteristics—including track pitch, track guide width, reference marks, and track numbering—for plastic, credit card-sized, optical memory cards. User data capacity is set at 2.86 megabytes.

Despite an initially enthusiastic reception by computer industry observers, the LaserCard's progress toward widespread commercial availability has been disappointly slow. One of the most widely publicized LaserCard licensees—Blue Cross and Blue Shield of Maryland—discontinued its LaserCard development activities in 1986, and a number of others have declined to renew their licenses. Industry analysts typically point to the absence of LaserCard-compatible equipment as the principal reason for the technology's limited acceptance; although the LaserCard itself was introduced in 1981, compatible reader/writers were still not widely available a decade later. At the time this report was prepared, only about 300 optical card reader/writers had reportedly been installed. Such devices have been produced in small quantities by certain Drexler licensees for use in product demonstrations and field trials. Nipponinco, for example, announced a LaserCard reader/writer in late 1987; it has been used in several optical card field trials. Other optical card reader/writers have been manufactured by Canon, Kyocera, Olympus Optical, and Omron. Their characteristics are described by Gocho (1988), Pierce (1988), Takagi et al (1989), Tsutsui (1990), and Yoda et al (1989). Under the terms of the previously mentioned agreement, the participants in Optical Card Business Company Limited are expected to make a major commitment to the production of optical card equipment, thereby increasing product availability, lowering prices, and providing the hardware infrastructure that is essential to the development and growth of optical card installations and applications. To promote its technology and facilitate the implementation of optical card applications, Drexler Technology Corporation itself has established a subsidiary, LaserCard Systems Corporation, which markets "plug and play" microcomputer-based systems which permit the use of LaserCards with MS-DOS application programs. Drexler has demonstrated such systems in a variety of information management applications, including medical recordkeeping, electronic publishing, maintenance logs, identification systems, and financial transactions. Canon offers similar preconfigured systems consisting of a microcomputer, an optical card reader/writer, and software to interface with existing application programs.

Other optical memory cards have not been as widely publicized as the LaserCard, and none were commercially available at the time this report was prepared. Optical Recording Corporation (ORC) has been developing an optical card system, called the Hi-Lite Card, for several years. Its patented technology is based on research performed at Battelle Memorial Institute's Pacific Northwest Laboratory and at Digital Recording Corporation. That research is described by Russell and De Forest (1983). The Hi-Lite Card is discussed by Adamson (1987, 1987a, 1988), Marks (1988), and Russell (1988). It features a write-once recording medium coated on a plastic, wallet-size carrier. The Hi-Lite system utilizes thermal recording methodologies; a laser raises the temperature of the medium's dye coating to form spots that represent digitally-coded information. When the card is canned by a retrieval unit, a laser detects differences in the reflectivity of recorded and unrecorded areas. Polycarbonate is used for the card's base material and protective covering. Cory (1990) discusses the relationship between Hi-Lite technology and optical card patents held by Drexler Technology Corporation, noting that LaserCard patents are limited to optical card systems with pit sizes larger than twenty-five microns. Hi-Lite cards employ smaller pit sizes which permit capacities up to 200 megabytes per side. Like their LaserCard counterparts, Hi-Lite card reader/writer units are peripheral devices designed primarily for microcomputer configurations, but no such devices were commercially available at the time this report was prepared.

Several Japanese companies are reportedly experimenting with optical card technology. Recognizing that optical memory cards face stiff competition from so-called "smart" cards which utilize integrated circuits for information storage, Nippon Telegraph and Telephone has developed a hybrid card which combines the attributes of an optical memory card and an integrated circuit card; it features one megabyte of optical storage plus integrated circuit components capable of storing 800 kilobytes. A prototype was demonstrated in 1991, but commercial availability has not been scheduled. Hayashi and Ogawa (1991) of Asahi Chemical Industries describe a silver metallic recording material that is suitable for optical cards and flexible media, such as tapes and diskettes. Toyota et al (1990) of Sony Corporation describe a new type of optical memory card that does not require preformatting. Dai Nippon Printing has demonstrated read-only and read/write optical cards which feature a double-layered thin metallic film of telluride. Data is recorded by burning microscopic pits into the metallic film. Since Dai Nippon Printing, as the principal investor in Optical Card Business Company Limited, has obtained a LaserCard manufacturing license, the status of its own optical card development efforts is uncertain.

OPTICAL CARD APPLICATIONS

As information storage products, optical cards can be utilized in any application for which compact, write-once recording media with several megabytes of capacity are appropriate. Drexler Technology Corporation has actively and extensively promoted its LaserCards in a wide variety of applications ranging from medical records management to alternative driver's licenses. As previously noted, the optical card's commercial development has been disappointing; LaserCard technology has been utilized, however, in a number of interesting demonstration projects and pilot installations implemented by Drexler licensees and others. It is expected that some of these pilot implementations will lead to commercially viable optical card applications in the 1990s.

Health care applications have dominated LaserCard field trials. As discussed by Bouldon and Haddock (1990), Brown (1989), Brown and Vallbona (1988), Brown et al (1989), Shoda et al (1990), and Vallbona et al (1989), the potential of LaserCards as portable, high capacity "medical passports" has attracted the attention of hospitals, clinics, health maintenance organizations, and other health care providers. Baylor College of Medicine, for example, has utilized LaserCards to record patient information in an ambulatory care application at a neighborhood clinic in metropolitan Houston. The LaserCards store personal information, patient histories, test results, laboratory reports, physicians' treatment notes, and other data, including disease codes and occupational codes. Patients carry their cards with them and present them at the clinic prior to medical consultations. Cards are updated with treatment notes after each visit; laboratory test reports are entered as they become available. Backup cards are maintained at the treatment site.

Siedband (1988), Siedband and Grenzow (1989), Siedband and Zhang (1989), and Siedband et al (1990) discuss the use of LaserCards to store digitized x-ray images in a demonstration project at the University of Wisconsin. When data compression techniques are employed, eight or more x-rays can be stored on a single card. The x-ray images are also archived onto a write-once optical disk. Demetriades and Gomez (1990) describe a prototype optical card system for patient data and images being implemented by the Department of Veterans Affairs. At the time this report was prepared, field tests were being conducted in two Veterans Affairs hospitals in the eastern United States; if the trials are successful, optical card systems could eventually be installed in over 170 VA hospitals and clinics. In 1988, British Telecommunications PLC implemented a LaserCard field test for records of obstetrics patients at a London hospital. The cards store medical histories, test results, and reports of physicians' consultations. The equipment configuration includes Nippon Conlux reader/writer units attached to British Telecom microcomputers. The LaserCard workstations operate on a local area network which permits communication with a mainframe computer for the automatic transmission of selected statistics required centrally by the National Health Service. British Telecommunications uses the trade name RecallCard for its LaserCard implementation. Olisis, a company under Olivetti management, has joined with Numera, a member of the Sassari Banca Popolare Group, and SIS Integrated Health Systems to develop LaserCard systems for medical applications in Europe. In 1990, Olivetti ordered 26,000 LaserCards for use in a test program involving hospitals, clinics, and physicians' offices in Sardinia.

In 1991, Drexler Technology Corporation received an order for 20,000 optical memory cards for use in a Japanese field trial implemented by the Ministry of Health and Welfare. The field trial involves the provision of twenty-four-hour health care services to elderly persons. Participants will carry a LaserCard containing information about their medical condition and previous treatment record. The program's services will include nursing care, health checkups, patient transportation services, and an emergency alarm system. Among other Japanese implementations, Hara (1989) discusses the use of optical cards in mass health examinations. Nishibori and Shiina (1990) of Tokyo Medical and Dental University describe a system for automated transfer of personal health records from a source data base to optical cards. Takahashi et al (1987) and Hinohara et al (1988) describe an optical card installation at Tokai University Hospital. Similar tests have been conducted by Olympus Optical at a medical clinic in Shirascu-cho, by Omron Tateisi at the Mikage Medical Office in Ohmiya, and by CSK Corporation at Kurashiki Chuo Hospital. Olympus Optical has introduced a dialysis data management system which uses LaserCards to store diagnostic and treatment records. Matsushita has announced a computerized hospital system which combines LaserCards with centralized optical disk storage. Garois Corporation has developed a microcomputer-based system which stores x-ray images on optical cards. It is reportedly planning a similar system for images generated by CT scanners.

Quinn (1988) discusses the potential of optical cards for the medical insurance industry, as well as in automotive and life insurance applications. A number of vendors and industry analysts have suggested the use of optical cards to store vehicle maintenance records. As noted above, optical card equipment enjoys potential advantages over disk drives in military installations and other applications requiring ruggedized devices. Kerlin (1988) discusses the use of optical cards for the delivery of health care to wounded soldiers in battlefield settings. Walker (1988) surveys the potential of optical cards for personnel records, procurement documentation, engineering information, training program certification, and other applications in the aerospace industry.

Sumitomo Bank has tested a cashless funds transfer system using LaserCards. Hertel (1989) discusses the use of optical cards in such consumer marketing applications as electronic coupon distribution. Barnes (1988) suggests that optical cards might replace CD-ROM in certain applications, although that seems unlikely given the enormous disparity in storage capacity between the two media. Optical cards, however, do offer a potentially attractive alternative to floppy disks for software distribution. Several analysts have also suggested the use of optical cards as microfiche substitutes to store digitized document images in records management and publishing applications. With just 2.86 megabytes of recording capacity, however, a read/write LaserCard can only store about fifty letter-size document images digitized at 200 pixels per horizontal and vertical inch with a compression factor of ten to one. In contrast, the most common microfiche format for source documents can store ninety-eight letter-size pages. In late 1991, Drexler Technology Corporation announced plans to develop and market a LaserCard recording, storage, and retrieval system for images generated or received by Group III facsimile machines. A single LaserCard can store approximately 100 images at the normal facsimile resolution of 200 by 100 pixels per inch. The system can archive facsimile images sequentially or combine images with data and text files pertaining to particular topics or transactions.

OPTICAL TAPE

As its name suggests, an optical tape is a flexible, ribbon-shaped substrate coated with an optical recording material. While optical tape systems are at an earlier stage of development than optical cards, their information storage potential has been discussed for more than a decade. Schmitt and Lee (1979) and Lee et al (1979), for example, describe research on thermoplastic optical recording tapes at Honeywell Corporation in the 1970s. As described by Drexler (1981, 1983a), the Drexon recording materials employed by optical cards have been coated onto tape substrates, but such media were never commercialized. Altman et al (1986) propose the development of optical tape recorders for high-volume data storage in aerospace and avionics applications. Langeveld (1987) discusses the potential of optical tape for large-scale data collection in high-energy physics research.

Optical tape systems are designed for magnetic tape replacement in mainframe and minicomputer installations requiring very high media capacities. CREO systems, a Canadian firm established in 1984 to design and manufacture innovative electronics products, is the first and—at the time this report was prepared—the only company to have implemented an operational optical tape recorder. As described by Gelbart (1990) and Spencer (1988, 1988a, 1990), the CREO 1003 tape drive employs a thirty-five millimeter optical tape packaged on a twelve-inch reel in 880-meter lengths. The optical recording material is Digital Paper, which was developed by Imperial Chemical Industries and is being marketed by ICI ImageData. As discussed by Abbott (1988, 1989, 1989a, 1990), Desmarais (1989), Owen (1988, 1989), Pountain (1989), Ruddick (1989), Ruddick and Duffy (1991), Strelitz (1989), Terry (1991), Vander (1989), and Williams (1988, 1989), Digital Paper is the trade name for a write-once optical recording material which consists of infrared-sensitive, dye-polymer coated on a flexible polyester substrate. In addition to tape, Digital Paper can be coated onto diskettes, cards, cylinders, strips, and other supports. It has also been utilized in a research project involving holographic identification tags for machine-tool workbits and other industrial products.

The CREO tape drive employs multiple laser diode array to read and write multiple tracks of data in thirty-two-bit increments. Its recording capacity is one terabyte (one trillion bytes) of data per reel, the equivalent of about 5,000 reels of nine-track magnetic tape recorded at 6,250 bits per inch or of 100 of the highest-capacity write-once optical disk cartridges. At the time this report was prepared, no other computer storage technology offered comparable recording capacity on a single medium. CREO delivered the first Model 1003 optical tape recorder to the Canada Centre for Remote Sensing in 1990. Intended to replace magnetic tape units for data archiving and backup, it will be used to record and store images beamed from earth observation satellites. With its high capacity, the CREO's optical tape system is expected to significantly reduce the Centre's media expenditures, which exceed one million dollars per year for magnetic tape. Vault space requirements for archived media will likewise be reduced.

Among similar products reportedly in development, Conover and Parris (1990) of Laser-Tape Systems Incorporated describe an optical tape system based on IBM 3480-type cartridges. As with the CREO Model 1003, it utilizes Digital Paper as its recording material. Control signals are recorded simultaneously with data, thereby eliminating the need for media formatting prior to use. Models with fifty gigabytes of cartridge capacity have reportedly been developed to the prototype stage; in contrast, the storage capacity of conventional 3480-type magnetic tape cartridges is 200 megabytes. Commercialization is possible in 1992. In the Netherlands, DOCdata N.V. has demonstrated an optical tape cassette with six gigabytes of data capacity. Its polyester-based, write-once recording material features a dielectric layer of nonconductive polymer. Recording is performed by an array of lasers. DOCdata has also proposed an automated tape library which will store 128 cassettes and offer unattended access to over 750 gigabytes of data. Commercial availability has not been scheduled.

Like the first generation of optical disks, the optical tape recorders described above employ write-once media. As might be expected, however, various companies are said to be exploring rewritable optical tape technologies. Dancygier (1987) and Neubert et al (1989), for example, discuss Schlumberger's experiments with an erasable magneto-optical tape system employing ironterbium alloys coated on Kapton. Reporting on research performed by the 3M Company, Vogelgesang and Hartmann (1988) likewise examine the feasibility of magneto-optical tape. Castera and Lehureau (1986) discuss a device for optical reading of magnetic tape using thin-film garnet transducers. Such technologies are at early experimental stages; commercialization is not expected for some time.

Bibliography

Abbott, S. (1985). Dye-based media for optical data storage. In IEE Colloquium on Optical Mass Data Storage. London: IEE, pp. 6/1-3.

Abbott, S. (1988). Digital paper: flexible optical data storage media. Polymer Preprints, vol. 29, no. 2, pp. 213-14.

Abbott, S. (1989). Digital paper: flexible optical data storage media. In Proceedings of the ACS Division of Polymeric Materials Science and Engineering, vol. 59. Washington, DC: American Chemical Society, p. 1220.

Abbott, S. (1989a). Flexible optical data storage. In COMPEURO 89: Third Annual European Computer Conference. New York: IEEE, pp. 1/66-67.

Abbott, S. (1990). Digital paper: flexible optical data storage media. SMPTE Journal, vol. 99, no. 2, pp. 142-44.

Abe, M. and Gomi, M. (1990). Magneto-optical recording on garnet films. Journal of Magnetism and Magnetic Materials, vol. 84, no. 3, pp. 222-28.

Abe, M. and Gomi, M. (1990a). Advanced materials for magneto-optic disk. In Proceedings of the SPIE, vol. 1316. Bellingham, WA: International Society for Optical Engineering, pp. 216-20.

Abe, S. et al (1987). The correlation of pit shape with the valence state of Ti in Te-Se-Ti alloy thin films for optical recording disks. Journal of Vacuum Science and Technology, vol. 5, no. 6, pp. 1966-67.

Abeytunga, P. (1990). CD-ROM coming of age in Canada. CD-ROM End User, vol. 2, no. 4, pp. 28-31.

Abid, A. (1989). CD-ROM and access to information in the south. In Impact of CD-ROM on Library Operations and Universal Availability of Information: Eleventh International Essen Symposium. Essen, West Germany: Essen University Library, pp. 1-12.

Abt, C. (1989). Market opportunities for CD-ROM. In OPTICALINFO 89: the International Meeting for Optical Publishing and Storage. Oxford: Learned Information, pp. 1-6.

Adams, R. (1990). The development of the Dawson Technology/Leicester Polytechnic librarians' workstation. In Online Information Retrieval: Today and Tomorrow. Oxford: Learned Information, pp. 113-17.

Adamson, J. (1987). Overview of Hi-Lite card technology: read/write drive and media. In Optical Information Systems 87: Conference Proceedings. Westport, CT: Meckler Corporation, pp. 68-71.

Adamson, J. (1987a). Optical Recording Corporation: ongoing business program. In Optical Information Systems 87: Conference Proceedings. Westport, CT: Meckler Corporation, pp. 72-73.

Adamson, J. (1988). Market applications and business relationships. In Electronic Imaging 88: International Electronic Imaging Exposition and Conference. Waltham, MA: Institute for Graphic Communication, vol. 2, pp. 854-57.

Addink, M. and Mullen, J. (1990). AS/400 ImagePlus system view. IBM Systems Journal, vol. 29, no. 3, pp. 451-66.

Adkins, A. (1987). An overview of TOPIX: CD-ROM premaster/encoding system. Optical Information Systems, vol. 7, no. 6, pp. 406-11.

Ai, T. et al (1990). Controller and interface of optical disk drive. National Technical Report, vol. 36, no 5, pp. 582-89.

Akeroyd, J. (1991). CD-ROM networks. Electronic Library, vol. 9, no. 1, pp. 21-25.

Alberico, R. (1988). Workstations for reference and retrieval. Small Computers in Libraries, vol. 8, no. 4, pp. 4-10.

Albin, S. et al (1990). An erasable optical memory using stimulated electronic transition (SET) concept. In Proceedings of the SPIE, vol. 1316. Bellingham, WA: International Society for Optical Engineering, pp. 358-62.

Albrecht, R. et al (1990). The European Science Data Archive for the Hubble Space Telescope. ESO Messenger, no. 59, pp. 61-63.

Alegiani, J. et al (1989). An in-vehicle navigation and information system utilizing defined software services. In Conference Record of Papers Presented at the First Vehicle Navigation and Information Systems Conference. New York: IEEE, pp. A3-A8.

Alesandrini, K. (1989). The latest in interactive graphics. In NCGA 89 Conference Proceedings: Tenth Annual Conference and Exposition Dedicated to Computer Graphics. Fairfax, VA: National Computer Graphics Association, vol. 3, pp. 193-220.

Ali, S. (1990). Databases on optical discs and their potential in developing countries. Journal of the American Society for Information Science, vol. 41, no. 4, pp. 238-44.

Allan, A. (1990). Chasing MARC: searching in BiblioFile, Dialog, OCLC, and RLIN. Journal of Academic Librarianship, vol. 15, no. 6, pp. 339-43.

Allen, G. (1990). Database selection by patrons using CD-ROM. College and Research Libraries, vol. 51, no. 1, pp. 69-75.

Allen, G. (1990a). CD-ROM training: what do the patrons want? RQ, vol. 30, no. 1, pp. 88-93.

Allen, R. (1989). Integrated text and image management. In OIS International 1989: Proceedings of the Sixth Annual Conference on Optical Information Systems. London: Meckler Corporation, pp. 223-29.

Allin, P. (1989). Optical or magnetic drives: which way is the mass storage market going? In IEE Colloquium on New Advances in Optical Recording Technology. London: IEE, pp. 6/1-5.

Altman, W. et al (1986). Optical storage for high performance applications in the late 1980s and beyond. RCA Engineer, vol. 3, no. 1, pp. 46-55.

Ammon, G. (1983). An optical disk jukebox mass memory system. In Proceedings of the SPIE, vol. 4121. Bellingham, WA: Society of Photo-Optical Instrumentation Engineers, pp. 2-9.

Ammon, G. and Siryj, B. (1983). Automatic handling mechanisms for an optical disc mass memory system. In Proceedings of the SPIE, vol. 385. Bellingham, WA: Society of Photo-Optical Instrumentation Engineers, pp. 14-16.

Anders, S. and Hardt, B. (1987). Injection molding of compact discs. Kunststoffe, vol. 77, no. 1, pp. 3-6.

Anderson, G. et al (1990). ImagePlus workstation program. IBM Systems Journal, vol. 29, no. 3, pp. 398-407.

Anderson, K. (1990). Methods of data compression after the manner of Lempel and Ziv. Optical Information Systems, vol. 10, no. 1, pp. 40-43.

Andrews, C. (1990). Understanding CD-ROM software. CD-ROM Professional, vol. 3, no. 4, pp. 59-62.

Andrews, C. (1991). Mastering the CD-ROM mastering and replication process. CD-ROM Professional, vol. 4, no. 4, pp. 17-22.

Apperson, G. and Doherty, R. (1987). Displaying images. In CD ROM: Optical Publishing. Redmond, WA: Microsoft Press, pp. 121-68.

Arai, R. and Itao, K. (1990). Network file for ISDN. In Digest of Papers: Tenth IEEE Symposium on Mass Storage Systems. Washington, DC: IEEE Computer Society Press, pp. 149-53.

Arai, S. and Maeda, T. (1990). OD321 series 12-inch large capacity WORM optical disk drive. Hitachi Review, vol. 39, no. 5, pp. 273-76.

Aratani, K. et al (1985). Magnetic and magneto-optic properties of Tb-FeCo-Al films. Journal of Applied Physics, vol. 57, no. 8, pp. 3903-5; also in IEEE Translation Journal on Magnetics in Japan, vol. 1, no. 3, pp. 333-34.

Aratani, K. et al (1987). Aging changes of some properties of amorphous TbFeAl thin films as magneto-optical recording medium. IEEE Translation Journal on Magnetics in Japan, vol. 2, no. 5, pp. 393-94.

Aratani, K. et al (1991). Unique MO disk attains super resolution. JEE, vol. 28, no. 293, pp. 74-76.

Arimune, H. et al (1987). Thermal stability and reliability of magneto-optical media with periodic structures. IEEE Translation Journal on Magnetics in Japan, vol. 2, no. 3, pp. 401-403.

Arink, G. (1982). Electronic image management for medicine. In First International Conference and Workshop on Picture Archiving and Communications Systems (PACS) for Medical Applications. Bellingham, WA: Society of Photo-Optical Instrumentation Engineers, pp. 441-45.

Armento, G. et al (1990). Maps and CD-ROM: a partnership for the future. Laserdisk Professional, vol. 3, no. 1, pp. 65-71.

Armstrong, A. (1987). Premastering and mastering. In CD ROM: Optical Publishing. Redmond, WA: Microsoft Press, pp. 217-26.

Armstrong, P. (1987). Beyond Domesday: an idea for interactive broadcasting. Television: the Journal of the Royal Television Society, vol. 24, no. 1, pp. 30-34.

Arps, M. (1991). Hardware and media options for CD-ROM publishing. CD-ROM Professional, vol. 4, no. 4, pp. 66-68.

Arundale, J. (1991). Newspapers on CD-ROM: the European perspective. In Twelfth National Online Meeting Proceedings. Medford, NJ: Learned Information, pp. 17-21.

Asami, N. et al (1987). The CD-ROm navigation system for automobile started operations. Nikkei Electronics, no. 434, pp. 119-30.

Asano, M. et al (1987). Magneto-optical recording media with new protective films. IEEE Transactions on Magnetics, vol. 23, no. 5, pp. 2520-22.

Asano, M. et al (1990). Cu/sub 3/N thin film for a new light recording media. Japanese Journal of Applied Physics, part 1, vol. 20, no. 10, pp. 1985-86.

Asari, S. et al (1987). Preparation of a magneto-optical disk using a rare earth-transition metal alloy target. Journal of Vacuum Science and Technology, vol. 5, no. 4, pp. 1949-51.

Asari, S. et al (1989). process for large-scale production of magneto-optical disks. Journal of Vacuum Science and Technology,

Ashikaga, Y. et al (1990). CD-ROM premastering system using CD-Write Once. Fujitsu Scientific and Technical Journal, vol. 26, no. 3, pp. 214-23.

Atkins, S. (1985). The Domesday Project. Media in Education and Development, vol. 18, no. 3, pp. 110-13. vol. 7, no. 2, pp. 170-75.

Attaran, E. and Grundy, P. (1989). magnetic, magneto-optical and structural properties of PtMnSb thin films. Journal of Magnetism and Magnetic Materials, vol. 78, no. 1, pp. 51-55.

Attinger, M. (1990). Imaging systems and records management. ARMA Records Management Quarterly, vol. 24, no. 1, pp. 9-11.

Au, K. (1989). CD-ROM LANs: multi-user and multi-source access: a status report. In OpticalInfo

89: the International Meeting for Optical Publishing and Storage. Oxford: Learned Information, pp. 7-19.

Augsburger, W. (1988). Innovations in optical disk jukeboxes. In Electronic Imaging 88: International Electronic Imaging Exposition and Conference. Waltham, MA: Institute for Graphic Communication, vol. 1, pp. 406-408.

Augsburger, W. (1988a). Jukebox Interface Management Systems (JIMS) software. In Optical Information Systems '88: Conference Proceedings. Westport, CT: Meckler Corporation, pp. 67-70.

Augsburger, W. (1990). A flexible jukebox for 5.25-inch WORM and rewritable optical disk drives. Optical Information Systems, vol. 10, no. 1, pp. 28-34.

Avers, C. and Probst, R. (1990). ImagePlus as a model for application solution development. IBM Systems Journal, vol. 29, no. 3, pp. 356-70.

Babbitt, W. and Mossberg, T. (1988). Time-domain frequency-selective optical data storage in a solid-state material. Optical Communications, vol. 65, no. 3, pp. 185-88.

Backus, J. (1989). MEDLINE on CD-ROM: a checklist. Laserdisk Professional, vol. 2, no. 4, pp. 74-81.

Bagg, T. (1987). Digitizing documents: guidelines for image quality. Inform, vol. 1, no. 11, pp. 6-9.

Bagg, T. (1989). Criteria for the use of CD-ROM. International Journal of Micrographics and Video Technology, vol. 7, no. 2, pp. 47-53.

Bakker, S. et al (1989). Medicine on CD-ROM: a comparison. Online Review, vol. 13, no. 1, pp. 39-50.

Balafas, D. (1990). File architectures for MO jukeboxes. In 1990 UniForum Conference Proceedings. Washington, DC: UniForum, pp. 199-208.

Balafas, D. (1991). Meeting the challenges of optical storage on UNIX networks. Computer Technology Review, vol. 11, no. 9, pp. 67-71.

Bales, K. (1987). The BBC advanced interactive video system. In NAV 87: Data Dissemination and Display — Electronics in Navigation. London: Royal Institute of Navigation, pp. 34/1-9.

Bardes, D. (1986). Implications of CD-Interactive: directions, specifications, and standards. Optical Information Systems, vol. 6, no. 4, pp. 324-28.

Barnes, R. (1984). Storage of computer data on optical media configured in credit card size. In IEEE Region 5 Conference: Electrical Engineering — a Century of Serving Society. New York: IEEE, pp. 116-19.

Barnes, R. (1984a). There's a LaserCard in your future. Electronic Publishing Review, vol. 4, no. 2, pp. 119-23.

Barnes, R. (1986). The optical memory card: the complementary alternative. In Optical Information Systems 86: Conference Proceedings. Westport, CT: Meckler Corporation, pp. 60-75.

Barnes, R. (1987). The optical memory card: a unique publishing medium. In Optical Publishing and Storage: Products that Work — Proceedings of Optical Publishing and Storage 87. Medford, NJ: Learned Information, pp. 1-3.

Barnes, R. (1987a). Desktop publishing: is all that paper really necessary. Paper presented at the 11th Annual TechDoc Conference of the Graphic Communications Association. Available from Drexler Technology Corporation.

Barnes, R. (1988). Optical memory cards: will they replace CD-ROM? In Electronic Imaging 88: International Electronic Imaging Exposition and Conference. Waltham, MA: Institute for Graphic Communication, vol. 1, pp. 483-84.

Barnes, R. and Field, R. (1987). The optical memory card: a unique publishing medium. In Optica 87: the International Meeting for Optical Publishing and Storage. Oxford: Learned Information, pp. 121-31.

Barnes, R. and Kilty, T. (1986). The driver's license for the nineties. Paper presented at the International Driver License/Driver Control Workshop, American Association of Motor Vehicle Administrators. Available from Drexler Technology Corporation.

Barnes, R. and Sukernick, F. (1985). LaserCard automated publications and maintenance records. In 1985 Videodisc, Optical Disk, and CD-ROM Conference and Exposition. Westport, CT: Meckler Publishing, pp. 15-23.

Barnes, R. and Sukernick, F. (1985a). LaserCard encoding, applications, and security. Paper presented at the National Bureau of Standards. Available from Drexler Technology Corporation.

Barnes, R. and Sukernick, F. (1986). Files on a card: small format, high capacity digital storage/retrieval. Journal of Information and Image Management, vol. 19, no. 10, pp. 34-38, 40.

Barnes, R. and Sukernick, F. (1986a). The optical memory card: its role in distributing digital information from large databases. In Proceedings of the SPIE, vol. 695. Bellingham, WA: Society of Photo-Optical Instrumentation Engineers, pp. 353-61.

Barnes, R. and Sukernick, F. (1986b). The optical memory card's role in the distribution of technical information. Optical Information Systems, vol. 6, no. 6, pp. 504-508.

Barnes, R. and Sukernick, F. (1986c). The Drexon LaserCard optical card data system for the automation industry. Paper presented at the Seventh Annual Conference on Automation Technology, CAD/CAM, and Engineering Data Handling. Available from Drexler Technology Corporation.

Barrett, B. (1990). Hit rates with the OCLC CD450 cataloging system: a test with recent, academic approval books. Cataloging and Classification Quarterly, vol. 12, no. 2, pp. 63-81.

Bartholomeusz, B. (1989). Thermo-magnetic marking of rare-earth transition-metal thin films. Journal of Applied Physics, vol. 65, no. 1, pp. 262-65.

Barton, R. et al (1986). New phase change material for optical recording with short erase time. Applied Physics Letters, vol. 48, no. 19, pp. 1255-57.

Bate, G. (1987). Materials challenges in metallic, reversible, optical recording media: a review. IEEE Transactions on Magnetics, vol. 23, no. 1, pp. 151-61.

Bate, G. (1989). Alternative storage technologies. In Digest of Papers: COMPCON Spring '89 Thirty-Fourth IEEE Computer Society International Conference. Washington, DC: Ieee Computer Society Press, pp. 151-57.

Baycroft, M. (1990). Public access CD-ROM workstations: design and management. In Computers in Libraries '90: Proceedings of the Fifth Annual Computers in Libraries Conference. Westport, CT: Meckler Corporation, pp. 3-5.

Beaumont, J. and Campbell, B. (1990). BiblioDisc: creating a database for Canada and the world. CD-ROM Professional, vol. 3, no. 4, pp. 42-49.

Beauvais, J. et al (1989). Optical recording characteristics of implanted tellurium films. Thin Solid Films, vol. 182, no. 1, pp. 47-52.

Bechevet, B. et al (1991). Rapid thermal annealing of CeDyGaIG films for magneto-optical disk storage. Journal of Applied Physics,

Becker, H. (1991). Encyclopedias on CD-ROM: two orders of magnitude more than any other educational software has ever delivered before. Educational Technology, vol. 31, no. 2, pp. 7-20.

Befeler, M. (1988). Electronic document distribution using CD-ROM. In Electronic Imaging 88: International Imaging Exposition and Conference. Boston: Institute for Graphic Communication, vol. 2, pp. 613-16.

Befeler, M. and Einberger, J. (1988). CD-ROM standardization. Laserdisk Professional, vol. 1, no. 2, pp. 70-72. vol. 69, no. 8, pt. 2A, pp. 4767-69.

Behara, B. (1991). Jukebox cost performance modelling. Document Image Automation, vol. 11, no. 3, pp. 150-55.

Behara, B. and Singh, H. (1990). Optical storage performance modeling and evaluation. Optical Information Systems, vol. 10, no.

Beheshti, J. (1991). Retrieval interfaces for CD-ROM bibliographic data bases. CD-ROM Professional, vol. 4, no. 1, pp. 50-53.
5, pp. 275-86.

Beiser, K. (1987). MaineCat fact sheet. In SCIL 1987 Proceedings. Westport, CT: Meckler Corporation, pp. 16-17.

Beiser, K. and Nelson, N. (1989). CD-ROM public access catalogs: an assessment. Library Technology Reports, vol. 25, no. 2, pp. 279-453.

Belanger, A. and Hoffman, S. (1990). Factors related to frequency of use of CD-ROM: a study of ERIC in an academic library. College and Research Libraries, vol. 51, no. 2, pp. 153-62.

Belani, R. (1991). Jane's CD-ROM project: step-by-step through the development process. CD-ROM Professional, vol. 4, no. 3, pp. 69-72.

Bell, A. (1980). Optical disks for information storage. Nature, vol. 287, no. 6, pp. 583-85.

Bell, A. (1983). Optical data storage technology: status and prospects. Computer Design, vol. 22, no. 1, pp. 133-38.

Bell, A. (1986). Materials for reversible optical data storage. In IEE Colloquium on Optical Mass Storage. London: IEE, pp. 5/1-5.

Bell, S. (1990). Spreading CD-ROM technology beyond the library: applications for remote communications software. Special Libraries, vol. 81, no. 3, pp. 189-95.

Beltrami, G. and Kulkarni, D. (1989). Data compression scheme for large databases on CD-ROM. In OpticalInfo 89: Proceedings of the International Meeting for Optical Publishing and Storage. Oxford: Learned Information, pp. 21-28.

Beltrami, G. and Ramana, R. (1989). Computer manuals on CD-ROM. In OPTICALINFO 89: the International Meeting for Optical Publishing and Storage. Oxford: Learned Information, pp. 29-35.

Bender, A. (1987). Text/image management and optical disk system design. Inform, vol. 1, no. 2, pp. 20-23.

Bender, A. (1988). An optical disk-based information retrieval system. Library Hi Tech, vol. 6, no. 3, pp. 81-86.

Benjamin, C. (1990). The role of optical storage technology for NASA's image storage and retrieval systems. In Proceedings of the SPIE, vol. 1248. Bellingham, WA: International Society for Optical Engineering, pp. 10-17.

Bennett, M. (1988). Rewritable optical technology and applications. In Proceedings of the Fifty Annual Conference on Optical Information Systems. London: Meckler Corporation, pp. 221-28.

Berezhnoy, A. and Popov, Y. (1991). Optical memory in electrooptical crystals. In Proceedings of the SPIE, vol. 1248. Bellingham, WA: International Society for Optical Engineering, pp. 44-49.

Berg, B. (1988). The impact of SCSI on optical storage. In Optical Information Systems '88: Conference Proceedings. Westport, CT: Meckler Corporation, pp. 58-62.

Berg, B. (1989). Implementing WORM storage in the Unix environment. In Software for Optical Storage. Westport, CT: Meckler Corporation, pp. 69-74.

Berg, B. (1990). The impact of SCSI on optical storage. In Seventh Annual OIS International 1990: Proceedings of the Seventh Annual Conference on Optical Information Systems. London: Meckler Corporation, p. 82.

Berg, B. (1990a). Software considerations for rewritable and multifunction optical disk drives. Optical Information Systems, vol. 10, no. 6, pp. 316-19.

Bernal, N. (1991). Local journal holdings availability messages on CD+ MEDLINE: impact on users and interlibrary loan patterns. CD-ROM Professional, vol. 4, no. 3, pp. 26-28.

Bernal, N. and Renner, I. (1990). CD-ROM Medline's impact on mediated online searches when patron cost is not a variable. Laserdisk Professional, vol. 3, no. 2, p. 25-27.

Bernstein, P. and Gueugnon, C. (1985). Properties of amorphous rare earth-transition metal thin films for magneto-optical recording. IEEE Transactions on Magnetics, vol. 21, no. 5, pp. 1613-17.

Berra, P. et al (1989). The impact of optics on data and knowledge base systems. IEEE Transactions on Knowledge Data Engineering, vol. 1, no. 1, pp. 111-32.

Berry, D. (1991). Post-processing data from Compact Disclosure using spreadsheets. Database, vol. 14, no. 2, pp. 58-63.

Berthreux, D. (1990). Interactive digital video. In IDATE: Twelfth International Conference Proceedings — Key Technologies, Experiments, New Concepts. Montpellier, France: IDATE, pp. 359-65.

Beshore, E. (1989). Sector striping techniques for WORM drives. Optical Information Systems, vol. 9, no. 4, pp. 187-89.

Bessette, O. and Sullivan, M. (1984). Operation of jukebox optical disk over a local area network. In Fifth Symposium on Automation Technology in Engineering Data Handling and CAD/CAM. Pebble Beach, CA: Automation Technology Institute, pp. 1-4.

Bessette, O. and Thomas, D. (1990). 2500 gigabyte capacity, 6 Mbyte/sec. data rate, dual port NASA optical disk jukebox. In Proceedings of the SPIE, vol. 1316. Bellingham, WA: International Bibi, A. (1990). CD-ROM for retrospective conversion: selection of a source data base — the BRAZNET experience. CD-ROM Librarian, vol. 5, no. 1, pp. 21-25. Society for Optical Engineering, pp. 42-47.

Bills, L. and Helgerson, L. (1989). CD-ROM catalog production products. Library Hi Tech, vol. 7, no. 1, pp. 67-92.

Bills, L. and Helgerson, L. (1988). CD-ROM public access catalogs: database creation and maintenance. Library Hi Tech, vol. 6, no. 1, pp. 67-86.

Bills, L. and Helgerson, L. (1988a). User interfaces for CD-ROM PACs. Library Hi Tech, vol. 6, no. 2, pp. 73-81.

Binder, R. (1988). Videodiscs in Museums: a Project and Resource Directory. Falls Church, VA: Future Systems.

Binder, W. (1988). The public access catalog of the university library of Bielefeld: the first German CD-ROM project for library applications. ABI-Technik, vol. 8, no. 1, pp. 8-11.

Binder, W. et al (1988). CD-ROM and online public access catalogs. ABI-Technik, vol. 8, no. 2, pp. 107-20.

Binwal, J. and Rao, D. (1989). LegalTrac: a CD-ROM version of Legal Resource Index. IASLIC Bulletin, vol. 34, no. 2, pp. 73-79.

Birecki, H. et al (1985). Magnetooptic quadrilayer reliability and performance. In Proceedings of the SPIE, vol. 529. Bellingham, WA: Society of Photo-Optical Instrumentation Engineers, pp. 19-24.

Bjorklund, G. et al (1984). Progress in frequency domain optical storage. In Topical Meeting on Optical Data Storage. Washington, DC: Optical Society of America, pp. THC-D5/1-5.

Black, D. (1990). Dots per what kind of inch? Inform, vol. 4, no. 5, pp. 9-11.

Blackwelder, M. et al (1990). CD-ROM access via a VAX: one institution's experiment. CD-ROM Librarian, vol. 5, no. 10, pp. 24-29.

Blizzard, A. (1989). 1986 and all that: the BBC Domesday Project. School Librarian, vol. 37, no. 3, pp. 94-96.

Blom, G. (1982). Optical disk data storage. In Proceedings of the SPIE, vol. 385. Bellingham, WA: Society of Photo-Optical Instrumentation Engineers, pp. 42-44.

Blom, G. (1982a). Optical disk data storage for medical imaging. In First International Conference and Workshop on Picture Archiving and Communications Systems (PACS) for Medical Applications. Bellingham, WA: Society of Photo-Optical Instrumentation Engineers, pp. 449-52.

Blom, G. and Lou, D. (1984). Archival life of tellurium-based materials for optical recording. Journal of the Electrochemical Society, vol. 131, no. 1, pp. 146-51.

Bloom, M. (1989). Don't throw away your Winchester . . . yet. ESD: Electronic System Design Magazine, vol. 19, no. 4, pp. 42-50.

Blumer, A. et al (1987). Complete inverted files for efficient text retrieval and analysis. Journal of the Association for Computing Machinery, vol. 34, no. 3, pp. 578-95.

Bogage, A. (1991). Periodical Abstracts Ondisc. CD-ROM Professional, vol. 4, no. 1, pp. 43-46.

Bolzoni, F. et al (1986). Cobalt alloys for perpendicular magnetic recording. In Second Congress on Cobalt Metallurgy and Uses. Brussels: Cobalt Development Institute, pp. 480-87.

Bonime, A. (1991). The promise and the challenge of CD-I. CD-ROM Professional, vol. 4, no. 5, pp. 17-28.

Bonini, D. (1985). Design of a modular, high-capacity optical disk subsystem. In Digest of Papers: IEEE Symposium on Mass Storage Systems. New York: IEEE, pp. 91-93.

Bonomi, M. (1991). Multimedia and CD-ROM: an overview of JPEG, MPEG, and the future. CD-ROM Professional, vol. 4, no. 6, pp. 38-40.

Bonta, B. (1990). Library staffing and arrangements for CD-ROM service. INSPEL, vol. 24, no. 1, pp. 5-13.

Bostwick, S. et al (1988). Multivendor system extensions take a big byte out of the VAX. Hardcopy, vol. 8, no. 2, pp. 33-36.

Bouldin, E. and Haddock, R. (1990). Application of an optical memory card as a portable medical record. In Proceedings of the SPIE, vol. 1248. Bellingham, WA: International Society for Optical Engineering, pp. 196-203.

Bowers, R. (1987). Changing the publishing model with optical media. Electronic and Optical Publishing Review, vol. 7, no. 1, pp. 4-6.

Bowers, R. (1989). The Oxford English Dictionary on compact disc. Electronic Library, vol. 7, no. 2, pp. 102-105.

Bowry, C. and Bonnett, P. (1991). Liquid crystal polymer optical memories: analogue, digital, and holographic. Optical Computing and Processing, vol. 1, no. 1, pp. 13-21.

Bracker, W. (1987). Optical data storage: theory, hardware, software, and applications. In Proceedings of the National Computer Graphics Association: Graphics 87 Eighth Annual Conference. Fairfax, VA: National Computer Graphics Association, pp. 75-90.

Brahmi, F. and Tyler, J. (1990). The effect of CD-ROM MEDLINE on online end-user and mediated searching: a follow-up study. Medical Reference Services Quarterly, vol. 9, no. 3, pp. 15-20.

Braid, J. (1989). ADONIS: from myth to reality. In Impact of CD-ROM on Library Operations and Universal Availability of Information: Eleventh International Essen Symposium. Essen, West Germany: Essen University Library, pp. 149-61.

Brandle, H. et al (1990). Magneto-optical Kerr effect of UFe/1/OSi/2. IEEE Transactions on Magnetics, vol. 26, no. 5, pp. 2795-97.

Brandt, R. (1991). CD-ROM, CD-I, multimedia, and reality. CD-ROM Librarian, vol. 6, no. 8, pp. 23-25.

Brauer, G. et al (1988). Large scale in-line sputtering systems for magneto-optical data storage media. In Proceedings of the SPIE, vol. 899. Bellingham, WA: Society of Photo-Optical Instrumentation Engineers, pp. 146-51.

Brauer, G. et al (1990). Production of magneto-optical data storage media by static DC sputter processes. In Proceedings of the SPIE, vol. 1323. Bellingham, WA: International Society for Optical Engineering, pp. 151-61.

Brazas, J. (1988). Vacuum-coated organic recording media. Journal of Imaging Science, vol. 32, no. 2, pp. 56-59.

Brennan, C. (1989). LaserCat vs. Bibliofile: a comparison in the small public library. CD-ROM Librarian, vol. 4, no. 7, pp. 10-17.

Breuggeman, P. (1990). The versatile CD-ROM workstation: making information available to both IBM and Macintosh users. CD-ROM Librarian, vol. 5, no. 5, pp. 34-38.

Breuggeman, P. (1991). Memory management for CD-ROM workstations. CD-ROM Professional, vol. 4, no. 5, pp. 39-43.

Brito, C. (1989). The developing countries and CD-ROM. Information Development, vol. 5, no. 4, pp. 210-16.

Brito, C. (1989a). The Pan American Health Organization Project. In Information — Knowledge — Evolution: Proceedings of the Forty-Fourth FID Congress. Amsterdam: Elsevier Science Publishers, pp. 291-300.

Brody, H. (1981). Materials for optical storage: a state-of-the-art survey. Laser Focus, vol. 17, no. 8, pp. 47-52.

Brooks, M. (1989). Bowker's Ingram-Books In Print Plus: a case study. Laserdisk Professional, vol. 2, no. 4, pp. 46-52.

Brown, C. and Coleman, D. (1991). Testing and development of an efficient remote CD-ROM system. CD-ROM Librarian, vol. 6, no. 9, pp. 13-18.

Brown, J. (1989). A new computer memory for biology and medicine using the laser card. Computers in Biology and Medicine, vol. 19, no. 6, pp. 375-83.

Brown, J. and Vallbona, C. (1988). New patient record system using the laser card. In Proceedings: Twelfth Annual Symposium on Computer Applications in Medical Care. Piscataway, NJ: IEEE, pp. 602-605.

Brown, J. et al (1988). A new patient record system using the LaserCard. Optical Information Systems, vol. 8, no. 4, pp. 156-61.

Brown, K. (1989). CD-ROM technology from Hewlett-Packard: HP LaserRetrieve and HP Laser-ROM. Optical Information Systems, vol. 9, no. 3, pp. 135-37.

Brown, S. (1991). Managing a retirement system's records using optical disk technology. Government Finance Review, vol. 7, no. 1, pp. 7-10.

Brown, W. and Earman, M. (1988). Determining error management strategies. In Proceedings of the SPIE, vol. 899. Bellingham, WA: Society of Photo-Optical Instrumentation Engineers, pp. 93-103.

Browning, M. and Haas, L. (1991). Is Business Periodicals Ondisc the greatest thing since sliced bread? A cost analysis and user survey. CD-ROM Professional, vol. 4, no. 1, pp. 37-41.

Brunell, D. (1990). A LANtastic connection for CD-ROM systems. OCLC Micro, vol. 6, no. 1, p. 12.

Bruno, R. (1987). Making compact disks interactive. IEEE Spectrum, vol. 24, no. 11, pp. 40-45.

Bruno, R. and Mizushima, M. (1986). New developments in optical media: an outline of CD-I. Optical Information Systems, vol. 6, no. 4, pp. 318-23.

Buchbinder, R. (1988). Pilot version of the CD-ROM edition "Deutsche Bibliographie". ABI-Technik, vol. 8, no. 2, pp. 89-93.

Buckley, B. (1990). The European cooperative CD-ROM project. In Bibliographic Access In Europe: First International Conference. Aldershot, United Kingdom: Gower, pp. 190-97.

Buddine, L. and Young, E. (1987). The Brady Guide to CD-ROM. New York: Prentice-Hall Press.

Bunzel, M. and Morris, S. (1992). Multimedia Applications Development Using DVI Technology. New York: McGraw-Hill.

Burgess, A. et al (1987). Comparison of transient thermal conduction in tellurium and organic dye-based digital optical storage media. Journal of Applied Physics, vol. 61, no. 1, pp. 74-80.

Burgess, J. (1985). A system approach using optical data disks to solve the mass data storage problem. In Digest of Papers: Seventh IEEE Symposium on Mass Storage Systems. Washington, DC: IEEE Computer Society Press, pp. 74-78.

Burgess, J. (1987). Virtual library system: a general purpose mass storage archive. In Digest of Papers: Eighth IEEE Symposium on Mass Storage Systems. Washington, DC: IEEE Computer Society Press, pp. 72-76.

Burgess, J. and Ramsey, N. (1988). FileTek Storage Machine applications. In Digest of Papers: Ninth IEEE Symposium on Mass Storage Systems. Washington, DC: IEEE Computer Society Press, pp. 98-102.

Burke, B. (1990). SCI/SSCI on CD-ROM. CD-ROM Librarian, vol. 5, no. 9, pp. 31-40.

Burton, B. and Cheng, G. (1989). Replacing a MARC service with a bibliographic utility on CD-ROM: the Hong Kong experience. In Bibliographic Databases and Networks: Papers Presented at the International Conference. New Delhi: Tata McGraw-Hill, pp. 1/17-27.

Burwell, L. (1991). The interaction of learning styles with learner control treatments in an interactive videodisc lesson. Educational Technology, vol. 31, no. 3, pp. 37-43.

Buschow, K. (1988). Magneto-optical properties of alloys and intermetallic compounds. In Ferromagnetic Materials: a Handbook on the Properties of Magnetically Ordered Substances. Amsterdam: North-Holland Physics Publishing, pp. 493-595.

Buschow, K. (1989). Magneto-optical recording materials. Journal of Less-Common Metals, vol. 155, no. 2, pp. 307-18.

Butcher, S. (1990). The rewards and trials of networking. Database, vol. 13, no. 4, pp. 103-105.

Butler, M. (1990). Full-text CD-ROM libraries for international development. Microcomputers for Information Management, vol. 7, no. 4, pp. 273-91.

Buxton, J. et al (1991). The Travelpilot: a second-generation automotive navigation system. In IEEE Transactions on Vehicular Technology, vol. 40, no. 1, pt. 1, pp. 41-44.

Campbell, B. (1989). CD-ROM publishing in Canada. Laserdisk Professional, vol. 2, no. 5, pp. 31-34.

Campbell, K. (1989). Postcode address file on CD-ROM. BURISA, no. 90, pp. 2-5.

Caniglia, G. (1989). EKOD: European Kompass on disc. In OpticalInfo 89: the International Meeting for Optical Publishing and Storage. Oxford: Learned Information, pp. 37-45.

Capodaglia, J. et al (1988). MEDLINE on compact disc: end-user searching on Compact Cambridge. Bulletin of the Medical Library Association, vol. 76, no. 2, pp. 181-83.

Carasso, M. et al (1982). Compact disc digital audio system. Philips Technical Review, vol. 40, no. 1, pp. 151-55.

Carcia, P. et al (1988). Stability of Te-Cu amorphous alloy thin films for optical recording. Journal of Applied Physics, vol. 64, no. 4, pp. 1671-78.

Carcia, P. et al (1991). Dielectric enhancement layers for a Pt/Co multilayer magneto-optical recording medium. Applied Physics Letters, vol. 58, no. 2, pp. 191-93.

Carey, R. et al (1991). Using an expert system to interface mainframe computing resources with an interactive video system. In Proceedings of the SPIE, vol. 1464. Bellingham, WA: International Society for Optical Engineering, pp. 500-507.

Carey, R. et al (1991a). Thermo-magneto-optic materials for high density data storage. In IEE Colloquium on New Materials for Information Storage. London: IEE, pp. 5/1-3.

Carino, P. (1989). CD-ROM technology and new users of information technology in the Philippines: do they have a future together. International Forum for Information and Documentation, vol. 14, no. 3, pp. 27-31.

Carlson, H. and Falk, D. (1991). Effectiveness of interactive videodisc instructional programs in elementary teacher education. Journal of Educational Technology Systems, vol. 19, no. 2, pp. 151-63.

Carnine, D. et al (1987). Videodisc instruction in fractions. Focus on Learning Problems in Mathematics, vol. 9, no. 1, pp. 31-52.

Carpenter, A. and Mitz, O. (1989). CD-ROM image publishing for SEC filings. Inform, vol. 3, no. 2, pp. 26-28.

Carringer, M. (1988). Real world jukebox implementation for Digital's VAX/VMS. Computer Technology Review, vol. 8, no. 10, pp. 47-54.

Carter, T. et al (1987). Photon-gated spectral hole burning by donor-acceptor electron transfer. Optical Letters, vol. 12, no. 5, pp. 370-72.

Cassel, R. (1987). Pennsylvania's CD-ROM statewide union catalog. In SCIL 1987 Proceedings. Westport, CT: Meckler Corporation, pp. 34-35.

Castera, J. and Lehureau, J. (1986). Optical readout of magnetic tapes. In Proceedings of the SPIE, vol. 702. Bellingham, WA: Society of Photo-Optical Instrumentation Engineers, pp. 321-28.

Castle, R. (1989). Paper woes thwarted on Capitol Hill as House installs optical disk system. International Journal of Micrographics and Video Technology, vol. 7, no. 2, pp. 73-75.

Castro, R. et al (1989). LILACS/CD-ROM project: CD-ROM Latin American and Caribbean literature on health sciences. Revista Espanola de Documentacion Cientifica, vol. 12, no. 1, pp. 23-29.

Cathell, B. (1987). HP Source Reader. In Optical Publishing and Storage: Products that Work — Proceedings of Optical Publishing and Storage '87. Medford, NJ: Learned Information, pp. 17-23.

Cathell, B. et al (1989). A compiled source access sytem using CD-ROM and personal computers. Hewlett-Packard Journal, vol. 40, no. 6, pp. 50-57.

Cawkell, A. (1989). Automatic indexing in the Science and Social Science Citation Index CD-ROM. Electronic Library, vol. 7, no. 6, pp. 345-50.

Cawkell, A. (1991). Electronic document supply systems. Journal of Documentation, vol. 47, no. 1, pp. 41-73.

Celestre, M. (1990). Eight commandments for CD-ROM production: practical advice for doing it yourself. CD-ROM Professional, vol. 3, no. 3, pp. 41-43.

Chadwyck-Healey, C. (1989). Advanced cartographic and geographic information systems on CD-ROM. In OpticalInfo 89: Proceedings of the International Meeting for Optical Publishing and Storage. Oxford, United Kingdom: Learned Information, pp. 47-56.

Chadwyck-Healey, C. (1989a). MundoCart and Supermap: cartographic and statistical databases on CD-ROM. Information Services and Use, vol. 9, no. 3, pp. 139-47.

Chadwyck-Healey, C. (1989b). Two major British catalogues on CD-ROM. In Impact of CD-ROM on Library Operations and Universal Availability of Information: Eleventh International Essen Symposium. Essen, West Germany: Essen University Library, pp. 231-40.

Chamchuklin, A. (1990). An evaluation of CD-ROM MEDLINE use in Thailand. Bulletin of the Medical Library Association, vol. 78, no. 4, pp. 395-99.

Chao, D. (1989). Cost comparisons between bibliographic utilities and CD-ROM-based cataloging systems. Library Hi Tech, vol. 7, no. 3, pp. 49-52.

Chao, S. et al (1990). Multiple phase change of lead oxide film for optical storage. Journal of Physics D: Applied Physics, vol. 23, no. 7, pp. 955-58.

Charles, S. and Clark, K. (1990). Enhancing CD-ROM searches with online updates: an examination of end-user needs, strategies, and problems. College and Research Libraries, vol. 51, no. 4, pp. 321-28.

Chen, C. (1985). Micro-based optical videodisc applications. Microcomputers for Information Management, vol. 2, no. 4, pp. 217-40.

Chen, C. (1987). CD-ROM survey in American academic and college libraries. In Online Information 87: Proceedings of the Eleventh International Online Information Meeting. Medford, NJ: Learned Information, pp. 9-12.

Chen, C. (1991). CD-I and full motion video. Microcomputers for Information Management, vol. 8, no. 1, pp. 53-57.

Chen, K. and Livingston, D. (1988). Simulation of space-borne optical mass memory system. In Conference Proceedings: 1988 IEEE SOUTHEASTCON. New York: IEEE, pp. 98-102.

Chen, M. et al (1985). Reversibility and stability of tellurium alloys for optical data storage. Applied Physics Letters, vol. 46, no. 8, p. 734-36.

Chen, M. et al (1986). Compound materials for reversible, phase-change optical storage. Applied Physics Letters, vol. 49, no. 9, pp. 502-4.

Chen, M. and Rubin, K. (1989). Progress of erasable phase-change materials. In Proceedings of the SPIE, vol. 1078. Bellingham, WA: Society of Photo-Optical Instrumentation Engineers, pp. 150-56.

Chen, M. et al (1983). Characterization of optical recording disk noise. In Proceedings of the SPIE, vol. 420. Bellingham, WA: Society of Photo-Optical Instrumentation Engineers, pp. 306-12.

Chen, P. (1986). The compact disk ROM: how it works. IEEE Spectrum, vol. 23, no. 4, pp. 44-48.

Cheney, S. (1990). Urban Phytonarian Handbook CD-ROM. CD-ROM Librarian, vol. 5, no. 9, pp. 22-25.

Cheriyan, C. (1988). Developing erasable optical devices for the PC environment. In Optical Information Systems '88: Conference Proceedings. Westport, CT: Meckler Corporation, pp. 106-11.

Cherry, L. and Waldstein, R. (1989). Electronic access to full document text and images through LINUS. AT&T Technical Journal, vol. 68, no. 4, pp. 72-90.

Chester, S. (1989). The laserdisk lawyer. Legal Economics, vol. 15, no. 8, pp. 28-35.

Chou, N. (1990). Chinese MARC database on CD-ROM. INSPEL, vol. 24, no. 2, pp. 87-101.

Cichocki, E. and Ziemer, S. (1988). Design considerations for CD-ROM retrieval software. Journal of the American Society for Information Science, vol. 39, no. 1, pp. 43-46.

Choy, J. and O'Lear, B. (1983). Proposal for the integration of digital optical storage into the mass storage system (MSS) at the National Center for Atmospheric Research (NCAR). In Proceedings of the SPIE, vol. 382. Bellingham, WA: Society of Photo-Optical Instrumentation Engineers, pp. 59-62.

Christodoulakis, S. (1985). Issues in the architecture of a document archiver using optical disk technology. SIGMOD Record, vol. 14, no. 4, pp. 34-50.

Christodoulakis, S. and Ford, A. (1989). Retrieval performance versus disc space utilization on WORM optical discs. SIGMOD Record, vol. 18, no. 2, pp. 306-14.

Chung, C. et al (1984). Stability of 3M DRAW optical recording media. In Topical Meeting on Optical Data Storage: Technical Digest. Washington, DC: Optical Society of America, pp. B1/1-4.

Chung, H. et al (1989). The degradation and hole formation of Te-Se alloy thin films for the optical recording. Transactions of the Korean Institute of Electrical Engineers, vol. 38, no. 2, pp. 106-11.

Chung, T. (1987). Laser-induced fluid motion on a dye/polymer layer for optical data storage. AICHE Journal, vol. 33, no. 6, pp. 1041-44.

Cinelli, J. (1988). DuraSTORE: a ruggedized 14-inch erasable optical disk drive. In Proceedings of the SPIE, vol. 899. Bellingham, WA: Society of Photo-Optical Instrumentation Engineers, pp. 2-7.

Cinnamon, B. (1988). Optical Disk Document Storage and Retrieval Systems. Silver Spring, MD: Association for Information and Image Management.

Clark, J. (1991). Using image scanners to create and access electronically stored documents. ARMA Records Management Quarterly, vol. 25, no. 3, pp. 9-13, 16.

Clark, K. (1990). DIALOG OnDisc Thomas Register: a review. CD-ROM Professional, vol. 3, no. 4, pp. 108-14.

Clemens, J. (1982). Video disks: three choices. IEEE Spectrum, vol. 19, no. 3, pp. 38-42.

Co, F. (1990). Retrospective conversion on CD-ROM: a cost analysis. CD-ROM Librarian, vol. 5, no. 1, pp. 11-20.

Coe, T. (1990). Networking CD-ROMs. In Online Information Retrieval: Today and Tomorrow. Oxford: Learned Information, pp. 67-74.

Cohen, C. (1979). Amorphous AsTeSe thin film promises 20,000 pages on an optical disk. Electronics, vol. 52, no. 13, pp. 68-69.

Cohen, E. et al (1989). Storage hierarchies. IBM Systems Journal, vol. 28, no. 1, pp. 62-76.

Cohen, E. and Young, M. (1986). Cost comparison of abstracts and index on paper, CD-ROM, and on-line. Optical Information Systems, vol. 6, no. 6, pp. 485-90.

Cohen, J. et al (1988). A laser-disk based archive, review and communications system for magnetic resonance imaging. In Proceedings of the SPIE, vol. 914. Bellingham, WA: Society of Photo-Optical Instrumentation Engineers, pt. B, pp. 1344-48.

Colborne, D. and Nicholls, P. (1990). Biology on disk: CD-ROM databases for the non-medical academic life sciences collection. Laserdisk Professional, vol. 3, no. 1, pp. 91-96.

Colglazier, M. (1988). A book catalog produced from USMARC records using Bibliofile, Pro-Cite, Biblio-Link, and Word Perfect. Information Technology and Libraries, vol. 7, no. 4, pp. 417-29.

Colvin, G. (1987). Database retrieval and indexing. In CD ROM: Optical Publishing. Redmond, WA: Microsoft Press, pp. 103-20.

Condic, K. (1991). Biological Abstracts on CD. CD-ROM Librarian, vol. 6, no. 3, pp. 29-33.

Connell, G. (1986). Magneto-optics and amorphous metals: an optical storage revolution. Journal of Magnetism and Magnetic Materials, vol. 54, no. 3, pp. 1561-66.

Conover, C. and Parris, J. (1990). Acousto-optics enables optical tape technology. Computer Technology Review, vol. 10, no. 16, pp. 99-102.

Cooke, D. (1986). Maps, optical discs, and vehicle navigation. In CD-ROM: the New Papyrus. Redmond, WA: Microsoft Press, pp. 553-62.

Cooke, D. (1987). Map storage on CD-ROM. Byte, vol. 12, no. 8, pp. 129-38.

Cooper, A. (1989). Document image processing — realising the vision. In OIS International 1989: Proceedings of the Sixth Annual Conference on Optical Information Systems. London: Meckler Corporation, pp. 165-70.

Cooper, L. and Tharp, A. (1989). Inverted signature trees and text searching on CD-ROMs. Information Processing and Management, vol. 25, no. 2, pp. 161-69.

Cormouls, M. and Gaudin, F. (1988). An example of catalog management on CD-ROM: BiblioFile. Documentaliste, vol. 25, no. 3, pp. 122-28.

Cornet, J. (1983). Deformation recording process in polymer-metal bilayers and its use for optical storage. In Proceedings of the SPIE, vol. 420. Bellingham, WA: Society of Photo-Optical Instrumentation Engineers, pp. 86-95.

Cory, C. (1990). Implementing optical card technologies. Optical Information Systems, vol. 10, no. 1, pp. 44-52.

Costanzo, C. (1991). Image processing: Imaging's cost/benefit tug of war considerations. Bankers Monthly, vol. 108, no. 5, pp. 13-16.

Coufal, H. and Lee, W. (1987). Time resolved calorimetry of Te films during pulsed laser annealing. Applied Physics, vol. B44, no. 2, pp. 141-46.

Couture, J. and Lessard, R. (1988). Modulation transfer function measurements for thin layers of azo dyes in PVA matrix used as an optical recording material. Applied Optics, vol. 27, no. 18, pp. 3368-74.

Cowan, L. (1990). Liberated information and the future of optical disks. Optical Information Systems, vol. 10, no. 6, pp. 327-31.

Crane, M. (1990). The New England Law Library Consortium: resource sharing with CD-ROM technology. Microcomputers for Information Management, vol. 7, no. 3, pp. 205-16.

Crane, N. (1987). Dialog's OnDisc ERIC. CD-ROM Librarian, vol. 2, no. 4, pp. 26-35.

Crasemann, J. and Hansen, P. (1989). Reversible optical recording on rare-earth-transition-metal disks. Thin Solid Films, vol. 175, no. 1, p. 2, pp. 261-64.

Crasemann, J. et al (1989). Thermo-magnetic switching on rare-earth transition-metal alloy magneto-optic disks. Journal of Applied Physics, vol. 66, no. 3, pp. 1273-78.

Crawford, B. (1988). Pitfalls of CD manufacturing. Microcontamination, vol. 6, no. 1, pp. 39-42.

Crawford, R. (1990). CD-ROM in Australian capital territory libraries. LASIE, vol. 21, no. 3, pp. 74-82.

Crawley, J. and Adams, C. (1991). InfoAccess Project: comparing print, CD-ROM, and in-house indexes. Canadian Journal of Information Science, vol. 16, no. 1, pp. 29-41.

Croll, M. (1990). Broadcasters' use of optical discs for audio recording. In Eighth International Conference on Video, Audio, and Data Recording. London: IEE, pp. 140-43.

Croucher, M. and Hopper, M. (1987). Materials for optical disks. Chemtech, vol. 17, no. 7, pp. 426-33.

Cullen, G. (1991). Rules of thumb for backfile conversions on optical imaging systems. Document Image Automation, vol. 11, no. 3, pp. 163-65.

Curtis, M. (1987). CD-ROM publishing: new production and distribution channels. In OPTICA 87: the International Meeting for Optical Publishing and Storage. Oxford: Learned Information, pp. 85-93.

Daigle, J. et al (1990). Queuing analysis of an optical disk jukebox based office system. IEEE Transactions on Computers, vol. 39, no. 6, pp. 819-28.

Dallas, W. et al (1987). A prototype totally digital radiology department: cnception and initiation. In Proceedings of the SPIE, vol. 767. Bellingham, WA: Society of Photo-Optical Instrumentation Engineers, pp. 700-707.

D'Alleyrand, M. (1989). Image Storage and Retrieval Systems. New York: McGraw-Hill.

Dalrymple, P. (1990). CD-ROM MEDLINE use and users: information transfer in the clinical setting. Bulletin of the Medical Library Association, vol. 78, no. 3, pp. 224-32.

Dalto, G. (1989). The use of CD-ROM for the construction of a union catalogue. Bollettino d'Informazioni, vol. 29, no. 2, pp. 257-63.

Dancygier, M. (1987). Magnetic properties of TbFe amorphous alloys deposited on Kapton: optical tape feasibility. IEEE Transactions on Magnetics, vol. 23, no. 5, pt. 1, pp. 2608-10.

Daum, A. (1989). Developments in CD ROM in Europe. In SCIL 89 International: Proceedings of the Third Annual Conference on Small Computers in Libraries. London: Meckler Corporation, pp. 122-26.

Dauner, D. et al (1990). Mechanical design of an optical disk autochanger. Hewlett-Packard Journal, vol. 41, no. 6, pp. 14-23.

David, S. (1990). CD-ROM Europe '90 International Exhibition and Congress. CD-ROM Professional, vol. 3, no. 6, pp. 85-86.

Davies, D. (1988). The CD-ROM medium. Journal of the American Society for Information Science, vol. 39, no. 1, pp. 34-42.

Davies, D. and Clark, D. (1990). Application of image storage in CD formats. In Proceedings of the SPIE, vol. 1248. Bellingham, WA: International Society for Optical Engineering, pp. 210-13.

Davies, D. and Clark, D. (1991). Aspects of the application of image and data storage in compact disk formats. In Proceedings of the SPIE, vol. 1401. Bellingham, WA: International Society for Optical Engineering, pp. 2-8.

Davis, D. (1987). Optical archiving: where are we now and where do we go from here? Optical Information Systems, vol. 7, no. 1, pp. 66-71.

Davis, R. (1987). Optical data storage for space sensing applications. In International Geoscience and Remote Sensing Symposium 1987. New York: IEEE, p. 899.

Day, R. (1989). Where's the rot? A special report on CD longevity. Stereo Review, vol. 54, no. 4, pp. 23-24.

Dayhoff, R. (1988). WORM optical disk systems for medicine. M.D. Computing, vol. 5, no. 6, pp. 12-16.

DeBloois, M. (1987). Anticipating Compact Disc-Interactive (CD-I): ten guidelines for prospective authors. Educational Technology, vol. 27, no. 6, pp. 25-27.

De Caro, C. et al (1991). Hole burning, Stark effect, and data storage: 2. Holographic recording and detection of spectral holes. Applied Optics, vol. 30, no. 20, pp. 2890-98.

De Haan, M. (1987). Optical technology: what's mature and what's on the horizon. ESD: the Electronic System Design Magazine, vol. 17, no. 9, pp. 41-49.

Demarais, N. (1989). Write-on: the advantages of digital paper. Compu-ters in Libraries, vol. 9, no. 5, pp. 37-38.

Demetriades, J. and Gomez, E. (1990). Optical patient card prototype within the Department of Veterans Affairs. MUG Quarterly, vol. 20, no. 1, pp. 109-12.

DePompa, B. (1991). CD-ROM-based documentation: IBM's InfoExplorer. CD-ROM Professional, vol. 4, no. 5, pp. 104-105.

Deschanvres, J. et al (1989). Garnet thin films deposited by a new chemical vapour deposition. Thin Solid Films, vol. 175, no. 1, pp. 281-85.

Desmarais, N. (1987). Bowker's Books in Print Plus. CD-ROM Librarian, vol. 2, no. 5, pp. 26-31.

Desmarais, N. (1988). An examination of Ulrich's Plus. CD-ROM Librarian, vol. 3, no. 4, pp. 24-31.

Desmarais, N. (1989). The librarian's CD-ROM handbook. Westport, CT: Meckler Corporation.

Desmarais, N. (1989a). CD-ROM public access catalogs: a bibliography. CD-ROM Librarian, vol. 4, no. 10, pp. 26-33.

Desmarais, N. (1990). Tools for producing multimedia CD-ROMs. Laserdisk Professional, vol. 3, no. 2, pp. 53-55.

Desmarais, N. (1991). Bureau of Electronic Publishing makes history. CD-ROM Librarian, vol. 6, no. 2, pp. 24-28.

De Smet, E. (1989). Experiences with an evaluation of CD-ROM for end users. Bibliotheek -en Archiefgids, vol. 65, no. 3, pp. 286-97.

De Valk, J. et al (1985). Simulation of a feasible medical image storage hierarchy within the Dutch IMAGIS project. In Proceedings of the SPIE, vol. 529. Bellingham, WA: Society of Photo-Optical Instrumentation Engineers, pp. 240-45.

Devoy, J. et al (1988). Media, file management schemes facilitate WORM utilization. Computer Technology Review, vol. 8, no. 13, pp. 48-49.

Dewe, M. (1987). Local studies and the new technology: the British experience. Information Development, vol. 3, no. 1, pp. 23-29.

Dickinson, G. (1990). Choosing a CD-ROM encyclopedia: how to critically evaluate the product. Library Software Review, vol. 9, no. 5, pp. 277-82.

DiGuilio, M. et al (1988). Reactively sputtered TeO/sub x thin films for optical recording films. Journal of Vacuum Science and Technology, vol. 6, no. 2, pp. 243-45.

Dillon, J. (1990). Magnetic and optical properties of rare earth garnets. Journal of Magnetism and Magnetic Materials, vol. 84, no. 3, pp. 213-21.

Dinan, R. et al (1990). ImagePlus high performance transaction system. IBM Systems Journal, vol. 29, no. 3, pp. 421-34.

Dirschedl, F. (1987). File system for write-once optical disks. OPTICA '87: International Meeting for Optical Publishing and Storage. Oxford: Learned Information, pp. 49-58.

Dixon, D. (1987). DVI video/graphics. Computer Graphics World, vol. 10, no. 7, pp. 125-28.

Dixon, D. (1989). Life before the chips: simulating digital video interactive technology. Communications of the Association for Computing Machinery, vol. 32, no. 7, pp. 824-31.

Donsbach, D. (1988). Transparent optical disk jukebox support for the VAX/VMS environment. In Electronic Imaging '88: International ElectronicImaging Exposition and Conference. Boston: Institute for Graphic Communication, vol. 2, pp. 880-81.

Drexler, J. (1979). Drexon disc storage for laser printers. In Proceedings of the SPIE, vol. 169. Bellingham, WA: Society of Photo-Optical Instrumentation Engineers, pp. 11-16.

Drexler, J. (1981). Drexon optical memory media for laser recording and archival data storage. Journal of Vacuum Science and Technology, vol. 18, no. 1, pp. 87-91.

Drexler, J. (1982). Laser card for compact optical data storage system. In Proceedings of the SPIE, vol. 329. Bellingham, WA: Society of Photo-Optical Instrumentation Engineers, pp. 61-68.

Drexler, J. (1983). Drexon optical storage for digital picture archiving applications. In Proceedings of the Second International Conference and Workshop on Picture Archiving and Communication Systems (PACS II) for Medical Applications. New York: IEEE, pp. 30-35.

Drexler, J. (1983a). The Drexon product family for laser recording and digital data storage: a status report. In Proceedings of the SPIE, vol. 420. Bellingham, WA: Society of Photo-Optical Instrumentation Engineers, pp. 57-59.

Deurinckx, A. et al (1983). Digital picture archiving and communication systems in medicine. Computer, vol. 16, no. 8, pp. 14-16.

Du, H. et al (1987). Efficient file structure for document retrieval in the automated office environment. In Proceedings of the Third International Conference on Data Engineering. New York: IEEE, pp. 165-72.

Dundon, G. (1986). Integrating a multifunctional optical disc drive. Electronic Engineering, vol. 58, no. 711, pp. 125-27.

Dysart, J. (1990). CD-ROM products in Canada. CD-ROM End User, vol. 2, no. 4, pp. 32-34.

Earl, M. and Hamberg, C. (1991). Medical students as CD-ROM end-user trainers. Bulletin of the Medical Library Association, vol. 79, no. 1, pp. 65-67.

Eaton, N. et al (1989). CD-ROM and other Optical Information Systems: Implementation Issues for Libraries. Phoenix: Oryx Press.

Ebert, H. and Akai, H. (1990). Theoretical study of magnetic and magneto-optical properties of iron-based transition-metal alloys. Journal of Applied Physics, vol. 67, no. 9-IIA, p. 4798.

Eckwright, G. and Bolin, M. (1990). No card cat — no problem: WLN's LaserCat provides another opportunity for cooperation. RQ, vol. 29, no. 4, pp. 525-33.

Edmead, M. (1987). Interactive applications using CD-I. In Digest of Papers: COMPCON Spring 87, Thirty-Second IEEE Computer Society International Conference. New York: IEEE, pp. 410-11.

Edwards, J. et al (1990). 14-inch advanced erasable optical disk development. In Proceedings of the SPIE, vol. 1316. Bellingham, WA: International Society for Optical Engineering, pp. 252-58.

Eguchi, N. et al (1990). An 86 mm magneto-optical disk drive with a compact and fast-seek-time optical head. In Proceedings of the SPIE, vol. 1316. Bellingham, WA: International Society for Optical Engineering, pp. 2-10.

Eich, M. et al (1987). Reversible digital and holographic optical storage in polymeric liquid crystals. In Proceedings of the SPIE, vol. 682. Bellingham, WA: Society of Photo-Optical Instrumentation Engineers, pp. 93-96.

Eichlseder, M. and Eusemann, N. (1987). Production unit for compact disks. Kunststoffe, vol. 77, no. 2, pp. 9-11.

Einberger, J. (1987). CD ROM characteristics. In CD ROM: Optical Publishing. Redmond, WA: Microsoft Press, pp. 31-44.

Einberger, J. and Zoellick, B. (1987). High Sierra Group format description. In CD ROM: Optical Publishing. Redmond, WA: Microsoft Press, pp. 195-217.

Ekberg, K. et al (1990). An overview of the Pioneer CD-ROM minichanger DRM-600. Optical Information Systems, vol. 10, no. 5, pp. 287-90.

Ekberg, K. et al (1991). Answering the need for WORM and rewritable optical storage: the Pioneer multifunction optical disk drive. Optical Information Systems, vol. 11, no. 1, pp. 19-23.

Ekberg, K. et al (1991a). Tracking optical media: CCS, SS, and discrete block format compared. Computer Technology Review, vol. 11, no. 9, pp. 73-76.

El-Bibany, H. and Paulson, B. (1991). Microcomputer/videodisc system for construction education. Microcomputers in Civil Engineering, vol. 6, no. 2, pp. 149-60.

Elshami, A. (1990). CD-ROM Technology for Information Managers. Chicago: American Library Association.

Emmelius, M. et al (1989). Materials for optical data storage. Angewandte Chemie: International Edition in English, vol. 28, no. 11, pp. 1445-71.

Engler, E. (1990). Advanced materials for reversible optical storage. Advanced Materials, vol. 2, no. 4, pp. 166-73.

Ensor, P. (1990). Controlling CD-ROM growth in academic libraries. CD-ROM Librarian, vol. 5, no. 8, pp. 20-21, 24-25.

Ensor, P. and Hardin, S. (1991). Using CD-ROM to provide enhanced information services for university administrators and committees. CD-ROM Professional, vol. 4, no. 3, pp. 44-46.

Erkilla, J. (1990). CD-ROM vs. online: implications for management from the cost side. Canadian Library Journal, vol. 47, no. 6, pp. 421-28.

Erkilla, J. (1991). The basic economics of CD-ROM pricing. CD-ROM Professional, vol. 4, no. 1, pp. 85-88.

Erkkila, J. et al (1991). The case study of a small academic library with many CD-ROMs. CD-ROM Professional, vol. 4, no. 5, pp. 133-37.

Evans, K. (1988). Thermal stress mechanisms in optical storage thin films. Journal of Applied Physics, vol. 63, no. 10, pp. 4946-50.

Eventoff, A. (1983). Improved Philips air sandwich disk. In Proceedings of the SPIE, vol. 420. Bellingham, WA: Society of Photo-Optical Instrumentation Engineers, pp. 150-59.

Falk, H. (1990). CD-ROM drive units for personal computers. Electronic Library, vol. 8, no. 6, pp. 434-35.

Fand, J. (1987). Full-text retrieval and indexing. In CD ROM: Optical Publishing. REdmond, WA: Microsoft Press, pp. 83-102.

Fantini, M. (1990). An archive of digital images. Microcomputers for Information Management, vol. 7, no. 1, pp. 25-40.

Ferebee, M. and Kibler, J. (1989). The Earth radiation budget experiment optical disk archival system. Optical Information Systems, vol. 9, no. 1, pp. 2-8.

Fernhout, H. (1987). The CARIN car information and navigation system and the extension to CARMINAT. In Sixth International Conference on Automotive Electronics. London: IEE, pp. 19\39-43.

Ferraro, A. (1987). Ulrich's PLUS: a New serials reference technology. Serials Review, vol. 13, no. 3, pp. 19-23.

Ferraro, A. (1988). Ulrich's PLUS: a high-performance, low-cost alternative to online serials reference systems. Serials Librarian, vol. 14, no. 3, pp. 121-25.

Ferre, J. et al (1990). Magneto-optical studies of Co/Au ultrathin metallic films. Applied Physics Letters, vol. 56, no. 16, pp. 1588-90.

Ferrell, M. and Parkhurst, C. (1987). Using LaserQuest for retrospective conversion of MARC records. Optical Information Systems, vol. 7, no. 6, pp. 396-400.

Ferelli, M. (1991). CD/ROM changers aid in database access. Computer Technology Review, vol. 11, no. 2, pp. 18-19.

Field, R. (1985). EP and the LaserCard: there's a lot in store. In Electronic Publishing: Corporate and Commercial Publishing, Proceedings of the International Conference. Pinner, Middlesex, England: Online Publications, pp. 159-67.

Fisher, R. (1988). CD-ROM wooing the sleeping giant: MIS. Inform, vol. 2, no. 6, pp. 36-37.

Fisher, W. and Gilbert, J. (1987). FileNet: a distributed system supporting Workflo, a flexible office procedures control language. In IEEE Computer Society Office Automation Symposium. New York: IEEE, pp. 226-33.

Flanders, B. (1990). Spinning the hits: CD-ROM networks in libraries. American Libraries, vol. 21, no. 11, pp. 1032-33.

Flanders, B. (1991). General Periodicals Ondisc: UMI's one-stop wonder. CD-ROM Librarian, vol. 6, no. 4, pp. 27-32.

Flanders, B. (1991b). 1991 New Grolier Electronic Encyclopedia. CD-ROM Librarian, vol. 6, no. 11, pp. 32-33.

Fleischhauer, C. (1990). The American Memory Project: sharing unique collections electronically. In Online/CD-ROM '90: Proceedings of the Conference. Weston, CT: Online Incorporated, pp. 57-62.

Fleming, J. (1989). Optical recording in organic media: thickness effects. Journal of Imaging Science, vol. 33, no. 3, pp. 65-68.

Fletcher, P. (1990). A match made in heaven: PC, CD, and SCSI. Portable Computer Review, vol. 2, no. 2, pp. 36-37.

Fluty, S. (1988). CD-ROM linked to ZIP+4 success. Inform, vol. 2, no. 6, pp. 37-38.

Fody, B. (1990). Integrating LaserDisclosure into the corporate environment: a case study. Laserdisk Professional, vol. 3, no. 2, pp. 28-29.

Folmsbee, M. et al (1990). Developing inexpensive multiuser access to CD-ROM: LaserCat at Gonzaga University Law School Library. CD-ROM Professional, vol. 3, no. 3, pp. 34-38.

Force, R. (1987). WLN's LaserCat. Optical Information Systems/Library and Information Center Applications, vol. 2, no. 3, pp. 18-25.

Forer, P. (1987). Video and data in geography: an initial analysis of the Domesday Project design in the United Kingdom. New Zealand Journal of Geography, no. 82, pp. 19-23.

Foulds, M. and Foulds, L. (1990). Downloading CD-ROM search results into a database management system. CD-ROM Librarian, vol. 5, no. 9, pp. 13-18.

Fowler, L. and Loomis, M. (1988). Corporate and Industry Research Reports (CIRR): a case study report. CD-ROM Librarian, vol. 3, no. 4, pp. 14-16.

Fox, D. (1988). CD-ROM use in Canadian libraries: a survey. CD-ROM Librarian, vol. 3, no. 10, pp. 23-28.

Fox, D. (1991). The CD-ROM Market in Canadian Libraries. Westport, CT: Meckler Corporation and Canadian Library Association; excerpted in CD-ROM Librarian, vol. 6, no. 1, pp. 15-23; vol. 6, no. 2, pp. 30-38; vol. 6, no. 3, pp. 36-44; and vol. 6, no. 4, pp. 41-47.

Fox, E. (1989). Advances in text and image publishing for CD-ROM. In National Online Meeting Proceedings. Medford, NJ: Learned Information, pp. 165-70.

Francis, B. (1988). PC back-up's optical understudy. Datamation, vol. 34, no. 25, pp. 57-60.

Frank, D. (1989). Information systems: an integral part of future vehicles. In Conference Record of Papers presented at the First Vehicle Navigation and Information Systems Conference. New York: IEEE, pp. 85-88.

Fraser, D. et al (1991). A semi-realistic driving simulator based on a video disc. In Eighth International Conference on Automotive Electronics. London: IEE, pp. 155-59.

Freeman, J. (1991). ZCAV format delivers one gigabyte capacity magneto optical drives. Computer Technology Review, vol. 11, no. 9, pp. 61-64.

Freese, R. (1988). Optical disks become erasable. IEEE Spectrum, vol. 25, no. 2, pp. 41-45.

Freese, R. et al (1982). Characteristics of bubble-forming optical direct-read-after-write (DRAW) media. In Proceedings of the SPIE, vol. 329. Bellingham, WA: Society of Photo-Optical Instrumentation Engineers, pp. 174-80.

Frenkel, K. (1989). The next generation of interactive technologies. Communications of the Association for Computing Machinery, vol. 32, no. 7, pp. 872-81.

Frierson, E. (1989). The CGIAR preservation and dissemination project. Revista AIBDA, vol. 10, no. 1, pp. 53-73.

Fruchterman, J. (1988). Omnifont text-recognition: linking paper, electronic, and optical input. Inform, vol. 2, no. 5, pp. 16-19.

Fryer, K. et al (1989). Beyond MEDLINE: a review of ten non-MEDLINE CD-ROM databases for the health sciences. Laserdisk Professional, vol. 2, no. 3, pp. 27-39.

Fukuda, K. et al (1990). Hypermedia personal computer communication system: Fujitsu Habitat. Fujitsu Scientific and Technical Journal, vol. 26, no. 3, pp. 197-206.

Fruscione, J. (1988). Conceptual Design Guidelines for Optical Disk Document Management Systems. Silver Spring, MD: Association for Information and Image Management.

Fushiki, K. (1987). Proposed standard for map files. Nikkei Electronics/ Nikkei Erekutoronikusu, no. 420, p. 77.

Fujimori, S. et al (1988). Crystallization process of Sb-Te alloy films for optical storage. Journal of Applied Physics, vol. 64, no. 3, pp. 1000-1004.

Fujimori, S. et al (1988a). Laser-induced phase transformation of Sb-Te alloy films for optical storage. In Fundamentals of Beam-Solid Interactions and Transient Thermal Processing. Pittsburgh: Materials Research Society, pp. 671-74.

Fujimura, K. et al (1987). Ag-Zn alloyed film for optical recording: II. Preparation vacuum evaporation. Journal of the Vacuum Society of Japan, vol. 30, no. 5, pp. 495-99.

Fujino, S. et al (1987). An expressway traffic-surveillance system. Mitsubishi Denki Giho, vol. 61, no. 4, pp. 65-68.

Fujiwara, T. (1985). Perpendicular magnetic recording technology. Toshiba Review, no. 154, pp. 6-9.

Fujiwara, T. (1989). Layered media make good magneto-optical storage disks. Laser Focus World, vol. 25, no. 11, pp. 109-14.

Fukami, T. et al (1990). Novel direct overwriting technology for magneto-optical disks by exchange-coupled RE-TM quadrilayered films. Journal of Applied Physics, vol. 67, no. 9, pt. 2A, pp. 4415-16.

Fukushima, Y. et al (1990). A single beam direct-overwrite optical disk drive using a phase change medium. Journal of the Institute of Television Engineers of Japan, vol. 44, no. 10, pp. 1410-17.

Fulton, A. (1990). Images of the past: the use of optical disc as a storage medium in Aberdeen City Libraries. In Text Retrieval: the State of the Art. London: Taylor Graham, pp. 187-91.

Fulton, A. (1990a). The use of WORM optical disc storage for newspaper cutting in a public library. Electronic Library, vol. 8, no. 3, pp. 167-71.

Funkenbusch, A. (1991). Magneto-optic data storage in the 90's. In Proceedings of the SPIE, vol. 1396. Bellingham, WA: International Society for Optical Engineering, pp. 699-708.

Funkenbusch, A. et al (1987). Magneto-optics technology for mass storage systems. In Digest of Papers: IEEE Symposium on Mass Storage Systems. Washington, DC: IEEE Computer Society Press, pp. 101-106.

Furuhata, H. et al (1989). Development of an ISO sampled servo rewritable/write-once combination optical disk drive. Japanese Journal of Applied Physics, vol. 28, suppl. 28-3, pp. 77-80.

Gale, J. (1990). Multimedia: how we get from here to there. In Online Information 90: Fourteenth International Online Information Meeting Proceedings. Oxford: Learned Information, pp. 1-3.

Gall, B. (1987). CD-I: a powerful interactive audio/

video system. Bulletin of the American Society for Information Science, vol. 13, no. 6, pp. 24-25.

Gambino, R. et al (1989). Exchange-coupled CoPd/TbCo magneto-optic storage films. IEEE Transactions on Magnetics, vol. 25, no. 5, pp. 3749-51.

Gambogi, W. et al (1987). Conductive polymers as active optical storage media. In Topical Meeting on Optical Data Storage: Summaries of Papers. Washington, DC: Optical Society of America, pp. 159-62.

Garfinkel, S. (1991). Designing a write-once file system. Dr. Dobb's Journal, vol. 16, no. 1, pp. 78-86.

Garnham, C. and Brodie, K. (1990). A simple solution to providing remote access to CD-ROM. CAUSE/EFFECT, vol. 13, no. 4, pp. 47-51.

Garofolo, J. and Pallett, D. (1989). USe of CD-ROM for speech database storage and exchange. In Eurospeech 89: European Conference on Speech Communication and Technology. Edinburgh: CEP Consultants, vol. 2, pp. 309-12.

Gartshore, P. et al (1991). A multi-window hypermedia environment for the delivery of information to architects, engineers, and product designers. Hypermedia, vol. 3, no. 2, pp. 119-32.

Gartshore, T. (1987). BiblioFile and the school library. School Libraries in Canada, vol. 7, no. 2, pp. 36-40.

Gau, J. (1989). Magneto-optical recording materials. Materials Science and Engineering, vol. B3, no. 4, pp. 371-75.

Gazdar, K. (1991). WORM application: optical stores versus paper flood. Funkschau, no. 8, pp. 48-52.

Geensen, J. (1986). Videodisc mastering and associated LV-ROM hardware. In IEE Colloquium on The Domesday Project — Engineering Aspects. London: IEE, pp. 2/1-35.

Gelb, J. (1989). System-managed storage. IBM Systems Journal, vol. 28, no. 1, pp. 77-103.

Gelbart, D. (1990). An optical tape recorder using linear scanning. In Proceedings of the SPIE, vol. 1316. Bellingham, WA: International Society for Optical Engineering, pp. 65-68.

George, K. and Harden, D. (1990). Integrating DIP with mid-range and mainframe systems. Image Processing 90 Conference Proceedings. London: Blenheim Online, p. 16.

Gerstein, R. and Sasnett, R. (1987). Martial fracture: an interactive videodisc case study for the social sciences. Optical Information Systems, vol. 7, no. 2, pp. 120-24.

Geurts, T. and Borman, J. (1989). Dutch reference data bases on CD-ROM: report of a study project. Open, vol. 21, no. 11, pp. 390-92.

Ghislandi, P. and Campana, A. (1989). In touch with XA: some considerations on earlier experiences of CD-ROM XA production. In Online Information 89: Thirteenth International Online Information Meeting Proceedings. Oxford: Learned Information, pp. 211-26.

Gibson, M. and Cross, B. (1987). Dinosaurs of the information world. Journal of Information Systems Management, vol. 4, no. 3, pp. 57-60.

Gielda, S. (1989). CD-ROM drives: what's available and what to look for when buying one. Laserdisk Professional, vol. 2, no. 1, pp. 13-19.

Gielda, S. (1989a). Multi-user CD-ROM systems for schools and libraries. Laserdisk Professional, vol. 1, no. 4, pp. 14-17.

Giesbrecht, W. (1988). Comparison of three CD-ROM cataloguing tools: Bibliofile, LaserCat, LaserQuest. School Library Bulletin, vol. 9, no. 1, pp. 23-27.

Giesbrecht, W. and McCarthy, R. (1991). Staff resistance to library CD-ROM services. CD-ROM Professional, vol. 4, no. 3, pp. 34-38.

Gilliam, E. and Sluzenski, K. (1990). CD-ROM user groups: the experiences of Digital Equipment Corporation's Digital Library Network. Database, vol. 13, no. 6, pp. 105-108.

Gingras, B. (1991). Cost justification for an engineering drawing storage and retrieval system. Document Image Automation, vol. 11, no. 2, pp. 68-70.

Gist, T. et al (1989). The Air Force Academy Instructor Workstation (IWS). Journal of Educational Technology Systems, vol. 17, no. 4, pp. 273-95.

Gittleman, J. and Arie, Y. (1984). High performance Al:polymer: Al: tri- layer optical disk. Applied Optics, vol. 23, no. 6, pp. 3946-49.

Gladney, H. and Mantey, P. (1990). Essential issues in the design of shared document/image libraries. In Proceedings of the SPIE, vol. 1258. Bellingham, WA: International Society for Optical Engineering, pp. 54-65.

Glass, L. (1989). Digital video interactive. Byte, vol. 14, no. 5, pp. 283-89.

Glavitsch, H. (1989). IBM image directions. In SEAS: Proceedings of the Spring Meeting 1989 — End User Computing. Amsterdam: SHARE European Association, vol. 2, pp. 1257-75.

Glenn, W. and Marx, P. (1990). Low-cost medical image storage and manipulation using optical disc subsystems. In Proceedings of the SPIE, vol. 1248. Bellingham, WA: International Society for Optical Engineering, pp. 214-19.

Glitz, B. (1988). Testing the new technology: MEDLINE on CD-ROM in an academic health sciences library. Special Libraries, vol. 79, no. 1, pp. 28-33.

Glover, N. (1989). The coming revolution in error correction technology. Optical Information Systems, vol. 9, no. 4, pp. 170-86.

Gocho, N. (1988). The optical card system: description and applications. Optical Information Systems, vol. 8, no. 4, pp. 141-43.

Godwin, J. (1989). An introduction to the Insite 325 Floptical disk drive. In Proceedings of the SPIE, vol. 1078. Bellingham, WA: Society of Photo-Optical Instrumentation Engineers, pp. 71-79.

Gold, M. (1990). The MATHSCI CD-ROM at Purdue University: video instruction. In National Onine Meeting Proceedings, 1990. Medford, NJ: Learned Information, pp. 131-36.

Goldberg, H. et al (1989). STM analysis of pit formation in organic WORM media. In Proceedings of the SPIE, vol. 1078. Bellingham, WA: Society of Photo-Optical Instrumentation Engineers, pp. 170-78.

Goldfinch, R. (1990). The impact of end-user searching of CD-ROM on online use. In Online Information Retrieval: Today and Tomorrow. Oxford: Learned Information, pp. 75-83.

Goldmann, G. (1987). Investigations of applicability of magneto-optical media for erasable digital optical data memories. Siemens Research and Development Reports, vol. 16, no. 4, pp. 161-70.

Goldsmith, P. (1988). Electron trapping erasable media: a new technology. In Optical Information Systems '88 Conference Proceedings. Westport, CT: Meckler Corporation, pp. 44-47.

Goldsmith, P. and Lindmayer, J. (1990). Electron trapping: a breakthrough rewritable optical data storage technology. In Proceedings of the SPIE, vol. 1319. Bellingham: International Society for Optical Engineering, pp. 138-39.

Goldsmith, P. et al (1990). Electron trapping: a new approach to rewritable optical data storage. In Proceedings of the SPIE, vol. 1316. Bellingham: International Society for Optical Engineering, pp. 312-20.

Goldstein, C. (1982). Optical disk technology and information. Science, vol. 215, no. 11, pp. 862-88.

Goldstein, C. (1984). Storage technology: present and future. Microcomputers for Information Management, vol. 1, no. 2, pp. 79-93.

Gomex, E. and Demetriades, J. (1990). Online archiving using optical WORM for VA DHCP systems. MUG Quarterly, vol. 20, no. 1, pp. 105-108.

Gomez, E. et al (1991). A MUMPS based CD-ROM application: DHCP minimal patient dataset. MUG Quarterly, vol. 21, no. 1, pp. 29-31.

Gomez, J. (1990). HARLIC CD-ROM union catalog project. CD-ROM Professional, vol. 3, no. 6, pp. 62-65.

Gomi, M. et al (1988). Bi-substituted garnet films sputtered in Ar+H/sub 2 for magneto-optic memory. IEEE Translation Journal on Magnetics in Japan, vol. 3, no. 3, pp. 198-204.

Gomi, M. et al (1988a). Improvement in optical and magnetic properties of bi-substituted garnet sputtered films for magneto-optical recording. Journal of Applied Physics, vol. 63, no. 8, pt. 2B, pp. 3642-44.

Goodsitt, M. et al (1986). Digital workload in a large radiology department. In Application of Optical Instrumentation in Medicine XIV: Medical Imaging, Processing, and Display and Picture Archiving and Communications Systems (PACS IV) for Medical Applications. Bellingham, WA: Society of Photo-Optical Instrumentation Engineers, pp. 710-16.

Goodwin, B. (1989). A problem on the horizon: the proliferation of user interfaces for CD-ROM databases. Resource Sharing and Information Networks, vol. 4, no. 2, pp. 27-30.

Gonzalez, J. (1991). Evaluation of InfoTrac Magazine Index Plus and EBSCO Magazine Article Summaries. CD-ROM Librarian, vol. 6, no. 6, pp. 36-37.

Gordon, D. and Suer, S. (1990). The effective use of CD-ROM products with special emphasis on Biological Abstracts on CD-ROM. In Preprints: Second International Conference on the Effective Use of CD-ROM Databases. Tokyo: USACO, pp. 57-64.

Goto, Y. et al (1984). Tellurium and copper-phthalocynanine multilayer films for optical disk media. Fujitsu Scientific and Technical Journal, vol. 20, no. 3, pp. 411-29.

Gotoh, A. et al (1989). Long life twelve-inch W-O type optical disk. In Proceedings of the SPIE, vol. 1078. Bellingham, WA: Society of Photo-Optical Instrumentation Engineers, pp. 36-42.

Gotoh, A. et al (1990). Highly re-liable and durable 5.25-inch magneto-optical disks. In Proceedings of the SPIE, vol. 1316. Bellingham, WA: International Society for Optical Engineering, pp. 221-29.

Gotoh, H. et al (1990b). Write once recording by phase separation. In Proceedings of the SPIE, vol. 1316. Bellingham, WA: International Society for Optical Engineering, pp. 333-40.

Gotoh, N. et al (1989). Melt-erasing method of single beam overwrite for phase-change optical disk. In Proceedings of the SPIE, vol. 1078. Bellingham, WA: Society of Photo-Optical Instrumentation Engineers, pp. 15-26.

Gove, P. (1988). BBC advanced interactive video and the Domesday discs. In Aspects of Educational Technology: Designing New Systems and Technologies for Learning. London: Kogan Page, pp. 152-57.

Graham, M. (1986). RCA and the VideoDisc: the Business of Research. New York: Cambridge University Press.

Graham, R. (1987). Kodak optical storage system. In Topical Meeting on Optical Data Storage: Summaries of Papers. Washington, DC: Optical Society of America, pp. 78-81.

Grant, M. and Stalker, J. (1989). The MultiPlatter CD-ROM network at Boston College. Laserdisk Professional, vol. 2, no. 5, pp. 12-18.

Grant, M. and Weinschenk, A. (1990). The MultiPlatter statistical module: determining optimum staffing and training needs. In Computers in Libraries '90: Proceedings of the Fifth Annual Computers in Libraries Conference. Westport, CT: Meckler Corporation, pp. 68-71.

Gravesteijn, D. (1987). New material developments for write-once and erasable phase-change optical recording. In Topical Meeting on Optical Data Storage: Technical Digest Series, vol. 10. Washington, DC: Optical Society of America, pp. 40-43.

Gravesteijn, D. (1988). Materials developments for write-once and erasable phase-change optical recording. Applied Optics, vol. 27, no. 4, pp. 736-38.

Gravesteijn, D. (1989). Phase-change optical recording. Philips Technical Review, vol. 44, no. 8, pp. 250-58.

Gravesteijn, D. and Van der Veen, J. (1984). Organic dye films for optical recording. Philips Technical Review, vol. 41, no. 2, pp. 325-33.

Gravesteijn, D. et al (1987). Phase-change optical data storage in GaSb. Applied Optics, vol. 26, no. 22, pp. 4772-76.

Green, I. (1988). The new face of C-O-M: Arkive IV/CRS. Optical Information Systems, vol. 8, no. 2, pp. 84-85.

Greenblatt, J. (1988). Information technology: industry update on optical character recognition and image scanners. Information Management Review, vol. 3, no. 3, pp. 71-74.

Greidanus, F. (1990). Status and future of magneto-optical disk drive technologies. Philips Journal of Research, vol. 45, no. 1, pp. 19-34.

Greidanus, F. and Zeper, W. (1990). Magneto-optical storage materials. MRS Bulletin, vol. 15, no. 4, pp. 31-39.

Greidanus, F. and Klahn, S. (1989). Magneto-optical recording and data storage materials. Advanced Materials, no. 2, pp. 45-51.

Greidanus, F. et al (1989). Thermomagnetic writing in thin Co/Pt layered structures. Applied Physics Letters, vol. 54, no. 24, pp. 2481-83.

Griffith, C. (1989). West Publishing's legal databases on CD-ROM. Laserdisk Professional, vol. 2, no. 5, pp. 61-66.

Griffith, C. (1990). Legal information on CD-ROM: a survey. CD-ROM Professional, vol. 3, no. 3, pp. 80-85.

Griffith, C. (1990a). Legal specific laserdisks: not just a field of dreams. Laserdisk Professional, vol. 3, no. 2, pp. 18-21.

Grimshaw, A. and Williams, B. (1987). BBC Domesday: from parchment and quills to lasers and disks. Information Media and Technology, vol. 20, no. 2, pp. 164-66.

Grundy, P. (1990). Materials in Magnetic and Magneto-Optic Information Storage. Metallic Materials, vol. 6, no. 7, pp. 422-27.

Gupta, M. (1984). Laser recording on an overcoated organic dye-binder medium. Applied Optics, vol. 23, no. 6, pp. 3950-55.

Gupta, M. and Strome, F. (1985). Performance of an erasable organic dye-binder optical disk medium. In Topical Meeting on Optical Data Storage: Digest of Technical Papers. Washington, DC: Optical Society of America, pp. WBB1/1-4.

Gupta, M. and Strome, F. (1986). Erasable laser recording in an organic dye-binder optical disk medium. Journal of Applied Physics, vol. 60, no. 8, pp. 2932-37.

Guru Prasad, D. (1984). A hierarchical storage and imaging display system for picture archiving and communication systems (PACS). In Proceedings of the SPIE, vol. 454. Bellingham, WA: Society of Photo-Optical Instrumentation Engineers, pp. 99-102.

Guttuso, F. (1989). Technology and market in cataloguing choice. Bollettino d'Informazioni, vol. 29, nos. 2-3, pp. 251-55.

Haarer, D. (1987). Photochemical hole burning: a high density storage scheme. Japanese Journal of Applied Physics: Supplement, vol. 26, suppl. 26-4, pp. 227-32.

Hack, S. et al. (1986). Architecture for an image filing and indexing system. In Application of Optical Instrumentation in Medicine XIV: Medical Imaging, Processing, and Display and Picture Archiving and Communication Systems (PACS IV) for Medical Applications. Bellingham, WA: Society of Photo-Optical Instrumentation Engineers, pp. 666-75.

Hagan, D. (1987). The Tacoma debut of Books in Print Plus. Library Journal, vol. 112, no. 14, pp. 149-51.

Hall, J. (1990). Optical disk system automates records management at Star Bank Cincinnati. Remittance and Document Processing Today, vol. 12, no. 6, pp. 7-8, 11.

Hallgren, S. (1990). Developing your CD-ROM. Electronic Library, vol. 8, no. 5, pp. 331-35.

Hallgren, S. (1990a). CD-Kat in Swedish public libraries, or how to make a shared disc act as a local catalogue. In Bibliographic Access in Europe: First International Conference. Aldershot, United Kingdom: Gower, pp. 204-11.

Halper, S. (1988). Optical disk backup library facilities for microcomputers. EDPACS, vol. 15, no. 11, pp. 5-7.

Halperin, M. and Renfro, P. (1988). Online vs. CD-ROM onsite: high-volume searching — considering the alternatives. Online, vol. 12, no. 6, pp. 36-42.

Halter, J. and Iwamoto, N. (1988). Thermal-mechanical modeling of a reversible dye-polymer media. In Proceedings of the SPIE, vol. 899. Bellingham, WA: Society of Photo-Optical Instrumentation Engineers, pp. 201-10.

Hamada, E. et al (1989). CD-compatible write-once disc system with high reflectivity. In Proceedings of the SPIE, vol. 1078. Bellingham, WA: Society of Photo-Optical Instrumentation Engineers, pp. 80-88.

Hamana, S. et al (1990). CCD data acquisition system installed on the spectrograph at the Norikura Solar Observatory. Reports of the National Astronomical Observatory of Japan, vol. 1, no. 1, pp. 13-21.

Hammack, G. et al (1985). The computer controlled videodisk: a new technology for optometric education. Journal of Optometric Education, vol. 10, no. 4, pp. 8-11.

Hammamura, E. and Itsubo, A. (1988). Polydiacetylene as optical memory and information processor. In Proceedings of the SPIE, vol. 824. Bellingham, WA: Society of Photo-Optical Instrumentation Engineers, pp. 66-71.

Han, I. and Nicholls, P. (1990). Evaluation of KAware Disk Publisher and the KAware2 retrieval system. CD-ROM Professional, vol. 3, no. 3, pp. 45-50.

Hanna, J. et al (1986). Photo-induced memory effect on a charge-acceptance in organic films and its application to a laser recording. Electrophotography, vol. 25, no. 3, pp. 249-57.

Hansen, P. (1990). Magneto-optical recording materials and technologies. Journal of Magnetism and Magnetic Materials, vol. 83, no. 1, pp. 6-12.

Hansen, P. and Heitmann, H. (1989). Media for erasable magnetooptic recording. IEEE Transactions on Magnetics, vol. 22, no. 5, pp. 943-45.

Hansen, P. et al (1991). Magnetic and magneto-optical properties of rare-earth transition-metal alloys containing Dy, Ho, Fe, Co. Journal of Applied Physics, vol. 69, no. 5, pp. 3194-3207.

Hanson, T. (1990). A survey of European Communities databases. ASLIB Proceedings, vol. 42, no. 6, pp. 171-88.

Hanus, F. and Laude, L. (1990). Application to optical data storage of laser induced synthesis of

CuTe. In Proceedings of the SPIE, vol. 1279. Bellingham, WA: International Society for Optical Engineering, pp. 196-202.

Han Vinck, A. (1988). On the application of coding for storage systems. In Video, Audio, and Data Recording: Seventh International Conference. London: IERE, pp. 213-17.

Hao, W. et al (1989). The optical and electrical properties of Te-In-Sb films during their phase transition. Journal of Non-Crystalline Solids, vol. 112, no. 1-3, pp. 291-5.

Hara, S. et al (1988). Hardware design for high performance 130-mm optical disk storage system. Review of the Electronic Communications Laboratory, vol. 36, no. 2, pp. 253-60.

Hara, S. (1989). An application of optical cards to mass health examination. In MEDINFO 89: Proceedings of the Sixth Conference on Medical Informatics. Amsterdam: North-Holland, pp. 1164-68.

Hardin, S. (1990). American Business Disk. CD-ROM Librarian, vol. 5, no. 11, pp. 36-39.

Harding, W. et al (1990). Object storage hierarchy management. IBM Systems Journal, vol. 29, no. 3, pp. 384-97.

Harrington, J. (1990). Aquatic Sciences and Fisheries Abstracts. CD-ROM Librarian, vol. 5, no. 10, pp. 41-45.

Harrington, R. and Braunschweig, B. (1990). Applying electronic image processing to photostats. Inform, vol. 4, no. 5, pp. 31-34.

Harris, R. (1991). OPTI-NET CD-ROM LAN at Eastern Virginia Medical School Library. CD-ROM Professional, vol. 4, no. 1, pp. 25-26.

Hartman, J. and Lind, M. (1987). Erasable bilayer dye-polymer optical recording medium. In Topical Meeting on Optical Data Storage: Technical Digest Series. Washington, DC: Optical Society of America, pp. 155-58.

Hartman, J. et al (1989). Read channel optical modeling for a bump forming dye-polymer optical data storage medium. In Proceedings of the SPIE, vol. 1078. Bellingham, WA: Society of Photo-Optical Instrumentation Engineers, pp. 308-24.

Hartmann, M. et al (1984). Erasable magneto-optical recording media. IEEE Transactions on Magnetics, vol. 20, no. 4, pp. 1013-18.

Hartmann, M. et al (1986). Improvement of corrosion resistance of GdTbFe by metal coatings. IEEE Transactions on Magnetics, vol. 22, no. 5, pp. 943-45.

Harvey, D. (1991). CD-ROM drives: how good is the third generation? Byte, vol. 16, no. 9, pp. 268-75.

Harvey, D. and Reinhardt, A. (1990). State of the media. Byte, vol. 15, no. 12, pp. 275-81.

Hashimoto, S. et al (1990). Ultrathin Co/Pt and Co/Pd new magneto-optical recording media. In Proceedings of the SPIE, vol. 1248. Bellingham, WA: Society of Photo-Optical Instrumentation Engineers, pp. 36-48.

Hashimoto, Y. (1987). Experimental HDTV digital VTR with a bit rate of 1 gbps. IEEE Transactions on Magnetics, vol. 23, no. 5, pt. 2, pp. 3167-72.

Hashimoto, Y. et al (1990). Direct overwriting capability of magneto-optical disks. Journal of Applied Physics, vol. 67, no. 9, pt. 2A, pp. 4420-22.

Hattori, Y. (1990). An overview of CD-ROM XA with demonstration. In Preprints: Second International Conference on the Effective Use of CD-ROM Databases. Tokyo: USACO, pp. 66-81.

Hatwar, T. and Majumdar, D. (1988). Oxidation and corrosion resistance of TbFeCoPt alloy films. IEEE Transactions on Magnetics, vol. 24, no. 6, pp. 2449-51.

Hatwar, T. and Stinson, D. (1991). Improvement in the sensitivity of the magneto-optical media. Journal of Applied Physics, vol. 69, no. 8, pt. 2A, pp. 4963-65.

Haucom, R. and Malone, E. (1987). A survey of Level III videodisc delivery systems. In CD-I and Interactive Videodisc Technology. Indianapolis: Howard W. Sams, pp. 93-116.

Hawkins, H. and Skriba, T. (1986). Utilization of an in-house videodisc recorder in image intensive medical specialities and development of educational strategies for large image data bases. In Application of Optical Instrumentation in Medicine XIV: Medical Imaging, Processing, and Display and Picture Archiving and Communication Systems (PACS IV) for Medical Applications. Bellingham, WA: Society of Photo-Optical Instrumentation Engineers, pp. 748-54.

Hayashi, Y. and Ogawa, S. (1991). Optical recording properties and structure of new silver metallic particles system. In Transactions of the Institute of Electronics, Information, and Communication Engineers, vol. J74C-II, no. 3, pp. 187-93.

Hayashi, Y. and Ogawa, S. (1991). Optical recording properties and structure of new silver metallic particles system. In Transactions of the Institute of Electronics, Information, and Communication Engineers, vol. J74C-II, no. 3, pp. 187-93.

Hayashi, Y. and Ogawa, S. (1991). Optical recording properties and structure of new silver metallic particles system. Transactions of the Institute of Electronics, Information and Communication Engineers, vol. J74C-II, no. 3, pp. 187-93.

Haycock, P. et al (1990). Structural and magnetic properties of laser-annealed magneto-optica thin films. IEEE Transactions on Magnetics, vol. 26, no. 5, pp. 1921-23.

Haynes, D. (1989). BNB on CD-ROM. C&L Applications, vol. 3, no. 2, pp. 2-3.

Heacox, S. (1991). CD-ROM standards: can we make them a reality? In Twelfth National Online Meeting: Proceedings. Medford, NJ: Learned Information, pp. 129-34.

Hecht, J. (1982). Lasers store a wealth of data. High Technology, vol. 2, no. 3, pp. 60-67.

Hecht, J. (1987). Erasable optical disks: coming at last. Laser Optronics, vol. 6, no. 9, pp. 77-79.

Hecht, J. (1987a). Optical memories vie for data storage. High Technology, vol. 7, no. 8, pp. 43-47.

Hedge, S. et al (1986). AT&T PACS architecture. In Application of Optical Instrumentation in Medicine XIV: Medical Imaging, Processing, and Display and Picture Archiving and Communication Systems (PACS IV) for Medical Applications. Bellingham, WA: Society of Photo-Optical Instrumentation Engineers, pp. 618-25.

Hegarty, K. (1988). The compact disk-circulation system interface at Tacoma Public Library: beyond stand-alone CD-ROM. Library Hi Tech, vol. 6, no. 3, pp. 103-12.

Heimburger, A. (1991). CD-ROM news from the Nordic countries. CD-ROM Professional, vol. 4, no. 3, pp. 22-25.

Heitmann, H. et al (1985). Amorphous rare earth-transition metal films for magneto-optical storage. Journal of Physics, vol. 46, no. C6, pp. 9-18.

Helgerson, L. and Martens, H. (1988). In search of CD-ROM data. PC Tech Journal, vol. 6, no. 10, pp. 66-73.

Hellstern, E. et al (1990). In-line production of magneto-optical quadrilayers. In Proceedings of the SPIE, vol. 1316. Bellingham, WA: International Society for Optical Engineering, pp. 230-36.

Helsel, S. (1987). The curricular domain of educational interactive videodisc. Optical Information Systems, vol. 7, no. 2, pp. 107-12.

Helsel, S. (1989). Optical technologies in medical schools. Optical Information Systems, vol. 9, no. 2, pp. 93-97.

Henderson, R. and Landesman, E. (1989). Interactive videodisc instruction in pre-calculus. Journal of Educational Technology Systems, vol. 17, no. 2, pp. 91-101.

Hendley, T. (1987). CD-ROM and Optical Publishing Systems: an Assessment of the Impact of Optical Read-Only Memory Systems on the Information Industry and a Comparison Between Them and Traditional Paper, Microfilm, and Online Publishing. Westport, CT: Meckler Corporation.

Hennig, J. (1985). Substrates made from transparent plastics for optical storage discs. Feinwerktechnik und Messtechnik, vol. 93, no. 6, pp. 305-308.

Hensel, M. (1986). Data publishing on optical discs. In CD-ROM: the New Papyrus. Redmond, WA: Microsoft Press, pp. 487-94.

Hertel, J. (1989). Consumer marketing opportunities for the optical memory card industry. Optical Information Systems, vol. 9, no. 1, pp. 20-22.

Herther, N. (1988). CD-ROM in libraries: the view from OCLC; an interview with Edward Kurdyla. Laserdisk Professional, vol. 1, no. 1, pp. 50-55.

Herther, N. (1990). Turning raw technology into real products: CD-ROM at Hewlett-Packard — an interview with HP's Marc Hoff. Laserdisk Professional, vol. 3, no. 1, pp. 28-35.

Herther, N. (1990a). 1989 OCLC study shows continued CD-ROM growth in libraries. Laserdisk Professional, vol. 3, no. 2, pp. 22-24.

Herzog, D. (1980). Optical disk approaches as mass storage. In Digest of Papers: IEEE Symposium on Mass Storage Systems. New York: IEEE, pp. 29-32.

Heshiki, A. et al (1988). Teleradiology at Gunma University Hospital. Medical Informatics, vol. 13, no. 4, pp. 295-301.

Heu, R. et al (1986). First experiences with an electronic image storage system. In Application of Optical Instrumentation in Medicine XIV: Medical Imaging, Processing, and Display and Picture Archiving and Communication Systems (PACS IV) for Medical Applications. Bellingham, WA: Society of Photo-Optical Instrumentation Engineers, pp. 557-60.

Hewison, N. (1989). Evaluating CD-ROM versions of the MEDLINE database: a checklist. Bulletin of the Medical Library Association, vol. 77, no. 4, pp. 332-36.

Hibino, K. et al (1990). 3D HDTV videodisc system. IEEE Transactions on Consumer Electronics, vol. 36, no. 3, pp. 555-59.

Higgins, B. and Oesterreicher, H. (1987). Properties and stability of Nd sub2/Fe sub 14/B particles. IEEE Transactions on Magnetics, vol. 23, no. 1, pp. 92-93.

Hildreth, C. (1987). CD-ROM public access library catalogues: uses, advantages, problems. In Impact of New Information Technology on International Library Cooperation. Essen, West Germany: Universitatsbibliothek Essen, pp. 151-77.

Hindel, R. (1986). Review of optical storage for archiving digital medical images. Radiology, vol. 161, no. 2, pp. 257-62.

Hindel, R. (1990). Archiving radiological images on WORM optical storage. Optical Information Systems, vol. 10, no. 3, pp. 131-39.

Hinds, T. (1990). CD-ROM development systems: a tutorial. CD-ROM Professional, vol. 3, no. 6, pp. 56-61.

Hinohara, S. et al (1988). Medical applications of IC card and optical card. In Towards New Hospital Information Systems: Proceedings of the IFIP-IMIA Working Conference. Amsterdam: North-Holland Publishing Company, pp. 197-201.

Hioki, T. et al (1988). Hi-vision optical video disc. IEEE Transactions on Consumer Electronics, vol. 34, no. 1, pp. 72-77.

Hirata, S. (1989). Vehicle-mounted navigation system using satellite radiowaves: NAVSTAR/GPS. Shingo Hoan, vol. 44, no. 10, pp. 439-41.

Hirata, S. and Yokouchi, K. (1987). A car navigation system using satellites. Mitsubishi Denki Giho, vol. 61, no. 8, pp. 77-80.

Hoekstra, B. (1983). Optical disk systems. Physics Technology, vol. 14, no. 5, pp. 241-48.

Hoffman, L. (1989). Cox Enterprises depends on CD-ROM-based product to support Hewlett-Packard minicomputer system. Laserdisk Professional, vol. 2, no. 5, pp. 28-30.

Hoffman, R. and Potember, R. (1989). Organometallic materials for erasable optical storage. Applied Optics, vol. 28, no. 7, pp. 1417-21.

Hoffos, S. (1986). Medical and health care applications in the British market. Optical Information Systems, vol. 6, no. 4, pp. 303-305.

Holberger, K. (1990). Evaluating optical jukebox systems for imaging applications. Optical Information Systems, vol. 10, no. 5, pp. 247-51.

Holder, S. and Daynes, R. (1986). Interactive design strategies. In CD-I and Interactive Videodisc Technology. Indianapolis: Howard W. Sams, pp. 29-68.

Holland, M. (1990). IEEE/IEE on CD-ROM: a review from a beta test. CD-ROM Librarian, vol. 5, no. 2, pp. 34-42.

Hollens, D. and Rible, J. (1991). Answers on the disc: general encyclopedias on CD-ROM. CD-ROM Professional, vol. 4, no. 4, pp. 54-61.

Holloway, C. (1987). Books in Print and Ulrich's on CD-ROM: a preliminary review. Online, vol. 11, no. 5, pp. 57-61.

Holmes, C. (1989). The use of optical mass storage in a CAD environment. In OIS International 1989: Proceedings of the Sixth Annual Conference on Optical Information Systems. London: Meckler Corporation, pp. 63-77.

Holmes, R. (1988). Laser disc technology: the implications for medicine and medical information. Audiovisual Librarian, vol. 14, no. 4, pp. 201-10.

Holtslag, A. and Scholte, P. (1989). Optical measurement of the refractive index, layer thickness, and volume changes of thin films. Applied Optics, vol. 28, no. 23, pp. 5095-5104.

Holtz, F. (1988). CD-ROMs: Breakthrough in Information Storage. Blue Ridge Summit, PA: Tab Books.

Holzberg, C. (1990). Music CDs and the computer: powerful new teaching tools. Technology and Learning, vol. 11, no. 1, pp. 88-90.

Hon, D. (1986). Parameters for the design of interactive programs. In CD-I and Interactive Videodisc Technology. Indianapolis: Howard W. Sams, pp. 15-28.

Honey, S. and White, M. (1986). Cartographic databases. In CD-ROM: the New Papyrus. Redmond, WA: Microsoft Press, pp. 563-72.

Honma, S. (1987). Precision moulding vs. mould materials. Plastics Age, vol. 33, no. 3, pp. 109-17.

Hooten, P. (1990). A preliminary analysis of CAT CD450 for retrospective conversion for the mid-sized research library. OCLC Micro, vol. 6, no. 1, pp. 18-20.

Hoover, J. (1986). Simultaneous write and read operations on an optical disk drive at rates up to 3 MBytes/sec. In Proceedings of the SPIE, vol. 695. Bellingham, WA: Society of Photo-Optical Instrumentation Engineers, pp. 323-28.

Horiai, N. et al (1991). Be-Cr-doped high-corrosion-resistant magneto- optical disks. Journal of Applied Physics, vol. 69, no. 8, pt. 2A, pp. 4764-66.

Horie, K. and Furusawa, A. (1991). Photochemical hole burning (PHB) for the characterization of low energy excitation modes in amorphous polymers. In Polymeric Materials Science and Engineering: Proceedings of the ACS Division of Polymeric Materials and Science and Engineering, vol. 64. Washington, DC: American Chemical Society, Books and Journals Division, pp. 248-49.

Horstman, R. (1988). Videodisc and player for

HDMAC. IN IBC 1988: International Broadcasting Convention. London: IEE, pp. 224-27.

Hosaka, H. (1988). Advances in magnetic and optical recording card. Journal of the Institute of Television Engineering of Japan, vol. 42, no. 4, pp. 365-68.

Hosokawa, T. et al (1989). 5.25-inch rewritable optical disk system. National Technical Report, vol. 35, no. 2, pp. 46-52.

Houze, R. (1991). Radionavigation from satellites: the AVIC system. Auto-Volt Electrauto, no. 664, pp. 11-13.

Howe, D. and Marchant, A. (1983). Digital optical recording in infrared sensitive organic polymers. In Topical Meeting on Optical Data Storage: Summaries of Papers. Washington, DC: Optical Society of America, pp. 23-25.

Howe, D. and Meichle, M. (1987). Digital optical recording: the case for coding. In Topical Meeting on Optical Data Storage: Summaries of Papers. Washington, DC: Optical Society of America, pp. 106-10.

Howe, D. and Wrobel, J. (1981). Solvent-coated organic materials for high-density optical recording. Journal of Vacuum Science and Technology, vol. 18, no. 1, pp. 92-99.

Hoy, J. (1991). Write-once or not write-once. Optical Information Systems, vol. 11, no. 1, pp. 24-25.

Hughes, A. (1989). Using different CD-ROMs on the same nondedicated workstation: some problems and solutions. Program, vol. 23, no. 4, pp. 415-22.

Hughes, H. (1989). Conversion of a teacher-delivered course into an interactive videodisc-delivered program. Foreign Language Annals, vol. 22, no. 3, pp. 283-94.

Hume, A. (1988). The file motel: an incremental backup system for Unix. In Proceedings of the Summer 1988 USENIX Conference. Berkeley, CA: USENIX Association, pp. 61-72.

Hunter, T. (1989). Vehicle navigation and flett management using differential GPS. In Conference Record of Papers Presented at the First Vehicle Navigation and Information Systems Conference. New York: IEEE, p. 366.

Huntting, S. (1986). Open wide and say dataaa. In CD-ROM: The New Papyrus. Redmond, WA: Microsoft Press, pp. 529-38.

Hurst, R. (1988). Digital video interactive: the technology and its applications. In Proceedings of the SPIE, vol. 899. Bellingham, WA: Society of Photo-Optical Instrumentation Engineers, pp. 296-305.

Hurst, R. and Luther, A. (1988). DVI: digital video from a CD-ROM. Information Display, vol. 4, no. 4, pp. 8-10.

Hutchison, R. (1991). Benchmark testing of CD-ROM drives. CD-ROM Professional, vol. 4, no. 1, pp. 31-35; vol. 4, no. 2, pp. 46-49; vol. 4, no. 3, pp. 56-61; vol. 4, no. 4, pp. 48-52.

Hutchison, R. (1991a). Considerations of technical sheets and testing: the new Mitsumi drive. CD-ROM Professional, vol. 4, no. 5, pp. 81-85.

Ichiyama, Y. et al (1985). A disk handling system and optical disk jukebox storage. In Proceedings of the SPIE, vol. 529. Bellingham, WA: Society of Photo-Optical Instrumentation Engineers, pp. 89-94.

Iijima, T. (1987). Highly stable indium alloyed TbFe amorphous films for magneto-optic memory. Applied Physics Letters, vol. 50, no. 25, pp. 1835-37.

Iijima, T. and Hatakeyama, I. (1987). Stability properties of indium doped TbFe amorphous films for magneto-optic memory applications. IEEE Transactions on Magnetics, vol. 23, no. 5, pp. 2626-28.

Iijima, T. et al (1989). Magnetic and magneto-optical properties of In-alloyed TbFe amorphous films. Applied Physics Letters, vol. 54, no. 23, pp. 2376-77.

Iijima, T. et al (1989a). Crystallization characteristics of phase change optical disks. Japanese Journal of Applied Physics, vol. 28, no. 11, pp. 1985-87.

Iiyori, H. and Takayama, S. (1991). Triple-layered NdCo amorphous-alloy films for magneto-optical media. Journal of Applied Physics, vol. 69, no. 8, pt. 2A, pp. 4761-63.

Ikeda, T. et al (1990). 3.5-inch rewritable optical disk drive for DBF and media compatibility. Journal of the Institute of Television Engineers of Japan, vol. 44, no. 10, pp. 1418-24.

Ikegawa, S. et al (1988). Reversible change between metastable crystalline phases by laser beam irradiation in sputtered Au-Ge alloy films. Journal of Vacuum Science and Technology, vol. 6, no. 3, pt. 2, pp. 1855-58.

Ikemoto, H. et al (1990). The optical properties of liquid selenium and tellurium. Journal of Non-Crystalline Solids, vol. 117, no. 1, pp. 493-96.

Imamura, N. (1988). Magneto-optical recording. Solid State Physics, vol. 23, no. 7, pp. 494-500.

Imamura, N. (1990). Recent progress of optical disc recording technology. Journal of the Institute of Television Engineers of Japan, vol. 44, no. 10, pp. 1337-42.

Inamura, K. et al (1990). Trial of PACS employing magneto-optical disks. In Proceedings of the SPIE, vol. 1234. Bellingham, WA: International Society for Optical Engineering, pp. 50-59.

Inoue, H. et al (1990). Direct overwriting of magneto-optical disk. In Proceedings of the SPIE, vol. 1248. Bellingham, WA: International Society for Optical Engineering, pp. 60-64.

Inui, T. et al (1987). Development of optical disk substrates. Sharp Technical Journal, no. 37, pp. 77-81.

Inui, T. et al (1989). Magneto-optical disk by contact printing method. In Proceedings of the SPIE, vol. 1078. Bellingham, WA: Society of Photo-Optical Instrumentation Engineers, pp. 204-13.

Irwin, D. (1991). Integrating CD-CATSS into the cataloging workflow. Information Technology and Libraries, vol. 10, no. 2, pp. 133-39.

Isailovic, J. (1985). Videodisc and Optical Memory Systems. Englewood Cliffs, NJ: Prentice-Hall.

Isbouts, J. (1987). CD-I: an analysis of design and application strategies. Optical Information Systems, vol. 7, no. 4, pp. 145-50.

Ishigame, M. (1990). Image input technology of optical image file. Journal of the Institute of Television Engineers of Japan, vol. 44, no. 11, pp. 1516-25.

Ishii, K. et al (1990). Mass storage technology in networks. In Proceedings of the SPIE, vol. 1248. Bellingham, WA: International Society for Optical Engineering, pp. 2-9.

Ishii, O. et al (1989). Double-layered overwritable magneto-optic disk with magnetic recording and magneto-optic reproducing. Journal of Applied Physics, vol. 65, no. 12, pp. 5245-47.

Ismael, R. (1989). Creative CD-I authoring. In OpticalInfo 89: the International Meeting for Optical Publishing and Storage. Oxford: Learned Information, pp. 137-43.

Itao, K. et al (1987). High data transfer rate and high-speed accessing optical disk drive technology. In Topical Meeting on Optical Data Storage. Washington, DC: Optical Society of America, pp. 164-67.

Itao, K. et al (1988). High performance magneto-optical mass storage system. Review of the Electronic Communications Laboratory, vol. 36, no. 2, pp. 247-52.

Ito, H. and Kojima, T. (1991). Analysis of higher information density pregroove model by boundary element method. Electronics Letters, vol. 27, no. 17, pp. 1511-12.

Ito, O. et al (1987). High speed write-once optical memory using 130mm disk for computer use. Japanese Journal of Applied Physics: Supplement, vol. 26, suppl. 26-4, pp. 211-24.

Itoga, M. et al (1987). Wideband recording technology for high-definition baseband VCRs. IEEE Transactions on Consumer Electronics, vol. 33, no. 3, pp. 203-209.

Itoh, M. et al (1983). New organic dye medium for ablative optical recording. In Proceedings of the SPIE, vol. 420. Bellingham, WA: Society of Photo-Optical Instrumentation Engineers, pp. 332-335.

Itoh, U. (1990). Ultra high density optical memory. Journal of the Institute of Television Engineers of Japan, vol. 44, no. 2, pp. 162-67.

Itoh, Y. et al (1988). Analog full-motion video recording on magneto-optical disk. Sharp Technical Review, no. 39, pp. 49-53.

Ivey, M. et al (1991). Optical information storage and charge traps in PZT thin films. IEEE Transactions on Ultrasonics, Ferroelectrics, and Frequency Control, vol. 38, no. 4, pp. 337-43.

Iwasawa, A. et al (1986). Photopolymerization and the reversibility of phase-change erasable optical disks. In Proceedings of the SPIE, vol. 695. Bellingham, WA: Society of Photo-Optical Instrumentation Engineers, pp. 86-90.

Izumi, H. et al (1990). Overwrite characteristics of magneto-optical disks by magnetic field modulation. In Proceedings of the SPIE, vol. 1316. Bellingham, WA: International Society for Optical Engineering, pp. 260-66.

Jackson, K. (1988). Downloading provisions of CD-ROM software: are they as good as they should be? Laserdisk Professional, vol. 1, no. 3, pp. 76-79.

Jackson, K. (1990). CASSIS/CD-ROM makes patent searching easier. Laserdisk Professional, vol. 3, no. 2, pp. 60-66.

Jackson, K. (1990a). CD-ROM databases from the U.S. government — some with minimal software. Laserdisk Professional, vol. 3, no. 2, pp. 94-97.

Jackson, K. and Kinyon, W. (1989). Diskware — a status report: laserdisk retrieval software today. Laserdisk Professional, vol. 2, no. 2, pp. 90-92.

Jackson, M. (1989). Software information on compact disk: a review of Software-CD and the ICP Software Information Directory. Laserdisk Professional, vol. 2, no. 5, pp. 50-55.

Jacobs, B. (1985). Thin films requirements for optical recording. Vacuum, vol. 35, no. 4, pp. 445-46.

Jacobs, B. et al (1984). Aging characteristics of amorphous magneto-optic recording media. Applied Optics, vol. 23, no. 15, pp. 3979-82.

Jacobson, R. and Brown, K. (1989). Archival properties of holograms. In Proceedings of the SPIE, vol. 1051. Bellingham, WA: Society of Instrumentation Engineers, pp. 60-67.

Jacobson, S. (1990). The use of optical storage for patent image retrieval: the US Patent and Trademark Office's Automated Patent System. In Proceedings of the SPIE, vol. 1248. Bellingham, WA: International Society for Optical Engineering, pp. 18-25.

Jacso, P. (1989). CD-CATSS: UTLAS' serials compact disk database; a review and critique. Serials Review, vol. 15, no. 4, pp. 7-18.

Jacso, P. (1989b). Negotiating your way through the pitfalls of CD-ROM installation: a guide to system requirements. Electronic Library, vol. 7, no. 5, pp. 287-94.

Jacso, P. (1990). The ideal CD-ROM workstation for the 1990s. In Online Information 90: Fourteenth International Online Information Meeting. Oxford: Learned Information, pp. 25-32.

Jacso, P. (1991). Coverage and accessibility in Ulrich's Plus and EBSCO-CD. Serials Librarian, vol. 20, no. 1, pp. 1-35.

Jacso, P. (1991a). Data transfer capabilities of CD-ROM software. CD-ROM Professional, vol. 4, no. 1, pp. 63-66 (Part I); vol. 4, no. 2, pp. 61-66 (Part II).

Jaggi, B. et al (1987). Optical memory disks in large data-base management for cytometry. Applied Optics, vol. 26, no. 16, pp. 3325-29.

Jansson, P. (1987). Patterning CD-ROM. PC Tech Journal, vol. 5, no. 7, pp. 162-73.

Jasionowski, A. (1991). Using phase-change technology with direct overwrite in a multifunction optical disk drive. Optical Information Systems, vol. 11, no. 1, pp. 4-8.

Jewell, T. (1989). CD-ROM and end-users: the University of Washington experience. CD-ROM Librarian, vol. 4, no. 1, pp. 15-21.

Jiang, F. and Okuda, M. (1991). The effect of doping on the erasure speed and stability of reversible phase-change optical recording films. Japanese Journal of Applied Physics, part 1, vol. 30, no. 1, pp. 97-100.

Jiang, F. et al (1989). Optical recording properties of In/sub 47/Se sub 51/Pb/sub 2 thin films. In Proceedings of the SPIE, vol. 1078. Bellingham, WA: Society of Photo-Optical Instrumentation Engineers, pp. 165-69.

Jipson, V. and Jones, C. (1981). Infrared dyes for optical storage. Journal of Vacuum Science and Technology, vol. 18, no. 1, pp. 105-109.

Johnson, S. (1988). LaserQuest: laser technology from GRC for retrospective conversion and on-going cataloging. Information Retrieval and Library Automation, vol. 24, no. 5, pp. 1-4.

Johnson, S. (1989). CAT CD450: new from OCLC. Information Retrieval and Library Automation, vol. 24, no. 11, pp. 1-2.

Jones, K. and Bell, C. (1984). Automatic extraction of words from texts especially for input into information retrieval systems based on inverted files. In Research and Development in Information Retrieval: Proceedings of the Third Joint BCS and ACM Symposium. Cambridge: Cambridge University Press, pp. 409-20.

Jones, S. (1990). The electronic era of information delivery: challenges for the information industry. In Preprints: Second International Conference on the Effective Use of CD-ROM Databases. Tokyo: USACO, pp. 44-49.

Jordahl, G. (1989). CD-ROM makes itself at home in-house. Inform, vol. 3, no. 10, pp. 30-33.

Joy, A. and Keane, N. (1989). CDMARC Subjects: the Library of Congress Subject Headings on CD-ROM. CD-ROM Librarian, vol. 4, no. 9, pp. 36-45.

Jutamilia, S. et al (1989). Optical associative memory with nonzero diagonal interconnection matrix based on electron trapping materials. In ICJNN International Joint Conference on Neural Networks. New York: IEEE, p. 633.

Jutamilia, S. et al (1989a). Optical pattern recognition and associative memory using electron trapping materials. In Proceedings of the SPIE, vol. 1053. Bellingham, WA: Society of Photo-Optical Instrumentation Engineers, pp. 67-74.

Jutamulia, S. et al (1991). Use of electron trapping materials in optical signal processing. Applied Optics, vol. 29, no. 22, p. 4806; vol. 30, no. 20, pp. 2879-84.

Kaehler, M. and Theissing, U. (1989). Cartographic raster archives: the first step of an hybrid geographic information system concept. In GIS/LIS '89 Proceedings: Annual Conference. Bethesda, MD: American Society of Photogrammetry and Remote Sensing, vol. 2, pp. 804-13.

Kaempf, G. (1987). Special polymers for data memories. Polymer Journal, vol. 19, no. 2, pp. 257-68.

Kaempf, G. et al (1987). Polymers as substrates and media for data storage. Polymer Engineering Science, vol. 27, no. 19, pp. 1421-35.

Kahn, P. (1988). Making a difference: a review of the user interface features of six CD-ROM data base products. Optical Information Systems, vol. 8, no. 4, pp. 169-83.

Kaiman, A. (1988). Digital video interactive. In SID International Symposium: Digest of Technical Papers. Playa del Rey, CA: Society for Information Display, pp. 8-9.

Kakihara, M. (1989). Mazda Car Communication System. Systems, Control, and Information, vol. 33, no. 7, pp. 355-62.

Kalb, H. and Schmit, S. (1990). Archiving of documents on WORM disks: the NFS approach. In Proceedings of the Spring 1990 EUUG Conference. Buntingford, UK: EUUG, pp. 193-98.

Kalstrom, D. (1988). Manufacturing "platinum standard" optical disks. In Optical Information Systems '88 Conference Proceedings. Westport, CT: Meckler Corporation, pp. 51-52.

Kalstrom, D. (1991). Optical media design takes on the appearance of a moth's eye. Computer Technology Review, vol. 11, no. 6, pp. 67-72.

Kaltenborn, K. (1991). End user searching in the CD-ROM data base Medline. Nachrichten fuer Dokumentation, vol. 42, no. 2, pp. 107-114 (Part I); vol. 42, no. 3, pp. 177-90 (Part II).

Kalthoff, R. (1990). Buying Electronic Image Management Systems. Cincinnati, OH: Strategy Incorporated.

Kamisher, L. (1986). The images system: videodisc and database integration for architecture. Optical Information SYstems, vol. 6, no. 6, pp. 501-503.

Kanayama, K. and Kaizu, S. (1990). Recent tendency of traffic control systems. Information Processing Society of Japan, vol. 31, no. 2, pp. 255-64.

Kanazawa, Y. et al (1984). Development of large capacity optical disk. In Proceedings of the SPIE, vol. 490. Bellingham, WA: Society of Photo-Optical Instrumentation Engineers, pp. 12-19.

Kane, P. (1991). Alchemy, synergy, and other considerations in cost-justifying imaging systems. Inform, vol. 5, no. 5, pp. 24-27, 68-70.

Kaneko, R. (1987). Magnetic and optical disk storage technology. JSME International Journal, vol. 30, no. 260, pp. 215-20.

Kaneko, T. and Yamamoto, R. (1988). Rare earth superlattices. Kino Zairyo, vol. 8, no. 8, pp. 52-56.

Kangarloo, H. et al (1987). A PACS module for pediatric radiology: current status. In Proceedings of the SPIE, vol. 767. Bellingham: Society of Photo-Optical Instrumentation Engineers, pp. 548-53.

Kano, H. et al (1989). Optimized structure of sputtered garnet disks. IEEE Transactions on Magnetics, vol. 25, no. 5, pp. 3737-42.

Karch, L. (1990). Serials information on CD-ROM: a reference perspective. Reference Services Review, vol. 18, no. 2, pp. 81-86.

Karp, N. (1990). Private company information in selected CD-ROM databases. CD-ROM Professional, vol. 3, no. 4, pp. 36-40.

Kasai, M. et al (1987). New access method for a 12-inch optical disk using partial crosstrack count control. In Conference on Lasers and Electro-Optics: Digest of Technical Papers. Washington, DC: Optical Society of America, pp. 266-67.

Katayama, H. et al (1988). Recording sensitivity and lifetime estimate of a magneto-optical disk. IEEE Translation Journal on Magnetics in Japan, vol. 3, no. 2, pp. 126-31.

Katayama, R. et al (1989). Multi-beam magneto-optical disk drive for parallel read/write operation. In Proceedings of the SPIE, vol. 1078. Bellingham, WA: Society of Photo-Optical Instrumentation Engineers, pp. 98-104.

Kato, R. (1990). Error injection. Hewlett-Packard Journal, vol. 41, no. 6, p. 33.

Katz, E. and Brechtlein, R. (1988). Perpendicular

recording increases data density. Mini-Micro Systems, vol. 21, no. 3, pp. 85-91.

Kauffman, S. (1988). Laser disc applications for law libraries. CD-ROM Librarian, vol. 3, no. 1, pp. 17-24.

Kawabata, H. and Yamamoto, K. (1988). Advances in magnetic and optical recording: recent trends in erasable optical recording media. Journal of the Institute of Television Engineering in Japan, vol. 42, no. 4, pp. 323-39.

Kawabata, T. et al (1990). Advanced Mobile Traffic Information and Communication System. Sumitomo Electric Technical Review, no. 29, pp. 161-68.

Kawabe, T. et al (1990). Study of picture quality on magneto-optical disk for analog video recording. Sharp Technical Journal, no. 47, pp. 21-26.

Kawamoto, A. et al (1988). Corrosion-resistant rare earth-transition metal amorphous films with high recording sensitivity for magneto-optical disks. Journal of Applied Physics, vol. 63, no. 8, pt. 2B, pp. 3853-55.

Kawashima, H. (1991). Two major programs and demonstrations in Japan. IEEE Transactions on Vehicular Technology, vol. 40, no. 1, pt. 1, pp. 141-46.

Kay, D. et al (1984). Experimental measurements on long-term IR readout of data recorded in organic optical storage media. In Topical Meeting on Optical Data Storage: Technical Digest. Washington, DC: Optical Society of America, pp. B2/1-3.

Kearsley, G. and Frost, J. (1985). Design factors for successful videodisc-based instruction. Educational Technology, vol. 25, no. 3, pp. 7-13.

Keele, R. (1988). Optical storage: terabytes online for IBM mainframes. In Proceedings of the SPIE, vol. 899. Bellingham, WA: Society of Photo-Optical Instrumentation Engineers, pp. 262-71.

Keen, E. (1990). Transferring records from CD-ROM to an inhouse database; some practical experiences. Program, vol. 24, no. 2, pp. 187-91.

Kellough, J. (1989). Moody's 5000+ and Dialog OnDisc Standard and Poor's Corportions: a comparison of two full-text business databases. Laserdisk Professional, vol. 2, no. 6, pp. 78-89.

Kellough, J. and Gomez, J. (1990). Congressional Masterfile 1 and 2 on CD-ROM: a door opener to congressional publications. CD-ROM Professional, vol. 3, no. 3, pp. 73-79.

Kelly, B. et al (1986). The effectiveness of videodisc instruction in teaching fractions to learning-disabled and remedial high school students. Journal of Special Education Technology, vol. 8, no. 2, pp. 5-17.

Kelly, M. (1989). 5.25-inch jukeboxes for WORM and rewritable media and drives. In OIS International 1989: Proceedings of the Sixth Annual Conference on Optical Information Systems. London: Meckler Corporation, pp. 78-83.

Kelly, R. et al (1986). Technical aspects of the Domesday Project. Electronics and Power, vol. 32, no. 11, pp. 804-806.

Kemp, R. (1987). Compact Cambridge MEDLINE: a review of the MEDLINE CD-ROM. Electronic and Optical Publishing Review, vol. 7, no. 1, pp. 26-29.

Kenville, R. (1981). Fifteen years of laser recording: where we've been and where we're going. Optical Engineer, vol. 20, no. 3, pp. 330-34.

Kenville, R. (1982). Hardware issues of optical mass storage systems. In IEEE Symposium on Mass Storage Systems. New York: IEEE, pp. 56-57.

Keppler, M. and Goldmann, G. (1988). Analysis of magneto-optic media for optical disk drives. In Proceedings of the SPIE, vol. 899. Bellingham, WA: Society of Photo-Optical Instrumentation Engineers, pp. 77-82.

Kercheval, R. (1989). CD-ROM pilot projects: new era in DoD publishing. CD-ROM End User, vol. 1, no. 8, pp. 46-48.

Kerlin, B. (1988). The Optical Memory Card as a Transportable Image Archiving Medium in a Digital Imaging Network. In Proceedings of the Spie, Vol. 914. Bellingham, WA: Society of Photo-optical Instrumentation Engineers, pp. 1088-96.

Khurshid, Z. (1991). BiblioFile versus CDMARC Bibliographic. CD-ROM Librarian, vol. 6, no. 11, pp. 26-31.

Kilty, L. (1988). Notes on the capabilities of magnetic stripe, chip, and optical transaction cards. Optical Information Systems, vol. 8, no. 4, pp. 146-47.

Kim, S. et al (1987). Syntheses of phenothiazine-quinone infrared dyes from tetrasubstituted anthraquinones. Chemistry Express, vol. 2, no. 1, pp. 73-76.

Kimura, K. et al (1988). CD-ROM systems based on the NEWS workstation. In Digest of Papers: COMPCON Spring '88. New York: IEEE, pp. 274-76.

Kimura, K. (1989). Optical recording materials based on TeO/sub x films. Japanese Journal of Applied Physics, part 1, vol. 28, no. 5, pp. 810-13.

Kimura, K. (1989a). Crystallization of TeO/sub x/-Pd films for optical recording materials. Japanese Journal of Applied Physics, part 1, no. 28, no. 11, pp. 2223-26.

King, A. (1991). Full text and CD-ROM: variations on a theme. Online, vol. 15, no. 5, pp. 107-108.

King, N. et al (1990). MEDLINE and PsycLIT on CD-ROM: a survey of users in an academic medical library. Medical Reference Services Quarterly, vol. 9, no. 1, pp. 43-58.

Kinney, J. (1989). The role for CD-ROM in information isolated areas. In Information — Knowledge — Evolution: Proceedings of the Forty-Fourth FID Congress. Amsterdam: North-Holland Publishing Company, pp. 279-89.

Kirino, F. et al (1991). Magnetic properties and corrosion resistance of magneto-optical recording film with nitric surface coating. Journal of the Japan Institute of Metals, vol. 55, no. 6, pp. 696-705.

Kittle, P. (1988). MEDLINE on CD-ROM: a review of six products. Laserdisk Professional, vol. 1, no. 3, pp. 18-28.

Kittle, P. (1989). Putting a medical library online: Phase III — remoe access to CD-ROMs. Laserdisk Professional, vol. 2, no. 2, pp. 15-18.

Kivits, P. and Bont, R. (1981). Laser induced melting and superheating in Te and In films for optical data storage. Applied Physics, vol. 24, no. 4, pp. 307-10.

Klahn, S. et al (1990). Recent advances in thin films for magneto-optic recording. Vacuum, vol. 41, no. 4, pp. 1160-65.

Klausmeier, J. (1986). The implications of CD-ROM for database producers. In National Online Meeting Proceedings. Medford, NJ: Learned Information, pp. 245-49.

Klein, S. et al (1989). String text retrieval systems on CD-ROM: compression and encryption considerations. ACM Transactions on Information Systems, vol. 7, no. 3, pp. 230-45.

Klein, S. et al (1989b). Storing text retrieval systems on CD-ROM: compression and encryption considerations. SIGIR Forum, vol. 23, no. 1, pp. 160-67.

Klimley, S. (1988). The Columbia CD-ROM experience: evaluation of map data on CD-ROM. Western Association of Map Libraries Bulletin, vol. 20, no. 1, pp. 19-22.

Kloosterboer, J. and Lippits, G. (1986). Replication of video discs using photopolymerization: process design and study of network formation. Journal of Imaging Science, vol. 30, no. 4, pp. 177-83.

Kobayashi, H. et al (1990). Corrosion study in TbFeCoCr amorphous magneto-optical films. IEEE Transactions on Magnetics, vol. 26, no. 5, pp. 1361-63.

Kobayashi, K. et al (1983). High density perpendicular recording on rigid disks. Fujitsu Science and Technology Journal, vol. 19, no. 1, pp. 99-126.

Kobayashi, K. et al (1987). Thin film head for perpendicular magnetic recording. IEEE Translation Journal on Magnetics in Japan, vol. 2, no. 1, pp. 35-47.

Kobayashi, M. and Kawamura, K. (1988). High corrosion resistant magneto-optical recording disk. Oki Technical Review, vol. 55, no. 131, pp. 33-38.

Kobayashi, M. et al (1987). Corrosion resistance of magneto-optical recording media. IEEE Translation Journal on Magnetics in Japan, vol. 2, no. 5, pp. 404-405.

Kobayashi, M. et al (1987a). High corrosion resistant magneto-optical recording media using TbFeCoTi films. Applied Physics Letters, vol. 50, no. 23, pp. 1694-95.

Kobayashi, M. et al (1988). Erasable optical memory media with thermoplastic/absorbent double layer. Applied Physics Letters, vol. 52, no. 21, pp. 1777-78.

Kobayashi, R. et al (1989). CD-ROM data processing. National Technical Report, vol. 35, no. 2, pp. 201-207.

Kobayashi, S. et al (1991). Organic optical storage medium with a read-out stability under 1 mW laser irradiation. Japanese Journal of Applied Physics, part 2, vol. 30, no. 1B, pp. L114-16.

Kobayashi, Y. et al (1990). General information control software for mobile navigation systems. Sumitomo Electric Technical Review, no. 30, pp. 39-44.

Kohler, W. et al (1989). Stability of frequency domain information bits in amorphous organic materials. Journal of Applied Physics, vol. 66, no. 7, pp. 3232-40.

Kohn, D. (1991). Current and future applications of optical storage technology in the health care industry. Document Image Automation, vol. 11, no. 3, pp. 143-49.

Kohn, D. (1991a). Optical technology demonstrates benefits. Computers in Healthcare, vol. 12, no. 5, pp. 22-26.

Koide, K. and Kitoh, K. (1989). Trends of automobile information and communication systems. Systems, Control and Information, vol. 33, no. 7, pp. 321-28.

Komori, M. et al (1987). Pilot PACS with on-line communication between an image workstation and CT scanners in a clinical environment. In Proceedings of the SPIE, vol. 767. Bellingham, WA: Society of Photo-Optical Instrumentation Engineers, pt. 2, pp. 744-51.

Korenjak, A. (1987). Digital video interactive (DVI). In INTERACT 87 Conference Proceedings. Peterborough, UK: PLF Communications, pp. 22-29.

Koshino, N. et al (1987). Phase-change type erasable optical disk. Fujitsu, vol. 38, no. 2, pp. 143-48.

Koshino, N. et al (1988). Selenium-indium-antimony alloy film for erasable optical disks. Fujitsu Scientific and Technical Journal, vol. 24, no. 1, pp. 60-69.

Kosmin, L. (1990). Resources for tracking CD-ROM in-house development options. CD-ROM Professional, vol. 3, no. 3, pp. 56-60.

Koumura, K. et al (1989). High speed accessing using split optical head. In Proceedings of the SPIE, vol. 1078. Bellingham, WA: Society of Photo-Optical Instrumentation Engineers, pp. 239-43.

Kovarick, A. (1989). High Sierra vs. ISO 9660: a summary. Laserdisk Professional, vol. 2, no. 5, pp. 20-22.

Kowel, S. et al (1987). Organic and polymeric thin films for nonlinear optics. Optical Engineering, vol. 26, no. 2, pp. 107-12.

Kozlovsksy, W. et al (1990). Compact blue lasers for optical recording applications. In Proceedings of the SPIE, vol. 1316. Bellingham, WA: International Society for Optical Engineering, pp. 194-98.

Kratzert, M. (1991). Installation of a CD-ROM local area network: the untold story. In Twelfth National Online Meeting Proceedings. Medford, NJ: Learned Information, pp. 201-207.

Kraus, D. and French, R. (1990). Automatic spectral database and archive system for optical spectroscopy. Applied Spectroscopy, vol. 44, no. 7, pp. 1221-26.

Kriz, H. et al (1991). An environmental approach to CD-ROM networking using off-the-shelf components. CD-ROM Professional, vol. 4, no. 4, pp. 24-31.

Kryder, M. (1985). Magneto-optic recording technology. Journal of Applied Physics, vol. 57, no. 8, pt. 2B, pp. 3913-18.

Kryder, M. (1990). Advances in magneto-optic recording technology. Journal of Magnetism and Magnetic Materials, vol. 83, no. 1, pp. 1-5.

Kryder, M. et al (1987). Control of parameters in rare earth transition metal alloys for magneto-optical recording media. IEEE Transactions on Magnetics, vol. 23, no. 1, pp. 165-67.

Kuder, J. (1986). Organic materials for optical data storage media: an overview. Journal of Imaging Technology, vol. 12, no. 3, pp. 140-43.

Kuder, J. (1988). Organic active layer materials for optical recording. Journal of Imaging Science, vol. 32, no. 2, pp. 51-56.

Kuder, J. and Nikles, D. (1985). Characterization of a dyed-polymer optical storage medium. In Topical Meeting on Optical Data Storage: Digest of Technical Papers. Washington, DC: Optical Society of America, pp. WBB3/1-4.

Kudou, R. et al (1990). F6443D magneto-optical disk drive subsystem. Fujitsu Scientific and Technical Journal, vol. 26, no. 4, pp. 330-36.

Kuhnert, L. (1986). A new optical photochemical memory device in a light-sensitive chemical active medium. Nature, vol. 319, no. 5, pp. 393-94.

Kume, M. et al (1987). Semiconductor lasers for WORM, erasable, and rewritable memory disks. JEE: Journal of Electronic Engineering, vol. 24, no. 248, pp. 44-47.

Kurdyla, E. (1988). 1987 OCLC compact disk study. Laserdisk Professional, vol. 1, no. 1, pp. 44-49.

Kurtenbach, G. (1988). The retrieval and display of patent images from optical storage. In National Online Meeting Proceedings, 1988. Medford, NJ: Learned Information, pp. 191-98.

Kurtz, C. (1987). Trends in optical recording. In Conference on Lasers and Electro-Optics: Digest of Technical Papers. Washington, DC: Optical Society of America, pp. 362-64.

Kurahashi, A. et al (1985). Development of the Erasable Magneto-Optical Disc Digital Audio Recorder. Audio Engineering Society Preprint 2296. New York: Audio Engineering Society.

Kushizaki, O. and Shigematsu, K. (1989). Rewritable optical disk subsystem 112 series. Hitachi Review, vol. 38, no. 5, pp. 253-56.

Kutt, P. and Balamuth, D. (1989). Operating experience with a multiple-processor system for data acquisition and reduction in nuclear physics. Computational Physics, vol. 2, no. 5, pp. 52-60.

Kutt, P. and Balamuth, D. (1989a). Operating experience with a VMEbus multiprocessor system for data acquisition and reduction in nuclear physics. IEEE Transactions on Nuclear Science, vol. 36, no. 5, p. 1725.

Kwok, C. (1989). Implementing WORM and erasable optical storage in the OS/2 environment. In

Software for Optical Storage. Westport, CT: Meckler Corporation, pp. 59-62.

LaBudde, E. et al (1985). Theoretical modeling and experimental characterization of Drexon recording media. In Topical Meeting on Optical Data Storage: Digest of Technical Papers. Washington, DC: Optical Society of America, pp. 1-2.

Lace, L. and Lee, H. (1988). PC based document imaging workstation and applications. In Electronic Imaging '88: International Electronic Imaging Exposition and Conference. Boston: Institute for Graphic Communication, vol. 1, pp. 309-14.

Ladner, B. and Barnett, M. (1990). MEDLINE on CD-ROM: comparison update. Laserdisk Professional, vol. 3, no. 2, pp. 67-71.

LaGuardia, C. et al (1991). CD-ROM networking in ARL academic libraries: a survey. CD-ROM Professional, vol. 4, no. 2, pp. 36-39.

Lam, L. and Lam, J. (1990). The impacts of CD-ROMs on the provision of information services in academic libraries. In Preprints: Second International Conference on the Effective Use of CD-ROM Databases. Tokyo: USACO, pp. 14-21.

Lamielle, J. and De Heaulme, M. (1986). A general bank of referential images using Laservision disk in biomedicine. In Optical Information Systems 86. Westport, CT: Meckler Corporation, pp. 184-91.

Lampton, C. (1987). CD ROMs. New York: F. Watts.

Landrum, H. (1988). The Intelligent Catalog in special libraries. CD-ROM Librarian, vol. 3, no. 10, pp. 21-22.

Lange, G. (1987). Practical specifications for characterizing write/read performance of optical disk media. In Topical Meeting on Optical Data Storage: Summaries of Papers. Washington, DC: Optical Society of America, pp. 54-57.

Langendorfer, H. et al (1986). Multimedia filing and retrieval based on optical and magnetic mass storage technologies. Microprocessing and Microprogramming, vol. 18, no. 5, pp. 505-12.

Langerman, S. (1990). CD-ROM in Israel: usage problems, prospects. Bulletin of the the Israel Society of Special Libraries and Information Centres, vol. 17, no. 2, pp. 24-30.

Langeveld, W. (1987). Optical storage and its possible use in high-energy physics. Computational Physics Communications, vol. 45, nos. 1-3, pp. 395-402.

Laskodi, T. et al (1988). A Unix file system for a write-once optical disk. In Proceedings of the Summer 1988 USENIX Conference. Berkeley, CA: USENIX Association, pp. 51-60.

Latham, J. (1989). LaserQuest: the General Research Corporation's CD-ROM catalog. Library Software Review, vol. 8, no. 4, pp. 201-203.

Law, K. and Johnson, G. (1983). Ablative optical recording using organic dye-in-polymer thin films: some mechanistic aspects. Journal of Applied Physics, vol. 54, no. 9, pp. 4799-4805.

Lau, T. (1990). Building a paperless office with document image processing system. In IPCC 90 — Communication Across the Sea: North American and European Practices, International Professional Communication Conference. New York: IEEE, pp. 40-42.

Lavender, T. (1986). CD-ROM servo systems. In CD ROM: the New Papyrus. Redmond, WA: Microsoft Press, pp. 91-102.

Lawson, W. (1989). CASSIS/CD-ROM: a project report. World Patent Information, vol. 11, no. 2, pp. 68-70.

Layton, T. (1991). The Electronic Eugenean: a multimedia yearbook project. Writing Notebook: Creative Word Processing in the Classroom, vol. 8, no. 4, p. 14.

Lealand, C. (1989). Production of the CD-ROM version of the British Library catalogue. OpticalInfo 89: the International Meeting for Optical Publishing and Storage. Oxford: Learned Information, pp. 85-91.

Lee, D. (1987). Indexing the Domesday Project. Indexer, vol. 15, no. 3, pp. 145-50.

Lee, J. and O'Connor, M. (1991). So you want to produce a CD-ROM?! Tips for successful data preparation. CD-ROM Professional, vol. 4, no. 1, pp. 81-84.

Lee, R. and Balthazar, L. (1991). The evolution and installation of an in-house CD-ROM LAN. Bulletin of the Medical Library Association, vol. 79, no. 1, pp. 63-65.

Lee, T. et al (1978). Development of thermoplastic-photoconductor tape for optical recording. Applied Optics, vol. 17, no. 4, pp. 2802-11.

Lee, W. (1989). Thin films for write-once and reversible optical data storage. In Proceedings of the Sino-US Joint Seminar on Vacuum and Surface Analysis. Singapore: World Scientific, vol. 2, pp. 249-78.

Lee, W. and Geiss, R. (1983). Degradation of thin tellurium films. Journal of Applied Physics, vol. 54, no. 3, pp. 1351-57.

Lee, W. and Weider, H. (1983). The stability of Te and Te-alloy films for optical data storage. In Topical Meeting on Optical Data Storage. Washington, DC: Optical Society of America, pp. B3/1-4.

Lee, Z. et al (1990). Enhancement and corrosion resistance improvement by AlN and AlSiN films. Journal of Applied Physics, vol. 67, no. 9, p. 5340.

Leeuwenburg, J. (19987). Supermap I: the census on CD-ROM. In Information Online 87: Worldwide Information at Your Fingertips — Preprints of the Second Australian Online Information Conference. Sydney: Library Association of Australia, pp. 106-108.

Legierse, P. (1987). Mastering technology and electroforming for optical disc systems. Transactions of Metal Finishing, vol. 65, no. 1, pp. 13-17; also in Galvanotechnik, vol. 78, no. 5, pp. 1269-78.

Lehmann, K. and Sledge, G. (1988). Optical storage devices for the publication of complete texts: cooperation between publishers and libraries. ABI-Technik, vol. 8, no. 1, pp. 59-63.

Lehr, J. (1983). Impact of manual and computer-assisted PACS for automated PACS. Radiology Management, vol. 5, no. 3, pp. 2-10.

Lenth, W. and Moerner, W. (1986). Gated spectral hole-burning for frequency domain optical recording. Optical Communications, vol. 58, no. 4, pp. 249-54.

Lenth, W. et al (1986). High-density frequency-domain optical recording. In Proceedings of the SPIE, vol. 695. Bellingham, WA: Society of Photo-Optical Instrumentation Engineers, pp. 216-23.

Leonard, W. (1989). A comparison of student reactions to biology instruction by interactive videodisc or conventional laboratory. Journal of Research in Science Teaching, vol. 26, no. 2, pp. 95-104.

Leuschke, C. (1989). Polycarbonate for optical applications. Kunststoffe, vol. 79, no. 10, p. 77.

Levene, M. (1985). High data rate, high-capacity optical disk buffer. In Digest of Papers: IEEE Symposium on Mass Storage Systems. New York: IEEE, pp. 17-21.

Levene, M. (1988). Applications for a high capacity, high data rate optical disk buffer. In Proceedings of the SPIE, vol. 899. Bellingham, WA: Society of Photo-Optical Instrumentation Engineers, pp. 279-93

Levene, M. (1989). Progress in the development of a high data rate, high capacity optical disk buffer. In Proceedings of the SPIE, vol. 1078 Bellingham, WA: Society of Photo-Optical Instrumentation Engineers, pp. 105-11.

Levene, M. (1990). High performance optical disk recorder: preliminary test results and spaceflight model projections. In Proceedings of the SPIE, vol. 1316. Bellingham, WA: International Society for Optical Engineering, pp. 48-57.

Levy, D. et al (1989). Applications of the sol-gel process for the preparation of photochromic information — recording materials: synthesis, properties, mechanisms. Journal of Non-Crystalline Solids, vol. 113, no. 2, pp. 137-45.

Levy, J. (1989). An operating system-independent WORM file system. In Software for Optical Storage. Westport, CT: Meckler Corporation, pp. 23-54.

Lichtenstein, T. (1983). Recording properties of Drexon optical memory disks. In Proceedings of the SPIE, vol. 420. Bellingham, WA: Society of Photo-Optical Instrumentation Engineers, pp. 96-101.

Liddell, D. (1990). IBM and imaging. Advanced Imaging, vol. 5, no. 4, pp. 30-34, 68.

Lieberman, D. (1988). Hierarchical file server puts archives on-line. Computer Design, vol. 27, no. 21, pp. 36-37.

Light, D. (1986). Mass storage estimates for the digital mapping era. Photogrammetric Engineering and Remote Sensing, vol. 53, no. 2, pp. 419-25.

Light, D. (1986a). Planning for optical disk technology with digital cartography. Photogrammetric Engineering and Remote Sensing, vol. 52, no. 3, pp. 551-57.

Lin, C. (1990). Critical assessment of the physics underlying direct overwrite in magneto-optic recording. Journal of Applied Physics, vol. 67, no. 9-IIA, pp. 4409-14.

Lin, C. and Do, H. (1990). Magneto-optical recording on evaporated Co/Pt multilayer films. IEEE Transactions on Magnetics, vol. 26, no. 5, pp. 1700-1702.

Lind, M. and Hartman, J. (1988). Performance of a reversible dye-polymer optical recording medium. In Proceedings of the SPIE, vol. 899. Bellingham, WA: Society of Photo-Optical Instrumentation Engineers, pp. 211-18.

Lindmayer, J. (1988). A new erasable optical memory. Solid State Technology, vol. 31, no. 8, pp. 135-38.

Lindmayer, J. and Wrigley, C. (1989). Electron trapping optical memory. In Summaries of Papers Presented at the Conference on Lasers and Electro-Optics. New York: IEEE, p. 96.

Lindmayer, J. et al (1989). Electronic optical storage technology approaches development phase. Laser Focus World, vol. 25, no. 11, pp. 119-27.

Lindmayer, J. et al (1991). Electron trapping for mass data storage memory. In Proceedings of the SPIE, vol. 1401. Bellingham, WA: International Society for Optical Engineering, pp. 103-12.

Line, M. (1989). The future of CD-ROMs for full text of journals. In Impact of CD-ROM on Library Operations and Universal Availability of Information: Eleventh International Essen Symposium. Essen, West Germany: Essen University Library, pp. 189-97.

Lippits, G. and Melis, G. (1986). High precision replication of Laservision video discs using UV-curable coatings. In Integration of Fundamental Polymer Science and Technology. London: Elsevier Applied Science Publishers, pp. 663-68.

Litman, J. (1987). Advances in microcomputing and their implications for business information retrieval: the death knell of online information? In National Online Meeting Proceedings. Medford, NJ: Learned Information, pp. 293-300.

Little, J. (1988). PDO and erasable technology. In OIS 88 Conference Proceedings. Westport, CT: Meckler Corporation, pp. 36-41.

Littlejohn, A. and Janousek, K. (1991). Company information on CD-ROM from 10K to 5000+. CD-ROM Professional, vol. 4, no. 3, pp. 50-55.

Livingston, D. (1988). Possible error control coding strategies for an optical disk buffer. In Proceedings of the SPIE, vol. 899. Bellingham, WA: Society of Photo-Optical Instrumentation Engineers, pp. 109-13.

Lloyd, P. (1990). Creating knowledge-based multimedia applications. In IEE Colloquium on Multimedia: the Future of User Interfaces. London: IEE, pp. 4/1-4.

Lobeck, M. (1989). The incorporation of CD-ROMs in a company information department. Nachrichten fuer Dokumentation, vol. 40, no. 3, pp. 137-50.

Lobeck, M. (1990). Patent information on CD-ROMs. World Patent Information, vol. 12, no. 4, pp. 200-211.

Lohrenz, M. and Ryan, J. (1990). Navy Standard Compressed Aeronautical Chart Database. Stennis Space Center, MS: Naval Oceanographic and Atmospheric Research Laboratory, NTIS Accession Number AD-A235 340/7/XAB.

Lomet, D. and Salzberg, B. (1989). Access methods for multiversion data. SIGMOD Record, vol. 18, no. 2, pp. 315-24.

Lou, D. (1977). A prototype optical disk recorder. IEEE Journal on Quantum Electronics, vol. 13, no. 9, p. 15.

Lou, D. (1981). The archival stability of tellurium films for optical information storage. Journal of the Electrochemical Society, vol. 128, no. 3, pp. 699-701.

Loveria, G. and Kinstler, D. (1990). Multimedia: DVI arrives. Byte, vol. 15, no. 11, pp. 105-108.

Lowe, J. (1987). Linking optical storage devices and local area networks. In SCIL 87: Second Annual Software/Computer/Database Conference and Exposition for Librarians and Information Managers. Westport, CT: Meckler Publishing, p. 100.

Lowe, L. (1986). CD-I: the medium of the future. In CD-I and Interactive Videodisc Technology. Indianapolis: Howard W. Sams, pp. 117-38.

Lowenthal, L. (1987). Integration of optical disk into mainframe system software. In Digest of Papers: COMPCON Spring 87. New York: IEEE, pp. 138-41.

Luborsky, F. et al (1985). Stability of amorphous transition metal-rare earth films for magneto-optic recording. IEEE Transactions on Magnetics, vol. 21, no. 5, pp. 1618-23.

Luettgen, A. et al (1991). CD-ROM: a Delivery Medium for CBT. Paper delivered at TITE '91: Ninth Annual Technology and Innovations in Training and Education Conference, sponsored by Department of Energy, March 11-15, 1991, NTIS Accession Number DE910000

Lunin, L. (1990). An overview of electronic image information. Optical Information Systems, vol. 10, no. 3, pp. 114-30.

Luther, A. (1987). New integrated video and graphics technology: digital video interactive. Optical Information Systems, vol. 7, no. 6, pp. 412-15.

Luther, A. (1991). Digital Video in the PC Environment, Second Edition. New York: Intertext Publications.

Luther, A. and Chaney, E. (1987). Digital video interactive technology. Library Software Review, vol. 6, no. 4, pp. 202-205.

Machovec, G. (1987). OCLC optical disc products for reference, cataloging and resource sharing. Online Libraries and Microcomputers, vol. 5, no. 5, pp. 1-3.

Machovec, G. (1991). CD-ROM and optical disc longevity. Online Libraries and Microcomputers, vol. 9, no. 5, pp. 1-3.

MacRae, I. (1989). Implementing WORM storage in the VAX/VMS environment. In Software for Optical Storage. Westport, CT: Meckler Corporation, pp. 75-82.

Madachy, R. et al (1988). Automatic digital ultrasound image acquisition and networking. In Proceedings of the Annual International Conference of the IEEE Engineering in Medicine and Biology Society. New York: IEEE, vol. 3, p. 1450.

Maeda, M. et al (1988). Reversible phase-change optical data storage in InSbTe alloy films. Journal of Applied Physics, vol. 64, no. 4, pp. 1715-19.

Maeda, M. et al (1989). Study on readout stability of TbFeCo magneto-optical disks. IEEE Transactions on Magnetics, vol. 25, no. 5, pp. 3539-41.

Maeda, M. et al (1989a). Single-beam overwriting with melt-erase process in InSbTe phase-change optical disk. Applied Physics Letters, vol. 54, no. 10, pp. 893-95.

Maeda, M. et al (1989b). Single-beam overwrite characteristics of InSbTe phase-change optical disks and the mechanism. Transactions of the Institute for Electronic, Information and Communication Engineers, vol. J72C-II, no. 10, pp. 893-900.

Maeda, S. et al (1990). New write-once optical media using near infrared absorbing metal complex dyes with indoaniline-type ligand. Molecular Crystals and Liquid Crystals, vol. 183, no. 1, pp. 491-94.

Maeda, S. et al (1991). Multimedia information system using a rewritable compact disc. Sharp Technical Journal, no. 48, pp. 27-36.

Maeda, T. et al (1991). High speed, large capacity optical disk using pit-edge recording and MCAV method. IEICE Transactions, vol. E74, no. 4, pp. 951-54.

Maeda, Y. et al (1991). Relationship between overwrite repeatability and the disk structure of InSbTe phase-change optical disks. Transactions of the Institute of Electronics, Information and Communication Engineers, vol. J74C-II, no. 4, pp. 243-49.

Maeno, Y. and Kobayashi, M. (1990). Fabrication of magnetic films for magneto-optical recording disk. Gijutsu, vol. 39, no. 6, pp. 321-28.

Maguire, D. (1989). The Domesday interactive videodisc system in geography teaching. Journal of Geography in Higher Education, vol. 13, no. 1, pp. 55-68.

Maher, J. (1987). Rigid optical disk assembly by Eastman Kodak Company. In Topical Meeting on Optical Data Storage: Summaries of Papers. Washington, DC: Optical Society of America, pp. 82-85.

Majumdar, D. and Hatwar, T. (1989). Effects of platinum and zirconium on the oxidation behavior of FeTbCo. Journal of Vacuum Science and Technology, vol. 7, no. 4, pp. 2673-77.

Mankovich, N. et al (1986). The software architecture of an integrated optical disk archive for digital radiographic images. In Proceedings of the SPIE, vol. 695. Bellingham, WA: Society of Photo-Optical Instrumentation Engineers, pp. 407-11.

Mankovich, N. et al (1986a). A general-purpose optical disk system with a radiological imaging application. In Application of Optical Instrumentation in Medicine XIV: Medical Imaging, Processing, and Display and Picture Archiving and Communications Systems (PACS IV) for Medical Applications. Bellingham, WA: Society of Photo-Optical Instrumentation Engineers, pp. 676-84.

Mankovich, N. et al (1988). Operational radiologic image archive on digital optical disks. Radiology, vol. 167, no. 1, pp. 139-42.

Mankovich, N. et al (1988a). Procedures, films, and images in a pediatric radiology image archive: one year's experience and projections. In Proceedings of the SPIE, vol. 914. Bellingham, WA: Society of Photo-Optical Instrumentation Engineers, pp. 1105-13.

Mano, Y. et al (1988). MUSE video disc. In Third International Colloquium on Advanced Television Systems: HDTV 87 Colloquium Proceedings. Montreal: Canadian Broadcasting Corporation, pp. 4/8/1-10.

Mano, Y. et al (1988). MUSE video disc. In Third International Colloquium on Advanced Television

Systems: HDTV 87 Colloquium Proceedings. Montreal: CBC Engineering, pp. 4/8/1-10.

Mansuripur, M. (1987). Magnetization reversal, coercivity, and the process of thermomagnetic recording in thin films of amorphous rare earth-transition metal alloys. Journal of Applied Physics, vol. 61, no. 4, pp. 1580-97.

Mansuripur, M. (1988). Magnetization reversal dynamics in the media of magneto-optical recording. Journal of Applied Physics, vol. 63, no. 12, pp. 5809-23.

Mansuripur, M. (1989). Detecting transition regions in magneto-optical disk systems. Applied Physics Letters, vol. 55, no. 8, pp. 716-17.

Mansuripur, M. et al (1985). Erasable optical disks for data storage: principles and applications. Industrial and Engineering Chemistry: Product Research and Development, vol. 24, no. 1, pp. 80-84.

Mardeusz, P. (1988). Oxford English Dictionary on compact disc. CD-ROM Librarian, vol. 3, no. 7, pp. 17-22.

Marinero, E. (1989). Structural properties and magnetism in magneto-optical alloys. In Proceedings of the MRS International Meeting on Advanced Materials. Pittsburgh: Materials Research Society, pp. 269-81.

Marks, H. (1988). An overview of the Hi-Lite optical card. Optical Information Systems, vol. 8, no. 4, pp. 162-63.

Marks, K. (1989). Input scanners: a growing impact in a diverse marketplace. In Proceedings of the SPIE, vol. 1082. Bellingham, WA: Society of Photo-Optical Instrumentation Engineers, pp. 73-88.

Marloth, H. (1989). CD-ROM products from the Library of Congress and the German Library. Bibliotheksdienst, vol. 23, no. 10, pp. 1061-66.

Marsh, E. (1988). How to evaluate and select an optical disk jukebox for integration in a mass storage system. In Optical Information Systems '88: Conference Proceedings. Westport, CT: Meckler Corporation, pp. 77-81.

Marsh, F. (1982). Videodisc technology. Journal of the American Society for Information Science, vol. 33, no. 4, pp. 237-44.

Marshall, M. and Voedisch, G. (1990). Compact discs: permanence and irretrievability may be synonymous in libraries as well as in Roget's. In National Online Meeting Proceedings. Medford, NJ: Learned Information, pp. 249-54.

Martin, M. (1990). Lotus CD/PROMPT: a well-heeled reference tool. Laserdisk Professional, vol. 3, no. 1, pp. 61-64.

Mason, P. (1991). Planning the National Agricultural Library's multimedia CD-ROM Ornamental Horiculture. Government Publications Review, vol. 18, no. 2, pp. 137-46.

Massey-Burzio, V. (1990). The MultiPlatter experience at Brandeis University. CD-ROM Professional, vol. 3, no. 3, pp. 22-26.

Masters, D. (1988). Implementation of a public access catalog on a compact disc: one library's experience. CD-ROM Librarian, vol. 3, no. 1, pp. 10-16.

Mastroddi, F. (1987). The European Community's electronic publishing programme: past achievements, future projects with respect to optical media. Liber News Sheet, no. 21, pp. 5-25.

Mathisen, R. (1991). Interactive multimedia and education: specifications, standards, and applications. Collegiate Microcomputer, vol. 9, no. 2, pp. 93-102.

Matick, R. (1977). Computer Storage Systems and Technology. New York: Wiley.

Matsuda, K. (1989). CD-ROM and LAN: construction of local online data base system. On-line Kensaku, vol. 10, no. 4, pp. 178-82.

Matsuda, T. et al (1990). Paperless patent system. Fujitsu, vol. 41, no. 6, pp. 491-97.

Matsui, F. et al (1988). An optical recording disk using an organic dye medium in regard to provide interchangeability to the disks using different organic dyes. IEEE Translation Journal on Magnetics in Japan, vol. 3, no. 11, pp. 789-98.

Matsushima, M. et al (1987). Aging properties of amorphous GdTbFeCo magnetic films and the effect of other elements added to them. IEEE Translation Journal on Magnetics in Japan, vol. 2, no. 5, pp. 399-400.

Matsushita, T. et al (1987). Effect of Ge addition on Ga-Se-Te system reversible optical recording media. Japanese Journal of Applied Physics, vol. 26, no. 1, pp. 62-64.

Matsuzawa, N. et al (1990). Optical recording characteristics of dye-polymer systems. Japanese Journal of Applied Physics, part 1, vol. 29, no. 10, pp. 1963-66.

Matthew, J. (1990). Data-packed CDs find favor with financial pros. Wall Street Computer Review, vol. 7, no. 10, pp. 45-54.

Mattson, R. (1974). Role of optical memories in computer storage. Applied Optics, vol. 13, no. 4, pp. 744-60.

Mattson, R. et al (1970). Evaluation techniques for storage hierarchies. IBM Systems Journal, vol. 9, no. 2, pp. 78-117.

Mayr, M. (1987). High vacuum equipment for compact disc coating. Metal Finishing, vol. 85, no. 1, pp. 37-39.

McCauley, J. (1987). A CD-ROM based distributed electronic repair manual. In National Online Meeting Proceedings. Medford, NJ: Learned Information, pp. 319-24.

McCormick, J. (1990). A Guide to Optical Storage Technology: using CD-ROM, WORM, Erasable, Digital Paper, and other High-Density Opto-Magnetic Storage Devices. Homewood, IL: Dow Jones-Irwin.

McCormick, J. (1991). Federal Register on CD-ROM: high volume, high frequency, and high tension meets CD-ROM. CD-ROM Professional, vol. 4, no. 4, pp. 70-71.

McCrary, L. (1988). Sputtering technology for CD manufacturing. Optical Information Systems, vol. 8, no. 3, pp. 118-19.

McCready, S. (1989). Insurance document management. Insurance Software Review, vol. 18-20, 22, 24, 26-30.

McDowell, A. (1989). A manufacturer's view of WORM software requirements. In Software for Optical Storage. Westport, CT: Meckler Corporation, pp. 13-21.

McFarlane, R. et al (1977). Optical disc data recorder. In Proceedings of the SPIE, vol. 220. Bellingham, WA: Society of Photo-Optical Instrumentation Engineers, pp. 45-47.

McGahan, W. and Woollam, J. (1989). Magnetooptics of multilayer systems. Applied Physics Communications, vol. 9, no. 1, pp. 1-25.

McGlynn, T. et al (1988). Connecting an optical disk archive with a relational database catalogue. In Online Information 88: Twelfth International Online Information Meeting. Oxford: Learned Information, vol. 2, pp. 535-41.

McIntire, G. and Hatwar, T. (1989). The corrosion protection behavior of aluminum nitride and silicon dioxide coatings on magneto-optical media. Corrosion Science, vol. 29, no. 7, pp. 811-21.

McIntyre, W. and Soane, D. (1990). Controlled phase separation of polymer liquid crystal mixtures for reversible optical data storage. Applied Optics, vol. 29, no. 11, pp. 1658-65.

McKnight, S. (1987). The use of BiblioFile at the University of Queensland Libraries. Cataloguing Australia, vol. 13, no. 3, pp. 54-58.

Mcleod, J. (1981). Optical disk storage technology. Optical spectra, vol. 15, no. 11, pp. 52-54.

McQueen, H. (1990). Networking CD-ROMs: implementation considerations. Laserdisk Professional, vol. 3, no. 2, pp. 13-16.

McQueen, H. (1990a). Remote dial-in patron access to CD-ROM LANs. CD-ROM Professional, vol. 3, no. 4, pp. 20-23.

McWhinnie, H. (1992). Development of visual languages with interactive video disks. Journal of Educational Technology Systems, vol. 20, no. 1, pp. 45-51.

Mead, M. (1989). Books in Print Plus. Technical Services Quarterly, vol. 6, no. 2, pp. 69-74.

Megarry, J. (1989). Hypertext and compact discs: the challenge of multimedia learning. In Aspects of Educational and Training Technology, Vol. XXII: Promoting Learning. London: Kogan Page, pp. 49-58.

Meiklejohn, W. (1986). Magneto-optics: a thermomagnetic recording technology. Proceedings of the IEEE, vol. 74, no. 11, pp. 1570-81.

Menasce, D. and Ierusalimschy, R. (1988). An object-oriented approach to interactive access to multimedia databases on CD-ROM. In RIAO 88 Program: Conference with Presentation of Prototypes and Operational Demonstrations, User-Oriented Content-Based Text and Image Handling. Paris: C.I.D., vol. 1, pp. 237-46.

Mendez, A. (1986). Application of a generalized mathematical model of noise sources to optical media evaluation. In Proceedings of the SPIE, vol. 695. Bellingham, WA: Society of Photo-Optical Instrumentation Engineers, pp. 373-85.

Mendez, A. (1988). A unified theory for WORM media modelling. In Proceedings of the SPIE, vol. 899. Bellingham, WA: Society of Photo-Optical Instrumentation Engineers, pp. 244-52.

Mergel, D. et al (1990). The switching process for thermo-magneto-optical recording and its relation to material properties and preparation conditions of thin films. In Proceedings of the SPIE, vol. 1274. Bellingham, WA: International Society for Optical Engineering, pp. 270-81.

Metz, R. (1991). Mounting CD-ROM products on a campus network: site licenses, training, and evaluation. In Twelfth National Online Meeting Proceedings. Medford, NJ: Learned Information, pp. 271-73.

Meyer, F. (1988). Networked CD-ROM. Inform, vol. 2, no. 8, p. 30.

Meyer, F. (1990). In-house CD-ROM publishing moves toward the desktop. Laserdisk Professional, vol. 3, no. 1, pp. 40-41.

Meyer, J. (1990). Error correction implementation and performance in a CD-ROM drive. Hewlett-Packard Journal, vol. 41, no. 6, pp. 42-48.

Meyer-Ebrecht, D. et al (1982). Laboratory prototype system for the archiving of computerized tomographic (CT) pictures on optical disks. In First International Conference and Workshop on Picture Archiving and Communication Systems (PACS) for Medical Applications. Bellingham, WA: Society of Photo-Optical Instrumentation Engineers, pp. 411-13.

Miceli, J. et al (1987). Head media interface tolerancing Kodak optical head and Kodak LWR media. In Topical Meeting on Optical Data Storage: Summaries of Papers. Washington, DC: Optical Society of America, pp. 86-89.

Milch, A. and Tasaico, P. (1980). The stability of tellurium films in moist air: a model for atmospheric corrosion. Journal of the Electrochemical Society, vol. 127, no. 4, pp. 884-91.

Miller, D. (1988). XPS oxidation study of TbFeCo films. Applied Surface Science, vol. 35, no. 1, pp. 153-63.

Miller, E. and Miller, W. (1991). Discovering CD-I. Des Moines: Microware Systems Corporation.

Miller, N. and Backus, J. (1991). Menu systems for CD-ROMs at the National Library of Medicine: using Direct Net and Direct Access. CD-ROM Professional, vol. 4, no. 5, pp. 48-52.

Miller, N. and Backus, J. (1991a). MAXX: maximum access to diagnosis and therapy. CD-ROM Librarian, vol. 6, no. 1, pp. 34-37.

Minemura, H. et al (1988). Erasing characteristics of optical disks using induction heating. Transactions of the Institute of Electronic Information and Communication Engineering, vol. J71C, no. 3, pp. 486-91.

Minemura, H. et al (1990). Three-dimensional analysis of overwritable phase-change optical disks. Journal of Applied Physics, vol. 67, no. 6, pp. 2731-35.

Miller, R. (1986). An overview of the interactive market. In CD-I and Interactive Videodisc Technology. Indianapolis: Howard W. Sams, pp. 1-14.

Minar, S. (1988). Preparing color images of CD-I. In Electronic Imaging 88: International Electronic Imaging Exposition and Conference. Boston: Institute for Graphic Communication, vol. 2, pp. 858-62.

Minemura, T. and Andoh, H. (1986). Reversible color change in alloys: application to thin film devices. Solid State Physics, vol. 21, no. 6, pp. 374-78.

Misaki, H. et al (1989). Hydrogen-containing SiCN protective films for magneto-optical media. IEEE Transactions on Magnetics, vol. 25, no. 5, pp. 4030-32.

Mitsuhashi, Y. (1990). Holographic memory. Journal of the Institute of Electronics, Information and Communication Engineers, vol. 73, no. 4, pp. 414-18.

Mitsunaga, M. (1991). Photon echo memory-principles and applications. Oyo Buturi, vol. 60, no. 1, pp. 21-28.

Mittelman, P. (1990). Compact disc interactive (CD-I): a new audiovisual technology. In NCGA 90 Conference Proceedings. Fairfax, VA: National Computer Graphics Association, vol. 1, pp. 314-16.

Miura, I. (1990). Distribution and sales of CD-ROMs in Japan: status and problems. Online, vol. 14, no. 4, pp. 106-108.

Miyauchi, M. (1988). Self-contained vehicle location and monitoring system of the Japanese police. In Proceedings of the 1988 Carnahan Conference on Security Technology: Electronic Crime Countermeasures. Lexington, KY: University of Kentucky Press, pp. 17-23.

Miyazaki, A. (1987). Systemized Hitachi mapping information system for diversified mapping needs. Pixel, no. 55, pp. 72-76.

Miyazaki, M. and Nishi, K. (1985). Hitachi optical disk subsystems. In Digest of Papers: IEEE Symposium on Mass Storage Systems. New York: IEEE, pp. 62-68.

Miyazaki, M. et al (1987). A new protective film for magneto-optical TbFeCo media. Journal of Applied Physics, vol. 61, no. 8, pp. 3326-28.

Miyazaki, T. et al (1987). New write-once optical media using azulenium dye. Japanese Journal of Applied Physics: Supplement, vol. 26, suppl. 26-4, pp. 33-36.

Mizuno, M. (1989). AMTICS car-mounted device. Systems, Control and Information, vol. 33, no. 7, pp. 363-70.

Moerner, W. (1985). Laser light-induced physical processes in optical materials: persistent spectral hole-burning. In Proceedings of the SPIE, vol. 541. Bellingham, WA: Society of Photo-Optical Instrumentation Engineers, pp. 60-68.

Moerner, W. (1985a). Molecular electronics for frequency domain optical storage: persistent spectral hole-burning — a review. Journal of Molecular Electronics, vol. 1, no. 2, pp. 55-71.

Moerner, W. (1988). Persistent Spectral Hole-Burning: Science and Applications. Berlin: Springer-Verlag.

Moerner, W. and Levenson, M. (1985). Can single-photon processes provide useful materials for frequency-domain optical storage? Journal of the Optical Society of America, vol. 2, no. 6, pp. 915-24.

Moerner, W. et al (1987). Frequency domain optical storage: the importance of photon-gated materials. In Topical Meeting on Optical Data Storage: Technical Digest Series. Washington, DC: Optical Society of America, pp. 151-54.

Moes, R. (1986). The CD-ROM puzzle: where do the pieces fit? Optical Information Systems, vol. 6, no. 6, pp. 509-11.

Molaire, M. (1988). Influence of melt viscosity on the writing sensitivity of organic dye-binder optical recording media. Applied Optics, vol. 27, no. 4, pp. 743-46.

Moller, T. (1990). Application issues in optical storage systems. In Proceedings of the SPIE, vol. 1248. Bellingham, WA: International Society for Optical Engineering, pp. 142-46.

Moore, C. (1989). Survey of CD-ROM users in the UK. Program, vol. 23, no. 4, pp. 385-93.

Moore, F. (1990). Spelling out the benefits of imaging. Inform, vol. 4, no. 2, pp. 29-32.

Moore, M. (1990). The effects of compact disk indexes on interlibrary loan services at a university library. Journal of Interlibrary Loan and Information Supply, vol. 1, no. 1, pp. 25-42.

Moore, N. (1988). Searching LISA on the SilverPlatter CD-ROM system. Program, vol. 22, no. 1, pp. 72-76.

Moran, R. (1988). Optical drives meet mainframes. Computer Decisions, vol. 20, no. 10, pp. 36-37.

Morgan, R. (1989). The growing requirement for electronic document management systems. In OIS International 1989: Proceedings of the Sixth Annual Conference on Optical Information Systems. London: Meckler Corporation, pp. 202-26.

Moribe, M. et al (1988). Bit-error reduction in magneto-optical disks. In Proceedings of the SPIE, vol. 899. Bellingham, WA: Society of Photo-Optical Instrumentation Engineers, pp. 88-92.

Morinaka, A. and Oikawa, S. (1986). Recording process on an optical recording medium with thermal coloration. Journal of Applied Physics, vol. 60, no. 6, pp. 1919-25.

Moritsugu, M. et al (1989). New optical head for magneto-optic library units. In Proceedings of the SPIE, vol. 1078. Bellingham, WA: Society of Photo-Optical Instrumentation Engineers, pp. 131-37.

Morris, S. (1987). Digital video interactive: a new integrated format for multi-media information. Microcomputers in Information Management, vol. 4, no. 4, pp. 249-61.

Morris, S. (1987a). Old ideas, new technologies and childhood. Educational Computing, vol. 3, no. 3, pp. 239-45.

Morris, S. (1988). Digital video interactive: one medium, many methods. In Fifth International Conference on Technology and Education. Edinburgh, UK: CEP Consultants, vol. 1, pp. 396-99.

Morris, S. (1988a). Digital video interactive: one medium, many methods. In Combined Proceedings: Third Conference on Applications of Artificial Intelligence and CD-ROM in Education and Training and Fourth Conference on Applications of Artificial Intelligence and CD-ROM in Education and Training. Warrenton, VA: Learning Technology Institute, pp. 1-2.

Morris, S. (1991). DVI multimedia applications and products. CD-ROM Professional, vol. 4, no. 6, pp. 33-36.

Morrow, B. (1988). Library Corporation's Bibliofile. CD-ROM Librarian, vol. 3, no. 1, pp. 25-29.

Morrow, B. (1989). SuperCAT cataloger's workstation. CD-ROM Librarian, vol. 4, no. 8, pp. 28-34.

Morrow, B. (1989). IMPACT public access catalog. CD-ROM Librarian, vol. 4, no. 1, pp. 22-25.

Morrow, B. (1990). Do-it-yourself CD-ROM LANs: a review of LANtastic and CD-connection. CD-ROM Librarian, vol. 5, no. 10, pp. 12-24.

Motley, S. (1990). The federal government and optical disk technology. Online, vol. 14, no. 2, pp. 105-107.

Mouton, J. (1986). Petroleum industry benefits today from optical disks. World Oil, vol. 202, no. 3, pp. 75-78.

Mueller, R. (1990). Rewriting the future: rewritable optical mass storage comes of age. Optical Information Systems, vol. 10, no. 6, pp. 1-10.

Mullan, N. and Blick, A. (1987). Initial experiences of untrained end users with a life sciences CD-ROM database: a salutary experience. Journal of Information Sciences Principles and Practices, vol. 13, no. 3, pp. 139-41.

Mun, S. et al (1988). Development and technology assessment of a comprehensive image management and communication network. Medical Informatics, vol. 13, no. 4, pp. 315-22.

Munakata, A. and Urano, N. (1989). Hypermedia personal computer FM TOWNS. Fujitsu, vol. 40, no. 6, pp. 343-51.

Murikami, T. et al (1989). Full-height magneto-optic rewritable disk drive. In Proceedings of the SPIE, vol. 1078. Bellingham, WA: Society of Photo-Optical Instrumentation Engineers, pp. 230-38.

Musikant, S. (1990). Thin films for active optics. In Proceedings of the SPIE, vol. 1323. Bellingham, WA: International Society for Optical Engineering, pp. 164-70.

Myers, E. (1988). Big Blue and the optical disk market. Inform, vol. 2, no. 4, pp. 38-41.

Myers, P. (1987). Publishing with CD-ROM: a Guide to Compact Disc Optical Storage Technologies for Providers of Publishing Services. Westport, CT: Meckler Corporation.

Myers, P. (1989). Using CD-ROM in science and medicine. Optical Information Systems, vol. 9, no. 2, pp. 65-73.

Nagano, S. (1990). Marketing prospect and network utilization of CD-ROM. In Preprints: Second International Conference on the Effective Use of CD-ROM Databases. Tokyo: USACO, pp. 19-33.

Nagasawa, M. (1990). Recent servo technology in optical recording equipment. Journal of the Institute of Television Engineers of Japan, vol. 44, no. 9, pp. 1186-93.

Nagy-Teti, B. (1990). The Science Citation Index in the multi-media environment. In National Online Meeting: Proceedings. Medford, NJ: Learned Information, pp. 305-308.

Naitoh, M. et al (1990). Write-once type CD recorder with swing head. Journal of the Institute of Television Engineers of Japan, vol. 44, no. 10, pp. 1403-1409.

Nakajima, H. (1989). The conception and evolution of digital audio. In IEEE International Solid-State Circuits Conference: Digest of Technical Papers. New York: IEEE, pp. 60-62.

Nakamura, E. and Itoh, K. (1990). Applications of rare earth metals for functional materials. Sumitomo Light Metal Technical Report, vol. 31, no. 2, pp. 46-58.

Nakamura, K. et al (1990). Magnetic and magneto-optical properties of Pd/Co multilayered films. IEEE Translation Journal on Magnetics in Japan, vol. 5, no. 6, pp. 522-28.

Nakamura, S. (1989). Suntory Limited presentation support system for liquor shops. Fujitsu, vol. 40, no. 6, pp. 372-75.

Nakamura, Y. (1985). Systems and materials for high density magnetic recording. Bulletin of the Japanese Institute of Metals, vol. 24, no. 8, pp. 646-52.

Nakamura, Y. and Iwasaki, S. (1984). Recording and reproducing characteristics of perpendicular magnetic recording. In Recent Magnetics for Electronics. Amsterdam: Elsevier Science Publishers, pp. 3-17.

Nakane, Y. et al (1985). Principle of laser recording mechanism by forming an alloy in the trilayer of thin metallic films. In Proceedings of the SPIE, vol. 529. Bellingham, WA: Society of Photo-Optical Instrumentation Engineers, pp. 76-82.

Nakane, Y. et al (1986). Optical write-once disk subsystem with higher data integrity. Journal of the Institute of Television Engineers of Japan, vol. 40, no. 6, pp. 508-13.

Nakashima, Y. et al (1990). 86 mm magneto-optical disk drive. In Proceedings of the SPIE, vol. 1316. Bellingham, WA: International Society for Optical Engineering, pp. 16-29.

Nakata, N. (1987). Laser diodes have low noise and low astigmatism. JEE: Journal of Electronic Engineering, vol. 24, no. 248, pp. 49-50.

Narayan, A. (1988). Thirty terabyte mass storage architecture. In Digest of Papers: Ninth IEEE Symposium on Mass Storage Systems. New York: IEEE, pp. 103-107.

Nash, S. and Wilson, M. (1991). Value-added bibliographic instruction: teaching students to find the right citations. Reference Services Review, vol. 19, no. 1, pp. 87-92.

Natraj, N. (1990). OCR integrated with imaging systems: reducing data entry costs. IMC Journal, vol. 26, no. 1, pp. 11-15.

Natraj, N. (1990a). Character recognition for document imaging applications. Remittance and Document Processing Today, vol. 13, no. 2, pp. 5-9.

Nawaoka, T. et al (1990). Development of a mapping and guidance database for mobile navigation systems. Sumitomo Electric Technical Review, no. 30, pp. 28-33.

Neame, L. (1990). Indexes on CD-ROM: integration and the end-user. CD-ROM Professional, vol. 3, no. 4, pp. 105-107.

Neary, A. (1990). CD-ROM resource sharing in Connecticut. CD-ROM Librarian, vol. 5, no. 10, pp. 31-37.

Nelson, N. (1989). On the cutting edge: Next Technology's CD-ROM jukebox. CD-ROM Librarian, vol. 4, no. 9, pp. 22-24.

Nelson, N. (1990). CD-ROM in European libraries. CD-ROM Librarian, vol. 5, (1): 26-28; vol. 5, no. 2, pp. 16-20.

Nesbit, K. (1990). CD Plus MEDLINE. CD-ROM Professional, vol. 3, no. 3, pp. 61-65.

Neubauer, K. (1988). Updating of online catalog on CD-ROM. In International Library Cooperation: Tenth Anniversary Essen Symposium. Essen, West Germany: Essen University Library, pp. 161-78.

Neubauer, K. (1989). Electronic library? The consequences of micros on data processing systems in libraries in the age of CD-ROM. In Impact of CD-ROM on Library Operations and Universal Availability of Information: Eleventh International Essen Symposium. Essen, West Germany: Essen University Library, p. 115-31.

Neubert, S. et al (1989). Use of magnetic tape as an optical storage media. In Proceedings of the SPIE, vol. 1018. Bellingham, WA: Society of Photo-Optical Instrumentation Engineers, pp. 102-108.

Neukirchner, E. (1991). Driver information and navigation system. Informatik Spektrum, vol. 14, no. 2, pp. 65-68.

Ng, S. (1991). Improving disk performance via latency reduction. IEEE Transactions on Computers, vol. 40, no. 1, pp. 22-30.

Nicholls, P. (1989). The cost of information: comparative economics of print, online, and laserdisk full-text media. Laserdisk Professional, vol. 2, no. 4, pp. 116-22.

Nicholls, P. (1990). A buyer's guide to CD-ROM selection: CD-ROM product directories and review tools. CD-ROM Professional, vol. 3, no. 3, pp. 13-21.

Nicholls, P. et al (1990). A framework for evaluating CD-ROM retrieval software. Laserdisk Professional, vol. 3, no. 2, pp. 41-46.

Nicholls, P. (1991). A survey of commercially available CD-ROM database titles. CD-ROM Professional, vol. 4, no. 2, pp. 23-28.

Nicholls, P. (1991a). The TFPL CD-ROM Directory 1991. CD-ROM Professional, vol. 4, no. 4, pp. 117-19.

Nicholls, P. and Van Den Elshout, R. (1990). Survey of databases available on CD-ROM: types, availability, and content. Database, vol. 13, no. 1, pp. 18-23.

Nickerson, G. (1991). Bibliographic instruction for CD-ROM: developing in-house tutorials. CD-ROM Professional, vol. 4, no. 5, pp. 45-47.

Nickerson, G. (1991b). The CD-ROM workstation: what it is and what to look for. CD-ROM Professional, vol. 4, no. 3, pp. 40-41.

Nicolosi, G. et al (1988). Optimized organization design for clinical patient data management of a cardiology department by a hybrid system. In Computers in Cardiology. Washington, DC: IEEE Computer Society Press, pp. 303-306.

Nieuwenhuysen, P. (1990). CD-ROM in Belgium. Electronic Library, vol. 8, no. 3, pp. 205-208.

Nieuwenhuysen, P. (1990a). CD-ROM in Flanders and Brussels. Bibliotheek en Archiefgids, vol. 66, no. 1, pp. 102-11.

Niihara, T. et al (1988). High corrosion-resistant magneto-optical film on a new plastic substrate. IEEE Transactions on Magnetics, vol. 24, no. 6, pp. 2437-42.

Niihara, T. et al (1990). Thermomagnetic recording mechanism on TbFeCo disks. Journal of Magnetism and Magnetic Materials, vol. 88, no. 1, pp. 177-82.

Niina, T. and Hamada, H. (1986). Development of laser diode indispensible to greter optical disk application. JEE: Journal of Electronic Engineering, vol. 23, no. 229, pp. 62-65, 73.

Nikles, D. et al (1989). Accelerated aging studies for organic optical data storage media. In Proceedings of the SPIE, vol. 1078. Bellingham, WA: Society of Photo-Optical Instrumentation Engineers, pp. 43-50.

Nikles, D. et al (1990). Naphthalocyanine chromophores for WORM-type optical data storage media. In Proceedings of the SPIE, vol. 1248. Bellingham, WA: International Society for Optical Engineering, pp. 65-73.

Nipp, D. (1991). Back to basics: integrating CD-ROM instruction with standard user education. Research Strategies, vol. 9, no. 1, pp. 41-47.

Nishibori, M. and Shiina, S. (1990). An automated data conversion and entry system for the medical optical card. In Biomedical Engineering Perspectives: Health Care Technologies for the 1990's and Beyond: Proceedings of the Annual Conference on Engineering in Medicine and Biology. Piscataway, NJ: IEEE, pp. 1262-63.

Nishida, T. et al (1987). Effect of Tl and metallic element addition to In-Se based phase-change optical recording film. Japanese Journal of Applied Physics: Supplement, vol. 26, suppl. 26-4, pp. 67-70.

Nishida, T. et al (1987a). Single-beam overwrite experiment using In-Se based phase-change optical media. Applied Physics Letters, vol. 50, no. 11, pp. 667-69.

Nishihara, H. (1990). Recent studies of miniaturization of optical disk pickups in Japan. In Proceedings of the SPIE, vol. 1248. Bellingham, WA: International Society for Optical Engineering, pp. 88-95.

Nishimori, K. et al (1987). Preparation and charsacterization of magnetron-sputtered Ag-Zn thin film for optical recording. Journal of the Vacuum Society of Japan, vol. 30, no. 4, pp. 175-81.

Nishimori, K. et al (1989). Ge-Te-Sb based overwritable phase change optical disk. Japanese Journal of Applied Physics: Supplement, vol. 28, no. 3, pp. 135-39.

Nishimura, T. et al (1989). Photochemical hole burning of the quinone derivatives in polymer matrices. Japanese Journal of Applied Physics: Supplement, vol. 28, suppl. 28-3, pp. 175-78.

Nishiuchi, H. et al (1990). Hypermedia operating system for FM TOWNS. Fujitsu Scientific and Technical Journal, vol. 26, no. 3, pp. 175-86.

Nisonger, T. (1990). Books in Print Plus as a tool for analyzing US in-print monographs. Library Resources and Technical Services, vol. 34, no. 4, pp. 477-91.

Nixon, P. (1990). A university library's OPAC on CD-ROM: various views on the technology. Inspel, vol. 24, no. 3, pp. 120-27.

Nogami, H. et al (1990). Modeling of crystallization of recording film for phase change optical disk with melt-erasing process. Transactions of the Institute of Electronics, Information, and Communication Engineers, vol. J73C-II, no. 5, pp. 328-37.

Noordzij, A. and Van De Pol, H. (1990). Implementation of CD-ROM databases in networks: some background aspects. In Online Information 90: Fourteenth International Online Information Meeting Proceedings. Oxford: Learned Information, pp. 33-42.

Nosaka, K. et al (1990). CD-ROM drive unit CDR-72, CDR-82. NEC Technical Journal, vol. 43, no. 9, pp. 131-33.

Nowak, K. (1989). The Deutsche Bibliographie and CD-ROM. In Impact of CD-ROM on Library Operations and the Universal Availability of Information: Eleventh International Essen Symposium. Essen, West Germany: Essen University Library, pp. 213-19.

Oba, H. et al (1985). Organic dye materials for optical recording medium. In Topical Meeting on Optical Data Storage: Digest of Technical Papers. Washington, DC: Optical Society of America, pp. WDD1/1-4.

Oba, H. et al (1986). Organic dye materials for optical recording media. Applied Optics, vol. 25, no. 22, pp. 4023-26.

Ochmann, P. (1991). Digital mapping on CD-ROM. INSPEL, vol. 25, no. 3, pp. 84-93.

O'Connor, M. (1991). What does it cost to develop a CD-ROM? CD-ROM Professional, vol. 4, no. 5, pp. 127-28.

O'Donnell, J. and Derksen, C. (1990). CD-ROM and floppy disk databases for the earth sciences. In Frontiers of Geoscience Information: Proceedings of the Twenty-Fourth Meeting of the Geoscience Information Society. Alexandria, VA: Geoscience Information Society, pp. 5-33.

Ogawa, M. et al (1987). Fast access method of optical disk memory. In Proceedings of the SPIE, vol. 817. Bellingham, WA: Society of Photo-Optical Instrumentation Engineers, pp. 17-23.

Ogawa, S. and Maeda, M. (1990). Magneto-optical recording enhanced by magnetic recording techniques. In Proceedings of the SPIE, vol. 1248. Bellingham, WA: International Society for Optical Engineering, pp. 28-35.

Ogoshi, K. et al (1985). An optical recording disk using an organic dye medium. In Topical Meeting on Optical Data Storage: Digest of Technical Papers. Washington, DC: Optical Society of America, pp. WDD2/1-4.

Ohara, S. et al (1990). A single beam overwrite optical disk memory using a phase change medium. In Proceedings of the SPIE, vol. 1248. Bellingham: International Society for Optical Engineering, pp. 74-85.

Ohe, H. et al (1988). Car navigation system. NEC Technical Journal, vol. 41, no. 13, pp. 149-59.

Ohkubo, K. et al (1990). Effects of dielectric layers on TbFeCo magneto-optical disk. IEEE

Translation Journal on Magnetics in Japan, vol. 5, no. 1, pp. 68-78.

Ohno, E. et al (1989). TeGeSnAu alloys for phase change type optical disk memories. Japanese Journal of Applied Physics, vol. 28, no. 7, pp. 1235-40.

Ohno, S. and Sugiura, Y. (1986). Application of high definition television system for electronic imaging. Journal of Imaging Technology, vol. 12, no. 5, pp. 261-66.

Ohta, K. et al (1989). Magneto-optical disk formed by contact printing. Journal of the Japanese Society for Precision Engineering, vol. 55, no. 8, pp. 1379-84.

Ohta, T. et al (1982). Optical storage media guidelines. In Topical Meeting on Optical Data Storage. Washington, DC: Optical Society of America, pp. 142-43.

Ohta, T. et al (1989). Phase change disk media having rapid cooling structure. Japanese Journal of Applied Physics: Supplement, vol. 28, no. 3, pp. 123-28.

Ohta, T. et al (1990). Accelerated aging studies for phase change type disc media. In Proceedings of the SPIE, vol. 1316. Bellingham: International Society for Optical Engineering, pp. 367-73.

Ohtani, N. et al (1990). Magneto-optical disk for analog video recording. Sharp Technical Journal, no. 46, pp. 17-22.

Ojima, M. and Ohta, N. (1988). Erasable optical disk technologies. Hitachi Review, vol. 37, no. 3, pp. 139-46.

Ojima, M. et al (1990). Performance and reliability of advanced magneto-optical disk drive. In Proceedings of the SPIE, vol. 1316. Bellingham: International Society for Optical Engineering, pp. 95-100.

Okada, M. et al (1989). Bit error analysis for magneto-optical disks under accelerated aging condition. NEC Research and Development, no. 94, pp. 49-56.

Okada, M. et al (1990). High performance magneto-optical recording for video file applications. In Proceedings of the SPIE, vol. 1316. Bellingham, WA: International Society for Optical Engineering, pp. 81-90.

Okamoto, H. (1989). Outline and results of experiments of advanced mobile traffic information and communication system. Systems, Control and Information, vol. 33, no. 7, pp. 337-45.

Okamoto, H. and Nakahara, T. (1988). An overview of AMTICS. In International Congress on Transportation Electronics: Proceedings. New York: IEEE, pp. 219-28.

Okazaki, A. et al (1990). Image based geographic information system using optical disks. In Proceedings of the SPIE, vol. 1258. Bellingham, WA: International Society for Optical Engineering, pp. 66-77.

Okazaki, H. et al (1989). A theoretical analysis for media life estimation using error rate. In Proceedings of the SPIE, vol. 1078. Bellingham, WA: Society of Photo-Optical Instrumentation Engineers, pp. 51-58.

Okuda, M. et al (1988). Studies on the amorphous-crystalline reversible phase transition of Te-Se-Ge thin film alloys. Applied Surface Science, vols. 33-34, pp. 797-803.

Okuno, I. and Ohtsuka, H. (1989). FM TOWNS application software. Fujitsu, vol. 40, no. 6, pp. 381-3.

O'Lear, B. and Kitts, D. (1985). Optical device interfacing for a mass storage system. Computer, vol. 18, no. 7, pp. 24-32.

Oliver, T. and Bianchi, M. (1990). Optical disk autochanger servomechanism design. Hewlett-Packard Journal, vol. 41, no. 6, pp. 24-34.

Olsen, R. (1988). Workstations change role of file servers. Computer-Aided Engineering, vol. 7, no. 10, p. 88

Olsen, R. and Kenley, G. (1989). Virtual optical disks solve the online storage crunch. Computer Decisions, vol. 28, no. 1, pp. 93-96.

Omachi, R. (1988). Hi-tech applications of rare earths. Material Science Forum, vol. 30, no. 1, pp. 147-53.

O'Malley, K. and List, J. (1987). Quality evaluation of images displayed on the AT&T CommView System at Abbott Northwestern Hospital. In Proceedings of the SPIE, vol. 767. Bellingham, WA: Society of Photo-Optical Instrumentation Engineers, pp. 782-86.

Ono, O. et al (1988). CD-ROM assisted navigation system. In IEEE 1988 International Conference on Consumer Electronics: Digest of Technical Papers. New York: IEEE, pp. 118-19.

Ooi, B. (1991). Fail-safe WORM file system. In Proceedings of the SPIE, vol. 1401. Bellingham, WA: International Society for Optical Engineering, pp. 27-34.

Oppenheim, C. (1988). CD-ROM: Fundamentals to Applications. London: Butterworths.

Oren, T. and Kildall, G. (1986). The compact disk ROM: applications software. IEEE Spectrum, vol. 23, no. 4, pp. 49-54.

Osterlund, S. (1987). Optical archiving systems. DEC Professional, vol. 6, no. 6, pp. 66-69.

Ouchi, K. and Iwasaki, S. (1984). Studies of perpendicular recording media. In Recent Magnetics for Electronics. Amsterdam: Elsevier Science Publishers, pp. 51-66.

Ovens, C. (1990). The genesis of a LAN at a third world university library. In National Online Meeting Proceedings. Medford, NJ: Learned Information, pp. 315-23.

Owechko, Y. (1989). Nonlinear holographic associative memories. IEEE Journal of Quantum Electronics, vol. 25, no. 3, pp. 619-34.

Owen, D. (1989). ICI Imagedata's digital paper. Optical Information Systems, vol. 9, no. 5, pp. 226-29.

Owen, P. (1988). Optical disk systems. In OIS International 1988: Proceedings of the Fifth Annual Conference. London: Meckler Corporation, pp. 105-11.

Pagell, R. (1990). New information technologies in libraries and information centers in third world countries. Online, vol. 14, no. 1, pp. 100-101.

Pahwa, A. and Rudd, G. (1991). Sending your CD-ROM data for mastering. CD-ROM Professional, vol. 4, no. 5, pp. 100-103.

Paisley, W. and Butler, M. (1987). The first wave: CD-ROM adoption in offices and libraries. Microcomputers for Information Management, vol. 4, no. 2, pp. 109-27.

Parker, E. (1985). The Library of Congress nonprint optical disk pilot program. Information Technology and Libraries, vol. 4, no. 3, pp. 288-99.

Parkes, J. and Wade, R. (1989). CLANN CD-CAT: the CLANN database on CD-ROM. LASIE, vol. 19, no. 6, pp. 120-31.

Parkin, A. et al (1990). Optical disk archiving using a personal computer: a solution to image storage problems in diagnostic imaging departments. Journal of Medical Engineering and Technology, vol. 14, no. 2, pp. 55-59.

Paul, D. et al (1991). The over-the-counter CD-ROM network solution. CD-ROM Librarian, vol. 6, no. 9, pp. 19-23.

Pearson, E. (1989). The impact of CD-ROM on library operations: to buy or to make — one library's experience producing a CD-ROM. In Impact of CD-ROM on Library Operations and Universal Availability of Information: Eleventh International Essen Symposium. Essen, West Germany: Essen University Library, pp. 133-39.

Pearson, E. and MacKinnon, R. (1988). CD-ROM in the library: its more than the fiche of the 21st century. In International Library Cooperation: Tenth Anniversary Essen Symposium. Essen, West Germany: Essen University Library, pp. 153-60.

Pearson, J. (1986). Polymeric optical disk recording media. CRC Critical Review of Solid State and Material Science, vol. 13, no. 1, pp. 1-26.

Pedemonte, C. et al (1991). CD-ROM access control: special software for a statistical survey. CD-ROM Professional, vol. 4, no. 4, pp. 40-43.

Pelz, N. (1991). On the way to multimedia: CD-I optical medium for interactive learning. Bulletin des Schweizeischen Elektrotechnischen Vereins et des Verbandes Schweizerischer Elektrizitaetswerke, vol. 82, no. 17, pp. 49-53.

Pemberton, A. (1991). Submitting artwork for CD-ROM label, booklet, and backliner. CD-ROM Professional, vol. 4, no. 3, pp. 66-68.

Pendlebury, J. and Lewis, M. (1989). CD-ROMs in a university library setting: the experiences of the first year. In Online Information 89: Proceedings of the Thirteenth International Online Information Meeting. Oxford: Learned Information, pp. 201-10.

Perlman, L. (1988). Can magnetic storage survive new technologies? Electronic Business, vol. 14, no. 18, pp. 133-34.

Perlov, C. (1991). Modeling the write process in direct overwrite magneto- optic media. Journal of Applied Physics, vol. 69, no. 8, pt. 2A, pp. 4945-47.

Perry, E. (1990). The Ezekiel effect: factors affecting development of local area networks for CD-ROM. Laserdisk Professional, vol. 3, no. 1, pp. 7-9.

Perry, W. (1990). End user's opinions and profiles: some lessons for disc and software developers. CD-ROM End User, vol. 2, no. 1, pp. 24-25.

Pesch, O. (1990). CD-ROM network software. CD-ROM Librarian, vol. 5, no. 11, pp. 9-16.

Peskin, A. (1985). On the role of optical disk at computing centers. In Proceedings of the SPIE, vol. 529. Bellingham, WA: Society of Photo-Optical Instrumentation Engineers, pp. 237-39.

Peters, C. (1987). Databased on CD-ROM: comparative factors for purchase. Electronic Library, vol. 5, no. 3, pp. 154-60.

Phillips, B. (1988). Floptical disk drive stores 20.8 megabytes of data. Electronic Design, vol. 36, no. 18, pp. 65-68.

Pierce, G. (1988). Development of the Drexler optical card reader/writer system. In Proceedings of the SPIE, vol. 899. Bellingham, WA: Society of Photo-Optical Instrumentation Engineers, pp. 31-33.

Pinsl, J. et al (1987). Liquid crystalline polysiloxanes for optical write-once storage. Journal of Molecular Electronics, vol. 3, no. 1, pp. 9-13.

Plesums, C. (1989). Implementation of a large scale document image system. In Reaping the Benefits of Technology: Proceedings of LOMA's Systems Forum 89. Atlanta: Life Office Management Association, pp. 19-23.

Plesums, C. and Bartels, R. (1990). Large-scale image systems: USAA case study. IBM Systems Journal, vol. 29, no. 3, pp. 343-55.

Pohlmann, K. (1988). The compact disc formats: technology and applications. Journal of the Audio Engineering Society, vol. 36, no. 4, pp. 250-58.

Pohlmann, K. (1989). The Compact Disc: a Handbook of Theory and Use. Madison, WI: A-R Editions.

Pollack, I. (1990). Books in Print Plus (BIP) CD-ROM on a communication network. ISLIC Bulletin, vol. 17, no. 1, pp. 16-21.

Polly, J. (1989). LAN sakes! CD ROM and sthe staff network at Liverpool Public Library. In Online '89 Conference Proceedings. Weston, CT: Online, pp. 132-33.

Popoff, P. and Ledieu, J. (1984). Towards new information systems: Gigadisc. In Proceedings of the

SPIE, vol. 490. Bellingham, WA: Society of Photo-Optical Instrumentation Engineers, pp. 20-26.

Potember, R. et al (1986). Electronic devices from conducting organics and polymers. Polymer Journal, vol. 19, no. 1, pp. 147-56.

Pountain, D. (1989). Digital paper. Byte, vol. 14, no. 2, pp. 274-80.

Pournelle, J. (1991). Jukebox computing. Byte, vol. 16, no. 1, pp. 73-88.

Pozza, E. (1990). The ADONIS experiment: the electronic serial. Australian and New Zealand Journal of Serials Librarianship, vol. 1, no. 4, pp. 31-44.

Price, C. (1989). Compact disks. Tax Adviser, vol. 20, no. 12, pp. 834-38.

Price, C. (1990). Compact disks: a new technology for finding answers to client's questions. CPA Journal, vol. 60, no. 3, pp. 62-64.

Price, M. (1991). Programming for CD-ROM. EXE, vol. 5, no. 11, pp. 72-80.

Prierson, E. and Zoellick, P. (1990). CIARL: the Compact International Agricultural Research Library — designing a library on CD-ROM. Revista AIBDA, vol. 11, no. 2, pp. 45-62.

Priestley, A. (1991). Integrating motion video with the PC. Interactive Learning International, vol. 7, no. 1, pp. 39-44.

Pritchard, J. (1989). Optical character recognition (OCR) and intelligent character recognition (ICR). Information Media and Technology, vol. 22, no. 1, pp. 21-24.

Prokupets, R. and Somers, D. (1990). Implementing WORM optical storage in a law enforcement environment. Optical Information Systems, vol. 10, no. 4, pp. 183-87.

Propps, J. (1990). Network CD-ROMs. OCLC Micro, vol. 6, no. 5, pp. 22-25.

Prussian, M. (1989). Issues for publishers and users of CD-ROM on networks. In OPTICAL INFO 89: the International Meeting for Optical Publishing and Storage. Oxford: Learned Information, pp. 93-97.

Psaltis, D. et al (1989). Parallel readout of optical disks. In Optical Computing 1989: Technical Digest Series, vol. 9. Washington, DC: Optical Society of America, pp. 58-61.

Pungel, W. (1988). Traffic control: beat the jam electronically. Funkschau, no. 18, pp. 43-45.

Put, P. (1990). Trends in optical disk mastering. MRS Bulletin, vol. 15, no. 4, pp. 52-56.

Puttapithakporn, S. (1990). Interface design and user problems and errors: a case study of novice searchers. RQ, vol. 30, no. 2, pp. 195-204.

Quinn, R. (1988). Insurance applications of optical card technology. Optical Information Systems, vol. 8, no. 4, pp. 148-50.

Ruddick, A. (1989). Digital paper: a write-once optical medium. In IEE Colloquium on New Advances in Optical Recording Technology. London: IEE, pp. 2/1-5.

Ruddick, A. and Duffy, J. (1991). ICI optical tape: the world's first commercial flexible WORM media. In IEE Colloquium on New Materials for Information Storage. London: IEE, pp. 3/1-4.

Radke, G. (1986). Car navigation: electronic pilots. Funkschau, no. 22, pp. 99-102.

Raitt, D. (1990). Laptop CD-ROM drives. Electronic Library, vol. 8, no. 5, pp. 328-30.

Raitt, D. and Chen, C. (1989). Optical products in European libraries and information centres: results of a survey. In Online Information 89: Proceedings of the Thirteenth International Online Information Meeting. Medford, NJ: Learned Information, pp. 227-32.

Raitt, D. and Chen, C. (1990). Use of CD-ROMs in West German libraries. In Developments in microcomputing: discovering new opportunities for libraries in the 1990s; Twelfth Essen Symposium. Essen, West Germany: Essen University Library, pp. 25-36.

Ralphs, J. (1990). Planning the distribution of technical documentation on CD-ROM. In Seventh Annual OIS International 1990: Proceedings of the Seventh Annual Conference on Optical Information Systems. London: Meckler Corporation, pp. 107-11.

Ramakrishnan, K. and Emer, J. (1989). Performance analysis of mass storage service alternatives for distributed systems. IEEE Transactions on Software Engineering, vol. 15, no. 2, pp. 120-33.

Ramamoorthy, C. and Chandy, K. (1970). Optimization of memory hierarchies in multiprogrammed systems. Journal of the ACM, vol. 17, no. 3, pp. 426-45.

Ramsay, N. (1990). Integration of the optical storage processor and the DBC/1012 database computer. In Digest of Papers: Tenth IEEE Symposium on Mass Storage Systems. Washington, DC: IEEE Computer Society Press, pp. 94-97.

Ranade, S. (1989). Benchmarking write-once drives: a systems integrator's perspective. Optical Information Systems, vol. 9, no. 2, pp. 58-64.

Ranade, S. (1990). Software for mass storage systems. Optical Information Systems, vol. 10, no. 5, pp. 256-69.

Ranade, S. (1991). Mass Storage Technologies. Westport, CT: Meckler Corporation.

Ranade, S. and Ng, J. (1990). Systems Integration for Write-Once Optical Storage. Westport, CT: Meckler Corporation.

Ranade, S. and Yee, F. (1989). Evaluation of optical disk jukebox software. Optical Information Systems, vol. 9, no. 3, pp. 120-26.

Ramsay, N. (1988). Using optical disk in non-image applications. Optical Information Systems, vol. 8, no. 4, pp. 164-68.

Rapp, B. et al (1990). Evaluating MEDLINE on CD-ROM: an overview of field tests in library and clinical settings. Online Review, vol. 14, no. 3, pp. 172-86.

Ravner, S. and Shull, T. (1990). High-performance optical disk mass storage for aerospace imaging systems. In Proceedings of the SPIE, vol. 1248. Bellingham, WA: International Society for Optical Engineering, pp. 170-75.

Raychaudhuri, P. (1989). Ge-Te-Ti thin films for high performance phase change optical recording. In Proceedings of the SPIE, vol. 1078. Bellingham, WA: Society of Photo-Optical Instrumentation Engineers, pp. 157-64.

Rebane, K. (1988). Photochemical hole-burning: basic principles and facts. In Proceedings of the Fourth International School on Condensed Matter Physics: Molecular Electronics. Singapore: World Scientific, pp. 467-506.

Rebane, K. (1990). Impurity doped low temperature solids as novel materials for optical data storage and processing. In Proceedings of the SPIE, vol. 1319. Bellingham, WA: International Society for Optical Engineering, pp. 146-47.

Rebane, K. et al (1988). Photoburning of persistent spectral holes and space-time domain holography of ultrafast events of nana- and picosecond duration. In Laser Optics of Condensed Matter: Proceedings of the USA-USSR Symposium. New York: Plenum, pp. 421-26.

Rees, F. (1986). A Plato-based videodisc self-instructional program for directing the development of string vibrato technique. Journal of Educational Technology Systems, vol. 14, no. 4, pp. 283-96.

Reese, J. (1987). A comparison and evaluation of three CD-ROM products. In Optical Information Systems 87. Westport, CT: Meckler Corporation, pp. 230-39.

Reese, J. (1987a). Vanderbilt's enhanced information access project: the OCLC CD/Search-CD450 component in test. Optical Information Systems Update/Library and Information Center Applications, vol. 2, no. 2, pp. 1-12.

Reese, J. (1989). Shareware and public domain software on CD-ROM. Laserdisk Professional, vol. 2 no. 6, pp. 15-34.

Reichardt, O. (1985). OSAR (optical storage and retrieval): a mass produced automated mass storage system. In Digest of Papers: Seventh IEEE Symposium on Mass Storage Systems. Washington, DC: IEEE Computer Society Press, pp. 69-73.

Reifsnyder, B. (1990). CD-ROM and online searching. Database, vol. 13, no. 1, pp. 94-96.

Reijns, G. et al (1988). Simulation and communication aspects of PACS. In Proceedings of the SPIE, vol. 914. Bellingham, WA: Society of Photo-Optical Instrumentation Engineers, pp. 1153-58.

Reim, W. and Weller, D. (1989). Magneto-optical properties of metallic bilayer thin films. IEEE Transactions on Magnetics, vol. 25, no. 5, pp. 3752-54.

Reno, C. and Tarzaiski, R. (1979). Optical disc recording at 50 megabits per second. In Proceedings of the SPIE, vol. 110. Bellingham, WA: Society of Photo-Optical Instrumentation Engineers, pp. 45-48.

Renn, A. et al (1989). Spectral hole burning and holography: multiple storage of holograms. Japanese Journal of Applied Physics: Supplement, vol. 28, suppl. 28-3, pp. 257-59.

Retzler, J. et al (1989). Optical disk radiation hardening considerations. Optical Engineering, vol. 28, no. 3, pp. 248-54.

Reynolds, G. and Halliday, J. (1987). Compact disc processing. In Sound Recording Practice. Third Edition. Oxford: Oxford University Press, pp. 440-52.

Reynolds, T. (1990). Optical disk records system frees claims company from paper. Remittance and Document Processing Today, vol. 13, no. 4, pp. 8-12.

Rhee, J. et al (1987). Write-erase characteristics of phase change optical recording in Ga-Se-Te systems. Japanese Journal of Applied Physics, vol. 26, no. 1, pt. 1, pp. 102-105.

Rhine, C. (1990). Implementing a local area network: the effect on present and future services at the Health Sciences Library. Information Technology and Libraries, vol. 9, no. 1, pp. 102-107.

Richards, D. (1989). Producer's view of CD-ROM for database distribution. In SCIL 89 International: Proceedings of the Third Annual Conference on Small Computers in Libraries. London: Meckler Corporation, pp. 111-14.

Richardson, J. (1991). Library user trials with a CD-ROM database. Computers in Libraries, vol. 11, no. 4, pp. 28-34.

Richman (1987). Dense media and the future of publishing. Electronic Publishing Business, vol. 5, no. 2, pp. 12-15; also in CD-ROM: the New Papyrus. Redmond, WA: Microsoft Press, pp. 445-52.

Richwine, P. and Switzer, J. (1990). CD-ROM MEDLINE training: a survey of medical school libraries. Medical Reference Services Quarterly, vol. 9, no. 3, pp. 21-29.

Rietdyk, R. (1990). CD-ROM networking developments in libraries. In Preprints: Second International Conference on the Effective Use of CD-ROM Databases. Tokyo: USACO, pp. 34-43.

Rio, F. et al (1990). Optical and magnetic properties of GdTbFe oxides thin films. Journal of Magnetism and Magnetic Materials, vol. 83, no. 1, pp. 35-36.

Rioux, M. (1988). interfacing BIP+ with a dBASE III+ acquisitions system. CD-ROM Librarian, vol. 3, no. 7, pp. 12-16.

Ripley, G. (1988). DVI interactivity in a universal all-digital medium. In Electronic Imaging 88: International Electronic Imaging Exposition and Conference. Boston: Institute for Graphic Communication, vol. 2, pp. 851-53.

Ripley, G. (1989). DVI: a digital multimedia technology. Communications of the Association for Computing Machinery, vol. 32, no. 7, pp. 811-22.

Ritzler, C. (1989). Databases on CD-ROM: what can this technology mean for developing countries in the future? Quarterly Bulletin of the International Association of Agricultural Librarians and Documentalists, vol. 34, no. 1, pp. 1-5.

Robbins, W. et al (1981). Bubble forming media for optical recording: a new approach. In CLEO 81: Conference on Lasers and Electronics. New York: IEEE, p. 122.

Roberts, W. et al (1988). Semiconductor laser marking studies on copper TCNQ thin films. Journal of Materials Science Letters, vol. 7, no. 3, pp. 198-202.

Robinson, P. (1990). The four multimedia gospels. Byte, vol. 15, no. 2, pp. 203-12.

Robinson, R. et al (1990). The service bureau concept. CD-ROM Professional, vol. 3, no. 3, pp. 39-40.

Robinson, R. et al (1990). Software for CD-ROM: a tutorial. Laserdisk Professional, vol. 3, no. 2, pp. 47-52.

Roby, C. (1991). Continuous composite multifunction optical storage. Optical Information Systems, vol. 11, no. 1, pp. 14-18.

Rodgers, D. (1990). Step-by-step through the CD-ROM production process. Laserdisk Professional, vol. 3, no. 1, pp. 36-39.

Rooijmans, C. and Verhoeven, J. (1983). Characteristics of the optical media laboratory disk. In Proceedings of the SPIE, vol. 420. Bellingham, WA: Society of Photo-Optical Instrumentation Engineers, pp. 18-21.

Rosen, L. (1990). CD-networks and CD-ROM: distributing data on disk. Online, vol. 14, no. 4, pp. 102-105.

Rosen, L. (1990). CD-ROM user interfaces: consistency or confusion? Database, vol. 13, no. 2, pp. 101-103.

Rosie, J. (1989). Standards and compatibility for CD-ROM. IN SCIL 89: International Proceedings of the Third Annual Conference on Small Computers in Libraries. London: Meckler Corporation, pp. 89-94.

Ross, S. (1991). Interactive videodiscs for science education. Journal of Computer Assisted Learning, vol. 7, no. 2, pp. 96-103.

Roth, J. (1986). The Essential Guide to CD-ROM. Westport, CT: Meckler Corporation.

Roth, J. (1986). The Essential Guide to CD-ROM. Westport, CT: Meckler Corporation.

Roth, J. (1988). CD-ROM Applications and Markets. Westport, CT: Meckler Corporation.

Roth, J. and Galloway, E. (1983). Basics of videodisc and optical disk technology. Journal of the American Society for Information Science, vol. 34, no. 6, pp. 408-16.

Rothchild, E. (1983). Optical memory media: how optical disks work, who makes the, and how much data they can hold. Byte, vol. 8, no. 3, pp. 86-106.

Rothchild, E. (1984). Optical memory: data storage by laser. Byte, vol. 9, no. 11, pp. 215-24.

Royce, I. (1986). CARIN: an application of CD-ROM. Optical Information Systems, vol. 6, no. 1, pp. 60-63.

Rubin, J. et al (1991). Survey of interactive language video discs. CALICO Journal, vol. 8, no. 4, pp. 65-94.

Rubin, K. and Chen, M. (1989). Progress and issues of phase-change erasable optical recording media. Thin Solid Films, vol. 181, no. 2, pp. 129-39.

Ruppert, J. and Gilbertson, M. (1988). CD-I, IV-D: the challenge for technical manuals. In IPCC

1988 Conference Record: a Pacific Rim Conference on Professional Technical Communication. New York: IEEE, pp. 21-24.

Rushton, A. et al (1989). Design and implementation of an optical disk-based astronomical data archive. Computer Physics Communications, vol. 57, nos. 1-3, pp. 427-31.

Rushton, A. et al (1990). The universe online: optical disks for astronomical archiving. Optical Information Systems, vol. 10, no. 1, pp. 35-39.

Russell, J. (1987). New optical memory card: Hi-Lite. Optical Information Systems, vol. 7, no. 6, pp. 416-20.

Russell, J. and De Forest, R. (1983). Stationary card optical digital storage system. In Proceedings of the Second International Conference and Workshop on Picture Archiving and Communication Systems (PACS II) for Medical Applications. New York: IEEE, pp. 42-44.

Rutherford, J. (1990). Improving CD-ROM management through networking. CD-ROM Professional, vol. 3, no. 5, pp. 20-27.

Ryan, B. (1990). Entering a new phase. Byte, vol. 15, no. 12, pp. 289-96.

Saeki, H. et al (1990). Optical video disc system for HDTV. In Signal Processing of HDTV: Proceedings of the Third International Workshop on HDTV. Amsterdam: Elsevier, pp. 519-26.

Safdie, E. (1988). Resolving the resolution issue: display considerations in imaging devices. Inform, vol. 2, no. 9, pp. 6-7, 33.

Saffady, W. (1988). Document indexing in CAR and optical filing systems: concepts and issues. Micrographics and Optical Storage Equipment Review, vol. 13, pp. 97-116.

Saffady, W. (1989). The cost of automated cataloging support: an analysis and comparison of selected products and services. Library Technology Reports, vol. 25, no. 4, pp. 461-628.

Saffady, W. (1989a). Text Storage and Retrieval Systems: a Technology Survey and Product Directory. Westport, CT: Meckler Corporation.

Saffady, W. (1989b). Electronic document imaging using write-once optical disks: an overview of concepts and components. International Journal of Micrographics and Video Technology, vol. 7, no. 3, pp. 91-97.

Saffady, W. (1990). Optical Disks vs. Magnetic Storage. Westport, CT: Meckler Corporation.

Saffady, W. (1990a). Micrographic Systems, Third Edition. Silver Spring, MD: Association for Information and Image Management.

Saffady, W. (1991). The market for optical disk products: a review of published forecasts, 1980-1990. Document Image Automation, vol. 11, no. 5, pp. 252-56.

Saffady, W. (1991a). Stability, Care, and Handling of Microforms, Magnetic Media, and Optical Disks. Library Technology Reports, vol. 27, no. 1, pp. 5-116.

Saito, A. et al (1987). High storage density optical disks using pit edge recording on Pb-Te-Se thin films. In Topical Meeting on Optical Data Storage: Summaries of Papers. Washington, DC: Optical Society of America, pp. 64-67.

Saito, M. and Nomura, K. (1989). A present status of CD-ROM XA and its future: introduction to Tibetan art in Ladakh. Joho Kanri, vol. 32, no. 8, pp. 653-63.

Saito, M. and Takeda, T. (1988). Optical disk redundancy design considering bit-error characteristics. Transactions of the Institute of Electronic Information and Communications Engineering, vol. J71C, no. 2, pp. 287-95.

Saldanha, K. and Howe, C. (1990). Qualification of an optical disk drive for autochanger use. Hewlett-Packard Journal, vol. 41, no. 6, pp. 35-37.

Salomon, K. (1990). Software-CD: a CD-ROM guide to software. CD-ROM Librarian, vol. 5, no. 5, pp. 42-44.

Samarajiva, R. (1989). Appropriate high tech: scientific communication options for small third world countries. Information Society, vol. 6, no. 1, pp. 29-46.

Sander, I. and Slovenka, S. (1987). Magneto-optic recording with a compact optical head. In Topical Meeting on Optical Data Storage: Summaries of Papers. Washington, DC: Optical Society of America, pp. 182-85.

Sao, Y. et al (1990). Overwritable phase-change optical disk using an In/sub 3/ SbTe/sub 2/ ternary compound. In Proceedings of the SPIE, vol. 1316. Bellingham: International Society for Optical Engineering, pp. 267-70.

Satchell, S. (1990). Megafloppies. Byte, vol. 15, no. 10, pp. 301-10.

Sato, M. et al (1987). Reliability of magneto-optical memory disks. IEEE Translation Journal on Magnetics in Japan, vol. 2, no. 5, pp. 395-96.

Sato, Y. et al (1989). 40db over-write-modulation phase-change optical disk using In-Sb-Te alloy. In Proceedings of the SPIE, vol. 1078. Bellingham, WA: Society of Photo-Optical Instrumentation Engineers, pp. 11-14.

Satoh, H. et al (1990). Signal characteristics of high definition video discs. Journal of the Institute of Television Engineers of Japan, vol. 44, no. 10, pp. 1376-82.

Satoh, I. and Kato, M. (1988). Holographic disk recording of digital data with fringe stabilization. Applied Optics, vol. 27, no. 14, pp. 2987-92.

Satyanarayanan, M. (1986). Modelling Storage Systems. Ann Arbor, MI: UMI Research Press.

Schankin, L. (1989) Air Force acquires data on disc. CD-ROM End User, vol. 1, no. 8, pp. 44-45.

Schein, A. (1989). Optical storage and OCR: key components of automated information management systems. Optical Information Systems, vol. 9, no. 1, pp. 9-15.

Schewe, M. (1989). Evaluating jukeboxes for optical disk systems. IMC Journal, vol. 25, no. 6, pp. 26-27.

Schiavone, L. et al (1984). Optical recording in amorphous hydrogenated tellurium. Applied Optics, vol. 23, no. 6, pp. 3954-55.

Schipma, P. (1989). A multi-database CD-ROM with graphics. In National Online Meeting Proceedings. Medford, NJ: Learned Information, pp. 387-91.

Schips, K. (1988). From brake light to navigation and telephone. Funkschau, no. 22, pp. 52-53.

Schitai, A. (1989). The design and development of an interactive videodisc for foreign language learning. Educational Technology, vol. 29, no. 7, pp. 48-52.

Schmidgall, R. (1990). Technical and economical advantages for inline production of magneto optical disks. In Proceedings of the Annual Technical Conference: Society of Vacuum Coaters. Washington, DC: Society of Vacuum Coaters, pp. 76-81.

Schmitt, F. and Lee, T. (1979). Developments in thermoplastic tape for optical recording. In Proceedings of the SPIE, vol. 177. Bellingham, WA: Society of Photo-Optical Instrumentation Engineers, pp. 89-96.

Schmitt, H. (1990). Magneto-optic devices. In Proceedings of the SPIE, vol. 1274. Bellingham: International Society for Optical Engineering, pp. 208-19.

Schnelling, H. (1989). Beyond online? Interactive public access to library files via CD-ROM. In Impact of CD-ROM on Library Operations and Universal Availability of Information: Eleventh International Essen Symposium. Essen, West Germany: Essen University Library, pp. 95-113.

Scholte, P. et al (1988). New materials for reversible optical storage applications. In Video, Audio, and Data Recording: Seventh International Conference. London: IERE, pp. 11-14.

Schreier, P. (1983. Plastic disk optical memory stores 1G bytes. EDN, vol. 28, no. 16, pp. 74, 76.

Schroeder, E. and Uhde, D. (1990). Extending the performance of the rewritable magneto-optical disc. IEEE Transactions on Consumer Electronics, vol. 36, no. 3, pp. 655-59.

Schroeder, J. (1984). A pedagogical mode of instruction for interactive videodisc. Journal of Educational Technology Systems, vol. 12, no. 4, pp. 311-17.

Schultz, K. (1989). BiblioMed: a CD-ROM version of MEDLINE. CD-ROM Librarian, vol. 4, no. 3, pp. 32-35.

Schultz, M. and Kryder, M. (1989). Erase process in direct overwrite magneto-optic recording material. Applied Physics Letters, vol. 54, no. 14, pp. 1371-73.

Schultz, K. and Salomon, K. (1990). End users respond to CD-ROM. Library Journal, vol. 115, no. 2, pp. 56-57.

Schwartz, C. (1989). Trends in interface design in the CD-ROM database environment. In Online 89 Conference Proceedings. Weston, CT: Online, pp. 139-42.

Schwerin, J. (1985). The potential role of Drexon LaserCards in optical publishing. Videodisc and Optical Disk, vol. 5, no. 4, pp. 288-93.

Sella, C. et al (1990). Structure and optical properties of Au-Cr films used in digital optical recording media. Vacuum, vol. 41, nos. 4-6, pp. 1172-75.

Sertic, K. and Mann, T. (1989). MOBAC CD-ROM union catalog project. Laserdisk Professional, vol. 2, no. 6, pp. 64-69.

Seshadri, S. et al (1990). Architecture of an optical jukebox image archive. In Proceedings of the SPIE, vol. 1234. Bellingham, WA: International Society for Optical Engineering, pp. 925-32.

Sever, S. (1989). CD-ROM and bridging of cultural and technological gaps in developing countries. In Impact of CD-ROM on Library Operations and Universal Availability of Information: Eleventh Essen Symposium. Essen, West Germany: Essen University Library, pp. 13-28.

Sharp, R. et al (1990). Improving image application performance of magneto-optic devices utilizing pre-erase. In Proceedings of the SPIE, vol. 1248. Bellingham, WA: International Society for Optical Engineering, pp. 49-59.

Sharpless, G. (1987). CD-I overview. In INTERACT 87: Conference Proceedings. Peterborough, UK: PLF Communications, pp. 3-12.

Shaw, A. (1988). Optical memory card: new technology or new application? Optical Information Systems, vol. 8, no. 4, pp. 154-55.

Sheets, C. (1991). NLSDBA: the national longitudinal surveys on compact disk. Behavior Research Methods, Instruments, and Computers, vol. 23, no. 2, pp. 212-13.

Shen, J. et al (1989). Magneto-optic properties of evaporated Mn-Bi-Al films. Journal of Magnetism and Magnetic Materials, vol. 81, no. 1, pp. 107-11.

Shepherd, J. (1988). Organic optical storage media for short wavelength systems. In Proceedings of the SPIE, vol. 1078. Bellingham, WA: Society of Photo-Optical Instrumentation Engineers, pp. 220-225.

Sherman, C. (1988). The CD ROM Handbook. New York: Intertext/McGraw-Hill.

Shieh, H. (1991). Time resolved thermomagnetic recording process in GdTbFeCo films. Journal of Applied Physics, vol. 69, no. 8, pt. 2A, pp. 4951-53.

Shiller, L. (1990). Selecting a CD-ROM drive. OCLC Micro, vol. 6, no. 5, pp. 26-27.

Shimada, J. and Kato, M. (1985). Trend in optical disc memory. Journal of the Society of Instrumentation and Control Engineers, vol. 24, no. 6, pp. 533-38.

Shimbori, S. (1987). CD-ROM: trends of file format standardization. Journal of Information Processing and Management, vol. 30, no. 2, pp. 137-48.

Shimidzu, N. and Ohno, S. (1989). Laser recording medium using dyestuff in polymer film. Journal of Imaging Technology, vol. 15, no. 1, pp. 19-22.

Shin, C. (1986). Optical autolibrary technology and its applications. In Proceedings of the SPIE, vol. 695. Bellingham, WA: Society of Photo-Optical Instrumentation Engineers, pp. 412-19.

Shiotani, H. et al (1990). Hi-Vision videograph. Sanyo Technical Review, vol. 22, no. 3, pp. 26-41.

Shiuh, C. et al (1988). Materials for multiple stages of archival optical recording. In Proceedings of the SPIE, vol. 899. Bellingham, WA: Society of Photo-Optical Instrumentation Engineers, pp. 240-43.

Shivaraman, M. and Engstrom, O. (1990). A sensitive MNMOS structure for optical storage. In ESSDERC 90: Twentieth European Solid State Device Research Conference. Bristol, England: Adam Hilger, pp. 575-58.

Shoda, J. et al (1990). Evaluation of optical memory card system for patient records. In Proceedings of the SPIE, vol. 1348. Bellingham, WA: International Society for Optical Engineering, pp. 536-44.

Shono, K. et al (1990). Sputtered garnet media for magneto-optic recording. Fujitsu Scientific and Technical Journal, vol. 26, no. 2, pp. 156-63.

Shrawagi, S. et al (1984). Defect measurements in digital optical disks. Journal of Vacuum Science and Technology, vol. 2, no. 2, pp. 346-49.

Shull, T. et al (1988). NASA spaceborn optical disk recorder development. In Proceedings of the SPIE, vol. 899. Bellingham, WA: Society of Photo-Optical Instrumentation Engineers, pp. 272-78.

Shumaker, L. (1990). Search Master Tax Library. CD-ROM Librarian, vol. 5, no. 10, pp. 46-49.

Siebourg, W. et al (1990). Birefringence: an important property of plastic substrates for magneto-optical storage disks. Polymer Engineering and Science, vol. 30, no. 18, pp. 1133-39.

Siedband, M. (1988). Filmless x-ray system using optical data cards. Optical Information Systems, vol. 8, no. 4, pp. 144-46.

Siedband, M. and Grenzow, F. (1989). Independent viewer for optical cards. In Image of the Twenty-First Century: Proceedings of the Annual International Conference of the IEEE Engineering in Medicine and Biology Society. New York: IEEE, vol. 2, pp. 775-76.

Siedband, M. and Zhang, H. (1989). Filmless medical imaging system. In MEDINFO 89: Proceedings of the Sixth Conference on Medical Informatics. Amsterdam: North-Holland Publishing Company, pp. 1160-63.

Siedband, M. et al (1990). Optical data card for medical imaging. In Proceedings of the SPIE, vol. 1248. Bellingham, WA: International Society for Optical Engineering, pp. 204-209.

Sieverts, E. 1989). Software for conversion of downloaded data: criteria for comparison and assessment. In Online Information 89: Thirteenth International Online Information Meeting Proceedings. Oxford: Learned Information, pp. 59-70.

Sijstermans, F. and Van der Meer, J. (1991). CD-I full-motion video encoding on a parallel computer. Communications of the Association for Computing Machinery, vol. 34, no. 4, pp. 81-91.

Silber, J. (1989). Implementation of DVI technology for high safety training. In Proceedings: Seventh Conference on Interactive Instruction Delivery. Warrenton, VA: Society for Applied Learning Technology, pp. 13-14.

Silver, H. and Dennis, S. (1990). Monitoring patron use of CD-ROM databases using SignIn-Stat.

Bulletin of the Medical Library Association, vol. 78, no. 3, pp. 252-57.

Simon, A. (1990). CD Plus PlusNet in a library consortium environment. CD-ROM Librarian, vol. 5, no. 11, pp. 28-33.

Simpson, D. (1989). Is write once the right choice? Systems Integration, vol. 22, no. 5, pp. 42-48.

Singarella, T. et al (1991). Videodisc technology trends in academic health sciences libraries. Bulletin of the Medical Library Association, vol. 79, no. 2, pp. 159-66.

Situ, H. et al (1989). Mechanism of transformations in phase-change optical recording media. Journal of Non-Crystalline Solids, vol. 113, no. 1, pp. 88-93.

Skelton, J. et al (1989). Document image processing: the new image processing frontier. In Proceedings of the SPIE, vol. 1153. Bellingham, WA: International Society for Optical Engineering, pp. 442-55.

Skupsky, D. (1991). Legal considerations in the design of an optical disk system. International Journal of Micrographics and Video Technology, vol. 9, no. 1, pp. 7-11.

Slater, G. (1988). The Hull Domesday textbase: a programmer's view. University Computing, vol. 10, no. 1, pp. 2-8.

Slicker, R. (1988). A software standard for write-once optical disks. Optical Information Systems, vol. 8, no. 2, pp. 81-83.

Sloan, S. (1990). The networked CD-ROM system: gathering information through the user interface. CD-ROM Professional, vol. 3, no. 4, pp. 25-29.

Sloan, S. (1990a). Expanded memory: one solution to networked CD-ROM memory problems. Computers in Libraries, vol. 10, no. 3, pp. 21-23.

Sloan, S. (1991). The ABCs of networking CD-ROMs: 26 depressing reasons why this may cost you more money than you think. CD-ROM Professional, vol. 4, no. 1, p. 29.

Smith, A. (1981). Long term file migration: development and evaluation of algorithms. Communications of the ACM, vol. 24, no. 8, pp. 521-32.

Smith, A. (1989). Prototyping a navigation data base of road network attributes. In Conference Record of Papers Presented at the First Vehicle Navigation and Information Systems Conference. New York: IEEE, pp. 331-36.

Smith, A. (1986). Research and development ofr memory hierarchies. In Proceedings of the Workshop on Future Directions in Computer Architecture and Software. Washington, DC: IEEE Computer Society Press, pp. 62-71.

Smith, R. (1989). British Library plans for CD-ROM. Laserdisk Professional, vol. 2, no. 2, pp. 58-61.

Smith, R. (1989a). CD-ROM for national bibliographies: a European project. In Impact of CD-ROM on Library Operations and Universal Availability of Information: Eleventh International Essen Symposium. Essen, West Germany: Essen University Library, pp. 221-30.

Smith, R. (1990). National libraries project on CD-ROM. Electronic Lib-rary, vol. 8, no. 6, p. 412-14.

Smith, R. and McSean, T. (1989). Planning and producing the British National Bibliography on CD-ROM. Program, vol. 23, no. 4, pp. 395-413.

Smith, T. (1981). The role of polymers in optical recording media. Journal of Vacuum Science and Technology, vol. 18, no. 1, pp. 100-104.

Smorch, T. (1990). CD-ROM public access catalogs: one way to get there. CD-ROM Librarian, vol. 5, no. 4, pp. 30-34.

Soffer, B. (1986). Associative holographic memory with feedback using phase-conjugate mirrors. Optical Letters, vol. 11, no. 2, pp. 118-20.

Soy, S. (1987). LePac product testing at Black Gold Cooperative Library System. Optical Information Systems Update/Library and Information Center Applications, vol. 2, no. 3, pp. 1-4.

Spencer, K. (1988). Terabyte optical tape recorder. In Digest of Papers: Ninth IEEE Symposium on Mass Storage Systems. Washington, DC: IEEE Computer Society Press, pp. 144-46.

Spencer, K. (1988a). Terabyte optical tape recorder. In Electronic Imaging 88: International Electronic Imaging Exposition and Conference. Waltham, MA: Institute for Graphic Communication, pp. 957-61.

Spencer, K. (1990). Optical tape recorder: easy data handling at less cost. Photonics Spectra, vol. 24, no. 2, pp. 115-16.

Spigai, F. (1987). Electronic publishing in the information age. Electronic Publishing Business, vol. 5, no. 2, pp. 4-11.

Spitz, C. (1991). Using CD-ROM to create computer-based training with audio. CD-ROM Professional, vol. 4, no. 3, pp. 73-75.

Spitz, C. (1991), Using CD-ROM to create computer-based training with audio. CD-ROM Professional, vol. 4, no. 3, pp. 73-75.

Sponheimer, E. (1990). Magnetooptical recording technology. Hewlett-Packard Journal, vl. 41, no. 6, pp. 8-9.

Sponheimer, E. (1991). The technology of magneto-optical recording. Elettronica Oggi, no. 120, pp. 95-101.

Sponheimer, E. and Santon, J. (1990). A CD-ROM drive for HP 3000 and HP 9000 computer systems. Hewlett-Packard Journal, vol. 41, no. 6, pp. 38-41.

Sporer, A. (1987). Reversible laser marking process in anthraquinone dye films. Applied Optics, vol. 26, no. 7, pp. 1240-45.

Stabler, K. (1991). A model for training academic librarians on CD-ROM. In Twelfth National Online Meeting Proceedings. Medford, NJ: Learned Information, pp. 361-65.

Stasek, M. and Sperry, L. (1989). Automating the catalog: CD-ROM in a public library. Journal of Educational Media and Library Sciences, vol. 26, no. 4, pp. 348-56.

Stavely, D. et al (1990). A rewritable optical disk library system for direct access secondary storage. Hewlett-Packard Journal, vol. 41, no. 6, pp. 6-7, 10-13.

Steen, B. (1989). ImagePlus: trends and directions. In Proceedings of the Thirteenth Annual G.U.I.D.E. Conference: Symposium on Storage. Lucerne, Switzerland: G.U.I.D.E., p. 403.

Steffey, R. (1991). Compton's MultiMedia Encyclopedia: bringing multimedia to the masses. CD-ROM Professional, vol. 4, no. 3, pp. 13-14, 17-20.

Stein, A. et al (1990). Silver sodalites: a chemistry approach towards reversible optical data storage. Journal of the Society of Photographic Science and Technology of Japan, vol. 53, no. 4, pp. 322-28.

Steinbrecher, D. (1987). Optical disks go head to head with traditional storage media. Today's Office, vol. 22, no. 5, pp. 24-30.

Stepnes, S. (1991). Photo CD technology makes 35mm cameras computer peripherals. Computer Technology Review, vol. 11, no. 14, pp. 53-56.

Stern, B. (1986). ADONIS: publishing on CD-ROM in mixed mode. In Tenth International Onine Information Meeting. Oxford: Learned Information, pp. 23-31.

Stern, B. (1990). ADONIS: a vision of the future. In Interlending and Document Supply: Proceedings of the First International Conference. Boston Spa, United Kingdom: British Library, pp. 23-33.

Stern, B. and Campbell, R. (1989). ADONIS: delivery of journal articles on CD-ROM. CD-ROM Librarian, vol. 4, no. 2, pp. 9-13.

Stern, B. and Compier, H. (1990). ADONIS: document delivery in the CD-ROM age. Interlending and Document Supply, vol. 18, no. 3, pp. 79-87.

Stevens, J. (1991). Rewritable media manufacturing for multifunctional drives. Optical Information Systems, vol. 11, no. 1, pp. 26-28.

Stewart, S. (1986). The use of optical storage technology in health care and medical science. Optical Information Systems, vol. 6, no. 4, pp. 298-302.

Stock, K. (1989). Cataloging and OPAC with compact disc in a local area network and in regional bibliographic utilities. ABI-Technik, vol. 9, no. 3, pp. 183-88.

Stockbridge, C. and Ravin, C. (1986). Phased implementation of AT&T PACS at Duke University Medical Center. In Proceedings of the SPIE, vol. 671. Bellingham, WA: Society of Photo-Optical Instrumentation Engineers, pp. 169-72.

Stocks, J. (1989). CD-ROM down under: a Delphi study of CD-ROM in Australian academic and special libraries. Laserdisk Professional, vol. 3, no. 1, pp. 18-22.

Stocks, J. (1989a). CD-ROM: a literature review and some results from a Delphi study. LASIE, vol. 20, no. 1, pp. 4-15.

Stolte, D. et al (1990). Integrating the optical library unit into the HP-UX operating system. Hewlett-Packard Journal, vol. 41, no. 6, pp. 11-12.

Storey, P. et al (1988). Environmental evaluation of rugged and long-life write-once optical disks. In Proceedings of the SPIE, vol. 899. Bellingham, WA: Society of Photo-Optical Instrumentation Engineers, pp. 226-32.

Storleer, R. (1989). CD-ROM in the library of the Norwegian University of Technology. Synopsis, vol. 20, no. 4, pp. 169-75.

Streets, S. (1990). The Asaca ADS-7800 HDTV magneto-optical disk stillstore. International Broadcast Engineer, vol. 21, no. 238, pp. 52-54.

Streets, S. and Tugwell, D. (1990). The Asaca AAM-800: an MO disk-based digital audio storage system. International Broadcast Engineer, vol. 21, no. 240, pp. 68-69.

Strelitz, M. (1989). Digital paper feeds at OA data banquet. Computer Technology Review, vol. 9, no. 2, pp. 26-29.

Stroot, S. et al (1991). Skill analysis utilizing videodisc technology. Computers in the Schools, vol. 8, nos. 1-3, pp. 271-91.

Sudou, R. et al (1988). Optical disc substrate using photo-curable casting resin. In Proceedings of the SPIE, vol. 899. Bellingham, WA: Society of Photo-Optical Instrumentation Engineers, pp. 129-33.

Sugiyama, Y. et al (1990). Crystallization process of In-Te alloy films for optical recording. Journal of Non-Crystalline Solids, vol. 122, no. 1, pp. 83-89.

Suh, S. (1985). Writing process in ablative optical recording. Applied Optics, vol. 24, no. 3, pp. 868-74.

Sukeda, H. et al (1990). High speed magnetic field modulation in pit-edge magneto-optic recording. IEEE Translation Journal on Magnetics in Japan, vol. 5, no. 1, pp. 79-86.

Sullivan, K. (1991). InfoTrac version 6.0. CD-ROM Professional, vol. 4, no. 4, pp. 44-47.

Suzuki, H. (1991). Fast, large-capacity wavelength-multiplexing memory materials based on photochemical hole burning. Solid State Physics, vol. 26, no. 2, pp. 139-46.

Suzuki, K. (1987). Toshiba high-power semiconductor laser for optical information processing. JEE: Journal of Electronic Engineering, vol. 24, no. 248, pp. 26-29.

Suzuki, M. et al (1990). Disk structure and writing method for high performance phase change erasable optical disk. In Proceedings of the SPIE, vol. 1316. Bellingham: International Society for Optical Engineering, pp. 374-81.

Suzuki, T. (1984). Perpendicular magnetic recording: its basics and potential for the future. IEEE Transactions on Magnetics, vol. 20, no. 5, pt. 1, pp. 675-80.

Suzuki, T. (1991). Magnetic and magneto-optic properties of rapid thermally crystallized garnet films. Journal of Applied Physics, vol. 69, no. 8, pt. 2A, pp. 4756-60.

Sypherd, A. (1990). Optical disk uses in criminal identification systems. In Proceedings of the SPIE, vol. 1248. Bellingham, WA: International Society for Optical Engineering, pp. 176-83.

Tachibana, K. and Takahashi, H. (1990). Signal processing in an HDTV video disc system using a two-channel recording method. Journal of the Institute of Television Engineers of Japan, vol. 44, no. 10, pp. 1383-90.

Tachibana, K. et al (1989). Optical disc system for wideband high definition video signal. IEEE Transactions on Consumer Electronics, vol. 35, no. 3, pp. 208-15.

Tada, J. et al (1986). Significant improvement of magnetic properties and corrosion resistance in evaporated Co-Ni recording media. IEEE Transactions on Magnetics, vol. 22, no. 5, pp. 343-45.

Takagi, T. et al (1989). Slit-shape edge emitting LED specially designed for optical card reader/writer. In Second Annual Meeting of the IEEE Lasers and Electro-Optics Society: LEOS 89. Piscataway, NJ: IEEE, p. 20.

Takahashi, T. et al (1987). A health care system using optical memory cards. In Proceedings of the Ninth Annual Conference of the IEEE Engineering in Medicine and Biology Society. New York: IEEE, pp. 243-44.

Takahashi, Y. et al (1990). CD-compatible write-once optical disc. Fuji Film: Research and Development, no. 35, pp. 58-65.

Tally, R. (1987). Creating a CD-ROM with the help of a simulator. Bulletin of the American Society for Information Science, vol. 13, no. 6, pp. 21-22.

Tamai, M. and Nakamoto, M. (1990). Hardware of hypermedia personal computer: FM TOWNS. Fujitsu Scientific and Technical Journal, vol. 26, no. 3, pp. 167-74.

Tamura, K. (1988). Bibliographic information service by CD-ROM. Joho Kanri, vol. 30, no. 11, pp. 1083-95.

Tamura, Y. et al (1987). CD-ROM premastering system development. Sanyo Technical Review, vol. 19, no. 1, pp. 46-54.

Tanaka, K. et al (1987). The technical trends in optical disk storage. Information Processing Society of Japan, vol. 28, no. 8, pp. 1075-83.

Takagi, K. (1987). Ring-closure of halogenonaphthoquinones with potassium 2-aminobenzenethiolate: tautomerism and substituent effects. Dyes and Pigments, vol. 8, no. 1, pp. 71-82.

Takahashi, A. et al (1990). High speed accessing of a 90 mm optical disk drive. In Proceedings of the SPIE, vol. 1316. Bellingham, WA: International Society for Optical Engineering, pp. 11-15.

Takahashi, M. et al (1991). Magneto-optic disks for high-density recording with a shorter wavelength laser. Journal of Applied Physics, vol. 69, no. 8, pt. 2A, p. 4773.

Takahashi, N. (1988). Digital still HDTV disc system. IEEE Transactions on Consumer Electronics, vol. 34, no. 1, pp. 64-71.

Takeda, T. and Isomura, Y. (1990). Image coded document retrieval from rewritable optical disks in remote file server on local area network. Journal of the Institute of Television Engineers of Japan, vol. 44, no. 10, pp. 1425-30.

Takeda, T. and Saito, M. (1988). Evaluation of sector alternation methods for optical disks. Transactions of the Institute for Electronic Information and Communications Engineering, vol. E71, no. 4, pp. 355-57.

Takeda, T. et al (1991). Higher area density recording technique for small, high-capacity optical disk subsystem. NTT R&D, vol. 40, no. 6, pp. 857-64.

Takenaga, M. et al (1982). Optical disc memory using tellurium suboxide thin films. National Technical Report, vol. 28, no. 6, pp. 1016-24.

Tamura, S. (1990). Photochemical hole burning. Journal of the Institute of Electronics, Information and Communication Engineers, vol. 73, no. 4, pp. 419-24.

Tanabe, T. et al (1989). Crystallization characteristics of phase-change media by laser pulse-train irradiation. Japanese Journal of Applied Physics, vol. 28, no. 10, pp. 1845-47.

Tanaka, F. and Suzuki, S. (1988). Analogue video recording on magneto-optical disk. KDD Technical Journal, no. 138, pp. 21-25

Tanaka, F. et al (1990). Advanced magneto-optical disk drive and media. In Proceedings of the SPIE, vol. 1316. Bellingham: International Society for Optical Engineering, pp. 245-51.

Tanaka, F. et al (1990a). Rewritable video disk drive. In Proceedings of the SPIE, vol. 1316. Bellingham: International Society for Optical Engineering, pp. 91-94.

Tanaka, K. and Sugawara, H. (1989). A 130mm rewritable optical disk drive and its media. Mitsubishi Electric Advances, vol. 48, no. 1, p. 29-32.

Tanaka, S. and Imamura, N. (1985). The effect of noble metals on oxidation resistance of TbFe. Japanese Journal of Applied Physics, vol. 2, no. 5, pp. 375-76.

Tanaka, S. et al (1987). Improvement of lifetimes of magneto-optical disks by alloying various elements. IEEE Translation Journal on Magnetics in Japan, vol. 2, no. 5, pp. 397-98.

Tanaka, T. (1986). Recent trends of optical recording materials. Journal of the Society for Photographic Science and Technology of Japan, vol. 49, no. 4, pp. 309-15.

Tani, T. et al (1987). Photochemical hole burning materials: dye molecules and matrices. Japanese Journal of Applied Physics: Supplement, vol. 26, suppl. 26-4, pp. 77-81.

Tao, H. and Chen, H. (1990). An experimental study of write-once-read-many (WORM) optical disks: I. Single dye system. MRL Bulletin of Research and Development, vol. 4, no. 1, pp. 1-8.

Tao, H. and Chen, H. (1990a). A new organic dye-in-polymer (DIP) medium for write-once-read-many (WORM) optical disks. Journal of Imaging Science, vol. 34, no. 6, pp. 255-58.

Tapper, R. (1986). The BBC Domesday Project: an educational review. Journal of Educational Television, vol. 12, no. 3, pp. 197-210.

Tapper, R. (1987). Building the Domesday data base: lessons for integrated database development. Aslib Proceedings, vol. 39, no. 4, pp. 107-21.

Tas, J. (1991). Commercial applications for optical data storage. In Proceedings of the SPIE, vol. 1401. Bellingham, WA: International Society for Optical Engineering, pp. 10-18.

Taylor, H. (1989). Science Citation Index print and CD: the best of both worlds from ISI. In Impact of CD-ROM on Library Operations and Universal Availability of Information: Eleventh International Essen Symposium. Essen, West Germany: Essen University Library, pp. 45-61.

Teger, N. (1991). MultiPlatter goes to school. CD-ROM Librarian, vol. 6, no. 6, pp. 21-28.

Tejedor, M. and Fernandez, A. (1986). Effect of the oxidation of the magnetic properties of vacuum evaporated Tb-Fe thin films. Journal of Magnetism and Magnetic Materials, vol. 59, no. 1, pp. 28-32.

Tennenhouse, M. (1987). MEDLINE on CD-ROM at the University of Manitoba Medical Library. Bibliotheca Medica Canadiana, vol. 8, no. 4, pp. 209-11.

Tenopir, C. and Smith, T. (1990). General periodical indexes on CD-ROM. CD-ROM Professional, vol. 3, no. 4, pp. 70-81.

Terao, M. (1985). Pb-Te-Se phase change recording film for optical disks. Solid State Physics, vol. 20, no. 1, pp. 132-38.

Terao, M. (1985a). Sn-Te-Se phase change recording film for optical disks. In Proceedings of the SPIE, vol. 529. Bellingham, WA: Society of Photo-Optical Instrumentation Engineers, pp. 46-50.

Terao, M. et al (1986). In-Se based phase change reversible optical recording film. In Proceedings of the SPIE, vol. 1078. Bellingham, WA: Society of Photo-Optical Instrumentation Engineers, pp. 105-109.

Terao, M. et al (1987). Oxidation resistance of Pb-Te-Se optical recording film. Journal of Applied Physics, vol. 62, no. 3, pp. 1029-34.

Terao, M. et al (1989). Progress of phase-change single-beam overwrite technology. In Proceedings of the SPIE, vol. 1078. Bellingham, WA: Society of Photo-Optical Instrumentation Engineers, pp. 2-10.

Terao, M. et al (1989a). Sn-Te-Se films for reversible phase-change optical recording. Japanese Journal of Applied Physics, vol. 28, no. 5, pp. 804-809.

Terao, M. et al (1989b). Effect of transition metal addition to a Ge-Sb-Te phase optical recording film. Optoelectronics: Devices and Technologies, vol. 4, no. 2, pp. 223-34.

Terasaki, A. et al (1991). Future trends and fundamental technologies for mobile communications: in recognition and perspective of the mobile communication systems. Joho Shori, vol. 32, no. 7, pp. 794-804.

Terasaki, H. et al (1991). High density MUSE videodisc. IEEE Transactions on Consumer Electronics, vol. 37, no. 3, pp. 418-23.

Terry, C. (1991). Digital-paper storage, flexible optical media boost data density. EDN, vol. 36, no. 9, pp. 77, 79-80, 85.

Terry, C. (1990). Drives accept WORM and rewritable media. EDN, vol. 35, no. 17, pp. 95-98, 100.

Tewell, T. (1989). The SCSI connectivity crisis. In Software for Optical Storage. Westport, CT: Meckler Corporation, pp. 169-76.

Thanhardt, E. and Harano, G. (1988). File migration in the NCAR mass storage system. In Digest of Papers: Ninth IEEE Symposium on Mass Storage Systems. New York: IEEE, pp. 114-21.

Thavendrarajah, A. et al (1989). Magnetic properties of sputtered Bi3Fe50. IEEE Transactions on Magnetics, vol. 25, no. 2, pp. 4015-17.

Therrien, D. (1991). Preparing for optical disk's next generation. Computer Technology Review, vol. 11, no. 9, pp. 18, 24, 26.

Thiel, T. et al (1990). CD-ROM Mastering for Information and Image Management. Silver Spring, MD: Association for Information and Image Management.

Thomas, G. (1985). High-speed data management system with on-line optical disk storage. In Digest of Papers: IEEE Symposium on Mass Storage Systems. New York: IEEE, pp. 38-42.

Thomas, G. (1987). Thin films for optical recording applications. Journal of Vacuum Science and Technology, part A, vol. 5, no. 6, pp. 1965-66.

Thomas, G. (1988). Future trends in optical recording. Philips Technical Review, vol. 44, no. 2, pp. 51-57.

Thompson, M. et al (1987). Two terabyte optical archival store. Computing in Physics Communications, vol. 45, no. 1, pp. 403-407.

Thoone, M. and Breukers, R. (1984). CARIN: a new dimension in car control. Elektronica, vol. 32, no. 18, pp. 19-29.

Thoone, M. (1987). CARIN: a car information and navigation system. Philips Technical Review, vol. 43, nos. 11-12, pp. 317-29.

Thorkildsen, R. et al (1986). Interactive videodisc: instructional design of a beginning reading program. Learning Disability Quarterly, vol. 9, no. 2, pp. 111-17.

Tiampo, J. (1987). CD-ROM disc titles. CD-ROM Review, vol. 1, no. 3, pp. 40-48.

Tiampo, J. (1987a). CD-ROM disc titles. CD-ROM Review, vol. 2, no. 4, pp. 48-57.

Tiampo, J. (1988). Update on retrieval software products. Optical Information Systems, vol. 8, no. 2, pp. 86-88.

Tibbetts, M. (1987). The BBC Domesday Project. In Electronic Publishing: the New Way to Communicate. London: Kogan Page, pp. 155-60.

Tibbetts, M. (1988). The BBC Domesday Project. In Micros Plus: Educational Peripherals; Proceedings of the IFIP TC 3/WG 3.3 Working Conference on the Educational Implications of Connecting Tools and Devices to Micro-Computers. Amsterdam: North-Holland Publishing Company, pp. 131-34.

Tinker, M. (1989). DVI parallel image compression. Communications of the Association for Computing Machinery, vol. 32, no. 7, pp. 844-51.

Tobe, M. and Kawabe, H. (1990). The application of map information in the customer-use phone information directory system. NTT R&D, vol. 30, no. 6, pp. 851-56.

Tobes, M. et al (1987). Teleradiology operations with a PACS environment. In Proceedings of the SPIE, vol. 767. Bellingham, WA: Society of Photo-Optical Instrumentation Engineers, pt. 2, pp. 849-52.

Toki, K. et al (1990). Sputtered Tb/FeCoTi multi-layered films for magneto-optical recording. IEEE Transactions on Magnetics, vol. 26, no. 5, pp. 1709-11.

Tokunaga, T. et al (1987). Stability of magnetic and magneto-optical properties of TbCo sputtered films. Electronics and Communication, vol. 70, no. 4, pp. 100-14.

Tokushima, T. et al (1989). Improvement of environmental stability by doping beryllium in TbFeCo magneto-optical recording media. IEEE Transactions on Magnetics, vol. 25, no. 1, pp. 687-91.

Tomisawa, S. et al (1991). CD-I player. Sanyo Technical Review, vol. 23, no. 1, pp. 90-101.

Tonosaki, M. (1990). Problems on usage of MEDLINE CD-ROM/ SilverPlatter version due to the production error of the U.S. National Library of Medicine. On-line Kensaku, vol. 11, no. 1, pp. 26-31.

Toyama, T. et al (1986). Optical videodisc for high definition television by the MUSE. SMPTE Journal, vol. 95, no. 1, pp. 25-29.

Toyama, T. et al (1987). Optical video disc for Hi-Vision. Sanyo Technical Review, vol. 19, no. 1, pp. 24-33.

Toyota, K. et al (1990). A new optical card requiring no preformatting. In Proceedings of the SPIE, vol. 1316. Bellingham, WA: International Society for Optical Engineering, pp. 345-55.

Trammell, B. (1989). Too little, too late? Not at USAA: big and early describes this organization's efforts in document processing. Inform, vol. 3, no. 7, pp. 24-26, 50-52.

Trapp, P. (1988). Hardware and software developments in 5.25-inch and 12-inch write-once optical disc jukeboxes. In OIS International 1988: Proceedings of the Fifth Annual Conference on Optical Information Systems. London: Meckler Corporation, pp. 213-16.

Traub, D. (1989). Multimedia down under: optical media in Australia and New Zealand. Optical Information Systems, vol. 9, no. 5, pp. 242-50.

Traub, D. (1990). Multimedia down under. CD-ROM Librarian, vol. 5, no. 3, pp. 16-23.

Troeltzsch, L. (1983). 3M optical videodisc project: part one — rationales and implementations. Videodisc/Videotex, vol. 3, no. 2, pp. 100-111.

Troeltzsch, L. (1984). 3M optical videodisc project: part two — preparing the master tape. Videodisc/Videotex, vol. 4, no. 1, pp. 54-62.

Tsuchiya, Y. et al (1991). High-density recording technology of optical video discs for Hi-Vision. Sanyo Technical Review, vol. 23, no. 1, pp. 80-89.

Tsuchiya, Y. et al (1991). High-density recording technology of optical video discs for Hi-Vision. Sanyo Technical Review, vol. 23, no. 1, pp. 80-89.

Tsujimura, K. et al (1990). CD software specifications for vehicle information display system, CD CRAFT. 1990 IEEE Workshop on Electronic Applications in Transportation. New York: IEEE, pp. 16-24.

Tsunoda, Y. and Ojima, M. (1987). Advanced technologies for the next generation optical disks. In Topical Meeting on Optical Data Storage: Summaries of Papers. Washington, DC: Optical Society of America, pp. 60-63.

Tsutsui, K. et al (1990). Optical card tracking servo system utilizing two light sources. In Proceedings of the SPIE, vol. 1316. Bellingham, WA: international Society for Optical Engineering, pp. 341-44.

Tsutsumi, K. and Umesaki, M. (1990). Novel direct-overwrite technology for magneto-optical disks. Mitsubishi Electric Advances, vol. 51, no. 1, pp. 8-11.

Tsuzawa, M. and Okamoto, H. (1989). Advanced Mobile Traffic Information and Control System — AMTICS. In Conference Record of Papers Presented at the First Vehicle Navigation and Information Systems Conference. New York: IEEE, pp. 475-83.

Tu, K. et al (1981). Silicide films for archival optical storage. Applied Physics Letters, vol. 39, no. 11, pp. 927-28.

Turley, R. (1989). User experience of the BBC Domesday discs in an academic library. Audiovisual Librarian, vol. 15, no. 2, pp. 76-79.

Turner, I. (1988). Error management in optical disk recording. In Digest of Papers: COMPCON Spring 88, 33rd IEEE Computer Society International Conference. Washington, DC: IEEE Computer Society Press, pp. 132-34.

Turner, P. (1991). CDMARC Names: the Library of Congress' name authority data base. CD-ROM Professional, vol. 4, no. 4, pp. 82-86.

Turtur, A. et al (1990). IDB: an integrated image data base system on local area network. In Proceedings of the SPIE, vol. 1259. Bellingham, WA: International Society for Optical Engineering, pp. 279-90.

Tyan, Y. et al (1987). Recent advances in phase-change media. In Topical Meeting on Optical Data Storage: Summaries of Papers. Washington, DC: Optical Society of America, pp. 44-49.

Ueda, S. (1990). Hypertext system: TownsGEAR. Fujitsu Scientific and Technical Journal, vol. 26, no. 3, pp. 187-96.

Ueno, F. (1987). Observation of fast microscopic phase change phenomena of chalcogenide thin films. Japanese Journal of Applied Physics: Supplement, vol. 26, suppl. 26-4, pp. 55-60.

Ueno, H. et al (1989). Development of a mobile mapping system for use in emergency gas line maintenance vehicles. In Conference Record of Papers Presented at the First Vehicle Navigation and Information Systems Conference. New York: IEEE, pp. 177-84.

Umehara, M. et al (1985). Application of organic dyes to optical disk memory. Journal of Synthetic Chemistry, vol. 43, no. 2, pp. 334-43.

Uricchio, W. et al (1990). From amoeba to re-Quest: a history and case study of Connecticut's CD-ROM-based statewide database. Library Hi Tech, vol. 8, no. 2, pp. 7-21.

Urita, K. (1987). Semiconductor lasers for optical memory disks: high output and low noise required. JEE: Journal of Electronic Engineering, vol. 24, no. 248, pp. 31-34.

Urrows, H. and Urrows, E. (1988). The chemistry of optical disk materials. Optical Information Systems, vol. 8, no. 5, pp. 202-15.

Urrows, H. and Urrows, E. (1989). The chemistry of optical disk materials. Optical Information Systems, vol. 8, no. 5, pp. 202-15.

Urrows, H. and Urrows, E. (1989b). The future of transactional card technologies. Optical Information Systems, vol. 9, no. 4, pp. 190-208.

Urrows, H. and Urrows, E. (1990). Erasable-rewritables now and promised: introductory notes. Optical Information Systems, vol. 10, no. 1, pp. 14-27.

Urrows, H. and Urrows, E. (1990a). Jukeboxes ascend: headlong growth ahead. Optical Information Systems, vol. 10, no. 5, pp. 220-24.

Urrows, H. and Urrows, E. (1991). Children's encyclopedias on CD-ROM. CD-ROM Librarian, vol. 6, no. 2, pp. 9-20.

Urrows, H. and Urrows, E. (1991a). Comparisons of CD-ROMs, electronic dictionaries, and other language aids. CD-ROM Librarian, vol. 6, no. 4, pp. 14-23.

Urrows, H. and Urrows, E. (1991b). Children's Encyclopedias on CD-ROM. CD-ROM Librarian, vol. 6, no. 2, pp. 9-20.

Urrows, H. and Urrows, E. (1991c). CD-ROMs for lawyers and accountants. CD-ROM Librarian, vol. 6, no. 9, pp. 24-34.

Urrows, H. and Urrows, E. (1991d). Kodak's photo CD and proposed PhotoYCC color standard. Computers in Libraries, vol. 11, no. 4, pp. 16-19.

Utsumi, K. et al (1988). Erasable phase change optical disk using a SeInSb alloy film for high-density recording. In Proceedings of the SPIE, vol. 899. Bellingham, WA: Society of Photo-Optical Instrumentation Engineers, pp. 196-200.

Valk, A. (1987). Compact disc interactive. Electronic and Optical Publishing Review, vol. 7, no. 2, pp. 64-68.

Vallbona, C. et al (1989). Pilot test and preliminary evaluation of an optical memory card medical record system. In MEDINFO 89: Proceedings of the Sixth Conference on Medical Informatics. Amsterdam: North-Holland Publishing Company, pp. 809-12.

Van Brakel, P. (1987). The electronic encyclopedia: facts on CD-ROM. Electronic and Optical Publishing Review, vol. 7, no. 4, pp. 186-91.

Van der Poel, C. et al (1986). Phase-change optical recording in TeSeSb alloys. Journal of Applied Physics, vol. 59, no. 6, pp. 1819-21.

Van der Walt, H. (1989). Effectiveness of information retrieval software for CD-ROM data bases: special emphasis on comprehensiveness. In OpticalInfo 89: the International Meeting for Optical Publishing and Storage. Oxford: Learned Information, pp. 125-29.

Van Engelen, P. and Buschow, K. (1990). Note on the magneto-optical properties of Fe/sub 3X compounds (X = B, P, Ge, Sn). Journal of Less-Common Metals, vol. 159, no. 1, pp. L1-L4.

Van Geider, T. (1991). Magneto-optical audio. Elektronica, vol. 39, no. 5, pp. 14-15, 17, 19-21, 23-25.

Van Halm, J. and Danczak, J. (1990). Evaluation of pilot discs with national bibliographic information. CD-ROM Librarian, vol. 5, no. 4, pp. 8, 10, 12-18.

Van Hartevelt, J. (1989). Economics of the production and use of agricultural databases on CD-ROM. Quarterly Bulletin of the International Association of Agricultural Librarians and Documentalists, vol. 34, no. 2, pp. 59-65.

Vanker, A. (1989). Digital paper: mass storage revolution? Laserdisk Professional, vol. 2, no. 1, pp. 38-41.

Van Kervel, S. (1988). Laservision ROM systems for digital data and video storage. Computer Standards and Interfaces, vol. 8, no. 1, pp. 83-88.

Van Luyt, B. and Zegers, L. (1989). The compact disc interactive system. Philips Technical Review, vol. 44, no. 11, pp. 326-33.

Van Luyt, B. and Zegers, L. (1990). The Compact Disc Interactive system: active dialogue with the user. Electrotechnology, vol. 1, no. 2, pp. 112-15.

Van Rijsewijk, H. et al (1982). Manufacture of Laser Vision video discs by a Photopolymerization process. Philips Technical Review, vol. 40, no. 10, pp. 287-97.

Van Tongeren, H. and Sens, M. (1987). Write-once phase-change recording in GaSb. In Topical Meeting on Optical Storage: Summaries of Papers. Washington, DC: Optical Society of America, pp. 50-53.

Van Uijen, C. (1985). Reversible optical recording: phase-change media and magneto-optics. In Proceedings of the SPIE, vol. 529. Bellingham, WA: Society of Photo-Optical Instrumentation Engineers, pp. 2-5.

Van Uijen, C. (1987). Measured performance of modulation strategies for digital optical recording media. In Topical Meeting on Optical Data Storage: Summaries of Papers. Washington, DC: Optical Society of America, pp. 102-105.

Vane-Tempest, S. (1990). Storage considerations assessing drive performance and optical technology. In Seventh Annual OIS International 1990: Proceedings of the Seventh Annual Conference on Optical Information Systems. London: Meckler Corporation, pp. 92-101.

Ventress, A. (1989). Networks and CD-ROMs. Information Service and Use, vol. 9, no. 2, pp. 93-100.

Vogelgesang, P. and Hartmann, J. (1988). Erasable optical tape feasibility study. In Proceedings of the SPIE, vol. 899. Bellingham, WA: Society of Photo-Optical Instrumentation Engineers, pp. 172-77.

Von den Berg, H. (1990). Direct-overwrite system for magneto-optical storage systems with circularly magnetized control layer. IEEE Transactions on Magnetics, vol. 26, no. 1, pp. 190-92.

Vries, L. and Jacobs, B. (1984). Digital optical recording with tellurium alloys. Philips Technical Review, vol. 41, no. 2, pp. 313-24.

Wachter, M. et al (1991). Local networks: local networks in the library, networking with CD-ROMs at the Dauphine University and Dunkirk's information network. Documentaliste: Sciences de l'Information, vol. 28, no. 2, pp. 95-101.

Wagner, A. and Little, M. (1989). Design of a CD-ROM index product. In National Online Meeting: Proceedings. Medford, NJ: Learned Information, pp. 449-52.

Wai-Hon, L. (1988). HOEs for optical storage systems. In Proceedings of the SPIE, vol. 884. Bellingham, WA: Society of Instrumentation Engineers, pp. 90-94.

Walker, F. and Thoma, G. (1989). Techniques for creating and accessing a document image archive. In National Online Meeting Proceedings. Medford, NJ: Learned Information, pp. 453-62.

Walker, F. and Thoma, G. (1990). Access techniques for document image databases. Library Trends, vol. 38, no. 4, pp. 751-86.

Walker, M. (1988). Aerospace manufacturing applications. Optical Information Systems, vol. 8, no. 4, pp. 150-53.

Wallgren, K. (1986). Supercomputing and storage. In Proceedings of the SPIE, vol. 899. Bellingham, WA: Society of Photo-Optical Instrumentation Engineers, pp. 334-41.

Wallgren, K. and Michael, G. (1988). Storage for supercomputers: a limiting issue. In Proceedings of the SPIE, vol. 899. Bellingham, WA: Society of Photo-Optical Instrumentation Engineers, pp. 292-95.

Walter, G. (1990). Trends in systems architectures of optical disk based document management systems (OD/DMS). International Journal of Micrographics and Optical Technology, vol. 8, no. 1, pp. 1-14.

Walters, J. (1989). EBSCO's Serials Directory: a comparison of information access in three formats. Serials Librarian, vol. 17, no. 1, pp. 81-99.

Wang, Y. et al (1987). The annealing effect and the origin of perpendicular anisotropy in amorphous GdTbFe film. Journal of Magnetism and Magnetic Materials, vol. 66, no. 1, pp. 84-90.

Warner, M. (1990). Library cooperatives: developing a CD-ROM union catalog for law libraries. In Computers in Libraries '90: Proceedings of the Fifth Annual Computers in Libraries Conference. Westport, CT: Meckler Corporation, pp. 204-206.

Warren, C. (1986). SCSI bus eases device integration. In CD-ROM: the New Papyrus. Redmond, WA: Microsoft Press, pp. 85-90.

Waruszewski, H. (1987). Sperry digital map system. In Proceedings of the IEEE 1987 National Aerospace and Electronics Conference. New York: IEEE, pp. 88-96.

Watabe, A. et al (1988). High-speed recording technology for optical disk comptible between write-once and magneto-optical media. Review of the Electronic Communications Laboratory, vol. 36, no. 2, pp. 261-66.

Watanabe, Y. et al (1987). Magneto-optical disk with alumina based oxide layer. IEEE Transactions on Magnetics, vol. 23, no. 5, pp. 2623-25.

Watson, M. and Meystre, P. (1990). Direct overwrite on a preformatted bilayer magneto-optical disk. In Proceedings of the SPIE, vol. 1316. Bellingham, WA: International Society for Optical Engineering, pp. 299-304.

Watson, P. and Golden, G. (1987). Distributing an online catalog on CD-ROM: the University of Illinois experience. Online, vol. 11, no. 2, pp. 65-74.

Weide, J. (1990). Electromap World Atlas. CD-ROM Librarian, vol. 5, no. 7, pp. 27-29.

Weide, J. (1990b). LePac. CD-ROM Librarian, vol. 5, no. 4, pp. 36-39.

Weide, J. (1991). Corporate and Industry Research Reports (CIRR) on Disc. CD-ROM Librarian, vol. 6, no. 4, pp. 39-41.

Weisenfeld, M. (1987). A manual on every desk: how CD-ROM solves the online documentation dilemna. In Optical Publishing and Storage: Products that Work — Proceedings of Optical Publishing and Storage '87. Medford, NJ: Learned Information, pp. 193-97.

Weller, D. and Reim, W. (1989). Spectroscopic study of potential magneto-optic storage layers. Applied Physics, vol. A49, no. 6, pp. 599-618.

Wetzler, F. (1990). Integrating image scanning and recognition. Advanced Imaging, vol. 5, no. 5, pp. 58-61.

Weyer, S. and Borning, A. (1985). A prototype electronic encyclopedia. ACM Transactions on Office Information Systems, vol. 3, no. 1, pp. 63-88.

Whittall, J. (1989). CD-ROM in a specialist environment. In SCIL 89 International: Proceedings of the Third Annual Conference on Small Computers in Libraries. London: Meckler Corporation, pp. 119-21.

Wiggins, R. (1990). Document image processing: new light on an old problem. International Journal of Information Management, vol. 10, no. 4, pp. 297-318.

Wilkins, T. (1990). Jukeboxes: meeting the reliability expectations. Optical Information Systems, vol. 10, no. 5, pp. 252-55.

Williams, B. (1986). CD-ROM: a new medium for publishing. Information Media and Technology, vol. 19, no. 3, pp. 107-109.

Williams, B. (1991). CD-ROM at British Airways. Information Media and Technology, vol. 24, no. 1, pp. 22-24.

Williams, C. (1989). Creating multimedia CD-ROM. In Proceedings of the Seventh Conference on Interactive Instructional Delivery. Warrenton, VA: Society for Applied Learning Technology, pp. 88-92.

Williams, E. (1991). An introduction to sputtering of magnetic and magneto-optic thin films for data recording. Journal of magnetism and magnetic materials, vol. 95, no. 3, pp. 356-64.

Williams, R. and Adkisson, J. (1989). Increasing diskette capacity with FLOPTICAL technology. In Digest of Papers: IEEE Computer Society International Conference. New York: IEEE, pp. 148-50.

Williams, T. (1987). Optical storage opens new applications for system design. Computer Design, vol. 26, no. 16, pp. 37-42.

Williams, T. (1989). Digital paper emerges as low cost archival storage option. Computer Decisions, vol. 28, no. 7, pp. 41-42.

Wilson, K. (1988). Palenque: an interactive multimedia digital video interactive prototype for children. In Combined Proceedings: Third Conference on Applications of Artificial Intelligence and CD-ROM in Education and Training and Fourth Conference on Applications of Artificial Intelligence and CD-ROM in Education and Training. Warrenton, VA: Learning Technology Institute, pp. 15-18.

Wiltgen, M. et al (1990). PACS: a pilot system in routine operation. Electromedica, vol. 58, no. 4, pp. 124-29.

Wingert, M. (1991). Multifarious mechanisms for multifunction drives. Inform, vol. 5, no. 4, pp. 43-47.

Wismer, D. (1988). The politics of CD-ROM: the legislative perplex. Laserdisk Professional, vol. 1, no. 1, pp. 76-79.

Wissbrun, K. (1987). Thermal expansion and flow model for pit formation in laser marking of polymeric films optical disks. Journal of Applied Physics, vol. 62, no. 3, pp. 1123-24.

Witt, R. et al (1986). Evaluation of digital image file storage requirements and creation rates. In Application of Optical Instrumentation in Medicine XIV: Medical Imaging, Processing, and Display and Picture Archiving and Communications Systems (PACS IV) for Medical Applications. Bellingham, WA: Society of Photo-Optical Instrumentation Engineers, pp. 724-28.

Wolf, D. (1989). German bibliography today on CD-ROM. Bibliotheksdienst, vol. 23, no. 6, pp. 701-702.

Womack, A. (1990). Religion Indexes on CD-ROM: a review. CD-ROM Professional, vol. 3, no. 4, pp. 84-87.

Woods, L. (1989). CD-ROM innovation: New South Wales TAFE Library Services research librarian special projects. LASIE, vol. 19, no. 6, pp. 132-36.

Wright, C. et al (1987). Stability phenomena in amorphous rare earth-transition metal films. IEEE Transactions on Magnetics, vol. 23, no. 1, pp. 162-64.

Wright, C. and Friend, L. (1991). A mobile online/CD-ROM workstation for demos and instruction. Online, vol. 15, no. 3, pp. 74-76.

Wright, M. (1988). SCSI host adapters offer super speed to personal computer I/O subsystems. EDN, vol. 33, no. 18, pp. 59-68.

Wrobel, J. (1989). Development of organic recording materials for optical disks. Solid State Technology, vol. 32, no. 6, pp. 103-105.

Wu, E. et al (1990). PC based CD-ROM access via a VAX: an experiment. In Computers in Libraries '90: Proceedings of the Fifth Annual Computers in Libraries Conference. Westport, CT: Meckler Corporation, pp. 215-17.

Wyrowski, F. and Bryngdahl. O. (1989). Digital holograms for optical memories. In Proceedings of the SPIE, vol. 1052. Bellingham, WA: Society of Instrumentation Engineers, pp. 126-30.

Yak, A. et al (1991). High speed swing arm three-beam optical head. In Proceedings of the SPIE, vol. 1401. Bellingham, WA: International Society for Optical Engineering, pp. 74-81.

Yamada, N. et al (1986). Te-Ge-Sn-Du phase change recording film for optical disk. Proceedings of the SPIE, vol. 695. Bellingham, WA: Society of Photo-Optical Instrumentation Engineers, pp. 79-85.

Yamada, N. et al (1989). High speed overwritable phase change optical disk material. Japanese Journal of Applied Physics: Supplement, vol. 26, no. 4, pp. 61-66.

Yamada, N. et al (1989b). High speed overwritable phase-change optical disk with GeTe-Sb/sub 2/Te/sub 3 thin films. National Technical Report, vol. 35, no. 2, pp. 110-17.

Yamada, N. et al (1991). Rapid-phase transitions of GeTe-Sb/sub 2/Te/sub 3/ pseudobinary amorphous thin films for an optical disk memory. Journal of Applied Physics, vol. 69, no. 5, pp. 2849-56.

Yamamoto, M. and Mons, H. (1988). CD-write once: the standard. Optical Information Systems, vol. 8, no. 5, pp. 246-47.

Yamaoka, H. (1989). Magneto-optical rewritable disk system. Sharp Technical Journal, no. 41, pp. 7-14.

Yamashita, T. et al (1988). An optical disk-based data acquisition system for the MX series minicomputers. Mitsubishi Denki Giho, vol. 62, no. 7, pp. 596-99.

Yamazaki, H. and Yagi, S. (1987). Study on high-density recording of an ablative-type optical disk. Journal of Applied Physics, vol. 62, no. 5, pp. 1605-1609.

Yamazaki, H. et al (1987). Reversible phase change Sb-Te films for optical disks. In Proceedings of the SPIE, vol. 818. Bellingham, WA: Society of Photo-Optical Instrumentation Engineers, pp. 217-20.

Yamazaki, S. (1990). Use of CD-ROM MEDLINE and end user education in the Jikei University School of Medicine. In Preprints: Second International Conference on the Effective Use of CD-ROM Databases. Tokyo: USACO, pp. 22-28.

Yan, B. et al (1990). The effect of terbium and gadolinium composition on the corrosion resistance of sputtered GdTbFeCo thin films. Journal of Applied Physics, vol. 67, no. 9, pp. 5310-12.

Yan, J. and Lin, S. (1990). CD-ROM and its applications in China. Reference Services Review, vol. 18, no. 2, pp. 93-96.

Yardy, R. et al (1990). Read stability in magneto-optical storage. In Proceedings of the SPIE, vol. 1316. Bellingham, WA: International Society for Optical Engineering, pp. 106-16.

Yariv, A. et al (1986). Demonstration of an all-optical associative holographic memory. Applied Physics Letters, vol. 48, no. 6, pp. 1114-17.

Yasuda, K. et al (1989). Magneto-optical properties of highly Al-substituted (y,Bi)(Fe,Al) sputtered films in short wavelength region. IEEE Transactions on Magnetics, vol. 25, no. 5, pp. 4012-14.

Yasui, S. et al (1986). Characteristics of the mass-produced optical disks. In Proceedings of the SPIE, vol. 299. Bellingham, WA: Society of Photo-Optical Instrumentation Engineers, pp. 33-37.

Yasuoka, H. et al (1987). Novel 1-beam-overwriting method for phase-change erasable disk. Japanese Journal of Applied Physics: Supplement, vol. 26, sup. 26-4, pp. 171-76.

Yazawa, T. (1991). Developing and choosing multifunctional optical storage: problems and solutions. Optical Information Systems, vol. 11, no. 1, pp. 9-13.

Yochum, K. (1988). Optical disk jukeboxes: how they work, what they can do. IMC Journal, vol. 24, no. 5, pp. 50-51.

Yoda, S. (1989). A write-once optical card reader/writer using two optical sources. Japanese Journal of Applied Physics Supplement, vol. 38, suppl. 28-3, pp. 91-94.

Yokomizo, K. (1987). CD-ROM map information system. Joho Kanri, vol. 30, no. 8, pp. 700-713.

Yokozeki, T. et al (1989). A virtual optical disk method to realize rewritability and revision control on a write-once optical disk. Transactions of the Institute of Electronic Information and Communications Engineering, vol. J72D-I, no. 6, pp. 414-22.

Yonezawa, S. (1979). High density optical disc: today and future. Journal of the Institute of Electronic and Communications Engineering of Japan, vol. 62, no. 1, pp. 81-82.

York, C. (1990). Compact Cambridge Medline. CD-ROM Librarian, vol. 5, no. 10, pp. 37-40.

Yoshihara, K. et al (1990). Digital video recording system using multi-beam magneto-optical disk drive. In Proceedings of the SPIE, vol. 1316. Bellingham: International Society for Optical Engineering, pp. 58-64.

Yoshikawa, T. et al (1990). Characteristics of MO-type rewritable video disk. In Proceedings of the SPIE, vol. 1316. Bellingham: International Society for Optical Engineering, pp. 237-44.

Yoshimura, M. et al (1989). Ultra-high density optical memory by photochemical hole burning (PHB) and multi-layered PHB system. In Proceedings of the SPIE, vol. 1078. Bellingham, WA: Society of Photo-Optical Instrumentation Engineers, pp. 326-30.

Yoshino, K. et al (1988). Spectral of polymer film containing poly 3-alkyl-thiophene with temperature and its application as optical recording media. Japanese Journal of Applied Physics, vol. 27, no. 3, pp. 454-56.

Yoshino, K. et al (1990). Optical recording utilizing conducting polymers, poly(p-phenylene vinylene) and its derivatives. Japanese Journal of Applied Physics, part 2, vol. 29, no. 8, pp. L1514-16.

Young, R. et al (1986). Effects of transition-metal elements on tellurium alloys for reversible optical data storage. Journal of Applied Physics, vol. 60, no. 12, pp. 4319-22.

Young, R. et al (1986a). Tellurium alloys for reversible optical data storage. In Materials Issues in Amorphous Semiconductor Technology Symposium. Pittsburgh: Materials Research Society, pp. 697-703.

Yu, C. et al (1989). Efficient placement of audio data on optical disks for real-time applications. Communications of the Association for Computing Machinery, vol. 32, no. 7, pp. 862-71.

Yuk, T. and Palais, J. (1991). Analysis of wavelength division multiplexing technique for optical data storage. In Proceedings of the SPIE, vol. 1401. Bellingham, WA: International Society for Optical Engineering, pp. 130-37.

Zak, J. et al (1990). Universal approach to magneto-optics. Journal of Magnetism and Magnetic Materials, vol. 89, nos. 1-2, pp. 107-23.

Zech, R. (1988). Systems, applications, and implications of optical storage. In Digest of Papers: COMPCON Spring 88. Washington, DC: IEEE Computer Society Press, pp. 135-40.

Zelinger, S. (1987). The optical disk jukebox: issues, choices, and options. Inform, vol. 1, no. 12, pp. 34-38.

Zeper, W. et al (1990). Co/Pt and Co/Pd multilayers as a new class of magneto-optical recording materials. In Proceedings of the SPIE, vol. 1274. Bellingham, WA: International Society for Optical Engineering, pp. 282-92.

Zeper, W. et al (1991). Co/Pt and Co/Pd multilayers as new magneto- optical recording media. Journal of Applied Physics, vol. 69, no. 8, pt. 2A, p. 4966.

Zimmerman, P. (1988). DVI technology and video production considerations. In Proceedings of the NCGA 88: Ninth Annual Conference and Exposition. Fairfax, VA: National Computer Graphics Association, vol. 3, pp. 644-49.

Zink, S. (1991). Toward more critical reviewing and analysis of CD-ROM user software interfaces. CD-ROM Professional, vol. 4, no. 1, pp. 16-22.

Zoellick, B. (1988). CD-ROM software architecture to promote interchangeability. Journal of the American Society for Information Science, vol. 39, no. 1, pp. 47-53.

Zwick, R. (1989). Implementing WORM storage in the MS-DOS environment. In Software for Optical Storage. Westport, CT: Meckler Corporation, pp. 55-58.

Index

AAM-8000 71
ABC-CLIO 96
Aberdeen City Libraries 56
ABI/Inform 95
ablative recording 4, 5-6, 8, 18
Abridged Index Medicus 93
Abt Books 111-112
Academic American Encyclopedia 93
Accell Computer Corporation 47
ADA 103
Adaptive Differential Pulse Code Modulation 114, 115
Adaptive Information Systems 69
ADONIS Project 89
ADPCM: See Adaptive Differential Pulse Code Modulation.
Advanced Data Management Incorporated 64
Advanced Graphics Applications 47, 69, 88
Advanced Mobile Traffic Information and Communication System 102
Advanced Projects International 64
Advanced Storage Concepts 47
Advanced Systems Development Incorporated 64
Advanced Technology Incorporated 64
AGANET 88
AGRICOLA 94, 109
AGRIS 94
AGRI/STATS 95
AIIM: See Association for Information and Image Management.
AIM: See American Interactive Media.
AIMS: See HP Advanced Image Management System
air sandwich 5
Airwave Adventure 113
Albany Medical College 51
Alcatel Thomson Gigadisc 8, 17
Alde Publishing 103
Alliance Plus 99, 100
Allied Health Literature Database 94
Alpharel Incorporated 64
Alphatronix 47
aluminum 12
Amazing Moby CD-ROM 93
Ambertek Systems 47

American Business Disc 95
American Digital Systems 47
American Interactive Media 117
American Management Systems 64
American Memory Project 113
American National Standards Institute 21-22, 24, 35, 44, 105-106
America: History and Life 96
Amiga 80, 112-113
Amitech Corporation 64
AMTICS: See Advanced Mobile Traffic Information and Communication System.
analog optical video disc systems 72
ANSI: See American National Standards Institute.
antimony 7, 12, 13
Apple Computer 103, 105
Apple II 103
Applied Computer Technology 64
Applied Optical Media 118
Applied Programming Technologies 47
Applied Science and Technology Index 94
Apunix Computer Services 47
Aquidneck Systems International 46, 53
Aries Systems Corporation 107
Arix Computer Corporation 47
Artecon 47
Artisoft 88
Arthur Anderson and Company 64, 91
Arthur Young and Company 64, 91
Artroom 104
Asaca 71
Asahi Chemical Industries 125
ASFA database 94
Association for Information and Image Management 27
ATG Gigadisc 8, 17, 22, 23, 24, 41
AT&T 52, 114
Audio Visual Information Communication system 102
autochangers 36-42, 48, 49, 50, 52, 53, 64, 68, 70, 88-89, 112
Automated Patent System 54, 95
Automated Solutions Incorporated 47
Auto-Graphics 91
AVIC: See Audio Visual Information Communication

system.
Background Music system 115
Baker and Taylor 100
Bank Street College 118
barcode 62
barium-ferrite 10, 34
Battelle Memorial Institute 125
Baylor College of Medicine 126
Bay MicroSystems 47
BCS-Mac Software Exchange Library 103
BDM International 64
Bell and Howell 9, 59, 69
Bering Industries 47
Bernoulli Box 34
Bertelsmann Computer Beratungsdienst 107
BETACORP 103
Bible 93
BiblioDisc 97
Bibliofile 99, 100, 107
Bibliographie Nationale Francaise 98
Bibliotheque Nationale 97
Biological and Agricultural Index 94
Biological Abstracts 94
BIP Plus: See Books in Print Plus.
bismuth 7
bi-metallic alloy recording: See dual alloy recording.
Blackwell North America 100
Blue Cross and Blue Shield of Maryland 124
BNB: See British National Biography
Books in Print Plus 94, 100
Books in Print with Book Reviews Plus 100
Books Out of Print Plus 100
BookBank 98, 100
Bookshelf 92
Bosch 102
Boston Computer Society 103
Boston Globe 98
Bowker 100
British Books in Print 98, 100
British Broadcasting Company 120
British Library 89, 97
British National Biography 98
British Telecommunications PLC 98, 126
Brodart 99, 100
BRS 107
Buchhandler Vereinigung 101
Bull 66, 68
Bureau Marcel van Dijk 98
Business Periodicals Ondisc 89, 95
Buttonware 103
CAB Abstracts 94
cache memory 26, 83, 84
CACI Image Support Services 64

Calera Recognition Systems 62
California Practice Library 96
California State University at Fullerton 88
Canada Centre for Remote Sensing 128
Canadian Business and Current Affairs Index 97
Canadian Center for Occupational Health and Safety 97
Canadian Library Association 97
Canadian Post Corporation 90
Canadian Secretary of State 97
Canadian Telebook Agency 97
CANCERLIT 94
Canon 11, 27, 30, 59, 69, 124, 125
CANSIM 97
Capacitance Electronic Disk 118
Capital Software Incorporated 64
CAR: See Computer-assisted microfilm retrieval
CARIN: See Car Information and Navigation system.
Car Information and Navigation system 102-103
CASSIS CD-ROM 95
Cataloging in Publication 100
CAT CD450 99, 100
CAV: See constant angular velocity.
CBIS 88
CCD: See charge coupled device
C CD-ROM 103
CCINFO Chemical Information disc 97
CCINFO Occupational Health and Safety Information disc 97
CCITT: See Consultative Committee on International Telephony and Telegraphy
CD Companion series 113
CDMARC Bibliographic 99, 100
CD Media and Reference Technology 96
CD NET 88
CDP: See Compound Document Processor
CD Plus 88, 93
CDTV: See Commodore Dynamic Total Vision system.
CD4X format 74
CD/BANKING 95
CD/CORPORATE 95
CD/CORPTECH 95
CD/PRIVATE+ 95
CD-Answer 107
CD-CATSS 97, 99, 100
CD-Connection 88
CD-DA 73, 74, 76, 78, 80, 82, 83, 84, 113, 115, 116, 117
CD-FOREX 99
CD-Formatter 77
CD-I 114-117, 118, 119
CD-Image-Build 77
CD-Kat 92
CD-MAP 101

CD-R 78-80
CD-ROM 3, 48, 51, 53, 54, 68
    applications 89-104
    autochangers 88-89
    disc production 76-80
    drives 80-89
    equipment configurations 80-82
    library support products 99-101
    maps 101-103
    multimedia 112-114
    networks 86-88
    private implementations 89-92
    production 76-84
    reference products 92-99
    software distribution 103-104
    standards and software 104-109
    storage characteristics 74-76
    technology 73-85
    user experiences 109-111
    vs. online systems 110-111
CD-ROM Extended Architecture 114
CD-ROM Public Domain Library 103
CD-ROM XA: See CD-ROM Extended Architecture.
CD-RTOS: See Compact Disc-Real Time Operating System.
CD-Single 76
CD-W: See CD-WO.
CD-WO 78, 79
CD-WORM: See CD-WO.
CD-3 format 76
CD*STAR system 69
CED: See Capacitance Electronic Disk.
Census Bureau 95
Centel Federal Systems 64
Central Connecticut State University 88
Century Disc 78
Century Media 7
Chadwyk-Healey 95, 96, 98, 101
charge-coupled device 57
Cherokee Data Systems 25
Chicago Tribune 98
Chinon America 80
CHOIX database 97
chromium dioxide 11
Chrysler 91
CINAHL-CD 94
CIP: See Cataloging in Publication.
Citibase 95
Claris 107
clip art 104
Club Mac 103
CLV: See constant linear velocity.
CMC ReSearch 94, 96, 113

cobalt 11, 12
COBRA 107
COINS: See Computer Output Information System
COLD: See Computer-Output Laser Disk.
Colorado Revised Statutes 96
COM: See Computer-Output Microfilm.
CommDisc Telefax 98
Commodore 80
Commodore Dynamic Total Vision system 112-113
Communications Infodisk 104
Compact Cambridge 94
Compact Deutschland 98
Compact disc 73
Compact Disclosure Europe 98
Compact Disc-Digital Audio: See CD-DA.
Compact Disc-Interactive: See CD-I.
Compact Disc-Read Only Memory: See CD-ROM.
Compact Disc-Real Time Operating System 116
Compact Disc-Recordable: See CD-R.
Compact Disc-Write Once: See CD-WORM.
Compact International Agricultural Research Library 99
Compact Library 94
Compact Cambridge 93
Compact Disclosure 95
COMPENDEX PLUS 94
Compound Document Architecture 66
Compound Document Processor 62
Compressed Aeronautical Chart 91
Compton's MultiMedia Encyclopedia 93, 113
CompuAdd 114
Compustat PC-Plus 95
Computer Clinical Information System 94
Computer Horizons Corporation 64
Computer Output Information System 53
Computer Sciences Corporation 64
computer-assisted microfilm retrieval 54, 64, 68, 69, 70
Computer-Output Laser Disk 52-53
Computer-Output Microfilm 52-53, 89, 91
Computron Technologies Corporation 53
Comstock Desktop Photography 104
COM-Squared Alternative 54
COM Squared Systems Incorporated 53, 69
Concise Encyclopedia of Science and Technology 94
Congressional Information Service 95
Congressional Masterfile 96
Congressional Record 96
Consan Incorporated 47
constant angular velocity 23, 24
constant linear velocity 23, 24
Consultative Committee on International Telephony and Telegraphy 58, 60, 70
Consultative Group on International Research 99

CONSU/STATS 95
continuous composite servo format 25, 30, 34
Conversion Dynamics Incorporated 69
Coopers and Lybrand 64
copper-technetium alloy 9
CorelDraw 104
Corel Systems 47, 104
Corporate Industry Research Reports 94
Corporate Snapshots 95
Corptech database 94
CREO 127-128
Cross-Cultural CD 96
Crowninshield Software 77, 107
CSK Corporation 126
CSSI 64
Cumulative Index to Nursing 94
Curie temperature 10
Cygnet Systems 41, 42
C. Itoh Electronics 46
Dainihon Computer Systems 101
Dai Nippon Printing 124, 125
Darkroom 104
Data DiscMan 76
Data General 46, 66
DataImage Incorporated 64
Data Management Design Incorporated 64
Datapro Software Finder 104
DataWare Technologies 107
Datawest 113
DataWorld Infodisk 104
Data/Ware Development 46, 53
Dauphine University 88
DAVID database 97
David Sarnoff Research Center 117
dBASE product line 109
DBF: See discrete block format.
DDP: See Disk Description Protocol.
DEC: See Digital Equipment Corporation
DECimage Express 66
DECUS 103
Defense Mapping Agency 101
Defense Technical Information Center 90
DELA: See Drexler European Licensees Association.
Delaware Code Annotated 96
Del Mar Avionics 52
Deltaic Systems 47
Dennoh Shokai 113
Denon 80
desktop publishing 104, 111
Deutsche Bibliographie Aktuell 98
Deutsche Bibliothek 97
Dialog 93, 107, 111
Dictionary of Scientific and Technical Terms 94

Dictionnaires Le Robert 98
Dictionnaire Vidal 98
Digipress 78
digital audio tape 48, 54, 43
Digital Diagnostics 93
Digital Equipment Corporation 46, 66, 68, 70, 80, 82, 91, 103, 105
Digital Paper 127
Digital Recording Corporation 125
Digital Video Interactive: See DVI.
direct seal disks 7
Directory of American Research and Technology 94
DiscLit: American Authors 96
Disc of Discs 92
discrete block format 34
DISCUS 1000 Systems 69
Disk Description Protocol 114
display terminals 69
DOCdata N.V. 128
DocuFile 47
Documentacion De Medios CD ROM 98
document digitization 56-59
Document Image Systems Corporation 64
document imaging 54-70
document scanners 3, 4, 56-59, 64, 66, 69
Document Technologies Incorporated 69
DocuPoint 69
Dolphin Systems Technology 47
Domesday Book 120
Dover Clip-Art 104
DoveSystem 91
Drexler European Licensees Association 124
Drexler Technology Corporation 123-127
Drexon 123, 127
DSI-Data Service and Information 95
dual alloy recording 4, 7, 18
Duetsche Bibelgesellschaft 93
Du Pont Safety Services 118
DVI 117-118
dye-based recording 4, 5, 6-7, 14, 18, 19, 20
DynaTek Automation Systems 47
dysprosium 11
Eastern Computers Incorporated 69
Eastman Kodak 6, 8, 17, 18, 18-22, 24, 41, 42, 66, 68, 69, 80, 112
EBSCO 98, 101
ECMA: See European Computer Manufacturers Association.
ECODISC 120
ECON/STATS 95
Editions Quebec/Amerique 113
EDS Corporation 64
Educorp Computer Services 103

eight-millimeter data cartridges 43, 48, 54, 77, 87
EIM: See European Interactive Media.
Electromap World Atlas 101
Electronic Map Cabinet 101
Electronic Text Corporation 107
Electron Trapping Optical Memory 15
Ellis Enterprises 93
EMBASE 94
EMC Corporation 46
Emulex 46
Encyclopedia Brittanica 113
English Poetry Full-Text Database 96
ENKAIOH disc 113
Epoch Systems 50
erasable optical disks: See rewritable optical disks.
ERIC 96, 106, 109, 111
Ernst and Young 64
ESPACE CD-ROM 98
Etak Corporation 102
Ethernet 68
ETOM: See Electron Trapping Optical Memory.
Euro-CD 92
European Commission 97
European Computer Manufacturers Association 104
European Interactive Media 117
European Patent Office 95, 98
Excel 103
Excerpta Medica 94
Executive Technologies 69, 107
Exxon 91
Eye-COM 69
FACOM 81
facsimile 58, 60, 70, 127
Facts On File 103, 113
Faraday effect 11
FAST TRACK Digital Directory 95
Faulkner Technical Reports 104
FDA-on CD-ROM 96
FD Incorporated 96
Federal Register 96
ferrite-cobalt 12
ferrite-silicon 12
ferrite-terbium 12
ferrite-terbium-gadolinium 12
ferrite-terbium-indium 12
FileMark Corporation 53
file migration 49
FileNet 41
Filequest 69
file servers 47, 48, 50, 88
Filetek 49-50
FindIt 107
FindIt Webster CD-ROM 93

FINN-COIN 98
First Canadian Shareware Disc 103
floppy disks 3, 10, 26, 34, 48, 53, 76, 80, 83, 103, 116, 127
floptical disks 34
FM TOWNS 113
Follett Software 99, 100
FOOD/STATS 95
Ford Motor Company 91
FORMTEK 64
Foundation for Advanced Biblical Studies 93
Frankfort Consortium 79
FSTA 94
Fuji 79
Fujitsu 5, 17, 18, 25, 28, 59, 79, 81, 113, 114
Fuji Xerox 8
Fulcrum Technologies 107
Full Spectrum Clip-Art 104
FulText 107
FWB Incorporated 47
gadolinium 11, 12, 13
gallium antimonide 13
gamma ferric oxide 11
Garois Corporation 126
Gaylord Information Systems 99
General Electric 51, 117
General Periodicals Index 93
General Research Corporation 92, 99, 100
General Science Index 94
Genesis game system 114
Genesis Imaging Technologies 62, 64
GEOdisc Georgia Atlas 101
GEOdisc U.S. Atlas 101
GEOVISION 101
germanium 13, 79
German Postcode Address File 98
Gigapage System 53
G.K. Hall 96
Goal Systems International 53
gold 12, 78
Goldstar 80
gold-chromium films 8
gold-germanium alloy 13
Grand Robert de la Langue Francaise 98
Greatest Books Ever Written 96
Greek Telephone Book on CD-ROM 98
Green Book 115
Grolier 93, 117
Group L 107
Grumman InfoConversion 64
GTX Corporation 64
Guardian on CD-ROM 98
Guinness Disc of World Records 93, 113

Harcourt Brace Jovanovich 117
Harmonie Park Press 96
HDTV: See High Definition Television
Helecon on CD-ROM 98
helical-scan tapes 77
Helsinki School of Economics and Business 98
Hewlett-Packard 11, 27, 28, 31, 46, 52, 59, 66, 68, 80, 87, 88, 91, 113
HFCA-ON CD-ROM 96
hierarchical storage configurations 48-50
High Definition Television 72, 119
Highlighted Data Incorporated 101, 113
High Sierra Group 105-106
Historical Abstracts 96
Hitachi 5, 11, 17, 18, 24, 25, 26, 27, 28, 41, 42, 59, 69, 71, 80, 101, 105, 114, 118
Hi-Lite Card 125
Honda 91
Honeywell 127
Hopkins Technology 95
Hoppenstedt CD-ROM 98
HP Advanced Image Management System 68
HP OfficeShare 88
HPTS: See ImagePlus High-Performance Transaction System
HSG: See High Sierra Group.
Hubble Space Telescope 50
Hutchinson Electronic Encyclopedia 93
HyperCard 107
H.W. Wilson 96, 107
IBIS Service AG 98
IBM 11, 16, 18, 34, 46, 53, 66, 69, 70, 77, 80, 82, 86, 91, 92, 100, 101, 103, 104, 105, 107, 111, 112, 114, 117, 121
ICI ImageData 127
ICP Software Information Directory 104
ICR: See Intelligent Character Recognition.
IMA: See Interactive Multimedia Association.
Image Business Systems Corporation 64
Image Club Graphics 104
Image Conversion Technologies 64
Image Data Corporation 64, 66
Image Data Systems 66
Image Gallery 104
Image Management Technologies 47
ImagePlus System 66
ImagePlus High-Performance Transaction System 66
IMNET Corporation 66, 69
IMPACT 91
Imperial Chemical Industries 127
Improvision 59
IMTECH Optical Systems Incorporated 53
INCOM 89

Independent on CD-ROM 98
index data entry 61-63
Index Medicus 93
Index to Legal Periodicals 96
Indiana University Medical Center 51
Indiana University School of Medicine 109
indium 13, 79
indium antimonide 13
indium-selenium-antimony
indium-selenium-cobalt 13
indium-selenium-lead 13
indium-selenium-thallium 13
Infinite Storage Architecture 50
Infomark Laser PC System 95, 120
Information Access Company 93, 120
Information Finder 93
Information Industry Association 105
Information Storage Incorporated 17, 25
Information Technology Group Incorporated 72
InfoTrac 93, 120
Ingram-Books in Print Plus 100
Innotech Incorporated 93
Insite Peripherals 34
INSPEC database 94
Institute for Scientific Information 96
Institute of Electrical and Electronics Engineers 94
integrated circuit cards 125
integrated services digital network 48
Intel 69, 117, 118
Intelligent Character Recognition 62
Interactive Multimedia Association 114
International Standardization Organization 20, 21, 22, 29, 34, 35, 54, 104, 106, 120
Iomega 34
IRISTER: See Iris Thermal Eclipse Reading.
Iris Thermal Eclipse Reading 35
iron-garnet 12
ISDN: See integrated services digital network.
Ishiyaku Shuppan 99
ISO: See International Standardization Organization.
Italian Yellow Pages for the U.S.A. 98
Iwanami Shotem 99
I-Mode Retrieval Systems 107
I-Search 107
Japan Airlines 91
Japanese Ministry of Health and Welfare 126
Japanese Patent Office 56
Japan External Trade Organization 99
Japan Interactive Media 117
JAPAN/MARC 92
Jasmine 47
JETRO ACE 99
JIM: See Japan Interactive Media.

INDEX 213

Joint Technical Commission on Permanence of Optical and Magnetic Systems 44
Josten's Learning Corporation 113
Journal of the American Medical Association 94
jukeboxes: See autochangers.
Juris Datenbanken 99
J. Whitaker and Sons 98, 100
J-DISC 99
Kapton 128
KAWare 2 Retrieval System 107
KDD 28, 71
Kenwood U.S.A. 79
Kerr effect 11
KIMS 3000 System
Kirk-Othmer Encyclopedia of Chemical Technology 94
Kluwer Datalex 99
Knowledge Access International 107
Knowledge Finder 107
Knowledge Retrieval System 107
KnowledgeSet Corporation 107
Kokusai Denshin Denwa: See KDD.
KOM Incorporated 46
Kompass Europe 98
KRS: See Knowledge Retrieval System.
Kubic Enterprises 89
Kurashiki Chuo Hospital 126
Kwickee In-House Graphic System 104
Kyocera 124
Kyoto University Hospital 52
K.G. Saur 98
LABOR/STATS 95
LaCie Limited 47
LANtastic 88
Laser Access Corporation 53
Laser Art CD-ROM 104
LaserCard Systems Corporation 125
LaserCards 123-127
LaserCAT 92, 99, 111
Laser Data 68, 69, 105, 107, 120
LaserDisclosure 112
LASERDOS 105
LaserDrive Limited 25
LASERFILE 105
Laserkey 107
Laser Magnetic Storage International 5, 11, 17, 18, 22-23, 25, 27, 36, 41, 42, 80, 81
Laser Optical Technology 103
laser printers 70
LaserQuest 99, 100
Laser Recording Systems 66
LaserTape Systems Incorporated 128
Laservision 118
Laser-Guide 92

Laser-Optic 2500 system 69
Lawbase CD-ROM
LC MARC data base 100
LC Name Authority data base 100
LC Subject Headings 100
LD-ROM 120-121
lead-zirconium-titanate films 9
Legal Databank 99
Legal Resources Index 96
LegalTrac 96
LePac 107
LeRobert Electronique 98
LetterPress CD-ROM 104
Library and Information Science Abstracts 98
Library Association (United Kingdom) 98
Library Corporation 99, 100
Library of Congress 99, 100, 113, 119
Library of the Future Series 96
LILACS 99
liquid crystalline polysiloxanes 9
liquid crystal polymers 16
LISA: See Library and Information Science Abstracts
Literal Corporation 5, 11, 17, 18, 25, 41
Little, Brown and Company 94
Litton Industries 66
Liverpool Public Library 88
LMSI: See Laser Magnetic Storage International.
long-playing phonograph records 74
Los Alamos National Laboratory 90
Lotus Development 95, 105, 107, 109, 117
LQ-4000 71
LV-ROM 120
Macademic Disc 103
MacApp disc 103
Mac Guide USA 103
machine-readable media 76
Macintosh 66, 69, 77, 80, 82, 88, 93, 100, 101, 103, 104, 107, 111, 112, 113, 121
Macintosh Programmer's Workshop 103
maganese 12
Magazine Article Summaries 93
Magazine Index 120
Magnavox 81
magneto-optical disks 10-12, 13, 14, 15, 28-36, 54, 70, 71, 123
magnetic storage devices and media 3, 9, 22, 42-44, 46-47, 48, 49, 50, 53, 59, 64, 69, 74, 76, 77, 80, 82, 83, 87, 89, 103, 128
Main Economics Indicators 95
Mammals: a Multimedia Encyclopedia 113
MARC 99
Marcive/PAC 92
Mark Encyclopedia of Polymer Science and Engineer-

ing 94
MARS System 69
Marshall Space Flight Center 50
Martin Marietta Corporation 72
Martindale-Hubble 96
Massachusetts General Hospital 51
Massachusetts Medical Society 94
MASS Microsystems 47
Mass Optical Storage Technologies 34
Matthew Bender and Company 96, 107
Matsushita 8, 11, 13, 17, 18, 69, 71, 81, 126
Maxell 18
Maximum Storage 17
Maxoptix 11, 27, 30, 31
Maxtor 6, 17, 18, 24, 34
MAXX 94
Mazda Car Communication System 102
MCAV: See modified constant angular velocity.
McGraw-Hill CD-ROM Science and Technical Reference Set 94
MediaBase 107
Medlin Accounting 103
MEDLINE 51, 93, 99, 106
MegaROM 103
Melbourne University 101
Merck Manual 94
Meridian Data 77, 80, 88, 105
Merriam Webster's Ninth New Collegiate Dictionary 93
Metafile Information Systems 66
Michie Company 96
MicroBASIS 107
microcomputer-based turnkey systems 53, 70
microcomputer implementations 77
MicroData Infodisk 104
Micro Design International 47
Micro Dynamics Limited 62, 69
microforms 59, 127
MicroMall Incorporated 117
Micromodex 94
Micronet S.A. 98
MicroNet Technology 47
MicroPatent 95
Microsoft CD-ROM Extensions 86, 106
Microsoft Corporation 69, 80, 86, 93, 103, 105, 114, 117
Microsoft Mail 103
Microsoft Office 103
Microsoft Windows 69, 80, 108, 114
Microsoft Word 103
Microtech International 47
MicroVAX workstations 91
Microware 116, 117

Microx 9
MIDI 112, 116
Mikage Medical Office 126
Mini Disc 71
Minolta 69
Mirror Technologies 47
Misawa Home Research Laboratory 113
Mitsubishi 5, 11, 16, 25, 41, 102
Mitsubishi Kasei 31
Mitsui Petrochemical Industries 31
Mitsumi 80
MH: See Modified Huffman
MMR: See Modified Modified Read
MNMOS materials 16
modified constant angular velocity 24
Modified Huffman 60
Modified Modified Read 60
Monthly Export Data 95
Monthly Import Data 95
Moody's Investors Service 95
MOST: See Mass Optical Storage Technologies.
Motion Picture Experts Group 116
Motorola 103
MPC: See Multimedia Personal Computer.
MPEG: See Motion Picture Experts Group.
MS-DOS 53, 66, 68, 69, 80, 86, 105, 125
multifunctional drives 27-28
Multi-Media Audubon's Mammals 113
Multi-Media Birds of America 113
MultiPlatter system 88
Multi-Ad Services 104
Multimedia Personal Computer 114
multimedia technologies 111-121
MUMPS
Mundocart/CD 101
Music Index on CD-ROM 96
MVS 53
MVS/ESA 66
Nakamichi 11, 34
NAS: See Network Aplication Support
National Aeronautics and Space Administration 50
National Agricultural Library 113, 120
National Air and Space Museum 119
National Central Library 99
National Computer Conference 32
National Decision Systems 95, 120
National Diet Library 99
National Gallery of Art 119
National Geographic Society 113
National Information Services Corporation 96
National Information Standards Organization 105
National Institute of Standards and Technology 106
National Library of Canada 97

National Portrait Gallery 111-112
National Trade Data Bank 95
Navigation Systems Research Society 102
NCR 66, 68, 87
Nebraska Statutes 96
NEC 12, 26, 69, 71, 81, 102, 104, 114
neodymium 11
Network Application Support 66
New England Journal of Medicine 94
New Grolier Electronic Encyclopedia 113
New Mexico Law on Disc 96
NEWS 81
New York Amateur Computer Club 103
New York Times, The 93, 98
NeXT systems 27, 80, 89
Next Technology 88
Nimbus Information Systems 77
Nimbus Records 74
Nippon Columbia 101
Nippon Conlux 124, 126
Nipponinco 124
Nippon Medical School 109
Nippon Telegraph and Telephone 26, 99, 101, 125
NISO: See National Information Standards Organization.
Nissan 91, 102
Nixdorf 66
Non-Print Pilot Project 119
Norikura Solar Observatory 50
NTSC 71
NTT: See Nippon Telegraph and Telephone.
Numera 126
NYNEX Information Resources Company 95
N/Hance Systems 47
OCEAN Microsystems 47
OCLC 92, 96, 99, 100, 107, 111
OCR: See optical character recognition
OFS: See Optical Fiche Systems
OGDEN/ERC Government Systems 66
Olisis 126
Olivetti 114, 126
Olympus Optical 124, 126
Omron Corporation 124
Omron Tateisi 126
OnDisc 111
Online Computer Systems 47, 88, 101, 107
Onsite Instruments Incorporated 50-51
OPERATE 81
Opsedale Civile 52
Optex 15
Optima Technology 47
Optical Card Business Company Limited 124, 125
optical cards 123-127

optical character recognition 62, 68
Optical Data Incorporated 14
Optical Fiche Systems 53
optical file servers 48, 69
Optical Media International 77
optical memory cards: See optical cards.
Optical Memory Disc Recorder 71
Optical Read Only Memory: See OROM.
Optical Recording Corporation 125
Optical Storage Corporation 31
Optical Storage International 17
Optical Storage Solutions 66
optical tape 127-128
Optimem 8, 17, 22
OPTI-NET 88
Optotech 17
Orange Book 79
Orange Free State 88
Oregon State University 88
OROM 35, 54
Oshare Cooking disc 113
Oster and Associates 96
OS/2 66, 68, 107
OS-9 116
OTC Plus 95
Oxford English Dictionary 93
Oxford Textbook of Medicine 94
Pacific Regional Aquaculture Information Service 88
PACS: See Picture Archiving and Communication Systems.
PAIS database 96
palladium 12
Pan American Health Organization 99
Panasonic 8, 17, 24, 27, 29, 31, 41, 59, 71, 72, 80
PATOS CD-ROM 98
PCX 104
PC: See polycarbonate.
PC-Blue 103
PC-SIG 103
PDO: See Philips and Du Pont Optical.
Pediatric Infectous Disease Journal 94
Pentax 59
Perceptics 46
Pergamon Compact Solutions 93
Periodical Abstracts Ondisc 93
Peripheral Land Incorporated 47
Petroconsultants CES Limited 101
phase-change recording
    write-once variety 4, 5, 7-8, 20
    rewritable variety 8, 13-14, 15, 27, 31
Philips 69, 73, 78, 79, 80, 102, 104, 105, 112, 114, 115, 116, 118, 120
Philips and Du Pont Optical 14, 18, 31

Philips Medical Systems 52
Philips Subsystems and Peripherals 80
Phone Base 98
PhoneDisc Business Reference Disc 95
PhoneDisc USA Corporation 95
phonograph records 76
Photo CD 112
Photo Gallery 104
photon-gated compounds 15-16
Picture Archiving and Communication Systems 51-52
Pinnacle Micro 47
Pioneer 6, 11, 17, 18, 25, 28, 71, 89, 118, 120
Pirelli Tire Catalog 91
PixelPaint Art 104
PixelPaint Professional 104
PKware 103
Plasmon Data Systems 8, 18
platinum 11, 12, 78
Plexus Computers 62
Plexus Software 66
PlusNet 88
Plus System 107
PMMA: See polymethyl methacrylate.
polycarbonate 4, 12, 79
polydiacetylene crystals 9
PolyGram 117
polymethyl methacrylate 4, 118
Pork Industry Handbook 120
POSIX 106
Postcode Address File 90
Postreklame CmbH 98
Powerpoint 103
PPDM: See Product and Process Document Management
Precision One Disc 99
Predicasts 95
premastering services 76
Prime Computer 46, 68
PRIMOS 68
ProArt disc 104
Procom Technology 47
Product and Process Document Management 68
Programmer's Library 103
Psychological Abstracts 96
PsycLit 96
Psyndex 96
PS/2 Ultimedia 114
Public Domain Shareware Hypercard Stack 103
Public Domain Software on File 103
Public Employees Retirement Association of Colorado 56
Public Library 93
Public Safety Management System 68

Publique Arte 104
Publishers Data Service Corporation 107
QL Tech 103
Qualogy 46
Quanta Press 96, 103, 104
Quantel Limited 51
Quantum Access 103, 107
Quantum Leap 107
Questar 107
Quicksoft 103
R & TA on CD-ROM 96
Radio Shack 84
Rand McNally 117
rare-earths 11-12
RCA 117, 118
read-only optical disks 3, 73, 89-122
read/write optical disks 3-72, 77, 119
    COM replacement 52-53
    data distribution 53-54
    data storage applications 42-52
    document imaging 54-70
    scientific applications 50-52
Readers Guide To Periodical Literature 93
RecallCard 126
Rechtsprechung des Bundesfinanzhofs 98-99
Recognition Equipment Incorporated 66
Red Book 104
ReferenceSet 77
Reference Technology 77, 105, 107, 120
Relax Technology 47
Religion Indexes 96
Religious and Theological Abstracts Incorporated 96
Renal Tumors of Children 94
Repertorio del Foro Italiano 98
Research 107, 108
Reteaco 107
rewritable optical disks 8, 48, 53, 54, 60, 61, 71, 73, 78
    drives and media 27-36
    technology 9-17
    5.25-inch systems 28-32, 73, 87
    3.5-inch systems 28, 33-36, 54, 73
Reflection Systems 8, 32
Review and Analysis of Companies in Holland 98
Ricoh 6, 11, 17, 18, 24, 27, 29, 36, 41, 59, 69, 79, 80
RILM database 96
Rock Ridge Group 106
Russian Karta series 101
Saishin Igaku Daijiten 99
sampled servo format 25, 34
Sanyo 80, 115
SAR: See SYS-OUT Archival and Retrieval System
Sassari Banca Popolare Group 126
Science Applications International Corporation 66

Scientific Micro Systems 46
SCISEARCH 94
SCI-TECH REFERANCE PLUS CD-ROM 94
Search CD450 107
Searcher 107
Search Express 107
SearchMaster Tax Library 96, 107
Sears 100
SEAT 98
Securities and Exchange Commission 112
Sega 114
Seiko Epson 34
SelectWare Technologies 104
selenium 7, 8, 13
Serials Directory CD-ROM 101
Services Documentaires Multimedia Incorporated 97
SET: See simulated electronic transition.
Shakespeare on Disc 96
Shareware Gold CD-ROM 103
Shareware Grab Bag 103
Sharp 11, 27, 29, 71, 79
Sherlock Holmes on Disc 96
Shugart 17
Sigma Imaging Systems 66
silicon 8
silver 78
silver-zinc alloy 13
SilverPlatter Information Incorporated 88, 93, 94, 95, 98, 104, 107, 109, 111
SilverPlatter Information Retrieval System 107
simulated electronic transition 16
SIRS: See SilverPlatter Information Retrieval System.
SIS Integrated Health Systems 126
Slater Hall Information Products 95, 107
smart cards 125
Smithsonian Institution 112, 117
Social Sciences Citation Index 96
Social Sciences Index 96
Social Security Administration 90
SocioFile 96
Sociological Abstracts 96
Software-CD 104
Somak Software 104
Sony 7, 11, 16, 17, 18, 22, 23, 27, 29, 34, 35, 41, 42, 71, 73, 76, 78, 79, 80, 81, 91, 104, 105, 114, 115, 118, 125
Space Station Program 50
Space Telescope Institute 50
Space Time Research 101
Spectrum Ownership 95
Standard and Poor 95
Statistics Canada 97
STA/FILE 105

STA/F TEXT 107
Storage Dimensions 47
Storage Machine 49-50
Storage Technology Corporation 18-19
Strategic Information 46
ST Systems Corporation 66
Sumitomo Bank 127
Sumitomo Electric 102
Summit Software 69
Summus Computer Systems 47
Sun Microsystems 80, 91, 103
Sun Moon Star 81
Suntory Limited 113
Super Blue 103
SuperCat 99, 100
SuperMac Technology 104
Supermap 101
Super Nintendo Entertainment System 114
Super Odyssey 113
Super VGA 81
Super VHS 71
SUSP: See System Use Sharing Protocol.
Swiss Federal Court decisions 98
Syquest 34
SYS-OUT Archival and Retrieval System 53
System Development Corporation 66
Systemhouse Incorporated 66
System Use Sharing Protocol 106
Tab Products 69
Taiyo Yuden Company 79, 80
Tandem Computer 46, 68
Tandy Corporation 14, 70, 80, 81, 84, 114
Tandy High-Intensity Optical Recorder 14
Teac 71, 80
Tecmar 47, 105
Teijin 14
TEI of Kozani KIIA 98
Telefax-Verlag Jaeger & Waldman 98
Teleflora 91
Tele-Info Verlag 98
tellurium 4, 5-6, 7, 8, 13, 18, 27
Ten X Technology 47
Teradata 50
Terminal Data Corporation 59
Termium 97
terbium 11, 12
Texel 80
Textbank/PC 107
Textware 107
TFPL 92
thermal bubble recording 4, 8, 18
Thomas Register of American Manufacturers 95
Thomson Consumer Electronics 71

THOR: See Tandy High-Intensity Optical Recorder.
3M Company 69, 105, 128
TIF format 104
Tiger Media 113
Time-Life Incorporated 117
tin 13
TIPS: See Tandem Image Processing System
titanium 11, 13
TMS 105, 107, 108, 120
Town-Page Map 99, 101
Tokai University Hospital 126
Tokyo Economic Press 99
TOM 93
Toppan Printing Company 99
Toshiba 5, 11, 17, 22, 24, 69, 80
transition metals 8, 11-12
TravelPilot 102
Tresor de la Langue Francaise 76
Trident Systems 66
Tri Star Publishing 93
TROPAG 94
TRW 66
TSC 66
turnkey optical filing systems 69-70
Twayne's United States Author Series 96
Type Gallery 104
UCLA: See University of California-Los Angeles.
Ulrich's Plus 94, 101
Unbound Incorporated 46
Unibase Systems 107
UNI-FILE 105
University Clinic for Radiology (Graz, Germany) 52
University Microfilms International 89, 93, 95, 112
University of California 16
University of California-Los Angeles 51
University of Cincinnati 71
University of Guelph 92
University of Michigan 89
University of Pennsylvania 52
University of Wisconsin 50, 126
Unisys 66
United Kingdom Department of Trade and Industry 120
Unix 48, 53, 66, 106, 107
Urban Phytonarian Handbook 111
USA Wars 96
Utlas 97, 99, 100
U.S. Air Force 90
U.S. Army Corps of Engineers 90
U.S. Army Health Facility Planning Agency 90
U.S. Department of Transportation 103
U.S. Design 46
U.S. History on CD-ROM 96
U.S. House of Representatives 56

U.S. Marine Corps 90
U.S. Navy 91
U.S. Operational Navigation Charts 101
U.S. Patent and Trademark Office 49, 55, 56, 95
U.S. Postal Service 90
U.S. Presidents on CD-ROM 96
Verband der Vereine Creditreform 98
Verbatim 32
Verlag Hoppenstedt 98
Verzeichnis Lieferbarer Bucher 101
Veterans Administration Medical Center (Indianapolis) 51
VHD: See Video High Density system.
Vidal Sur Dusque 98
videocassete recorders 71
Videodisc Catalogue 119
video disc recorders 3, 28, 70-72
video disc systems 51, 71, 117, 118-121
Video High Density system 118
video terminals 70
ViewStar Corporation 66, 69
Viral Hepatitis Discs 94
Virginia Polytechnic Institute 88
Virginia State Legal Code 96
Vision Three 66
Visual Dictionary 113
VMS 107
Voyager Company 113
VR Publisher 77
Wall Street Journal 98
Wang Integrated Information System 68, 69
Wang Laboratories 46, 62, 66, 68, 69
Warchest CD-ROM 90
Wavetrain 113
Webster's Ninth New Collegiate Dictionary 113
Weizmann Institute of Sciences in Israel 88
Wer Liefert Was? 98
West Coast Information Systems 66
Western Library Network 92, 99, 111
West Publishing 96
Wheeler Quick Art CD-ROM 104
White Sands Missile Range 103
WIIS: See Wang Integrated Information System
Wila Verlag 98
WilsonDisc 93, 107
WLN: See Western Library Network
WNET-TV 117
Word Cruncher 107
World Book's Information Finder 93
World Library Incorporated 96
WorldScope database 95
WORM disks: See write-once optical disks.
Wraptop Kojien 99

Wright Investors' Service 95
write-once optical disks 3, 9, 10, 27-28, 34, 60, 61, 68, 73
    drives and media 17-36
    fourteen-inch systems 18-22
    recording technology 4-9
    twelve-inch systems 22-24, 52, 53, 54, 70
    5.25-inch systems 24-25, 54, 70, 73, 78, 87
Xebec 105
Xerox 66, 105
Xyxis Corporation 47
Yamaha 79
Yellow Book 104, 105
ZCAV: See zoned constant angular velocity.
Zenith Data Systems 114
Zetaco 46
ZIP+4 90
zirconium 11
zoned constant angular velocity 30-31
Zyindex 107
Zylab 107